Management Information System

MANAGEMENT INFORMATION SYSTEM

By

ANURANJAN MISRA

Associate Professor
ABES Engineering College,
Ghaziabad (UP)

UNIVERSITY SCIENCE PRESS

(An Imprint of Laxmi Publications Pvt. Ltd.)

BANGALORE • CHENNAI • COCHIN • GUWAHATI • HYDERABAD
JALANDHAR • KOLKATA • LUCKNOW • MUMBAI • RANCHI
NEW DELHI • BOSTON, USA

Published by

UNIVERSITY SCIENCE PRESS

(*An Imprint of Laxmi Publications Pvt. Ltd.*)
113, Golden House, Daryaganj,
New Delhi-110002

Phone : 011-43 53 25 00
Fax : 011-43 53 25 28

www.laxmipublications.com
info@laxmipublications.com

First Edition: 2013

OFFICES

✆ **Bangalore**	080-26 75 69 30	✆ **Chennai**	044-24 34 47 26
✆ **Cochin**	0484-237 70 04, 405 13 03	✆ **Guwahati**	0361-254 36 69, 251 38 81
✆ **Hyderabad**	040-24 65 23 33	✆ **Jalandhar**	0181-222 12 72
✆ **Kolkata**	033-22 27 43 84	✆ **Lucknow**	0522-220 95 78
✆ **Mumbai**	022-24 91 54 15, 24 92 78 69	✆ **Ranchi**	0651-220 44 64

UMI-9577-195-MANAGEMENT INFO SYSTEM-MIS **C—**

Typesetted at Shubham Composer, New Delhi. Printed at : Repro Knowledgecast Limited, Thane

CONTENTS

CHAPTER 1. Fundamentals of Information System **1–40**

1.0 Introduction 1
1.1 Why Information Systems 1
1.2 Brief History of Information Systems 2
1.3 What is an Information System? 2
1.4 New Role of Information Systems in Organizations 3
1.5 Nature/Feature/Characteristics of Information System 5
1.6 Key Components of Information System 6
1.7 Basics of Information Systems 6
1.8 Classification of Information Systems 8
1.9 Artificial Intelligence 35
1.10 Neural Networks 38
1.11 Fuzzy Logic 39
Exercise 40

CHAPTER 2. Developing MIS Systems **41–75**

2.0 Introduction to Software Life Cycle Models 41
2.1 Activities Involved Software Development Life Cycle Model 41
2.2 Different Types of Software Development Life Cycle Models (SDLC) 50
2.3 Iterative Enhancement Life Cycle Model 53
2.4 The Spiral Life Cycle Model 54
2.5 Object Oriented Methodology Life Cycle Model 56
2.6 Dynamic System Development Method (DSDM) 59
2.7 Case Tools 61
2.8 System Description Techniques 63
Exercise 69
Multiple Choice Questions 69

CHAPTER 3. Introduction to MIS **76–88**

3.0 Introduction 76
3.1 What is Management Information System 78
3.2 Nature/Feature/Characteristics of Management Information System 78
3.3 Key Components of Management Information System 79
3.4 Advantages of MIS 79
3.5 Limitations of MIS 79

3.6	Management Information System Versus Data Processing System	80
3.7	Management Information System Versus Decision Processing System	81
3.8	Decision Making and Information Systems for an Organization	82
3.9	Organization Information Strategy	84
3.10	End User Computing	85
	Exercise	88
CHAPTER 4.	**Concept of Planning and Control**	**89–96**
4.0	Organizational Planning	89
4.1	The Planning Process	90
4.2	Types of Plans	90
4.3	Planning Principles	91
4.4	Characteristics of Control Process	91
4.5	Elements of an Organization Planning Process	92
4.6	Your Organization Three Years from Now...	92
4.7	Mission Statement	93
4.8	Considerations in Making a Planning Calendar	93
4.9	Developing Goals and Objectives	94
4.10	Organization Control	94
4.11	Nature of Control in Organization	95
4.12	Relationship between Control and Organization	95
	Exercise	96
CHAPTER 5.	**Introduction to Value Chain**	**97–104**
5.0	Porter's Value Chain Model	97
5.1	Linking Value Chain Analysis to Competitive Advantage	99
5.2	Steps in Value Chain Analysis	99
5.3	Uses of Value Chain Model	100
5.4	Technology and the Value Chain	101
5.5	Linkages between Value Chain Activities	102
5.6	Analyzing Business Unit Interrelationships	102
5.7	Outsourcing Value Chain Activities	103
5.8	The Value Chain System	103
	Exercise	104
CHAPTER 6.	**Managing Knowledge in Information System**	**105–126**
6.0	Introduction	105
6.1	System as Planned Organizational Change	105
6.2	Business Process Reengineering and Process Improvement	107
6.3	TQM and Six Sigma	108
6.4	Knowledge Management in the Organization	116
6.5	Creating a Virtual Company	122

6.6	Becoming an Angle Company	123
6.7	Building a Knowledge Creating Company	124
	Exercise	125
	Further Reading and References	126
Chapter 7.	**Business Applications of IT**	**127–147**
7.0	Internet and Electronic Commerce	127
7.1	Intranets and Extranet	133
7.2	Fundamentals of Strategic Advantage	135
7.3	Strategic Applications and Issues in Information Technology	139
7.4	Key Terms and Concepts	144
	Exercise	147
Chapter 8.	**Introduction to Enterprise Resource Planning**	**148–160**
8.0	Introduction	148
8.1	History	148
8.2	Definition of ERP	151
8.3	ERP as System Perspective	151
8.4	ERP Software	152
8.5	Functional Modules of ERP Software	152
8.6	ERP Systems	153
8.7	ERP Systems and Business Continuity Management	154
8.8	Force Fuelling ERP	156
8.9	The Cost of ERP	158
8.10	Advantages of ERP	158
8.11	Disadvantages of ERP	159
8.12	Common Myths of ERP	160
	Exercise	160
Chapter 9.	**Customer Relationship Management**	**161–173**
9.0	Introduction	161
9.1	Definitions	162
9.2	CRM Software	165
9.3	ECRM or Web Based CRM	165
9.4	Key Features of CRM Tools	169
9.5	Issues in Customer Relation Management	170
9.6	Goals of CRM	172
	Exercise	173
Chapter 10.	**Introduction to Supply Chain Management**	**174–190**
10.0	Intranet and Supply Chain Management	174
10.1	Fundamentals of Supply Chain Management	175
10.2	Managing Retail Supply Chains	177

10.3	Supply Chain Decisions	178
10.4	Supply Chain Modeling Approaches	179
10.5	Supply Chain Application Software's	181
10.6	Examples of Supply Chain Application Software's	188
	Exercise	190
CHAPTER 11.	**Procurement Management**	**191–193**
11.0	Introduction	191
11.1	Definition of E-Procurement	192
11.2	Benefits of Adopting an E-Procurement System	192
11.3	Typical Adoption Strategies	193
11.4	Pitfalls to Avoid	193
	Exercise	193
CHAPTER 12.	**Enterprise and Global Management**	**194–204**
12.0	Introduction	194
12.1	Managing IT Infrastructure and Architecture: Enterprise Computing	194
12.2	Managing the New IT Infrastructure	198
12.3	Enterprise Systems	200
12.4	Industrial Networks and Extended Enterprise Systems	201
12.5	Global Enterprise Solutions	202
	Summary	204
	Exercise	204
CHAPTER 13.	**Security and Ethical Challenges of IT**	**205–223**
13.0	Information Securities and Control	205
13.1	Why Break IT System Security?	209
13.2	Information System Security Threats	209
13.3	Ethical and Social Dimensions	213
13.4	Business Ethics	215
	Exercise	222
CHAPTER 14.	**Quality Assurance and Testing**	**224–233**
14.0	Introduction	224
14.1	Quality Assurance	224
14.2	Growth of International Information Systems	230
14.3	Ethical and Social Dimensions	230
	Summary	232
	Exercise	232
	Further Reading	233
CHAPTER 15.	**Cyber Crimes and Privacy Issues**	**234–242**
15.0	Introduction	234
15.1	Why Cyber Laws at all	234

15.2 Cyber Crimes 235
15.3 Basic Approaches for Creation of Cyber Laws 236
15.4 Establishing a Suitable Framework 236
15.5 Cyber Legislations Worldwide 237
15.6 Defining Cyber Laws 238
15.7 The Legal Issues 238
Exercise 242

Appendix I. Basics of Management 243

Appendix II. Basics of Information 257

Appendix III. Basics of System 268

Appendix IV. Computers and IT Related Techniques 277

Appendix V. Glossary on Management Information System 298

PREFACE

The system provides information on the past, present and project future and on relevant events inside and outside the organization. It may be defined as a planned and integrated system for gathering relevant data, converting it into right information and supplying the same to the concerned executives. The main purpose of MIS is to provide the right information to the right people at the right time.

Management Information system is sets of inter-related procedures using IT infrastructure in a business enterprise to generate and disseminate desired information. Such systems are designed to support decision-making by the people associated with the enterprise in the process of attainment of its objectives. The business information system gets data and other resources of IT infrastructure as input from the environment and process them to satisfy the information needs of different entities associated with the business enterprise.

This book incorporates following 15 chapters as well as Examples, Multiple Choice questions, and review questions.

1. Fundamentals of information System
2. Developing MIS Systems
3. Introduction to MIS
4. Concept of Planning and control
5. Introduction to Value Chain
6. Managing knowledge in Information System
7. Business Applications of IT
8. Introduction to Enterprise Resource Planning
9. Customer Relationship Management
10. Introduction to Supply Chain Management
11. Procurement Management
12. Enterprise and Global Management
13. Security and Ethical Challenges of IT
14. Quality Assurance and Testing
15. Cyber Crimes and Privacy Issues

The book also contains six appendixes: Basics of Management, Basics of Information, Basics of System, Computers & IT Related Techniques, Introduction to Decision Making and Glossary on Management Information System.

Since rapid changes can be witnessed in the area of Information Technology and Management Information System is not left untouched. I have taken my best efforts to incorporate the latest updates taking in the Management Information System. Furthermore your views, suggestions, comments and recommendations are invited & will be highly appreciable. Simultaneously please do not hesitate to write me at e-mail anuranjanmisra@gmail.com, and I promise you to revert at earliest. I have tried to bring the book free from errors. However, it is not unusual that certain flaws might have crept into the body of the text. I take personal responsibility for the same and request to let know of those misprints or mistakes. I assure the readers to remove them in the next addition of this book.

—Author

1

Fundamentals of Information System

1.0 INTRODUCTION

The initial concept of information system was to process data from the organization and present it in the form of reports at regular intervals. The system was mostly capable of handling the data from collection to processing. It was more unfriendly, requiring each individual to pick and choose the processed data and use it for his requirements. This concept was further modified when a distinction was made between data and information. The information is a product of an analysis of data. This concept is similar to a raw material and the finished product. What are needed are information and not a mass of data. However, the data can be analyzed in a number of ways, producing different shades and specifications of the information as a product. It was, therefore, demanded that the system concept be an individual-oriented, as each individual may have a different orientation. Towards the information. This concept was further modified, that the system should present information in such a form and format that it creates an impact on its user, provoking a decision or an investigation.

A system or process that provides the information necessary to manage an organization effectively is known as Management information system. MIS and the information it generates are generally considered essential components of prudent and reasonable business decisions.

1.1 WHY INFORMATION SYSTEMS

The system provides information on the past, present and project future and on relevant events inside and outside the organization. Information system may be defined as a planned and integrated system for gathering relevant data, converting it in to the right information and supplying the same to the concerned executives. As long as organizations are small and have limited operational goals manual information system are satisfactory. Many trends in the development of industry and commerce have made computer based information system essential to efficiently run organizations. Need of information systems arises rapidly because of the following reasons:

- The size of organizations is becoming larger. This is due to increase in population and rapid rate of industrial development.
- Computer based processing enables the same data to be processed in many ways based on needs, thereby allowing managers to look at the performance of an organization from different angles.
- As the volume of data has increased and the variety of information and their timeliness is now of great importance, computer based information processing has now become essential for effectively managing organizations.
- Organizations are now distributed with many branches.
- Markets are becoming competitive. To maintain favorable balance of payments in a country, organizations have to be internationally competitive.
- The general socio-economic environment depends more up to date and accurate information. Human Society is changing faster than ever before. Governmental regulations have become complex. Organizations have to interact with many other interested parties such as a consumer groups, environmental protection groups, financial institutions etc., which did not exist before.

1.2 BRIEF HISTORY OF INFORMATION SYSTEMS

- 1950's : Electronic Data Processing/Automatic Data Processing
- 1960's : Management Information Systems (*i.e.*, Report generating systems)
- 1970's : Decision Support Systems (DSS), Office Automation Systems
- 1980's : Information as strategic tool, End-User Computing, Managerial control
- 1990's : Integration: Core activities + Information as a product
- 2000's : Knowledge based expert systems

1.3 WHAT IS AN INFORMATION SYSTEM?

An information system is a collection of hardware, software, data, people and procedures that are designed to generate information that supports the day-to-day, short-range, and long-range activities of users in an organization. Information systems generally are classified into five categories: office information systems, transaction processing systems, management information systems, decision support systems, and expert systems.

Some other definitions of information system are as follows:

In a general sense, the term information system (IS) refers to a system of people, data records and activities that process the data and information in an organization, and it includes the organization's manual and automated processes. In a narrow sense, the term information system (or computer-based information system) refers to the specific application software that is used to store data records in a computer system and automates some of the information-processing activities of the organization. Computer-based information systems are in the field of information technology. The discipline of business process modelling describes the business processes supported by information systems.

(http://en.wikipedia.org)

An organized collection, storage, and presentation system of data and other knowledge for decision-making, progress reporting, and for planning and evaluation of programs. It can be either manual or computerized, or a combination of both.

(www.ojp.usdoj.gov)

Information System is a combination of database, human and technical resources that together with the appropriate organization skills produce information needed to support certain economic activity, management of resources and/or decision-making procedures.

(**www.costg9.plan.aau.dk**)

1.4 NEW ROLE OF INFORMATION SYSTEMS IN ORGANIZATIONS

The organizational structure is a central aspect in becoming a successful and agile market player who is fulfilling the business goals of an organization. Organizations had to realize that their goals can not be fulfilled by only adapting their systems landscape and implementing smooth business processes.

Information systems organizations come in various shapes and sizes. Each of these organizations is built around major macro processes that they perform or support. These processes generally fulfill specific, IT-related needs for internal customers. Although each information systems organization has a unique structure and individual processes, they may have many elements in common.

The information systems organization is typically led by a chief information officer (CIO). As the CIO is responsible for setting the strategic direction of the information systems organization, he or she has to choose an appropriate organization structure. A centralized approach was primarily dictated by mainframes in the 1960's. Mainframes resided in one physical location and required centralized decision-making and local staff that operate and maintain these systems. During the 1980's, personal computers allowed computing power to be spread beyond the raised-floor, air-conditioned rooms of mainframes. This was the very beginning of a decentralization approach to the information systems organization. Today the strategies, processes and structures of information systems organizations exist along a continuum from centralization to decentralization. Organizations should weight benefits and drawbacks against these two approaches. Some companies may combine the two approaches and choose a federal approach, found in the middle of the continuum [Pear06].

The information systems organization basically constitutes a central entity along a value chain of service providers and service customers. On the supply side, you can identify external service providers such as systems integrators, technology providers and professional services providers. On the demand side are customers of the information systems organization, mostly represented by company-internal business units.

Today many of these organizations are under tremendous pressure being in a marketplace that continuously demands "producing" more while spending less. IT divisions of publicly traded companies are often challenged by increasing regulatory standards (*e.g.*, the Sarbanes-Oxley Act) and compliance efforts (*e.g.*, technology to enable sustainable compliance with these regulations). While information systems organizations have to manage an increased complexity in their IT environments, they additionally have to offer cost-efficient and convenient business solutions. These demands on IT have prompted information systems organizations to find an innovative answer in order to quickly and effectively meet these challenges. The answer consists of two main issues: outsourcing of selective IT services and shifting IT activities to business units. The result is a transformation of the structure of this organization toward a lean information systems organization.

Todays organizations face isues such as challenging informational needs, diverse management styles, and heightened security requirements.MIS and the Role of Database in an Organization is constantly changing.Management and organizations facing constantly changing problems, diverse managerial styles, and ever present information needs offer a challenging context for developing computer based information systems. MIS uses computer technology to provide information and decision support to managers, helping them becomes more effective. Developments in the young computer industry are changing corporate management style.

Computer technology, including DBMS's, is the motivating and enabling basis for the rapidly expanding field of MIS. A management information system is an integrated, user machine system for providing information to support operations, management, analysis, and decision making functions in an organization. The system utilizes computer hardware and software, manual procedures, models for analysis, planning, control and decision making and a data base.

Managers at all levels use similar data. Operating managers require data, which is timely, precise, detailed, internal and historical. Upper level managers need data which is aggregated, external as well as internal, future oriented as well as historical and covering a longer span time. An effective MIS cannot be built without viable data management tools. Such tools were not generally available previously. Moreover, most organizations did not effectively use DBMS technology until two decades before. An important key to a successful MIS is the effective management of an organization's data resources.

Role of the Database in an Organization

An organization is traditionally viewed as a three level pyramid-operational activities at the bottom, management planning and control activities in the middle and strategic planning and policy making in top management. The corporate database contains data relating to the organization, its operations, its plan and its environment.

State of Database Management in Organizations

The needs of organizations and management are changeable, diverse and often ill-defined, yet they must be met. Added to these are outside pressures from federal taxing authorities, federal securities agencies and legislators making privacy laws. Both internal and external forces demand that organizations exercise control over their data resources.

Decisions and actions in the organization are based upon the image contained in the corporate database. Managerial decisions direct the actions at the operational level and produce plans and expectations, which are formally captured and stored in the corporate database. Transactions record actual results of organizational activities and environmental changes and update the database to maintain a current image.

People in the organization query the database for information to conduct the daily operations. Middle management receives reports comparing actual results to previously recorded plans and expectations. The corporate database provides data for modeling and forecasting which support top management needs. The corporate database supports all levels of an organization and is vital for operations, decision-making and the management process.

While management seeks to control data resources, computer applications grow. When a corporation achieves comprehensive support of its operations, for instance, computer applications begin to penetrate into higher management levels. With comprehensive database support of operations, an MIS can mature as a tool for planning, control and decision making. Earlier, in the development of an MIS, an organization must appoint a DBA to manage its data resources.

While an organization's move toward the database approach can be hastened by the acquisition of a DBMS, the latter is not necessary. Most commercially available DBMS's fall substantially short of ideal capabilities, making their acquisition an interim measure — a move to help the organization learn how to operate in a managed data environment. In seeking DBMS capability, building one's own system is unrealistic except for large organizations with special needs, such as a very large database or large volumes of known transactions requiring rapid online response.

Data is a vital resource in an organization and must be managed. The organizational database is an essential component in a management information system. Of the four components of a data processing system, attention to data has lagged behind the development of machines and programming technology. Taking a database approach requires an organization to focus on data as a valued resource. Data is separate from programs and application systems, which use it.

1.5 NATURE/FEATURE/CHARACTERISTICS OF INFORMATION SYSTEM

The basic characteristics of information system are as follows:

1. The Information systems are subject to the dynamics of business environment and need to be flexible enough to absorb the inevitable changes in the information of business. They have to be efficient to satisfy the demanding and hard task matters.
2. Information system needs to be proactive. They should anticipate changes in information needs of users and accordingly adapt themselves to suit their needs. This has become important because of the fact that the mangers get involved in the runtime activities to the extent that the decision making becomes a matter of imitating what competitors are doing or planning to do, rather than making an informed choice.
3. The purpose of Information system is to cater to the information needs for decision-making in business.
4. The Information systems have to design keeping in view the availability of financial and human resources to the business enterprise.
5. The cost effectiveness is a matter of prime concern in the development and maintenance of Information system. Economic justification for investment in IT infrastructure for Business Information system is a pre-condition for its existence and sustenance.

1.6 KEY COMPONENTS OF INFORMATION SYSTEM

Information systems can be described by four key components; they are as follows:

1. Decision
2. Transaction and processing
3. Information and flow
4. Individuals or functions involved
5. Types of Information systems.

It is difficult to observe the decision process through which we can see and review the results of a decision. Transactions are usually more visible, though many current systems use computer programs, principles, an observer can see information and its flows. Individuals can be observed too.

1.7 BASICS OF INFORMATION SYSTEMS

Data

Raw data are numbers, characters, images or other outputs from devices to convert physical quantities into symbols, in a very broad sense. Such data are typically further processed by a human or input into a computer, stored and processed there, or transmitted (output) to another human or computer. *Raw data* is a relative term; data processing commonly occurs by stages, and the "processed data" from one stage may be considered the "raw data" of the next.

Data is raw. It simply exists and has no significance beyond its existence (in and of itself). It can exist in any form, usable or not. It does not have meaning of itself. In computer parlance, a spreadsheet generally starts out by holding data.

Information

Information is data that has been given meaning by way of relational connection. This "meaning" can be useful, but does not have to be. In computer parlance, a relational database makes information from the data stored within it. When the data is processed, grouped, organized, sequences and presented in an easy to understand manner become information.

Knowledge

Knowledge is the appropriate collection of information, such that it's intent is to be useful. Knowledge is a deterministic process. When someone "memorizes" information (as less-aspiring test-bound students often do), then they have amassed knowledge. This knowledge has useful meaning to them, but it does not provide for, in and of itself, integration such as would infer further knowledge. For example a pre school child can answer only those questions whose answers are written in his/her answer book, like $3 \times 2 = 6$. If we ask a typical question like "3216×23" the child can not answer it correctly, because it is not written in his/her answer book and student could not have knowledge.

Understanding

Understanding is an interpolative and probabilistic process. It is cognitive and analytical. It is the process by which I can take knowledge and synthesize new knowledge from the previously held knowledge. The difference between understanding and knowledge is the difference between "learning" and "memorizing". People who have understanding can undertake useful actions because they can synthesize new knowledge, or in some cases, at least new information, from what is previously known (and understood). That is, understanding can build upon currently held information, knowledge and understanding itself. In computer parlance, AI systems possess understanding in the sense that they are able to synthesize new knowledge from previously stored information and knowledge.

Wisdom

Wisdom is an extrapolative and non-deterministic, non-probabilistic process. It calls upon all the previous levels of consciousness, and specifically upon special types of human programming (moral, ethical codes, etc.). It beckons to give us understanding about which there has previously been no understanding, and in doing so, goes far beyond understanding itself. It is the essence of philosophical probing. Unlike the previous four levels, it asks questions to which there is no (easily-achievable) answer, and in some cases, to which there can be no humanly known answer period. Wisdom is therefore, the process by which we also discern, or judge, between right and wrong, good and bad. I personally believe that computers do not have, and will never have the ability to posses wisdom. Wisdom is a uniquely human state, or as I see it, wisdom requires one to have a soul, for it resides as much in the heart as in the mind. And a soul is something machines will never possess (or perhaps I should reword that to say, a soul is something that, in general, will never possess a machine).

Data Vs Information

Even data is not meaningless but it is not as relevant to a decision maker as information. Data is not easily understood because it is not organized in an intuitive manner, complex and unclear. So we can say data is a row material for information, after passing through in many processes data becomes information.

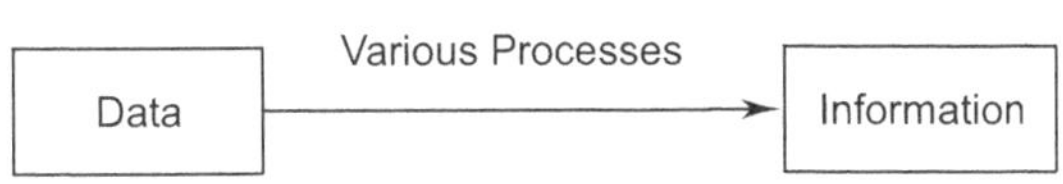

Data

- Facts, statistics used for reference or analysis.
- Numbers, characters, symbols, images etc., which can be processed by a computer.
- Data must be interpreted, by a human or machine, to derive meaning
- "Data is a representation of information"
- Latin 'datum' meaning "that which is given"
- Data plural, datum singular.

Information

- Knowledge derived from study, experience (by the senses), or instruction.
- Communication of intelligence.
- "Information is any kind of knowledge that is exchangeable amongst people, about things, facts, concepts, etc., in some context".
- "Information is interpreted data".

Information Vs Knowledge

Knowledge refers to the practical use of information. While information can be transported, stored or shared without many difficulties the same can not be said about knowledge. Knowledge necessarily involves a personal experience. Referring back to the scientific experiment, a third person reading the results will have information about it, while the person who conducted the experiment personally will have knowledge about it.

1.8 CLASSIFICATION OF INFORMATION SYSTEMS

Information System can be categorized into many types. The main Information System is as follows:

1.8.1 Operations Support System (OSS)

Many OSS systems were initially not linked to each other and often required manual intervention. For example, consider the case where a customer wants to order a new telephone service. The ordering system would take the customer's details and details of their order, but would not be able to configure the telephone exchange directly - this would be done by a switch management system. Details of the new service would need to be transferred from the order handling system to the switch management system - and this would normally be done by a technician re-keying the details from one screen into another - a process often referred to as "swivel chair integration". This was clearly another source of inefficiency, so the focus for the next few years was on creating automated interfaces between the OSS applications - OSS integration. Cheap and simple OSS integration remains a major goal of most telecom companies.

Operations Support Systems (also called **Operational Support Systems** or **OSS**) are computer systems used by telecommunications service providers. The term OSS most frequently describes "network systems" dealing with the telecom network itself, supporting processes such as maintaining network inventory, provisioning services, configuring network components, and managing faults. The complementary term Business Support Systems or **BSS** is a newer term and typically refers to "business systems" dealing with customers, supporting processes such as taking orders, processing bills, and collecting payments. The two systems together are often abbreviated **BSS/OSS** or simply **B/OSS**.

1.8.2 Management Support System

Management support system is a Subset of management information system (MIS), it extends the information retrieval capabilities of the end-users with 'query and analysis functions' for searching a database, generating 'what if' scenarios, and other such purposes.

1.8.3 Transaction Processing System

A **Transaction Processing System** (TPS) is a type of information system. TPSs collect, store, modify, and retrieve the transactions of an organization. A transaction is an event that generates or modifies data that is eventually stored in an information system. To be considered a transaction processing system the computer must pass the ACID test.

1.8.3.1 Types of Transaction Processing Systems

Batch processing: Batch processing is a transaction where information is gathered and stored but not processed immediately. Advantages of batch processing is being able to share information among users and avoiding idling computer systems by processing transactions when the computer's resources are less busy. Examples include cheques in a banking system or the billing of a credit card where you receive one bill for a month's worth of purchases.

Real-time processing: Real-time processing is a transaction where information is processed immediately and the operator has access to an online catalogue. Real-time processing is mostly used in Online transaction processing. For example a withdrawal from a bank account or library loans.

1.8.3.2 Features of Transaction Processing Systems

Rapid response: Fast performance with a rapid response time is critical. Businesses cannot afford to have customers waiting for a TPS to respond, the turnaround time from the input of the transaction to the production for the output must be a few seconds or less.

Reliability: Many organisations rely heavily on their TPS; a breakdown will disrupt operations or even stop the business. For a TPS to be effective its failure rate must be very low. If a TPS does fail, then quick and accurate recovery must be possible. This makes well-designed backup and recovery procedures essential.

Inflexibility: A TPS wants every transaction to be processed in the same way regardless of the user, the customer or the time for day. If a TPS were flexible, there would be too many opportunities for non-standard operations, for example, a commercial airline needs to consistently accept airline reservations from a range of travel agents, accepting different transactions data from different travel agents would be a problem.

Controlled processing: The processing in a TPS must support an organisation's operations. For example if an organisation allocates roles and responsibilities to particular employees, then the TPS should enforce and maintain this requirement.

1.8.3.3 ACID Test Properties: First Definition

Atomicity: A transaction's changes to the state are atomic: either all happen or none happen. These changes include database changes, messages, and actions on transducers.

Consistency: A transaction is a correct transformation of the state. The actions taken as a group do not violate any of the integrity constraints associated with the state. This requires that the transaction be a correct program.

Isolation: Even though transactions execute concurrently, it appears to each transaction T, that others executed either before T or after T, but not both.

Durability: Once a transaction completes successfully (commits), its changes to the state survive failures.

Storing and retrieving: Storing and retrieving information from a TPS must be efficient and effective. The data is stored in warehouses or other databases, the system must be well designed for its backup and recovery procedures.

Databases and files: The storage and retrieval of data must accurate as it is used many times throughout the day. A database is a collection of data neatly organised, which stores the accounting and operational records in the database. Databases are always protective of its delicate data, so it usually has a restricted view of certain data. Databases are designed using hierarchical, network or relational structures; each structure is effective in its own sense.

- *Hierarchical structure:* organises data in a series of levels, hence why it is called hierarchal. Its top to bottom like structure consists of nodes and branches; each child node has branches and is only linked to one higher level parent node.
- *Network structure:* Similar to hierarchical, network structures also organises data using nodes and branches. But, unlike hierarchical, each child node can be linked to multiple, higher parent nodes.
- *Relational structure:* Unlike network and hierarchical, a relational database organises its data in a series of related tables. This gives flexibility as relationships between the tables are built.

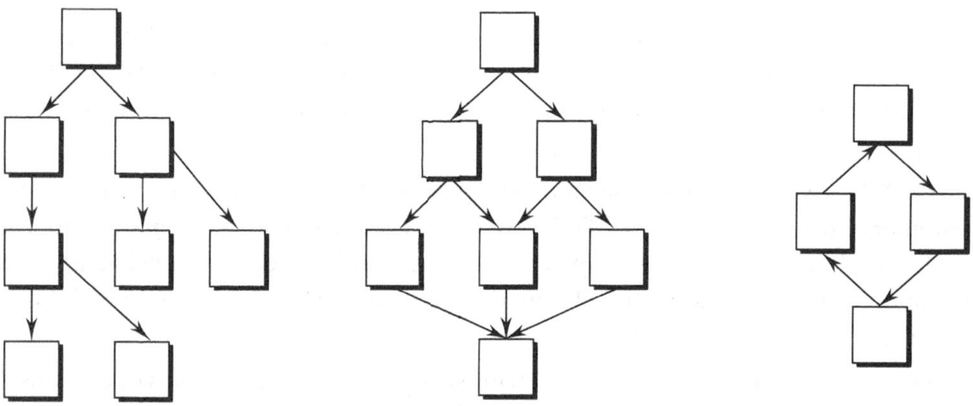

A Hierachical Structure **A Network Structure** **A Relational Structure**

Fig. 1.1

The following features are included in real time transaction processing systems:

- *Good data placement:* The database should be designed to access patterns of data from many simultaneous users.
- *Short transactions:* Short transactions enables quick processing. This avoids concurrency and paces the systems.
- *Real-time backup:* Backup should be scheduled between low times of activity to prevent lag of the server.

- *High normalisation:* This lowers redundant information to increase the speed and improve concurrency, this also improves backups.
- *Archiving of historical data:* Uncommonly used data is moved into other databases or backed up tables. This keeps tables small and also improves backup times.
- *Good hardware configuration:* Hardware must be able to handle many users and provide quick response times.

In a TPS, there are 5 different types of files, the TPS uses the files to store and organise its transaction data:

- *Master file:* Contains information about an organisation's business situation. Most transactions and databases are stored in the master file.
- *Transaction file:* It is the collection of transaction records. It helps to update the master file and also serves as audit trails and transaction history.
- *Report file:* Contains data that has been formatted for presentation to a user.
- *Work file:* temporary files in the system used during the processing.
- *Program file:* Contains the instructions for the processing of data.

Data Warehousing

A data warehouse is a database that collects information from different sources. When it's gathered in real-time transactions it can be used for analysis efficiently if it's stored in a data warehouse. It provides data that is *consolidated, subject-orientated, historical* and *read-only*:

- **Consolidated:** Data is organised with consistent naming conventions, measurements, attributes and semantics. It allows data from a data warehouse from across the organisation to be effectively used in a consistent manner.
- **Subject-orientated:** Large amounts of data is stored across an organisation, some data could be irrelevant for reports and makes querying the data difficult. It organises only key business information from operational sources so that it's available for analysis.
- **Historical:** Real-time TPS represent the current value at any time, an example could be stock levels. If past data is kept, querying the database could return a different response. It stores series of snapshots for an organisation's operational data generated over a period of time.
- **Read-only:** Once data is moved into a data warehouse, it becomes read-only, unless it was incorrect. Since it represents a snapshot of a certain time, it must never be updated. Only operations which occur in a data warehouse are loading and querying data.

Backup Procedures

Since business organisations have become very dependent on TPSs, a breakdown in their TPS may stop the business' regular routines and thus stopping it's operation for a certain amount of time. In order to prevent data loss and minimise disruptions when a TPS breaks down a well-designed backup and recovery procedure is put into use. The recovery process can rebuild the system when it goes down.

Recovery Process

A TPS may fail for many reasons. These reasons could include a system failure, human errors, hardware failure, incorrect or invalid data, computer viruses, software application errors or natural disasters. So it is logical to assume that it's not possible to keep a TPS from never failing, however because it may fail time to time, it must be able to cope with failures. The TPS must be able to detect and correct errors when they occur. A TPS will go through a recovery of the database to cope when the system fails, it involves the backup, journal, checkpoint and recovery manager:

- **Backup:** A backup copy is usually produced at least once a day. It should be tored in a secure location, protected from damage and loss.
- **Journal:** A journal maintains an audit trail of transactions and database changes. Transaction logs and Database change logs are used, a transaction log records all the essential data for each transactions, including data values, time of transaction and temrinal number. A database change log contains before and after copies of records that have been modified by transactions.
- **Checkpoint:** A checkpoint record contains necessary information to restart the system. These should be taken frequently, such as several times an hour. It is possible to resume processing from the most recent checkpoint when a failure occers with only a few minutes of processing work that needs to be repeated.
- **Recovery manager:** A recovery manager is a program which restores the database to a correct condition which can restart the transaction processing.

Depending on how the system failed, there can be two different recovery procedures used. Generally, the procedures involes restoring data that has been collected from a backup device and then running the transaction processing again. Two types of recovery are *backward recovery* and *forward recovery*:

- **Backward recovery:** used to undo unwanted changes to the database. It reverses the changes made by transactions which have been aborted. It involves the logic of reprocessing each transaction - which is very time consuming.
- **Forward recovery:** it starts with a backup copy of the database. The transaction will then reprocess according to the transaction journal that occured between the time the backup was made and the present time. It's much faster and more accurate.

1.8.3.4 Types of Back-up Procedures

There are two main types of Back-up Procedures: *Grandfather-father-son* and *Partial backups*:

Grandfather-father-son

This procedure refers to at least three generations of backup master files. Hence, the most recent backup is the son, the oldest backup is the grandfather. It's commonly used for a *batch transaction processing system* with a magnetic tape. If the system fails during a batch run, the master file is recreated by using the son backup and then restarting the batch. However if the son backup fails, is corrupted or destroyed, then the next generation up backup (father) is required. Likewise, if that fails, then the next generation up backup (grandfather) is required. Of course the older the generation, the more the data may be out of date. Organizations can have up to twenty generations of backup.

Partial backups

This only occurs when parts of the master file are backed up. The master file is usually backed up to magnetic tape at regular times, this could be daily, weekly or monthly. Completed transactions since the last backup are stored separately and are called **journals**, or **journal files**. The master file can be recreated from the journal files on the backup tape if the system is to fail.

Updating in a batch

This is used when transactions are recorded on paper (such as bills and invoices) or when it's being stored on a magnetic tape. Transactions will be collected and updated as a batch at when it's convenient or economical to process them. Historically, this was more widely used as the information technology did not exist to allow real-time processing.

The two stages in batch processing are:

- Collecting and storage of the transaction data into a transaction file - this involves sorting the data into sequential order.
- Processing the data by updating the master file - which can be difficult, this may involve data additions, updates and deletions that may require to happen in a certain order. If an error occurs, then the entire batch fails.

Updating in batch requires sequential access - since it uses a magnetic tape this is the only way to access data. A batch will start at the beginning of the tape, then reading it from the order it was stored; it's very time-consuming to locate specific transactions.

The information technology used inclues a secondary storage medium which can store large quantities of data inexpensively (thus the common choice of a magnetic tape). The software used to collect data does not have to be online - it doesn't even need a user interface.

Updating in real-time

This is the immediate processing of data. It provides instant confirmation of a transaction. This involves a large amount of users who are simultaneously performing transactions to change data. Because of advances in technology (such as the increase in the speed of data transmission and larger bandwidth), real-time updating is now possible.

Steps in a real-time update involve the sending of a transaction data to an online database in a master file. The person providing information is usually able to help with error correction and receives confirmation of the transaction completion.

Updating in real-time uses direct access of data. This occurs when data is accessed without accessing previous data items. The storage device stores data in a particular location based on a mathematical procedure. This will then be calculated to find an approximate location of the data. If data is not found at this location, it will search through sucessive locations until it's found.

The information technology used could be a secondary storage medium that can store large amounts of data and provide quick access (thus the common choice of a magnetic disk). It requires a user-friendly interface as it's important for rapid response time.

1.8.4 Process Control System

Process control is a statistics and engineering discipline that deals with architectures, mechanisms, and algorithms for controlling the output of a specific process. For example, heating up the temperature in a room is a process that has the specific, desired outcome to reach and maintain a defined temperature (*e.g.*, 20°C), kept constant over time. Here, the temperature is the **controlled variable**. At the same time, it is the **input variable** since it is measured by a thermometer and used to decide whether to heat or not to heat. The desired temperature (20°C) is the **setpoint**. The state of the heater (*e.g.*, the setting of the valve allowing hot water to flow through it) is called the **manipulated variable** since it is subject to control actions.

A commonly used control device called a programmable logic controller, or a PLC, is used to read a set of digital and analog inputs, apply a set of logic statements, and generate a set of analog and digital outputs. Using the example in the previous paragraph, the room temperature would be an input to the PLC. The logical statements would compare the setpoint to the input temperature and determine whether more or less heating was necessary to keep the temperature constant. A PLC output would then either open or close the hot water valve, an incremental amount, depending on whether more or less hot water was needed. Larger more complex systems can be controlled by a Distributed Control System (DCS) or SCADA system.

In practice, process control systems can be characterized as one or more of the following forms:

- ***Discrete:*** Found in many manufacturing, motion and packaging applications. Robotic assembly, such as that found in automotive production, can be characterized as discrete process control. Most discrete manufacturing involves the production of discrete pieces of product, such as metal stamping.
- ***Batch:*** Some applications require that specific quantities of raw materials be combined in specific ways for particular durations to produce an intermediate or end result. One example is the production of adhesives and glues, which normally require the mixing of raw materials in a heated vessel for a period of time to form a quantity of end product. Other important examples are the production of food, beverages and medicine. Batch processes are generally used to produce a relatively low to intermediate quantity of product per year (a few pounds to millions of pounds).
- ***Continuous:*** Often, a physical system is represented though variables that are smooth and uninterrupted in time. The control of the water temperature in a heating jacket, for example, is an example of continuous process control. Some important continuous processes are the production of fuels, chemicals and plastics. Continuous processes, in manufacturing, are used to produce very large quantities of product per year(millions to billions of pounds).

Statistical Process Control

Statistical Process Control (SPC) is an effective method of monitoring a process through the use of control charts. Much of its power lies in the ability to monitor both process center and its variation about that center. By collecting data from samples at various points within the process, variations in the process that may affect the quality of the end product or service can be detected and corrected, thus reducing waste as well as the likelihood that problems will be passed on to the customer. It has an emphasis on early detection and prevention of problems.

Examples

A thermostat is a simple example for a closed control loop: It constantly measures the current temperature and controls the heater's valve setting to increase or decrease the room temperature according to the user-defined setting. A simple method switches the heater either completely on, or completely off, and an overshoot and undershoot of the controlled temperature must be expected. A more expensive method varies the amount of heat provided by the heater depending on the difference between the required temperature (the "setpoint") and the actual temperature. This minimizes over/undershoot.An anti-lock braking system (ABS) is a more complex example, consisting of multiple inputs, conditions and outputs.

1.8.5 Enterprise Collaboration System

Enterprise collaboration systems refers to the use of groupware tools and the internet, intranets, extranets and other computer networks to support and enhance communication. Examples include enterprise communication tools such as e-mail, enterprise conferencing tools such as videoconferencing and collaborative work management tools such as task and project management.

ECS can be further divided into three types:

- Communication Tools
- Conferencing Tools
- Collaboration Tools

1.8.6 Management Information System

Management information systems is a general name for the academic discipline covering the application of people, technologies, and procedures -- collectively, the information system -- to business problems.

As an area of study it is also referred to as information technology management. The study of information systems is usually a commerce and business administration discipline, and frequently involves software engineering, but also distinguishes itself by concentrating on the integration of computer systems with the aims of the organization. The area of study should not be confused with computer science which is more theoretical in nature and deals mainly with software creation, and not with computer engineering, which focuses more on the design of computer hardware. IT service management is a practitioner-focused discipline centering on the same general domain.

In business, information systems support business processes and operations, decision-making, and competitive strategies.

1.8.6.1 The Decision Support Role

The Business decision-making support function goes one step further. It becomes an integral part -- even a vital part -- of decision-making. It allows users to ask very powerful "What if...?" questions: *What if* we increase the price by 5%? *What if* we increase price by 10%? *What if* we decrease price by 5%? *What if* we increase price by 10% now, then decrease it by 5% in three months? It also allows users to deal with contingencies: If inflation increases by 5% (instead of 2% as we are assuming), then what do we do? What do we do if we are faced with a strike or a new competitive threat? An organization succeeds or fails based on the quality of its decisions. The enhanced ability to explore "what if" questions is central to analyzing the likely results of possible decisions and choosing those most likely to shape the future as desired. "Business decision-making support function" is a phrase likely to quicken the pulse of no one but an accountant, but, in fact, it is all about turning wonderful dreams into solid realities.

1.8.6.2 The Performance Monitoring Role

MIS are not just statistics and data analysis, but also assessment of human capabilities. They have to be used as an MBO (Management by objectives) tool. They help:

- to establish relevant and measurable objectives
- to monitor results and performances (reach ratios)
- to send alerts, in some cases daily, to managers at each level of the organization, on all **deviations** between results and pre-established objectives and budgets.

1.8.6.3 Potential Benefits of MIS Investments

Investing in information systems can pay off for a company in many ways.

1. Such an investment can support a core competency. Great companies invariably have one or two core competencies, something they can do better than anyone else. This could be anything from new product development to customer service. It is the heart of the business and no matter what it is, information technology can support that core competency. An IT investment in a company's core competency can create a significant barrier to entry for other companies, defending the organization's primary turf and protecting its markets and profits.
2. It can build supply chain networks. Firms that are a part of an integrated supply chain system have established relationships of trust with suppliers. This means faster delivery times, problem-free delivery and an assured supply. It can also mean price discounts and other preferential treatment. The inability of new entrants to get onto a supply chain/ inventory management system can be a major barrier to entry.
3. It can enhance distribution channel management. As with supplier networks, investment in distribution channel management systems can ensure quicker delivery times, problem free delivery, and preferential treatments. When the distribution channel management system is exclusive, it can mean some control over access to retailers, and, once more, a barrier to entry.
4. Such an IT investment can help build brand equity. To build a brand, firms often invest huge sums in advertising. A huge brand name is a formidable barrier to enter and sustaining it can be facilitated by investment in marketing information systems and customer relationship management system.
5. Information systems can mean better production processes (1). Such systems have become essential in managing large production runs. Automated systems are the most cost efficient way to organize large scale production. These can produce economies of scale in promotion, purchasing, and production; economies of scope in distribution and promotion; reduced overhead allocation per unit; and shorter break-even times more easily. This absolute cost advantage can mean greater profits and revenue.
6. IT investment can boost production processes (2). Information systems allow a company flexibility in its output level. Michael Porter claims that economies of scale are a barrier to entry, aside from the absolute cost advantages they provide. This is because, a company producing at a point on the long-run average cost curve where economies of scale exist has the potential to obtain cost savings in the future, and this potential is a barrier to entry.
7. Implementing IT experience can leverage learning curve advantages. As a company gains experience using IT systems, it becomes familiar with a set of best practices that are more or less known to other firms in the industry. Firms outside the industry are generally not familiar with the industry specific aspects of using these systems. New entrants will

be at a disadvantage unless they can redefine the industries best practices and leap-frog existing firms.

8. IT investment can impact mass customization production processes. IT controlled production technology can facilitate collaborative, adaptive, transparent, or cosmetic customization. This flexibility can increase margins and increase customer satisfaction.
9. Leverage IT investment in computer aided design (1). CAD systems facilitate the speedy development and introduction of new products. This can create proprietary product differences. Product differentiation can be a barrier to entry. Proprietary product differences can be used to create incompatibilities between competing products. These incompatibilities increase consumers' switching costs. High customer switching costs is a very valuable barrier to entry.
10. It means expanded E-commerce. Company web sites can be personalized to each customers interests, expectations, and commercial needs. They can also be used to create a sense of community. Both of these tend to increase customer loyalty. Customer loyalty is an important barrier to entry.
11. Information systems leverage stability. Technologically sophisticated firms with multiple electronic points of contact with customers, suppliers, and others enjoy greater stability. This monumental appearance of stability can be a barrier to entry, especially in financial services.
12. The simple fact that IT investment takes a significant amount of money makes it a barrier to entry. Anything that increases capital requirements is a barrier to entry.

1.8.6.4 Historical Development

The role of business information systems has changed and expanded over the last four decades.

In the incipient decade (1950s and '60s), **"elecsystems"** could be afforded by only the largest organizations. They were used to record and store bookkeeping data such as journal entries, specialized journals, and ledems" *were used to generate a limited range of predefined reports, including income statements (they were called P & L's back then), balance sheets and sales reports. They were trying to perform a decision making support role, but they were not up to the task.*

By the 1970s **"decision support systems"** were introduced. They were interactive in the sense that they allowed the user to choose between numerous options and configurations. Not only was the user allowed to customize outputs, they also could configure the programs to their specific needs. There was a cost though. As part of your mainframe leasing agreement, you typically had to pay to have an IBM system developer permanently on site.

The main development in the 1980s was the introduction of **decentralized computing**. Instead of having one large mainframe computer for the entire enterprise, numerous PCs were spread around the organization. This meant that instead of submitting a job to the computer department for batch processing and waiting for the experts to perform the procedure, each user had their own computer that they could customize for their own purposes. Many poor souls fought with the vagaries of DOS protocols, BIOS functions, and DOS batch programming.

As people became comfortable with their new skills, they discovered all the things their system was capable of. Computers, instead of creating a paperless society, as was expected, produced mountains of paper, most of it valueless. Mounds of reports were generated just because it was possible to do so. This information overload was mitigated somewhat in the 1980s with the introduction of **"executive information systems"**. They streamlined the process, giving the executive exactly what they wanted, and only what they wanted.

The 1980s also saw the first commercial application of artificial intelligence techniques in the form of **"expert systems"**. These programs could give advice within a very limited subject area. The promise of decision making support, first attempted in management information systems back in the 1960s, had step-by-step, come to fruition.

The 1990s saw the introduction of the *Strategic information system*. These systems used information technology to enable the concepts of business strategy developed by scholars like M. Porter, T Peters, J. Reise, C. Markides, and J. Barney in the 1980s. The sustainability of these applications has since been called into question by N. Carr, which Piccoli and Ives, among others, have countered.

The role of business information systems had now expanded to include strategic support. The latest step was the commercialization of the Internet, and the growth of intranets and extranets at the turn of the century.

1.8.7 Decision Support Systems

Transaction processing and management information systems provide information on a regular basis. Frequently, however, users need information not provided in these reports to help them make decisions. A sales manager, for example, might need to determine how high to set yearly sales quotas based on increased sales and lowered product costs. Decision support systems help provide information to support such decisions.

A **Decision Support System (DSS)** is an information system designed to help users reach a decision when a decision-making situation arises. A variety of DSSs exist to help with a range of decisions.

A decision support system uses data from internal and/or external sources.

Internal sources of data might include sales, manufacturing, inventory, or financial data from an organization's database. Data from **external sources** could include interest rates, population trends, and costs of new housing construction or raw material pricing. Users of a DSS, often managers, can manipulate the data used in the DSS to help with decisions.

Some decision support systems include query language, statistical analysis capabilities, spreadsheets, and graphics that help you extract data and evaluate the results. Some decision support systems also include capabilities that allow you to create a model of the factors affecting a decision. A simple model for determining the best product price, for example, would include factors for the expected sales volume at each price level. With the model, you can ask what-if questions by changing one or more of the factors and viewing the projected results. Many people use application software packages to perform DSS functions. Using spreadsheet software, for example, you can complete simple modeling tasks or what-if scenarios.

A special type of DSS, called an **Executive Information System (EIS)**, is designed to support the information needs of executive management. Information in an EIS is presented in charts and tables that show trends, ratios, and other managerial statistics. Because executives usually focus on strategic issues, EISs rely on external data sources such as the Dow Jones News/Retrieval service or the Internet. These external data sources can provide current information on interest rates, commodity prices, and other leading economic indicators.

To store all the necessary decision-making data, DSSs or EISs often use extremely large databases, called data warehouses. A **data warehouse** stores and manages the data required to analyze historical and current business circumstances.

1.8.8 Human Resource Management System

Human Resource Management Systems (HRMS, EHRMS), Human Resource Information Systems (HRIS), HR Technology or also called **HR modules**, shape an intersection in between human resource management (HRM) and information technology. It merges HRM as a discipline and in particular its basic HR activities and processes with the information technology field, whereas the planning and programming of data processing systems evolved into standardised routines and packages of enterprise resource planning (ERP) software. On the whole, these ERP systems have their origin on software that integrates information from different applications into one universal database. The linkage of its financial and human resource modules through one database is the most important distinction to the individually and proprietary developed predecessors, which makes this software application both rigid and flexible.

1.8.8.1 The HR Function's Reality

All in all, the HR function is still to a large degree administrative and common to all organisations. To varying degrees, most organisations have formalised selection, evaluation, and payroll processes. Efficient and effective management of the "Human Capital" Pool (HCP) has become an increasingly imperative and complex activity to all HR professionals. The HR function consists of tracking innumerable data points on each employee, from personal histories, data, skills, capabilities, experiences to payroll records. To reduce the manual workload of these administrative activities, organisations began to electronically automate many of these processes by introducing innovative HRMS/HCM technology. Due to complexity in programming, capabilities and limited technical resources, HR executives rely on internal or external IT professionals to develop and maintain their Human Resource Management Systems (HRMS). Before the "client-server" architecture evolved in the late 1980s, every single HR automation process came largely in form of mainframe computers that could handle large amounts of data transactions. In consequence of the high capital investment necessary to purchase or program proprietary software, these internally developed HRMS were limited to medium to large organisations being able to afford internal IT capabilities. The advent of client-server HRMS authorised HR executives for the first time to take responsibility and ownership of their systems. These client-server HRMS are characteristically developed around four principal areas of HR functionalities: 1) "payroll", 2) time and labour management 3) benefits administration and 4) HR management.

The **payroll module** automates the pay process by gathering data on employee time and attendance, calculating various deductions and taxes, and generating periodic paycheques and employee tax reports. Data is generally fed from the human resources and time keeping modules to calculate automatic deposit and manual cheque writing capabilities. Sophisticated HCM systems can set up accounts payable transactions from employee deduction or produce garnishment cheques. The payroll module sends accounting information to the general ledger for posting subsequent to a pay cycle.

The **time and labour management module** applies new technology and methods (time collection devices) to cost effectively gather and evaluate employee time/work information. The most advanced modules provide broad flexibility in data collection methods, as well as labour distribution capabilities and data analysis features. This module is a key ingredient to establish organisational cost accounting capabilities.

The **benefit administration module** permits HR professionals to easily administer and track employee participation in benefits programs ranging from healthcare provider, insurance policy, and pension plan to profit sharing or stock option plans.

The **HR management module** is a component covering all other HR aspects from application to retirement. The system records basic demographic and address data, selection, training and development, capabilities and skills management, compensation planning records and other related activities. Leading edge systems provide the ability to "read" applications and enter relevant data to applicable database fields, notify employers and provide position management and position control.

Typically, HRMS/HCM technology replaces the four core HR activities by streamlining them electronically; 1) payroll, 2) time and labour management, 3) benefit administration and 4) HR management. While using the internet or corporate intranet as a communication and workflow vehicle, the HRMS/HCM technology can convert these into web-based HRMS components of the ERP system and permit to reduce transaction costs, leading to greater HR and organisational efficiency. Through employee or manager self-service (ESS or MSS), HR activities shift away from paper based processes to using self-service functionalities that benefit employees, managers and HR professionals alike. Costly and time consuming HR administrative tasks, such as travel reimbursement, personnel data change, benefits enrolment, enrolment in training classes (employee side) and to instruct a personnel action, authorise access to information for employees (manager's side) are being individually handled and permit to reduce HR transaction time, leading to HR and organisational effectiveness. Consequently, HR professionals can spend fewer resources in managing administrative HR activities and can apply freed time and resources to concentrate on strategic HR issues, which lead to business innovation.

1.8.8.2 EHRMS Vendors

Vendors of popular EHRMS enterprise level software packages include: SAP, Oracle, PeopleSoft, Microsoft, LogicaCMG and Exact Software.

A wide variety of other software vendors VSO provide various subsets of enterprise level functionality. For example, basic time and attendance software packages provide employee timekeeping functionality while other vendors focus primarily on payroll processing.

Open Source EHRMS' such as OrangeHRM are also available, however they lack end-to-end processes, functionalities and integration with common or open source ERP systems.

1.8.9 Integrated Information Systems

With today's sophisticated hardware, software and communications technologies, it often is difficult to classify a system as belonging uniquely to one of the five information system types discussed. Much of today's application software supports transaction processing and generates management information. Other applications provide transaction processing, management information, and decision support. Although expert systems still operate primarily as separate systems, organizations increasingly are consolidating their information needs into a single, integrated information system.

1.8.10 Strategic Information Systems

Strategic Information System (SIS) is systems that support or shape an organization's competitive strategy. An SIS is characterized by its ability to change significantly the manner in which business id done.

1.8.10.1 Role of It in Strategic Systems

Information technology contributes to Strategic Information Systems in several ways, they are:

- Information technology creates applications that provide direct strategic advantage to organizations.
- IT supports strategic changes such as reengineering. For example IT allows efficient decentralization by providing high - speed communication lines, and the it streamlines and short terms product design with computer added engineering tools.
- IT provides for technological innovations or art as an enabler of innovation. These can incorporated in the firm's goods or services, or can affect how those are provided.
- IT provides competitive intelligence by controlling and analyzing information about innovations, markets, competitors, and environmental changes. Such information provides strategic advantages: if a company knows something important before its competitors or if it can make correct interpretation of information before its competitors, then it can introduce changes first and benefit from them.

1.8.11 Expert System

An **expert system** also known as a knowledge based system, is a computer program that contains some of the subject-specific knowledge of one or more human experts. This class of program was first developed by researchers in artificial intelligence during the 1960s and 1970s and applied commercially throughout the 1980s. The most common form of expert systems is a program made up of a set of rules that analyze information (usually supplied by the user of the system) about a specific class of problems, as well as providing mathematical analysis of the problem(s), and, *depending upon their design*, recommend a course of user action in order to implement corrections. It is a system that utilizes reasoning capabilities to reach conclusions.

1.8.11.1 Types of Problems Solved by Expert Systems

Expert systems are most valuable to organizations that have a high-level of know-how experience and expertise that cannot be easily transferred to other members. They are designed to carry the intelligence and information found in the intellect of experts and provide this knowledge to other members of the organization for problem-solving purposes.

Typically, the problems to be solved are of the sort that would normally be tackled by a medical or other professional. Real experts in the problem domain (which will typically be very narrow, for instance "diagnosing skin in human teenagers") are asked to provide "rules of thumb" on how they evaluate the problems, either explicitly with the aid of experienced systems developers, or sometimes implicitly, by getting such experts to evaluate test cases and using computer programs to examine the test data and (in a strictly limited manner) derive rules from that. Generally expert systems are used for problems for which there is no single "correct" solution which can be encoded in a conventional algorithm — one would not write an expert system to find shortest paths through graphs, or sort data, as there are simply easier ways to do these tasks.

Simple systems use simple true/false logic to evaluate data, but more sophisticated systems are capable of performing at least some evaluation taking into account real-world uncertainties, using such methods as fuzzy logic. Such sophistication is difficult to develop and still highly imperfect.

1.8.11.2 Application

Expert systems are designed and created to facilitate tasks in the fields of accounting, medicine, process control, financial service, production, human resources etc. Indeed, the foundation of a successful expert system depends on a series of technical procedures and development that may be designed by certain technicians and related experts. When a corporation begins to develop and implement an expert system project, it will use selfsourcing, insourcing and / or outsourcing techniques.

While expert systems have distinguished themselves in AI research in finding practical application, their application has been limited. Expert systems are notoriously narrow in their domain of knowledge—as an amusing example, a researcher used the "skin disease" expert system to diagnose his rustbucket car as likely to have developed measles—and the systems were thus prone to making errors that humans would easily spot. Additionally, once some of the mystique had worn off, most programmers realized that simple expert systems were essentially just slightly more elaborate versions of the decision logic they had already been using. Therefore, some of the techniques of expert systems can now be found in most complex programs without any fuss about them.

An example of an expert system used by many people is the Microsoft windows operating system troubleshooting software located in the "help" section in the taskbar menu. Obtaining expert / technical operating system support is often difficult for individuals not closely involved with the development of the operating system. Microsoft has designed their expert system to provide solutions, advice, and suggestions to common errors encountered throughout using the operating systems.

Another 1970s and 1980s application of expert systems — which we today would simply call AI — was in computer games. For example, the computer baseball games Earl Weaver Baseball and Tony La Russa Baseball each had highly detailed simulations of the game strategies of those two baseball managers. When a human played the game against the computer, the computer queried the Earl Weaver or Tony La Russa Expert System for a decision on what strategy to follow. Even those choices where some randomness was part of the natural system (such as when to throw a surprise pitch-out to try to trick a runner trying to steal a base) were decided based on probabilities supplied by Weaver or La Russa. Today we would simply say that "the game's AI provided the opposing manager's strategy."

1.8.11.3 Expert Systems Versus Problem-Solving Systems

The principal distinction between expert systems and traditional problem solving programs is the way in which the problem related expertise is coded. In traditional applications, problem expertise is encoded in both program and data structures.

In the expert system approach all of the problem related expertise is encoded in data structures only; none is in programs. Several benefits immediately follow from this organization.

An example may help contrast the traditional problem solving program with the expert system approach. The example is the problem of tax advice. In the traditional approach data structures describe the taxpayer and tax tables, and a program in which there are statements representing an expert tax consultant's knowledge, such as statements which relate information about the taxpayer to tax table choices. It is this representation of the tax expert's knowledge that is difficult for the tax expert to understand or modify.

In the expert system approach, the information about taxpayers and tax computations is again found in data structures, but now the knowledge describing the relationships between them is encoded in data structures as well. The programs of an expert system are independent of the problem domain (taxes) and serve to process the data structures without regard to the nature of the problem area they describe. For example, there are programs to acquire the described data values through user interaction, programs to represent and process special organizations of description, and programs to process the declarations that represent semantic relationships within the problem domain and an algorithm to control the processing sequence and focus.

The general architecture of an expert system involves two principal components: a problem dependent set of data declarations called the knowledge base or rule base, and a problem independent (although highly data structure dependent) program which is called the inference engine.

1.8.11.4 Individuals Involved with Expert Systems

There are generally three individuals having an interaction with expert systems. Primary among these is the end-user; the individual who uses the system for its problem solving assistance. In the building and maintenance of the system there are two other roles: the problem domain expert who builds and supplies the knowledge base providing the domain expertise, and a knowledge engineer who assists the experts in determining the representation of their knowledge, enters this knowledge into an explanation module and who defines the inference technique required to obtain useful problem solving activity. Usually, the knowledge engineer will represent the problem solving activity in the form of rules which is referred to as a rule-based expert system. When these rules are created from the domain expertise, the knowledge base stores the rules of the expert system.

1.8.11.5 The End User

The end-user usually sees an expert system through an interactive dialog, an example of which follows:

1. *Do you know to which restaurant you want to go?*

Ans. No.

2. *Is there any kind of food you would particularly like?*

Ans. Unknown.

3. *Do you like spicy food?*

Ans. No.

4. *Do you usually drink wine with meals?*

Ans. Yes.

5. *When you drink wine, is it French wine?*

Ans. Why

As can be seen from this dialog, the system is leading the user through a set of questions, the purpose of which is to determine a suitable set of restaurants to recommend. This dialog begins with the system asking if the user already knows the restaurant choice (a common feature of expert systems) and immediately illustrates a characteristic of expert systems; users may choose not to respond to any question. In expert systems, dialogs are not pre-planned. There is no fixed control structure. Dialogs are synthesized from the current information and the contents of the knowledge base. Because of this, not being able to supply the answer to a particular questions does not stop the consultation.

Another major distinction between expert systems and traditional systems is illustrated by the following answer given by the system when the user answers a question with another question, "Why", as occurred in the above example. The answer is:

Ans. I am trying to determine the type of restaurant to suggest. So far Chinese is not a likely choice. It is possible that French is a likely choice. I know that if the diner is a wine drinker, and the preferred wine is French, then there is strong evidence that the restaurant choice should include French.

It is very difficult to implement a general explanation system (answering questions like Why and How) in traditional systems. The response of the expert system to the question WHY is an exposure of the underlying knowledge structure. It is a rule; a set of antecedent conditions which, if true, allow the assertion of a consequent. The rule references values, and tests them against various constraints or asserts constraints onto them. This, in fact, is a significant part of the knowledge structure. There are values, which may be associated with some organizing entity. For example, the individual diner is an entity with various attributes (values) including whether they drink wine and the kind of wine. There are also rules, which associate the currently known values of some attributes with assertions that can be made about other attributes. It is the orderly processing of these rules that dictates the dialog itself.

1.8.11.6 The Knowledge Engineer

Knowledge engineers are concerned with the representation chosen for the expert's knowledge declarations and with the inference engine used to process that knowledge. He / she can use the knowledge acquisition component of the expert system to input the several characteristics known to be appropriate to a good inference technique including:

1. A good inference technique is independent of the problem domain.

   In order to realize the benefits of explanation, knowledge transparency, and reusability of the programs in a new problem domain, the inference engine must not contain domain specific expertise.
2. Inference techniques may be specific to a particular task, such as diagnosis of hardware configuration. Other techniques may be committed only to a particular processing technique.
3. Inference techniques are always specific to the knowledge structures.
4. Successful examples of rule processing techniques include:
   (*a*) Forward chaining
   (*b*) Backward chaining

1.8.11.7 The Inference Rule

An understanding of the "inference rule" concept is important to understand expert systems. An inference rule is a statement that has two parts, an if-clause and a then-clause. This rule is what gives expert systems the ability to find solutions to diagnostic and prescriptive problems. An example of an inference rule is:

If the restaurant choice includes French, and the occasion is romantic,

Then the restaurant choice is definitely Paul Bocuse.

An expert system's rulebase is made up of many such inference rules. They are entered as separate rules and it is the inference engine that uses them together to draw conclusions. Because each rule is a unit, rules may be deleted or added without affecting other rules (though it should affect which conclusions are reached). One advantage of inference rules over traditional programming is that inference rules use reasoning which more closely resemble human reasoning.

Thus, when a conclusion is drawn, it is possible to understand how this conclusion was reached. Furthermore, because the expert system uses knowledge in a form similar to the expert, it may be easier to retrieve this information from the expert.

Chaining

There are two main methods of reasoning when using inference rules: backward chaining and forward chaining.

Forward chaining starts with the data available and uses the inference rules to conclude more data until a desired goal is reached. An inference engine using forward chaining searches the inference rules until it finds one in which the if-clause is known to be true. It then concludes the then-clause and adds this information to its data. It would continue to do this until a goal is reached. Because the data available determines which inference rules are used, this method is also called *data driven*.

Backward chaining starts with a list of goals and works backwards to see if there is data which will allow it to conclude any of these goals. An inference engine using backward chaining would search the inference rules until it finds one which has a then-clause that matches a desired goal. If the if-clause of that inference rule is not known to be true, then it is added to the list of goals. For example, suppose a rulebase contains two rules:

1. If Fritz is green then Fritz is a frog.
2. If Fritz is a frog then Fritz hops.

Suppose a goal is to conclude that Fritz hops.The rulebase would be searched and rule (2) would be selected because its conclusion (the then clause) matches the goal. It is not known that Fritz is a frog, so this "if" statement is added to the goal list. The rulebase is again searched and this time rule (1) is selected because its then clause matches the new goal just added to the list. This time, the if-clause (Fritz is green) is known to be true and the goal that Fritz hops is concluded. Because the list of goals determines which rules are selected and used, this method is called *goal driven*.

1.8.11.8 Confidences

Another advantage of expert systems over traditional methods of programming is that they allow the use of confidences. When a human reasons he does not always conclude things with 100% confidence. He might say, "If Fritz is green, then he is probably a frog" (after all, he might be a chameleon). This type of reasoning can be imitated by using numeric values called confidences. For example, if it is known that Fritz is green, it might be concluded with 0.85 confidence that he is a frog; or, if it is known that he is a frog, it might be concluded with 0.95 Confidence that he hops. These numbers are similar in nature to probabilities, but they are not the same. They are meant to imitate the confidences humans use in reasoning rather than to follow the mathematical definitions used in calculating probabilities.

The following general points about expert systems and their architecture have been illustrated.

1. The sequence of steps taken to reach a conclusion is dynamically synthesized with each new case. It is not explicitly programmed when the system is built.
2. Expert systems can process multiple values for any problem parameter. This permits more than one line of reasoning to be pursued and the results of incomplete (not fully determined) reasoning to be presented.
3. Problem solving is accomplished by applying specific knowledge rather than specific technique. This is a key idea in expert systems technology. It reflects the belief that human experts do not process their knowledge differently from others, but they do possess different knowledge. With this philosophy, when one finds that their expert system does not produce the desired results, work begins to expand the knowledge base, not to re-program the procedures.

There are various expert systems in which a "rulebase" and an "inference engine" cooperate to simulate the reasoning process that a human expert pursues in analyzing a problem and arriving at a conclusion. In these systems, in order to simulate the human reasoning process, a vast amount of knowledge needed to be stored in the knowledge base. Generally, the knowledge base of such an expert system consisted of a relatively large number of "if then" type of statements that were interrelated in a manner that, in theory at least, resembled the sequence of mental steps that were involved in the human reasoning process.

Because of the need for large storage capacities and related programs to store the rulebase, most expert systems have, in the past, been run only on large information handling systems. Recently, the storage capacity of personal computers has increased to a point where it is becoming possible to consider running some types of simple expert systems on personal computers.

In some applications of expert systems, the nature of the application and the amount of stored information necessary to simulate the human reasoning process for that application is just too vast to store in the active memory of a computer. In other applications of expert systems, the nature of the application is such that not all of the information is always needed in the reasoning process. An example of this latter type application would be the use of an expert system to diagnose a data processing system comprising many separate components, some of which are optional. When that type of expert system employs a single integrated rulebase to diagnose the minimum system configuration of the data processing system, much of the rulebase is not required since many of the components which are optional units of the system will not be present in the system. Nevertheless, earlier expert systems require the entire rulebase to be stored since all the rules were, in effect, chained or linked together by the structure of the rulebase.

When the rulebase is segmented, preferably into contextual segments or units, it is then possible to eliminate portions of the Rulebase containing data or knowledge that is not needed in a particular application. The segmenting of the rulebase also allows the expert system to be run with systems or on systems having much smaller memory capacities than was possible with earlier arrangements since each segment of the rulebase can be paged into and out of the system as needed. The segmenting of the rulebase into contextual segments requires that the expert system manage various intersegment relationships as segments are paged into and out of memory during execution of the program. Since the system permits a rulebase segment to be called and executed at any time during the processing of the first rulebase, provision must be made to store the data that has been accumulated up to that point so that at some time later in the process, when the system returns to the first segment, it can proceed from the last point or rule node that was processed. Also, provision must be made so that data that has been collected by the system up to that point can be passed to the second segment of the rulebase after it has been paged into the system and data collected during the processing of the second segment can be passed to the first segment when the system returns to complete processing that segment.

The user interface and the procedure interface are two important functions in the information collection process.

1.8.11.9 The User Interface

The function of the user interface is to present questions and information to the operator and supply the operator's responses to the inference engine.

Any values entered by the user must be received and interpreted by the user interface. Some responses are restricted to a set of possible legal answers, others are not. The user interface checks all responses to insure that they are of the correct data type. Any responses that are restricted to a legal set of answers are compared against these legal answers. Whenever the user enters an illegal answer, the user interface informs the user that his answer was invalid and prompts him to correct it. As explained in the cross referenced application, communication between the user interface and the inference engine is performed through the use of a User Interface Control Block (UICB) which is passed between the two.

1.8.11.10 Procedure Node Interface

The function of the procedure node interface is to receive information from the procedures coordinator and create the appropriate procedure call. The ability to call a procedure and receive information from that procedure can be viewed as simply a generalization of input from the external world. While in some earlier expert systems external information has been obtained, that information was obtained only in a predetermined manner so only certain information could actually be acquired. This expert system, disclosed in the cross-referenced application, through the knowledge base, is permitted to invoke any procedure allowed on its host system. This makes the expert system useful in a much wider class of knowledge domains than if it had no external access or only limited external access.

In the area of machine diagnostics using expert systems, particularly self-diagnostic applications, it is not possible to conclude the current state of "health" of a machine without some information. The best source of information is the machine itself, for it contains much detailed information that could not reasonably be provided by the operator.

The knowledge that is represented in the system appears in the rulebase. In the rulebase described in the cross-referenced applications, there are basically four different types of objects, with associated information present.

1. Classes--these are questions asked to the user.
2. Parameters--a parameter is a place holder for a character string which may be a variable that can be inserted into a class question at the point in the question where the parameter is positioned.

3. Procedures--these are definitions of calls to external procedures.
4. Rule Nodes--The inferencing in the system is done by a tree structure which indicates the rules or logic which mimics human reasoning. The nodes of these trees are called rule nodes. There are several different types of rule nodes.

The rulebase comprises a forest of many trees. The top node of the tree is called the goal node, in that it contains the conclusion. Each tree in the forest has a different goal node. The leaves of the tree are also referred to as rule nodes, or one of the types of rule nodes. A leaf may be an evidence node, an external node, or a reference node.

An evidence node functions to obtain information from the operator by asking a specific question. In responding to a question presented by an evidence node, the operator is generally instructed to answer "yes" or "no" represented by numeric values 1 and 0 or provide a value of between 0 and 1, represented by a "maybe."

Questions which require a response from the operator other than yes or no or a value between 0 and 1 are handled in a different manner.

A leaf that is an external node indicates that data will be used which was obtained from a procedure call.

A reference node functions to refer to another tree or subtree.

A tree may also contain intermediate or minor nodes between the goal node and the leaf node. An intermediate node can represent logical operations like And or Or.

The inference logic has two functions. It selects a tree to trace and then it traces that tree. Once a tree has been selected, that tree is traced, depth-first, left to right.

The word "tracing" refers to the action the system takes as it traverses the tree, asking classes (questions), calling procedures, and calculating confidences as it proceeds.

As explained in the cross-referenced applications, the selection of a tree depends on the ordering of the trees. The original ordering of the trees is the order in which they appear in the rulebase. This order can be changed, however, by assigning an evidence node an attribute "initial" which is described in detail in these applications. The first action taken is to obtain values for all evidence nodes which have been assigned an "initial" attribute. Using only the answers to these initial evidences, the rules are ordered so that the most likely to succeed is evaluated first. The trees can be further re-ordered since they are constantly being updated as a selected tree is being traced.

It has been found that the type of information that is solicited by the system from the user by means of questions or classes should be tailored to the level of knowledge of the user. In many applications, the group of prospective uses is nicely defined and the knowledge level can be estimated so that the questions can be presented at a level which corresponds generally to the average user. However, in other applications, knowledge of the specific domain of the expert system might vary considerably among the group of prospective users.

One application where this is particularly true involves the use of an expert system, operating in a self-diagnostic mode on a personal computer to assist the operator of the personal computer to diagnose the cause of a fault or error in either the hardware or software. In general, asking the operator for information is the most straightforward way for the expert system to gather information assuming, of course, that the information is or should be within the operator's understanding. For example, in diagnosing a personal computer, the expert system must know the major functional components of the system. It could ask the operator, for instance, if the display is a monochrome or color display. The operator should, in all probability, be able to provide the correct answer 100% of the time. The expert system could, on the other hand, cause a test unit to be run to determine the type of display. The accuracy of the data collected by either approach in this instance probably would not be that different so the knowledge engineer could employ either approach without affecting the accuracy of the diagnosis. However, in many instances, because of the nature of the information being solicited, it is better to obtain the information from the system rather than asking the operator, because the accuracy of the data supplied by the operator is so low that the system could not effectively process it to a meaningful conclusion.

In many situations the information is already in the system, in a form of which permits the correct answer to a question to be obtained through a process of inductive or deductive reasoning. The data previously collected by the system could be answers provided by the user to less complex questions that were asked for a different reason or results returned from test units that were previously run.

1.8.11.11 *Advantages and Disadvantages*

Expert systems exercise information technology to acquire and utilize human expertise. It can be beneficial for organizations that have clear objectives, rules and procedures. Expert systems can:

- Provide consistent answers for repetitive decisions, processes and tasks
- Hold and maintain significant levels of information
- Reduce employee training costs
- Centralize the decision making process
- Create efficiencies and reduce time needed to solve problems
- Combine multiple human expert intelligences
- Reduce the amount of human errors
- Give strategic and comparative advantages creating entry barriers to competitors
- Review transactions that human experts may overlook

Although significantly advantageous to many entities, limitations of expert systems may arise through:

- The lack of human common sense needed in some decision makings
- The creative responses human experts can respond to in unusual circumstances
- Domain experts not always being able to explain their logic and reasoning
- The challenges of automating complex processes
- The lack of flexibility and ability to adapt to changing environments
- Not being able to recognize when no answer is available.

1.8.11.12 *The Difference between Neural Networks and Expert Systems*

- Expert systems emulate human decision making
- Neural networks learn human thought processes and reasoning patterns
- Expert systems use rules and frames in which to make their decisions
- Neural networks adjust to inputs and outputs
- Expert systems require humans to update their database of information
- Neural networks continue to expand their own base of information

1.8.12 Executive Information System

An **Executive Information System** (EIS) is a computer-based system intended to facilitate and support the information and decision making needs of senior executives by providing easy access to both internal and external information relevant to meeting the strategic goals of the organization. It is commonly considered as a specialized form of Decision Support System (DSS).

The emphasis of EIS is on graphical displays and easy-to-use user interfaces. They offer strong reporting and drill-down capabilities. In general, EIS are enterprise-wide DSS that help top-level executives analyze, compare, and highlight trends in important variables so that they can monitor performance and identify opportunities and problems. EIS and data warehousing technologies are converging in the marketplace.

For the past few years, the term EIS has been little-used. A more common term used to describe this domain area is Business Intelligence (sub areas of reporting, analyitics, dashboards).

1.8.12.1 History of EIS

Traditionally, executive information systems were developed as mainframe computer-based programs. The purpose was to package a company's data and to provide sales performance or market research statistics for decision makers, as such financial officers, marketing directors, and chief executive officers, who were not well acquainted with computers. The objective was to develop computer applications that would highlight information to satisfy senior executives' needs. Typically, an EIS provides the data that would only need to support executive level decisions instead of the data for all the company. Today, the application of EIS is not only used in typical corporation hierarchies, but also installed at the personal computer levels or workstation levels on a local area network. EIS now cross computer hardware platforms and integrate information stored on mainframes, personal computer systems, and minicomputers. As some client service companies adopt the latest enterprise information systems, employees can now use their personal computers to get access to the company's data and decide which data are relevant for their decision makings. This arrangement makes all users capable to customize their access to the proper company's data and provide relevant information to both upper and lower levels in companies.

1.8.12.2 EIS Components

The components of an EIS can typically be classified into the following categories:

Hardware: When talking about hardware for an EIS environment, we should focus on the hardware that meet executive's needs. The executive must be put the first and the executive's needs must be defined before the hardware can be selected. The basic computer hardware needed for a typical EIS includes four components: (1) Input data-entry devices. These devices allow the executive to enter, verify, and update data immediately; (2) The central processing unit (CPU), which is the kernel because it controls the other computer system components; (3) Data storage files. The executive can use this part to save useful business information, and this part also help the executive to search historical business information easily; (4) Output devices, which provide a visual or permanent record for the executive to save or read. This device refers to the visual output device or printer. In addition, with the advent of local area networks (LAN), several EIS products for networked workstations became available. These systems require less support and less expensive computer hardware. They also increase access of the EIS information to many more users within a company.

Software: Choosing the appropriate software is vital to design an effective EIS. Therefore, the software components and how they integrate the data into one system are very important. The basic software needed for a typical EIS includes four components: (1) Text base software. The most common form of text is probably the word processing document; (2) Database. Heterogeneous databases residing on a range of vendor-specific and open computer platforms helps executives access to both company internal and external data; (3) Graphic base. Graphics can turn volumes of text and statistics into visual information for executives. Typical graphic types are: time series charts, scatter diagrams, maps, motion graphics, sequence charts, and comparison-oriented graphs (i.e., bar charts); (4) Model base. The EIS models contain routine and special statistical, financial, and other quantitative analysis. Now perhaps the more difficult problem to those executives is how to choose EIS software rather than how to use them, because the latest EIS software packages are more intelligible to nontechnicians, self-documenting, and more flexible. Therefore, when we evaluate EIS software, we should think about if the package is easy to use, if the package responds readily to the executive's requests, and if the package is reasonably priced. Furthermore, we need consider if the package can run on the current hardware we have.

Interface: An EIS needs to be efficient to retrieve relevant data for decision makers, so the interface is very important. Several types of interfaces can be available to the EIS structure, such as scheduled reports, questions/answers, menu driven, command language, natural language, and input/output. It is crucial that the interface must fit the decision maker's decision-making style. If the executive is not comfortable with the information questions/answers style, the EIS will not be fully utilized. The ideal interface for an EIS would be simple to use and highly flexible, providing consistent performance, reflecting the executive's world, and containing help information and error messages.

Telecommunications: As decentralizing is becoming the current trend in companies, telecommunications will play a pivotal role in networked information systems. Transmitting data from one place to another has become crucial for establishing a reliable network. In addition, telecommunications within an EIS can accelerate the need for access to distributed data.

1.8.12.3 EIS Applications

EIS enables executives to find those data according to user-defined criteria and promote information-based insight and understanding. Unlike a traditional management information system presentation, EIS can distinguish between vital and seldom-used data, and track different key critical activities for executives, both which are helpful in evaluate if the company is meeting its corporate objectives. After realizing its advantages, people have applied EIS in many areas, especially, in manufacturing, marketing, and finance areas.

Manufacturing: Basically, manufacturing is the transformation of raw materials into finished goods for sale, or intermediate processes involving the production or finishing of semi-manufactures. It is a large branch of industry and of secondary production. Manufacturing operational control focuses on day-to-day operations, and the central idea of this process is effectiveness and efficiency. To produce meaningful managerial and operational information for controlling manufacturing operations, the executive has to make changes in the decision processes. EIS provides the evaluation of vendors and buyers, the evaluation of purchased materials and parts, and analysis of critical purchasing areas. Therefore, the executive can oversee and review purchasing operations effectively with EIS. In addition, because production planning and control depends heavily on the plant's data base and its communications with all manufacturing work centers,

EIS also provides an approach to improve production planning and control. Following are some real-world EIS applications related to manufacturing.

Marketing: In an organization, marketing executives' role is to create the future. Their main duty is managing available marketing resources to create a more effective future. For this, they need make judgment s about risk and uncertainty of a project and its impact on company in short term and long term. To assist marketing executives in making effective marketing decisions, an EIS can be applied. EIS provides an approach to sales forecasting, which can allow the market executive to compare sales forecast with past sales. EIS also offers an approach to product price, which is found in venture analysis. The market executive can evaluate pricing as related to competition along with the relationship of product quality with price charged. In summary, EIS software package enables marketing executives to manipulate the data by looking for trends, performing audits of the sales data, and calculating totals, averages, changes, variances, or ratios. All of these sales analysis functions help marketing executives to make final decisions. Following are some real-world EIS applications related to marketing.

Financial: A financial analysis is one of the most important steps to companies today. The executive needs to use financial ratios and cash flow analysis to estimate the trends and make capital investment decisions. An EIS is a responsibility-oriented approach that integrated planning or budgeting with control of performance reporting, and it can be extremely helpful to finance executives. Basically, EIS focuses on accountability of financial performance and it recognizes the importance of cost standards and flexible budgeting in developing the quality of information provided for all executive levels. EIS enables executives to focus more on the long-term basis of current year and beyond, which means that the executive not only can manage a sufficient flow to maintain current operations but also can figure out how to expand operations that are contemplated over the coming years. Also, the combination of EIS and EDI environment can help cash managers to review the company's financial structure so that the best method of financing for an accepted capital project can be concluded. In addition, the EIS is a good tool to help the executive to review financial ratios, highlight financial trends and analyze a company's performance and its competitors. Following are some real-world EIS applications related to finance.

1.8.12.4 Advantages and Disadvantages of EIS

Advantages

- Easy for upper-level executives to use, extensive computer experience is not required in operations
- Provides timely delivery of company summary information
- Information that is provided is better understanding
- Filters data for management
- Improves to tracking information
- Offers efficiency to decision makers

Disadvantages

- Functions are limited, can not perform complex calculations
- Hard to quantify benefits and to justify implementation of an EIS
- Executives may encounter overloaded information
- System may become slow, large, and hard to manage

- Difficult to keep current data
- May lead to less reliable and secure data
- Small companies may encounter excessive costs for implementation.

1.8.12.5 Future Trends in EIS

The future of executive info systems will not be bound by mainframe computer systems. This trend allows executives escaping from learning different computer operating systems and substantially decreases the implementation costs for companies. Because utilizing existing software applications lies in this trend, executives will also eliminate the need to learn a new or special language for the EIS package. Future executive information systems will not only provide a system that supports senior executives, but also contain the information needs for middle managers. The future executive information systems will become diverse because of integrating potential new applications and technology into the systems, such as incorporating artificial intelligence (AI) and integrating multimedia characteristics and ISDN technology into an EIS.

1.8.13 Cross Functional Information Systems

The successful application of cross functional systems which would allow information sharing between managers is dependent on people and technological issues. People issues include corporate culture, work units and individual decision makers. Cooperation is an essential factor in corporate cultures and work units to encourage information sharing between managers that will be facilitated by cross functional systems. An abundance of useless or incorrect information in cross functional systems must also be avoided, for efficient decision making. Technological issues on the other hand, include information system elements and level of success. Management must compare the advantages of using information system elements such as inputs, processors and outputs with the costs involved. The level of access to be granted for each user must also be determined to guard against the misuse of information.

1.8.13.1 Cross Functional Team

In business, a "cross functional team" is a group of people with different functional expertise working toward a common goal. It may include people from finance, marketing, operations, and human resources departments. Typically, it includes employees from all levels of an organization. Members may also come from outside an organization (in particular, from suppliers, key customers, or consultants).

Cross functional teams often function as self-directed teams responding to broad, but not specific directives. Decision-making within a team may depend on consensus, but often is led by a manager/coach/team leader.

A non-business, yet good example of cross-functional teams are music bands, where each element plays a different instrument (or has a different role). Songs are the result of collaboration and participation, and the goals are decided by consensus. Skills to play all the instruments involved are not required since music provides a standard language that everybody in the team can understand. In short, music bands are clear examples of how these teams work. The Movie maker is the best example to show the relation between the team members from different experiences, The director actualy is the team leader but if he said action and at the same time the the sound manager found some distortion or noise or any thing which he is not convinced within his job he can take the decision to stop until this problem is solved, So In every expert is the leader or the manager of the whole operation when there is a problem related to his speciality.

The growth of self-directed cross-functional teams has influenced decision-making processes and organizational structures. Although management theory likes to propound that every type of organizational structure needs to make strategic, tactical, and operational decisions, new procedures have started to emerge that work best with teams.

1. *Less unidirectional:* Up until recently, decision making flowed in one direction. Overall corporate-level objectives drove strategic business unit (SBU) objectives, and these in turn, drove functional level objectives. Today, organizations have flatter structures, companies diversify less, and functional departments have started to become less well-defined. The rise of self-directed teams reflects these trends. Intra-team dynamics tend to become multi-directional rather than hierarchical. Interactive processes encourage consensus within teams. Also the directives given to the team tend to become more general and less prescribed.
2. *Greater scope of information:* Cross-functional teams require a wide range of information to reach their decisions. They need to draw on information from all parts of an organization's information base. This includes information from all functional departments. System integration becomes important because it makes all information accessible through a single interface.
3. *Greater depth of information:* Cross-functional teams require information from all levels of management. The teams may have their origins in the perceived need to make primarily strategic decisions, tactical decisions, or operational decisions, but they will require all three types of information. Almost all self-directed teams will need information traditionally used in strategic, tactical, and operational decisions. For example, new product development traditionally ranks as a tactical procedure. It gets strategic direction from top management, and uses operational departments like engineering and marketing to perform its task. But a new product development team would consist of people from the operational departments and often someone from top management.

   In many cases, the team would make unstructured strategic decisions — such as what markets to compete in, what new production technologies to invest in, and what return on investment to require; tactical decisions like whether to build a prototype, whether to concept-test, whether to test-market, and how much to produce; and structured operational decisions like production scheduling, inventory purchases, and media flightings. In other cases, the team would confine itself to tactical and operational decisions. In either case it would need information associated with all three levels.
4. *Greater range of users:* Cross-functional teams consist of people from many parts of an organization. Information must take a form that all users understand. Not only engineers use technical data and not only accountants use financial data and not only human resources personnel use HR data. Modern organizations lack middle managers to combine, sort, and prioritize the data. Technical, financial, marketing, and all other types of information must come in a form that all members of a cross-functional team can understand. This involves reducing the amount of specialized jargon, sorting information based on importance, hiding complex statistical procedures from the users, giving interpretations of results, and providing clear explanations of difficult concepts. Slicing and dicing techniques may prove useful in providing different views of the information to different users. Data visualization systems can present complex results in an intuitive manner.
5. *Less teleological:* Since the publication of Peter Drucker's views on "Management by Objectives", business decision-making has become more goal-oriented. Managers have come to view decision-making generally, and strategic thinking in particular, as a multi-stage process that starts with an assessment of the current situation, determines objectives,

then determines how to reach these objectives. Management by objectives took this basic scheme and applied it to virtually all significant decisions. Today many firms have started to opt for a less structured, more interactive approach. One way of implementing this involves using self-directed cross-functional teams. Proponents hope that these teams will develop strategies that will re-define industries and create new "best practices". They feel that mere incremental improvements do not suffice. Cross-functional teams, using unstructured techniques and searching for revolutionary competitive advantages, allegedly require information systems featuring increased interactivity, more flexibility, and the capability of dealing with fuzzy logic. Artificial intelligence holds out the promise of one day proving useful in this regard. Teams consist of members with variable levels of skills and experiences brought together to reach the objectives.

1.9 ARTIFICIAL INTELLIGENCE

1.9.1 Introduction

Artificial Intelligence (AI, for short) is an area which has over half a century of history. A began in earnest with the mergence of the computers during the late 1940s. It was the ability of these machines to store large amount of data and process it into information at very high speeds, hitherto unimaginable, that gave researchers the vision of building systems which could imitate/ emulate some, if not all, human abilities.

While some ground work had already been initiated earlier, it was not until the 1980s that AI received popular economic and managerial acclaim. It was during this period that AI went through the transition from a primary research area to potential commercial applications. It was only then that AI was accepted as an emerging technology and as such attracted considerable attention.

1.9.2 What is Artificial Intelligence?

Artificial Intelligence (AI) is basically a technology which helps/facilitates the application of computers to areas that require knowledge, perception, reasoning, understanding and cognitive abilities which distinguish the human behaviour from machines like computers.

Hence, before moving into further discussion about AI, it would be desirable to compare and understand the attributes of Natural (Human) Intelligence and Artificial (Machine) Intelligence.

Attributes	Natural Intelligence	Artificial Intelligence
• Ability to use sensors (eyes, ear, touch, smell)	High	Low
• Ability to be creative and imaginative	High	Low
• Ability to learn from past experiences	High	Low
• Ability to be adaptive	High	Low
• Ability to afford the cost of acquiring intelligence	High	Low
• Ability to use a variety of information sources	High	Low
• Ability to acquire a large amount of external information	High	Low
• Ability to make complex calculations	Low	High
• Ability to transfer information	Low	High
• Ability to make a series of calculations, rapidly and accurately	Low	High

1.9.3 Pre-requisites of AI

To be artificially intelligent and also be able to come out with human-like responses, computer must possess the following requisite features:

- Understand what is 'Common Sense'.
- Understand 'Facts' and relationships among 'Facts'
- Be able to manipulate 'Qualitative' data.
- Be able to deal with exceptions and discontinuity.
- Be able to interface with humans in a 'Free-Format' fashion.
- Be able to deal with new situations based on previous learning.

1.9.4 AI Definitions

AI has been defined differently by different people. Let us, therefore, not the various AI definitions.

'AI is a branch of computer science that is concerned with the automation of intelligent behaviour".

— George Luger and William Stablefied

'AI is a series of related technologies that attempt to simulate and reproduce human behaviour, including thinking, speaking, feeling and reasoning".

— Hussein Bidgoli

'AI is a branch of computer science concerned with the study and creation of computer systems that exhibit some form of intelligence: Systems that learn new concepts and tasks, systems that can reason and draw useful conclusions about the world around us, systems that can understand natural languages and perceive and comprehend a visual scene and systems that perform other types of feats that require human types of intelligence".

— Dan patterson

1.9.5 The AI Canvas

AI today not only focuses on computer science and computers, but encompasses a group of related technologies and speciality areas like:

- Expert System
- Fuzzy Logic
- Intelligent Agents
- Natural Language Processing
- Neural Networks
- Robotics
- Speech Recognition
- Vision recognized Systems
- Learning System

Nielson, a pioneer in the area of AI, likes to characterize the various areas/components of AI in terms of what he calls, 'ONION MODEL' as illustrated hereafter:

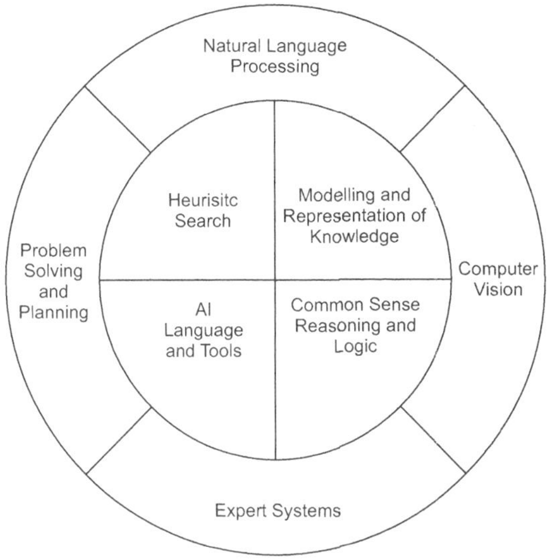

Fig. 6.3 *The AI Onion Model*

1.9.6 AI Applications

While the technology aspects of AI are almost in place by now, initial applications have clearly demonstrated that AI can provide great leverage for corporate organizations.

Some of the illustrative AI applications are as follows:

- Manufacturing/Production Planning and Scheduling
- Project Management
- Factory Management
- Sales, Distribution and Field Services
- Diagnosis and Trouble-shooting
- Financial Management
- Currency/Interest Rates SWAPs
- Portfolio Management
- Asset Liability Management
- Reading/Interpreting Financials
- Criminology
- Geology (Drilling/Oil Exploration Sites)

1.9.7 Precaution

Notwithstanding the advances in AI, it must be remembered that AI Systems are not a replace human decision-making completely. They are meant to replicate/emulate human decision-making for certain types of clearly and well-defined problems — the Chess Matches between Gary Kasporov (Natural Intelligence) and Deep Junior (Artificial Intelligence) being a classic example of AI/ES.

Like other computer-based information systems, the overall purpose of AI systems/applications in business is to help the organizations/managers achieve the goals.

AI has, no doubt, started getting acceptance and credibility. The success of AI as a mass-market technology, however, would depend upon a number of practical factors like:

- Cost
- Personnel with requisite skills
- Corporate Management attributes, and MOST IMPORTANTLY
- The demonstration of a variety of commercial AI success stories to be a role model for others to follow.

1.10 NEURAL NETWORKS

Let us first recap the most important features of the neural networks found in the brain. Firstly the brain contains many billions of very special kinds of cell - these are the nerve cells or neurons. These cells are organized into a very complicated intercommunicating network. Typically each neuron is physically connected to tens of thousands of others. Using these connections neurons can pass electrical signals between each other. These connections are not merely *on* or *off* - the connections have varying *strength* which allows the influence of a given neuron on one of its neighbors to be either very strong, very weak (perhaps even no influence) or anything in between. Furthermore, many aspects of brain function, particularly the learning process, are closely associated with the adjustment of these connection strengths. Brain activity is then represented by particular patterns of firing activity amongst this network of neurons. It is this simultaneous cooperative behavior of very many simple processing units which is at the root of the enormous sophistication and computational power of the brain.

Artificial neural networks are computers whose architecture is modeled after the brain. They typically consist of many hundreds of simple processing units which are wired together in a complex communication network. Each unit or node is a simplified model of a real neuron which fires (sends off a new signal) if it receives a sufficiently strong input signal from the other nodes to which it is connected. The strength of these connections may be varied in order for the network to perform different tasks corresponding to different patterns of node firing activity. This structure is very different from traditional computers.

The traditional computers that we deal with every day have changed very little since their beginnings in the 1940's. While there have been very significant advances in the speed and size of the silicon-based transistors, which form their basic elements - the hardware, the overall design or architecture has not changed significantly. They still consist of a central processing unit or CPU which executes a rigid set of rules (the program or software) sequentially, reading and writing data from a separate unit - the memory. All the "intelligence" of the machine resides in this set of rules - which are supplied by the human programmer. The usefulness of the computer lies in its vast speed at executing those rules - it is a superb machine but not a mind.

Neural networks are very different - they are composed of many rather feeble processing units, which are connected into a network. Their computational power depends on working together on any task - this is sometimes termed parallel processing. There is no central CPU following a logical sequence of rules - indeed there is no set of rules or program. Computation is related to a dynamic process of node firings. This structure then is much closer to the physical workings of the brain and leads to a new type of computer that is rather good at a range of complex tasks.

1.11 FUZZY LOGIC

Fuzzy logic is a powerful problem-solving methodology with a myriad of applications in embedded control and information processing. Fuzzy provides a remarkably simple way to draw definite conclusions from vague, ambiguous or imprecise information. In a sense, fuzzy logic resembles human decision making with its ability to work from approximate data and find precise solutions.

Unlike classical logic, which requires a deep understanding of a system, exact equations, and precise numeric values, Fuzzy logic incorporates an alternative way of thinking, which allows modeling complex systems using a higher level of abstraction originating from our knowledge and experience. Fuzzy Logic allows expressing this knowledge with subjective concepts such as very hot, bright red, and a long time, which are mapped into exact numeric ranges.

Fuzzy Logic has been gaining increasing acceptance during the past few years. There are over two thousand commercially available products using Fuzzy Logic, ranging from washing machines to high-speed trains. Nearly every application can potentially realize some of the benefits of Fuzzy Logic, such as performance, simplicity, lower cost, and productivity.

Fuzzy Logic has been found to be very suitable for embedded control applications. Several manufacturers in the automotive industry are using fuzzy technology to improve quality and reduce development time. In aerospace, fuzzy enables very complex real time problems to be tackled using a simple approach. In consumer electronics, fuzzy improves time to market and helps reduce costs. In manufacturing, fuzzy is proven to be invaluable in increasing equipment efficiency and diagnosing malfunctions.

Fuzzy Logical Control Systems

A **fuzzy control system** is a control system based on fuzzy logic - a mathematical system that analyzes analog input values in terms of logical variables that take on continuous values between 0 and 1, in contrast to classical or digital logic, which operates on discrete values of either 0 and 1 (true and false).

Fuzzy controllers are very simple conceptually. They consist of an input stage, a processing stage, and an output stage. The input stage maps sensor or other inputs, such as switches, thumbwheels, and so on, to the appropriate membership functions and truth values. The processing stage invokes each appropriate rule and generates a result for each, then combines the results of the rules. Finally, the output stage converts the combined result back into a specific control output value.

The most common shape of membership functions is triangular, although trapezoidal and bell curves are also used, but the shape is generally less important than the number of curves and their placement. From three to seven curves are generally appropriate to cover the required range of an input value, or the "universe of discourse" in fuzzy jargon.

Fuzzy control system design is based on empirical methods, basically a methodical approach to trial-and-error. The general process is as follows:

- Document the system's operational specifications and inputs and outputs.
- Document the fuzzy sets for the inputs.
- Document the rule set.

- Determine the defuzzification method.
- Run through test suite to validate system, adjust details as required.
- Complete document and release to production.

EXERCISE

1. What are information systems?
2. Why Information Systems are needed?
3. Give a Brief History of Information Systems.
4. What is the new Role of Information Systems in Organizations?
5. Describe Characteristics of Information system.
6. Describe Key Components of Information system.
7. Give a Classification of Information Systems.
8. What is Artificial Intelligence?
9. Describe AI Applications.
10. Define Neural Networks.
11. Describe Fuzzy Logical Control Systems.

2

DEVELOPING MIS SYSTEMS

2.0 INTRODUCTION TO SOFTWARE LIFE CYCLE MODELS

Nearly three decades ago the operations in an organization used to be limited and so it was possible to maintain them using manual procedures. But with the growing operations of organizations, the need to automate the various activities increased, since for manual procedures it was becoming very difficult and cumbersome. Like maintaining records for a thousand plus employees company on papers is definitely a cumbersome job. So, at that time more and more companies started going for automation.

Since there were a lot of organizations, which were opting for automation, it was felt that some standard and structural procedure or methodology be introduced in the industry so that the transition from manual to automated system became easy. The concept of system life cycle came into existence then. Life cycle model emphasized on the need to follow some structured approach towards building new or improved system. There were many models suggested. A waterfall model was among the very first models that came into existence. Later on many other models like prototype, rapid application development model, etc., were also introduced.

System development begins with the recognition of user needs. Then there is a preliminary investigation stage. It includes evaluation of present system, information gathering, feasibility study, and request approval. Feasibility study includes technical, economic, legal and operational feasibility. In economic feasibility cost-benefit analysis is done. After that, there are detailed design, implementation, testing and maintenance stages.

In this session, we'll be learning about various stages that make system's life cycle. In addition, different life cycles models will be discussed. These include Waterfall model, Prototype model, Object—Oriented Model, spiral model and Dynamic Systems Development Method (DSDM).

2.1 ACTIVITIES INVOLVED SOFTWARE DEVELOPMENT LIFE CYCLE MODEL

Problem solving in software consists of these activities:

1. Understanding the Problem
2. Deciding a Plan for a Solution

3. Coding the Planned Solution
4. Testing the Actual Program

For small problems these activities may not be done explicitly. The start end boundaries of these activities may not be clearly defined, and not written record of the activities may be kept. However, for large systems where the problem solving activity may last over a few years. And where many people are involved in development, performing these activities implicitly without proper documentation and representation will clearly not work. For any software system of a non-trival nature, each of the four activities for problem solving listed above has to be done formally. For large systems, each activity can be extremely complex and methodologies and precedures are needed to perform it efficiently and correctly. Each of these activities is a major task for large software projects.

Furthermore, each of the basic activities itself may be so large that it cannot be handled in single step and must be broken into smaller steps. For example, design of a large software system is always broken into multiple, distinct design phases, starting from a very high level design specifying only the components in the system to a detailed design where the logic of the components is specified. The basic activities or phases to be performed for developing a software system are:

1. Requirement Analysis/Determination of System's Requirements
2. Design of System
3. Development (Coding) of Software
4. System Testing

In addition to the activities performed during software development, some activities are performed after the main development is complete. There is often an installation (also called implementation) phase, which is concerned with actually installing the system on the client's computer systems and then testing it. Then, there is software maintenance. Maintenance is an activity that commences after the software is developed. Software needs to be maintained not because some of its components "wear out" and need to be replaced, but because there are often some residual errors remaining in the system which must be removed later as they are discovered. Furthermore, the software often must be upgraded and enhanced to include more "features" and provide more services. This also requires modification of the software, Therefore, maintenance in unavoidable for software systems.

In most commercial software developments there are also some activities performed before the requirement analysis takes place. These can be combined into a feasibility analysis phase. In this phase the feasibility of the project is analyzed, and a business proposal is put forth with a very general plan for the project and some cost estimates. For feasibility analysis, some understanding of the major requirements of the system is essential. Once the business proposal is accepted or the contract is awarded, the development activities begin starting with the requirements analysis phase.

Following topics describes the above—mentioned phases:

1. Preliminary Investigation
2. Requirement Analysis/Determination of System's Requirements
3. Design of System
4. Development (coding) of Software

5. System Testing
6. Software Maintenance
7. Error Distribution with Phases

2.1.1 Preliminary Investigation

Figure 2.1 shows different stages in the system's life cycle. It initiates with a project request. First stage is the preliminary analysis. The main aim of preliminary analysis is to identify the problem. First, need for the new or the enhanced system is established. Only after the recognition of need, for the proposed system is done then further analysis is possible.

Suppose in an office all leave-applications are processed manually. Now this company is recruiting many new people every year. So the number of employee in the company has increased. So manual processing of leave application is becoming very difficult. So the management is considering the option of automating the leave processing system. If this is the case, then the system analyst would need to investigate the existing system, find the limitations present, and finally evaluate whether automating the system would help the organization.

Once the initial investigation is done and the need for new or improved system is established, all possible alternate solutions are chalked out. All these systems are known as "candidate systems". All the candidate systems are then weighed and the best alternative of all these is selected as the solution system, which is termed as the "proposed system". The proposed system is evaluated for its feasibility. Feasibility for a system means whether it is practical and beneficial to build that system.

Feasibility is evaluated from developer and customer's point of view. Developer sees whether they have the required technology or manpower to build the new system. Is building the new system really going to benefit the customer. Does the customer have the required money to build that type of a system? All these issues are covered in the feasibility study of the system. The feasibility of the system is evaluated on the three main issues: technical, economical, and operational. Another issue in this regard is the legal feasibility of the project.

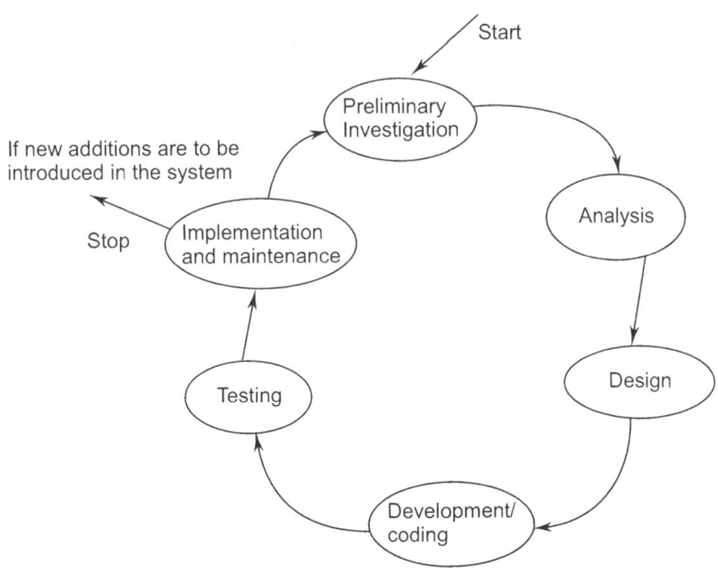

Fig. 2.1 *Various Stages in System Development*

1. **Technical feasibility:** Can the development of the proposed system be done with current equipment, existing software technology, and available personnel? Does it require new technology?
2. **Economic feasibility:** Are there sufficient benefits in creating the system to make the costs acceptable? An important outcome of the economic feasibility study is the cost benefit analysis.
3. **Legal feasibility:** It checks if there are any legal hassle in developing the system.
4. **Operational feasibility:** Will the system be used if it is developed and implemented? Will there be resistance from users that will undermine the possible application benefits?

The result of the feasibility study is a formal document, a report detailing the nature and scope of the proposed solution. It consists of the following:

- Statement of the problem
- Details of findings
- Findings and recommendations in concise form

Once the feasibility study is done then the project is approved or disapproved according to the results of the study. If the project seems feasible and desirable then the project is finally approved otherwise no further work is done on it.

2.1.2 Determination of System's Requirements: Analysis Phase

Requirements Analysis is done in order to understand the problem for which the software system is to solve. For example, the problem could be automating an existing manual process, or developing a completely new automated system, or a combination of the two. For large systems which have a large number of features, and that need to perform many different tasks, understanding the requirements of the system is a major task. The emphasis in requirements analysis is on identifying what is needed from the system and not how the system will achieve it goals. This task is complicated by the fact that there are often at least two parties involved in software development — a client and a developer. The developer usually does not understand the client's problem domain, and the client often does not understand the issues involved in software systems. This causes a communication gap, which has to be adequately bridged during requirements Analysis.

In most software projects, the requirement phase ends with a document describing all the requirements. In other words, the goal of the requirement specification phase is to produce the software requirement specification document. The person responsible for the requirement analysis is often called the analyst. There are two major activities in this phase — problem understanding or analysis and requirement specification in problem analysis; the analyst has to understand the problem and its context. Such analysis typically requires a thorough understanding of the existing system, the parts of which must be automated.

Once the problem is analyzed and the essentials understood, the requirements must be specified in the requirement specification document. For requirement specification in the form of document, some specification language has to be selected (example: English, regular expressions, tables, or a combination of these). The requirements documents must specify all functional and performance requirements, the formats of inputs, outputs and any required standards, and all design constraints that exits due to political, economic environmental, and security reasons. The phase ends with validation of requirements specified in the document. The basic purpose of validation is to make sure that the requirements specified in the document, actually reflect the actual requirements or needs, and that all requirements are specified. Validation is often done through requirement review, in which a group of people including representatives of the client, critically review the requirements specification.

Software Requirement or Role of Software Requirement Specification (SRS)

IEEE (Institute of Electrical and Electronics Engineering) defines as,

1. A condition of capability needed by a user to solve a problem or achieve an objective;
2. A condition or capability that must be met or possessed by a system to satisfy a contract, standard, specification, or other formally imposed document.

Note that in software requirements we are dealing with the requirements of the proposed system, that is, the capabilities that system, which is yet to be developed, should have. It is because we are dealing with specifying a system that does not exist in any form that the problem of requirements becomes complicated. Regardless of how the requirements phase proceeds, the Software Requirement Specification (SRS) is a document that completely describes what the proposed software should do without describing how the system will do it?. The basic goal of the requirement phase is to produce the Software Requirement Specification (SRS), which describes the complete external behavior of the proposed software.

2.1.3 Design of System (Software Design)

The purpose of the design phase is to plan a solution of the problem specified by the requirement document. This phase is the first step in moving from problem domain to the solution domain. The design of a system is perhaps the most critical factor affecting the quality of the software, and has a major impact on the later phases, particularly testing and maintenance. The output of this phase is the design document. This document is similar to a blue print or plan for the solution, and is used later during implementation, testing and maintenance.

The design activity is often divided into two separate phase—system design and detailed design. System design, which is sometimes also called top-level design, aims to identify the modules that should be in the system, the specifications of these modules, and how they interact with each other to produce the desired results. At the end of system design all the major data structures, file formats, output formats, as well as the major modules in the system and their specifications are decided.

During detailed design the internal logic of each of the modules specified in system design is decided. During this phase further details of the data structures and algorithmic design of each of the modules is specified. The logic of a module is usually specified in a high-level design description language, which is independent of the target language in which the software will eventually be implemented. In system design the focus is on identifying the modules, whereas during detailed design the focus is on designing the logic for each of the modules. In other words, in system design the attention is on what components are needed, while in detailed design how the components can be implemented in software is the issue.

During the design phase, often two separate documents are produced. One for the system design and one for the detailed design. Together, these documents completely specify the design of the system. That is they specify the different modules in the system and internal logic of each of the modules.

A design methodology is a systematic approach to creating a design by application of set of techniques and guidelines. Most methodologies focus on system design. The two basic principles used in any design methodology are problem partitioning and abstraction. A large system cannot be handled as a whole, and so for design it is partitioned into smaller systems. Abstraction is a concept related to problem partitioning. When partitioning is used during design, the design activity focuses on one part of the system at a time. Since the part being designed interacts with other parts of the system, a clear understanding of the interaction is essential for properly designing the part. For this, abstraction is used. An abstraction of a system or a part defines the overall behavior of the system at an abstract level without giving the internal details.

While working with the part of a system, a designer needs to understand only the abstractions of the other parts with which the part being designed interacts. The use of abstraction allows the designer to practice the "divide and conquer" technique effectively by focusing one part at a time, without worrying about the details of other parts.

Like every other phase, the design phase ends with verification of the design. If the design is not specified in some executable language, the verification has to be done by evaluating the design documents. One way of doing this is thorough reviews. Typically, at least two design reviews are held-one for the system design and one for the detailed and one for the detailed design.

2.1.4 Development of Software (Coding)

Once the design is complete, most of the major decisions about the system have been made. The goal of the coding phase is to translate the design of the system into code in a given programming language. For a given design, the aim of this phase is to implement the design in the best possible manner. The coding phase affects both testing and maintenance profoundly. A well written code reduces the testing and maintenance effort. Since the testing and maintenance cost of software are much higher than the coding cost, the goal of coding should be to reduce the testing and maintenance effort. Hence, during coding the focus should be on developing programs that are easy to write. Simplicity and clarity should be strived for, during the coding phase.

An important concept that helps the understandability of programs is structured programming. The goal of structured programming is to arrange the control flow in the program. That is, program text should be organized as a sequence of statements, and during execution, the statements are executed in the sequence in the program.

For structured programming, a few single-entry-single-exit constructs should be used. These constructs includes selection (if-then-else), and iteration (while - do, repeat - until etc). With these constructs it is possible to construct a program as sequence of single - entry - single - exit constructs. There are many methods available for verifying the code. Some methods are static in nature that is, that is they do not involve execution of the code. Examples of such methods are data flow analysis, code reading, code reviews, testing (a method that involves executing the code, which is used very heavily). In the coding phase, the entire system is not tested together. Rather, the different modules are tested separately. This testing of modules is called "unit testing". Consequently, this phase is often referred to as "coding and unit testing". The output of this phase is the verified and unit tested code of the different modules.

2.1.5 System Testing

Testing is the major quality control measure employed during software development. Its basic function is to detect errors in the software. During requirement analysis and design, the output is a document that is usually textual and non-executable. After the coding phase, computer programs are available that can be executed for testing phases. This implies that testing not only has to uncover errors introduced during coding, but also errors introduced during the previous phases. Thus, the goal of testing is to uncover requirement, design or coding errors in the programs.

Consequently, different levels of testing are employed. The starting point of testing is unit testing. In this a module is tested separately and is often performed by the coder himself simultaneously with the coding of the module. The purpose is to execute the different parts of the module code to detect coding errors. After this the modules are gradually integrated into subsystem, which are then integrated themselves eventually form the entire system. During integration of modules, integration testing is performed. The goal of this testing is to detect design errors, while focusing on testing the interconnection between modules. After the system is put together, system testing is performed. Here the system is tested against tech system requirements to see if all the requirements are met and the system performs as specified by the requirements. Finally, acceptance testing is performed to demonstrate to the client, on the real life data of the client, the separation of the system.

For testing to be successful, proper selection of test cases is essential. There are two different approaches to selecting test cases-functional testing and structural testing. In functional testing the software for the module to be tested is treated as black box, and then test cases are decided based on the specifications of the system or module. For this reason, this form of testing is also called "black box testing". The focus is on testing the external behavior of the system. In structural testing the test cases are decided based on the logic of the module to be tested. Structural testing is sometimes called "glass box testing". Structural testing is used for lower levels of testing and functional testing is used for higher levels.

Testing is an extremely critical and time-consuming activity. It requires proper planning of the overall testing process. Frequently the testing process starts with the test plan. This plan identifies all the testing related activities that must be performed and specifies the schedule, allocates the resources, and specify guidelines for testing. The test plan specifies manner in which the modules will integrate together. Then for different test units, a test case specification document is produced, which lists all the different test cases, together with the expected outputs, that will be used for testing. During the testing of the unit, the specified test cases are executed and actual result is compared with the expected output. The final output of the testing phases is to the text report and the error report, or set of such reports (one of each unit is tested). Each test report contains the set of such test cases and the result of executing the code with these test cases. The error report describes the errors encountered and action taken to remove those errors.

2.1.6 SDLC—Implementation and Maintenance

Maintenance includes all the activity after the installation of software that is performed to keep the system operational. As we have mentioned earlier, software often has design faults. The two major forms of maintenance activities are adaptive maintenance and corrective maintenance.

It is generally agreed that for large systems, removing all the faults before delivery is extremely difficult and faults will be discovered long after the system is installed. As these faults are detected, they have to be removed. Maintenance activities related to fixing of errors fall under corrective maintenance.

Removing errors is one of the activities of maintenance. Maintenance also needed due to a change in the environment or the requirements of the system. The introduction of a software system affects the work environment. This change in environment often changes what is desired from the system. Furthermore, often after the system is installed and the users have had a chance to work with it for sometime, requirements that are not identified during requirement analysis phase will be uncovered. This occurs, since the experience with the software helps the user to define the needs more precisely. There might also be changes in the input data, the system environment and output formats. All these require modification of the software. The maintenance activities related to such modification fall under adaptive maintenance.

Maintenance work is based on existing software, as compared to development work, which creates new software. Consequently maintenance resolves around understanding the existing software and spares most of their time trying to understand the software that they have to modify. Understanding the software involves not only understanding the code, but also the related documents. During the modification of the software, the effects of the change have to be clearly understood by the maintainer since introducing undesired side effects in the system during modification is easier.

To test whether those aspects in the system that are not supposed to be modified are operating as they were before modification, regression testing is done. Regression testing involves executing old test cases to test that no new errors have been introduced. Thus, maintenance involves understanding the existing software (code and related documents), understanding the effects of change, making the changes - both to the code and documents, testing the new parts (changes), and resetting of the old parts that were not changed.

Since often during development, needs of the maintainers are not kept in mind, little support documents are produced during development to aid the maintainer. The complexity of the maintenance task is coupled with the neglect of maintenance concerns during development which makes maintenance the most cost effective activity in the life of a software product.

2.1.7 Error Distribution with Phases

A typical software product may take months to a few years for development, and is in operation for five to twenty years before it is withdrawn. For software, the cost of development is the incurred during requirement analysis, design, coding and testing. Therefore, the development cost is the total cost incurred before the product delivery. The cost of maintenance is the cost of modifying the software due to residual faults in the software, for enhancing or for updating the software. This cost is spread over the operational years of the software. Software engineers generally agree that the total cost of maintenance is more than the cost of development of software. The ratio of development to maintenance cost has been variously suggested as 40/60, 30/70 or even lower. However, it is generally accepted that the cost of maintenance is likely to be higher than the development cost, and are often not at all concerned with the maintenance.

Since maintenance depends critically on the software characteristics that are decided during development, maintenance cost can be reduced if maintenance concerns are kept in forefront during development. One of the reasons why this is often not done is that the development cost is done by the developers while maintenance is often done by the users. Hence, the developers do not have much incentive for increasing the development effort in order to reduce the maintenance cost. However, for reduction in overall cost of software, it is imperative that the software be developed so the maintenance is easy.

The development cost, a typical distribution of effort with the different phases is

Requirement - 10%

Design - 20%

Coding - 20%

Testing - 50%

The exact number will differ with organization and the type of the project. There are some observation we can make from the data given above. The first is that the goal of design and coding should reduce the cost of design and coding, but should be to reduce the cost of testing and maintenance, at the expense of increasing design and coding cost. Both testing and maintenance depend heavily in the design and coding of the software. And these costs can be considerably reduced if the software is designed and coded to make testing and maintenance easier. Therefore, during design and implementation, the issues in our minds should be "can the design be easily tested", and "can it be easily modified". These require alternate designs and may increase the cost of the design and coding. But this additional costs pay dividends in the later phases.

Error Distribution

The notion that programming is the central of activity during software development is largely because normally programming has been considered to be difficult task and sometimes an "art". Another consequence of this kind of thinking is the belief that errors largely occur during programming, as it is the oldest activity in software development and offers many opportunities for commiting errors. It is now realized that errors can occur at any stage during development. A typical distribution of error occurrences is

Requirement Analysis - 20%

Design - 30%

Coding - 50%

As we can see, errors occur throughout the development process. However the cost of correcting different phases is not the same and depends on when the error is detected and correceted. As one old expect, the greater the delay in detecting an error after it occurs, the more expensive it is to correct it. Error that occur during the requirements phase, if corrected after coding is completed, can cost many times more than correcting the error during the requirements phase itself. The reason for this is fairly obvious. If there is an error in the requirements, then the design and the code will get affected.

To correct the error, the coding that is done would require both the design and the code to be changed there by increasing the correction. So we should attempt to detect errors in the previous phase and should not wait until testing to detect errors. This is not often practiced. In reality, sometimes testing is the sole point where errors are detected. Besides the cost factor, reliance on testing as the primary source for error detection, due to the limitations of testing, will also result in unreliable software. Error detection and correction should be a continous proces that is done throughout software development. In terms of the development phases what this means is that we should try to validate each phase before starting with the next.

2.2 DIFFERENT TYPES OF SOFTWARE DEVELOPMENT LIFE CYCLE MODELS (SDLC)

A Software Development Life Cycle Model is a set of activities together with an ordering relationship between activities which if performed in a manner that satisfies the ordering relationship that will produce desired product. Software Development Life Cycle Model is an abstract representation of a development process.

In a software development effort the goal is to produce high quality software. The development process is, therefore, the sequence of activities that will produce such software. A software development life cycle model is broken down into distinct activities. A software development life cycle model specifies how these activities are organized in the entire software development effort. We discuss each software development life cycle model in detail.

- Waterfall Software Development Life Cycle Model
- Prototyping Software Development Life Cycle Model
- Iterative Enhacement Model
- The Spiral Model
- Object Oriented Methodology
- Dynamic System Development Method

2.2.1 Waterfall Software Development Life Cycle Model

The simplest software development life cycle model is the waterfall model, which states that the phases are organized in a linear order. A project begins with feasibility analysis. On the successful demonstration of the feasibility analysis, the requirements analysis and project planning begins.

The design starts after the requirements analysis is done. And coding begins after the design is done. Once the programming is completed, the code is integrated and testing is done. On succeeful completion of testing, the system is installed. After this the regular operation and maintenance of the system takes place. The following figure demonstrates the steps involved in waterfall life cycle model.

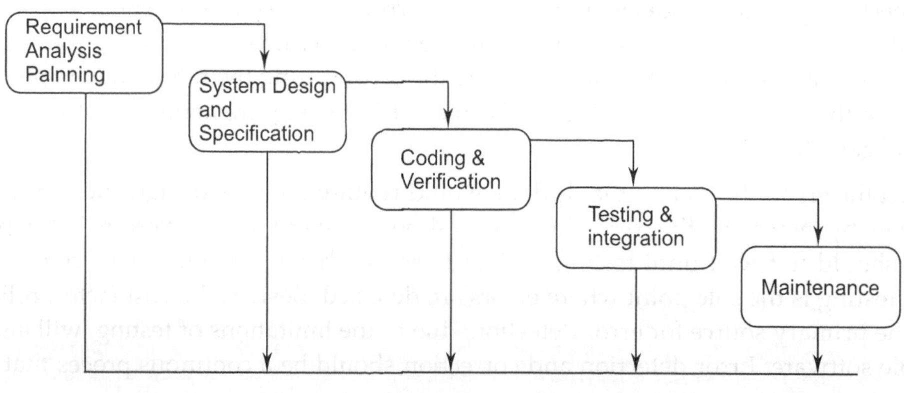

The Waterfall Software Life Cycle Model

With the waterfall model, the activities performed in a software development project are requirements analysis, project planning, system design, detailed design, coding and unit testing, system integration and testing. Linear ordering of activities has some important consequences. First, to clearly identify the end of a phase and beginning of the others. Some certification mechanism has to be employed at the end of each phase. This is usually done by some verification and validation. Validation means confirming the output of a phase is consistent with its input (which is the output of the previous phase) and that the output of the phase is consistent with overall requirements of the system.

The consequences of the need of certification is that each phase must have some defined output that can be evaluated and certified. Therefore, when the activities of a phase are completed, there should be an output product of that phase and the goal of a phase is to produce this product. The outputs of the earlier phases are often called intermediate products or design document. For the coding phase, the output is the code. From this point of view, the output of a software project is to justify the final program along with the use of documentation with the requirements document, design document, project plan, test plan and test results.

Another implication of the linear ordering of phases is that after each phase is completed and its outputs are certified, these outputs become the inputs to the next phase and should not be changed or modified. However, changing requirements cannot be avoided and must be faced. Since changes performed in the output of one phase affect the later phases, that might have been performed. These changes have to made in a controlled manner after evaluating the effect of each change on the project.This brings us to the need for configuration control or configuration management.

The certified output of a phase that is released for the best phase is called baseline. The configuration management ensures that any changes to a baseline are made after careful review, keeping in mind the interests of all parties that are affected by it. There are two basic assumptions for justifying the linear ordering of phase in the manner proposed by the waterfall model.

For a successful project resulting in a successful product, all phases listed in the waterfall model must be performed anyway.

Any different ordering of the phases will result in a less successful software product.

Project Output in a Waterfall Model

As we have seen, the output of a project employing the waterfall model is not just the final program along with documentation to use it. There are a number of intermediate outputs, which must be produced in order to produce a successful product.

The set of documents that forms the minimum that should be produced in each project are:

- Requirement document
- Project plan
- System design document
- Detailed design document
- Test plan and test report

- Final code
- Software manuals (user manual, installation manual etc.)
- Review reports

Except for the last one, these are all the outputs of the phases. In order to certify an output product of a phase before the next phase begins, reviews are often held. Reviews are necessary especially for the requirements and design phases, since other certification means are frequently not available. Reviews are formal meeting to uncover deficiencies in a product. The review reports are the outcome of these reviews.

Advantages of Waterfall Life Cycle Models

1. Easy to explain to the user
2. Stages and activities are well defined
3. Helps to plan and schedule the project
4. Verification at each stage ensures early detection of errors/misunderstanding

Limitations of the Waterfall Life Cycle Model

The waterfall model assumes that the requirements of a system can be frozen (*i.e.*, basedline) before the design begins. This is possible for systems designed to automate an existing manual system. But for absolutely new system, determining the requirements is difficult, as the user himself does not know the requirements. Therefore, having unchanging (or changing only a few) requirements is unrealistic for such project.

Freezing the requirements usually requires choosing the hardware (since it forms a part of the requirement specification). A large project might take a few years to complete. If the hardware is selected early, then due to the speed at which hardware technology is changing, it is quite likely that the final software will employ a hardware technology that is on the verge of becoming obsolete. This is clearly not desirable for such expensive software.

The waterfall model stipulates that the requirements should be completely specified before the rest of the development can proceed. In some situations it might be desirable to first develop a part of the system completely, an then later enhance the system in phase. This is often done for software products that are developed not necessarily for a client (where the client plays an important role in requirement specification), but for general marketing, in which the requirements are likely to be determined largely by developers.

2.2.2 Prototyping Software Life Cycle Model

The goal of prototyping-based development is to counter the first two limitations of the waterfall model discussed earlier. The basic idea here is that instead of freezing the requirements before a design or coding can proceed, a throwaway prototype is built to understand the requirements. This prototype is developed based on the currently known requirements. Development of the prototype obviously undergoes design, coding and testing. But each of these phases is not done very formally or thoroughly. By using this prototype, the client can get an "actual feel" of the system, since the interactions with prototype can enable the client to better understand the requirements of the desired system.

Prototyping is an attractive idea for complicated and large systems for which there is no manual process or existing system to help determining the requirements. In such situations letting the client "plan" with the prototype provides invaluable and intangible inputs which helps in determining the requirements for the system. It is also an effective method to demonstrate the feasibility of a certain approach. This might be needed for novel systems where it is not clear that constraints can be met or that algorithms can be developed to implement the requirements. The process model of the prototyping approach is shown in the figure below.

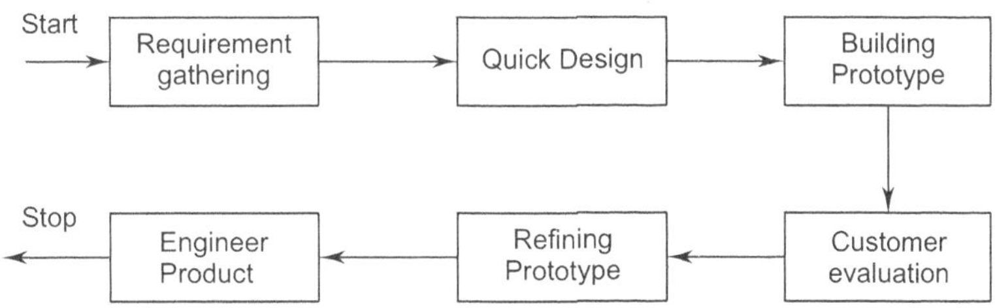

Prototyping Model

The basic reason for little common use of prototyping is the cost involved in this built-it-twice approach. However, some argue that prototyping need not be very costly and can actually reduce the overall development cost. The prototype are usually not complete systems and many of the details are not built in the prototype. The goal is to provide a system with overall functionality. In addition, the cost of testing and writing detailed documents are reduced. These factors helps to reduce the cost of developing the prototype. On the other hand, the experience of developing the prototype will very useful for developers when developing the final system. This experience helps to reduce the cost of development of the final system and results in a more reliable and better designed system.

Advantages of Prototyping

1. Users are actively involved in the development
2. It provides a better system to users, as users have natural tendency to change their mind in specifying requirements and this method of developing systems supports this user tendency.
3. Since in this methodology a working model of the system is provided, the users get a better understanding of the system being developed.
4. Errors can be detected much earlier as the system is mode side by side.
5. Quicker user feedback is available leading to better solutions.

Disadvantages

1. Leads to implementing and then repairing way of building systems.
2. Practically, this methodology may increase the complexity of the system as scope of the system may expand beyond original plans.

2.3 ITERATIVE ENHANCEMENT LIFE CYCLE MODEL

The iterative enhancement life cycle model counters the third limitation of the waterfall model and tries to combine the benefits of both prototyping and the waterfall model. The basic idea is that the software should be developed in increments, where each increment adds some functional capability to the system until the full system is implemented. At each step extensions and design modifications can be made. An advantage of this approach is that it can result in better testing, since testing each increment is likely to be easier than testing entire system like in the waterfall model. Furthermore, as in prototyping, the increments provides feedback to the client which is useful for determining the final requirements of the system.

In the first step of iterative enhancement model, a simple initial implementation is done for a subset of the overall problem. This subset is the one that contains some of the key aspects of the problem which are easy to understand and implement, and which forms a useful and usable system. A project control list is created which contains, in an order, all the tasks that must be performed to obtain the final implementation. This project control list gives an idea of how far the project is at any given step from the final system.

Each step consists of removing the next step from the list. Designing the implementation for the selected task, coding and testing the implementation, and performing an analysis of the partial system obtained after this step and updating the list as a result of the analysis. These three phases are called the design phase, implementation phase and analysis phase. The process is iterated until the project control list is empty, at the time the final implementation of the system will be available. The process involved in iterative enhancement model is shown in the figure below.

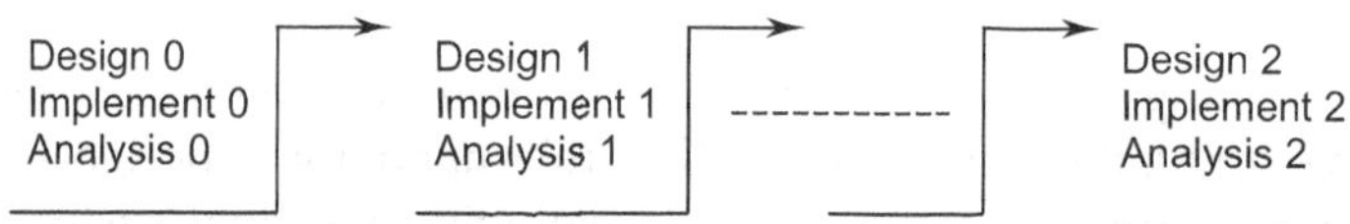

The Iterative Enhancement Model

The project control list guides the iteration steps and keeps track of all tasks that must be done. The tasks in the list can be include redesign of defective components found during analysis. Each entry in that list is a task that should be performed in one step of the iterative enhancement process, and should be simple enough to be completely understood. Selecting tasks in this manner will minimize the chances of errors and reduce the redesign work.

2.4 THE SPIRAL LIFE CYCLE MODEL

This is a recent model that has been proposed by Boehm. As the name suggests, the activities in this model can be organized like a spiral. The spiral has many cycles. The radial dimension represents the cumulative cost incurred in accomplishing the steps dome so far and the angular dimension represents the progress made in completing each cycle of the spiral. The structure of the spiral model is shown in the figure given below. Each cycle in the spiral begins with the identification of objectives for that cycle and the different alternatives are possible for achieving the objectives and the imposed constraints.

The next step in the spiral life cycle model is to evaluate these different alternatives based on the objectives and constraints. This will also involve identifying uncertainties and risks involved. The next step is to develop strategies that resolve the uncertainties and risks. This step may involve activities such as benchmarking, simulation and prototyping. Next, the software is developed by keeping in mind the risks. Finally the next stage is planned.

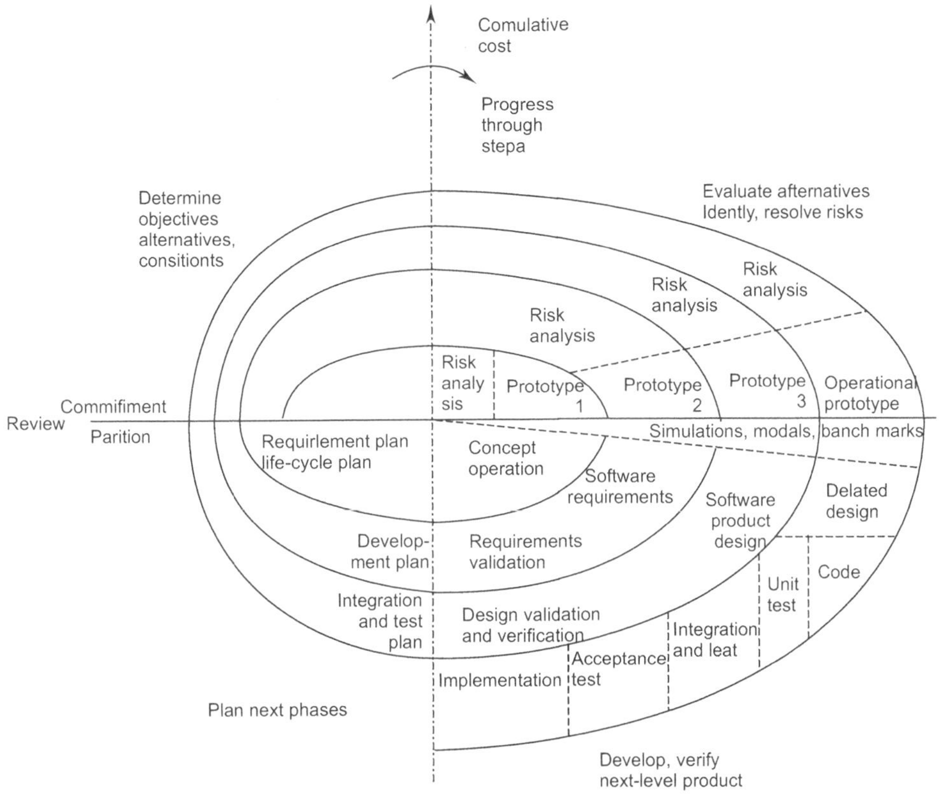

Fig. 2.2

The next step is determined by remaining risks. For example, its performance or user-interface risks are considered more important than the program development risks. The next step may be evolutionary development that involves developing a more detailed prototype for resolving the risks. On the other hand, if the program development risks dominate and previous prototypes have resolved all the user-interface and performance risks; the next step will follow the basic waterfall approach.

The risk driven nature of the spiral model allows it to accommodate any mixture of specification-oriented, prototype-oriented, simulation-oriented or some other approach. An important feature of the model is that each cycle of the spiral is completed by a review, which covers all the products developed during that cycle, including plans for the next cycle. The spiral model works for developed as well as enhancement projects.

In round one, a concept of operation is developed. The objectives are stated more precisely and quantitatively and the cost and other constraints are defined precisely. The risks here are typically whether or not the goals can be met within the constraints. The plan for the next phase will be developed which will involve defining separate activities for the project. In round two the top-level requirements are developed. In succeeding the rounds, the actual development may be done. This is a relatively new model and can encompass different development strategies. In addition to the development activities, it incorporates some of management and planning activities into the model. For high-risk projects this might be a preferred model.

2.5 OBJECT ORIENTED METHODOLOGY LIFE CYCLE MODEL

We live in a world of objects. These objects exist in nature, in man-made entities, in business, and in the products that we use. They can be categorized, described, organized, combined, manipulated and created. Therefore, an object-oriented view has come into picture for creation of computer software. An object-oriented approach to the development of software was proposed in late 1960s.

Object-Oriented development requires that object-oriented techniques be used during the analysis, and implementation of the system. This methodology asks the analyst to determine what the objects of the system are, how they behave over time or in response to events, and what responsibilities and relationships an object has to other objects. Object-oriented analysis has the analyst look at all the objects in a system, their commonalties, difference, and how the system needs to manipulate the objects.

Object Oriented Process

The Object Oriented Methodology of Building Systems takes the objects as the basis. For this, first the system to be developed is observed and analyzed and the requirements are defined as in any other method of system development. Once this is done, the objects in the required system are identified. For example in case of a Banking System, a customer is an object, a chequebook is an object, and even an account is an object.

In simple terms, Object Modeling is based on identifying the objects in a system and their interrelationships. Once this is done, the coding of the system is done. Object Modeling is somewhat similar to the traditional approach of system designing, in that it also follows a sequential process of system designing but with a different approach. The basic steps of system designing using Object Modeling may be listed as:

- System Analysis
- System Design
- Object Design
- Implementation

System Analysis

As in any other system development model, system analysis is the first phase of development in case of Object Modeling too. In this phase, the developer interacts with the user of the system to find out the user requirements and analyses the system to understand the functioning.

Based on this system study, the analyst prepares a model of the desired system. This model is purely based on what the system is required to do. At this stage the implementation details are not taken care of. Only the model of the system is prepared based on the idea that the system is made up of a set of interacting objects. The important elements of the system are emphasized.

System Design

System Design is the next development stage where the overall architecture of the desired system is decided. The system is organized as a set of sub systems interacting with each other. While designing the system as a set of interacting subsystems, the analyst takes care of specifications as observed in system analysis as well as what is required out of the new system by the end user.

As the basic philosophy of Object-Oriented method of system analysis is to perceive the system as a set of interacting objects, a bigger system may also be seen as a set of interacting smaller subsystems that in turn are composed of a set of interacting objects. While designing the system, the stress lies on the objects comprising the system and not on the processes being carried out in the system as in the case of traditional Waterfall Model where the processes form the important part of the system.

Object Design

In this phase, the details of the system analysis and system design are implemented. The Objects identified in the system design phase are designed. Here the implementation of these objects is decided as the data structures get defined and also the interrelationships between the objects are defined.

Let us here deviate slightly from the design process and understand first a few important terms used in the Object-Oriented Modeling.

As already discussed, Object Oriented Philosophy is very much similar to real world and hence is gaining popularity as the systems here are seen as a set of interacting objects as in the real world. To implement this concept, the process-based structural programming is not used; instead objects are created using data structures. Just as every programming language provides various data types and various variables of that type can be created, similarly, in case of objects certain data types are predefined.

For example, we can define a data type called pen and then create and use several objects of this data type. This concept is known as creating a class.

Class: A class is a collection of similar objects. It is a template where certain basic characteristics of a set of objects are defined. The class defines the basic attributes and the operations of the objects of that type. Defining a class does not define any object, but it only creates a template. For objects to be actually created instances of the class are created as per the requirement of the case.

Abstraction: Classes are built on the basis of abstraction, where a set of similar objects are observed and their common characteristics are listed. Of all these, the characteristics of concern to the system under observation are picked up and the class definition is made. The attributes of no concern to the system are left out. This is known as abstraction.

The abstraction of an object varies according to its application. For instance, while defining a pen class for a stationery shop, the attributes of concern might be the pen color, ink color, pen type etc., whereas a pen class for a manufacturing firm would be containing the other dimensions of the pen like its diameter, its shape and size etc.

Inheritance: Inheritance is another important concept in this regard. This concept is used to apply the idea of reusability of the objects. A new type of class can be defined using a similar existing class with a few new features. For instance, a class vehicle can be defined with the basic functionality of any vehicle and a new class called car can be derived out of it with a few modifications.

This would save the developers time and effort as the classes already existing are reused without much change.

Coming back to our development process, in the Object Designing phase of the Development Process, the designer decides onto the classes in the system based on these concepts. The designer also decides on whether the classes need to be created from scratch or any existing classes can be used as it is or new classes can be inherited from them.

Implementation

During this phase, the class objects and the interrelationships of these classes are translated and actually coded using the programming language decided upon. The databases are made and the complete system is given a functional shape.

The complete OO methodology revolves around the objects identified in the system. When observed closely, every object exhibits some characteristics and behavior. The objects recognize and respond to certain events. For example, considering a Window on the screen as an object, the size of the window gets changed when resize button of the window is clicked.

Here the clicking of the button is an event to which the window responds by changing its state from the old size to the new size. While developing systems based on this approach, the analyst makes use of certain models to analyze and depict these objects. The methodology supports and uses three basic models:

- **Object Model** - This model describes the objects in a system and their interrelationships. This model observes all the objects as static and does not pay any attention to their dynamic nature.
- **Dynamic Model** - This model depicts the dynamic aspects of the system. It portrays the changes occurring in the states of various objects with the events that might occur in the system.
- **Functional Model** - This model basically describes the data transformations of the system. This describes the flow of data and the changes that occur to the data throughout the system.

While the Object Model is most important of all as it describes the basic element of the system, the objects, all the three models together describe the complete functional system.

As compared to the conventional system development techniques, OO modeling provides many benefits. Among other benefits, there are all the benefits of using the Object Orientation. Some of these are:

- **Reusability** - The classes once defined can easily be used by other applications. This is achieved by defining classes and putting them into a library of classes where all the classes are maintained for future use. Whenever a new class is needed the programmer looks into the library of classes and if it is available, it can be picked up directly from there.
- **Inheritance** - The concept of inheritance helps the programmer use the existing code in another way, where making small additions to the existing classes can quickly create new classes.

- **Programmer** has to spend less time and effort and can concentrate on other aspects of the system due to the reusability feature of the methodology.
- **Data Hiding** - Encapsulation is a technique that allows the programmer to hide the internal functioning of the objects from the users of the objects. Encapsulation separates the internal functioning of the object from the external functioning thus providing the user flexibility to change the external behavior of the object making the programmer code safe against the changes made by the user.
- **The systems** designed using this approach are closer to the real world, as the real world functioning of the system is directly mapped into the system designed using this approach.

Advantages of Object Oriented Methodology

- Object Oriented Methodology closely represents the problem domain. Because of this, it is easier to produce and understand designs.
- The objects in the system are immune to requirement changes. Therefore, allows changes more easily.
- Object Oriented Methodology designs encourage more re-use. New applications can use the existing modules, thereby reduces the development cost and cycle time.
- Object Oriented Methodology approach is more natural. It provides nice structures for thinking and abstracting and leads to modular design.

2.6 DYNAMIC SYSTEM DEVELOPMENT METHOD (DSDM)

Dynamic System Development Method is another approach to system development, which, as the name suggests, develops the system dynamically. This methodology is independent of tools, in that it can be used with both structured analysis and design approach or object-oriented approach.

The Dynamic System Development Method (DSDM) is dynamic as it is a Rapid Application Development method that uses incremental prototyping. This method is particularly useful for the systems to be developed in short time span and where the requirements cannot be frozen at the start of the application building. Whatever requirements are known at a time, design for them is prepared and design is developed and incorporated into system. In Dynamic System Development Method (DSDM), analysis, design and development phase can overlap. Like at one time some people will be working on some new requirements while some will be developing something for the system. In Dynamic System Development Method (DSDM), requirements evolve with time.

Dynamic System Development Method (DSDM) has a five-phase life cycle as given the following figure.

Feasibility Study

In this phase the problem is defined and the technical feasibility of the desired application is verified. Apart from these routine tasks, it is also checked whether the application is suitable for Rapid Application Development (RAD) approach or not. Only if the RAD is found as a justified approach for the desired system, the development continues.

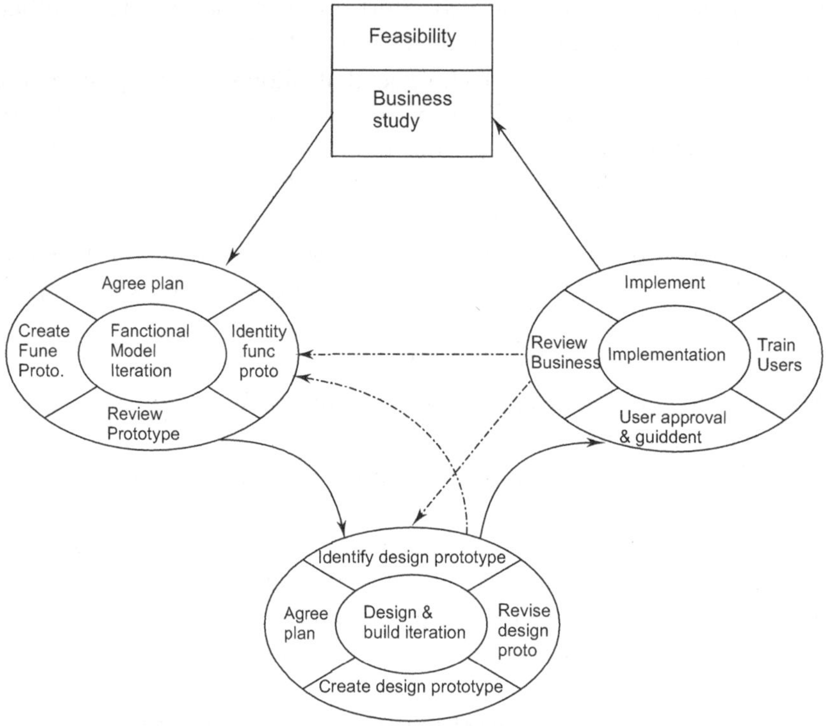

Fig. 2.3

Business Study

In this phase the overall business study of the desired system is done. The business requirements are specified at a high level and the information requirements out of the system are identified. Once this is done, the basic architectural framework of the desired system is prepared.

The systems designed using Rapid Application Development (RAD) should be highly maintainable, as they are based on the incremental development process. The maintainability level of the system is also identified here so as to set the standards for quality control activities throughout the development process.

Functional Model Iteration

This is one of the two iterative phases of the life cycle. The main focus in this phase is on building the prototype iteratively and getting it reviewed from the users to bring out the requirements of the desired system. The prototype is improved through demonstration to the user, taking the feedback and incorporating the changes. This cycle is repeated generally twice or thrice until a part of functional model is agreed upon. The end product of this phase is a functional model consisting of analysis model and some software components containing the major functionality.

Design and Build Iteration

This phase stresses upon ensuring that the prototypes are satisfactorily and properly engineered to suit their operational environment. The software components designed during the functional modeling are further refined till they achieve a satisfactory standard. The product of this phase is a tested system ready for implementation.

There is no clear line between these two phases and there may be cases where while some component has flown from the functional modeling to the design and build modeling while the other component has not yet been started. The two phases, as a result, may simultaneously continue.

Implementation

Implementation is the last and final development stage in this methodology. In this phase the users are trained and the system is actually put into the operational environment. At the end of this phase, there are four possibilities, as depicted by figure :

- Everything was delivered as per the user demand, so no further development required.
- A new functional area was discovered, so return to business study phase and repeat the whole process.
- A less essential part of the project was missed out due to time constraint and so development returns to the functional model iteration.
- Some non-functional requirement was not satisfied, so development returns to the design and build iterations phase.

Dynamic System Development Method (DSDM) assumes that all previous steps may be revisited as part of its iterative approach. Therefore, the current step need be completed only enough to move to the next step, since it can be finished in a later iteration. This premise is that the business requirements will probably change anyway as understanding increases, so any further work would have been wasted.

According to this approach, the time is taken as a constraint *i.e.*, the time is fixed, resources are fixed while the requirements are allowed to change. This does not follow the fundamental assumption of making a perfect system the first time, but provides a usable and useful 80% of the desired system in 20% of the total development time. This approach has proved to be very useful under time constraints and varying requirements.

DSDM Model Limitations

- It is a relatively new model. It is not very common. So it is difficult to understand.

DSDM Model Advantages

- Active user participation throughout the life of the project and iterative nature of development improves quality of the product.
- DSDM ensures rapid deliveries.
- Both of the above factors result in reduced project costs.

2.7 CASE TOOLS

What is Case?

CASE is an acronym for Computer Added Software Engineering or Computer Added Systems Engineering. Computer Aided System Engineering involves using software packages to accomplish and automate many of the activities of the Information System Development, including software development or programming. Computer Aided Software Engineering is same as CASE above, but the emphasis is more on software development.

According to Microsoft's Computer Dictionary, CASE is "a comprehensive label for software designed to use computers in all places of computer programme development, from planning and modeling through coding and documentation".

CASE, accordingly, represents a working environments consisting of programmes and other development tools that help Managers, System Analysts, Programmers and other to automate the design and procedures for business, engineering and scientific computer system.

Why Case?

CASE is basically call the automation of step-by-step methodologies for software and systems development to reduce the amount of repetitive work the developer/programmer needs do to. CASE takes away the drudgery of system development by automating many routine software development tasks and enforcing adherence to design rules/specifications. The use of CASE also helps the programmers to keep pace with the increasing sophistication in programming. The use of CASE revolutionizes the development process as it improves the design, significantly cuts down the time to design a new product and reduces the cost in the process. CASE is also useful in enhancing productivity, ensuring reliability and improving visibility during the development process.

CASE is, therefore, considered to be the WAVE and HOPE of the future.

What does the "CASE" Involve?

As has been stated earlier, the goal of CASE is to use computer technologies to facilitate the development of information system by automating the activities involved in the systems development life cycle. The activities encompass strategic system planning, system analysis, systems design, system management, project management, user interface design and database design etc.

"CASE" Tools

The software packages available in the areas/activities of automating the system development activities are known as CASE Tools. CASE Tools are available for varying purposes/activities as illustrated hereafter.

Further in certain quarters, CASE Tools are also referred to as 'Toolsets', and as stated by james o'brein, the Toolsets could be:

1. The Planning Toolsets which help begin the development process with information strategy planning from a high level, business vantage point.
2. The Analysis Toolset which focuses on correctly capturing detailed business requirements early in the development process.
3. The Design Toolset which provides detailed specifications of the system solution.
4. The Information Integrator which integrates system specifications, checks them for consistency and correctness and records in local or central repositories.
5. The Code Generation Toolset which produces a higher language programme code based on system specifications.
6. The Database Generation Toolset which generates system control information needed for data storage and access.
7. The Public Interface which provides for file transfers and query reporting.

The CASE Tools Capabilities

After discussing the CASE and CASE Tools, let us now discuss what CASE Tools can and can not do.

CASE Tools can …….	CASE Tools can not ………
Automate number of manual tasks involved in System Development.	Automatically provide a functional, relevant system.
Promote standardization based on a single methodology.	Easily interface with database and fourth-generation languages.
Promote greater consistency and co-ordination during a development project.	Automatically force analysis to use prescribed methodologies when one does not exist.
Generate a large portion of documentation for a system, such as Data Flow Diagram, Data Models and/or other specifications.	Radically transform the Systems Analysis and Design Process.

(Source: MIS, Lau don)

Can 'CASE' Do Everything?

It Is obvious that CASE does not and can not do anything and everything. It must be remembered that CASE is, at best, only a facilitator. It can certainly accelerate analysis and design and promote iterative design. But it still remains a methodology and a set of tools for developing system with, as stated earlier, enhanced productivity, reliability and visibility. CASE is not automated system development and it does not enable system to be designed automatically to meet business requirements.

Let us remember that CASE is neither a magic wand nor a magic cure-all. CASE is exactly that it sounds like.

2.8 SYSTEM DESCRIPTION TECHNIQUES

Graphical representation of any process is always better and more meaningful than its representation in words. Moreover, it is very difficult to arrange and organise the large amount of data into meaningful interpretation of the whole. System Analysis and Design makes use of the various tools for representing and facilitating comprehension of the complex processes and procedure involved. In this lesson, we present some details about Flowcharts, data flow diagram (DFD), Decision Tables and Decision Trees.

2.8.1 Flowcharts

The pictorial representation of the programs or the algorithm is known as flowcharts. It is nothing but a diagrammatic representation of the various steps involved in designing a system. Some of the boxes which are used in flowcharts are:

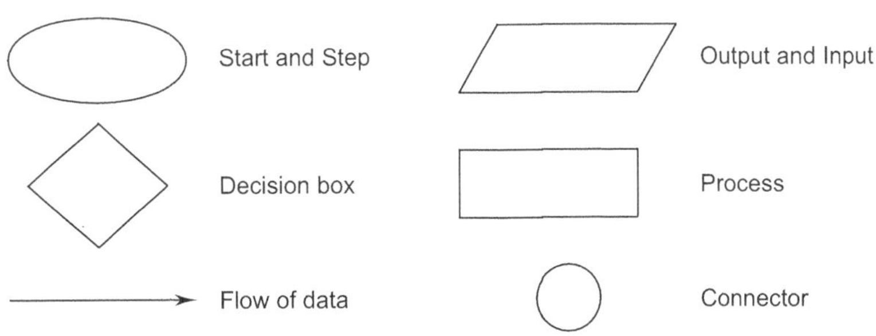

A flowchart consists of a set of 'flowchart symbols' connected by arrows. Each symbol contains information about what must be done at that point and the arrow shows the 'flow of execution' of the algorithm *i.e.,* they show the order in which the instructions must be executed. The purpose of using flowcharts is to graphically present the logical flow of data in the system and defining major phases of processing along with the various media to be used.

Flowcharts are of three types:

- System flowcharts
- Run flowcharts
- Program flowcharts

(*a*) **System flowcharts:** System flowchart describes the data flow for a data processing system. It provides a logical diagram of how the system operates. It represents the flow of documents, the operations performed in data processing system. It also reflects the relationship between inputs, processing and outputs. Following are the features of system flowcharts:

- the sources from which data is generated and device used for this purpose
- various processing steps involved
- the intermediate and final output prepared and the devices used for their storage

Figure 2.3 is a sample of system flowchart for the following algorithm:

1. Prompt the user for the centigrade temperature
2. Store the value in C
3. Set F to 32+(9 × C/5)
4. Print the value of C, F
5. Stop

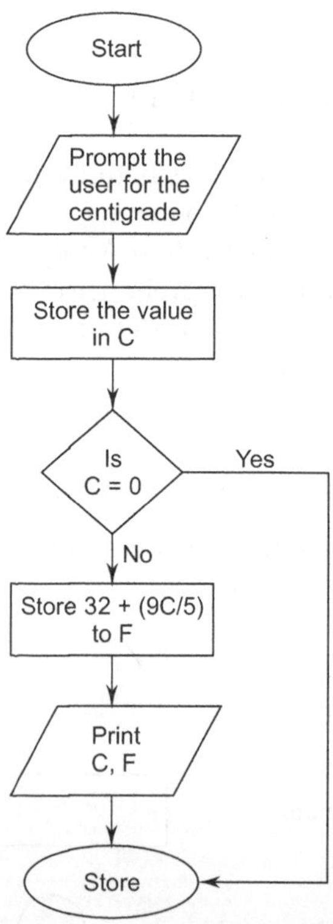

Fig. 2.4 *System Flowchart*

(*b*) **Run flowcharts:** Run flowcharts are used to represent the logical relationship of computer routines along with inputs, master files, transaction files and outputs. Figure 2.5 illustrates a run flowchart.

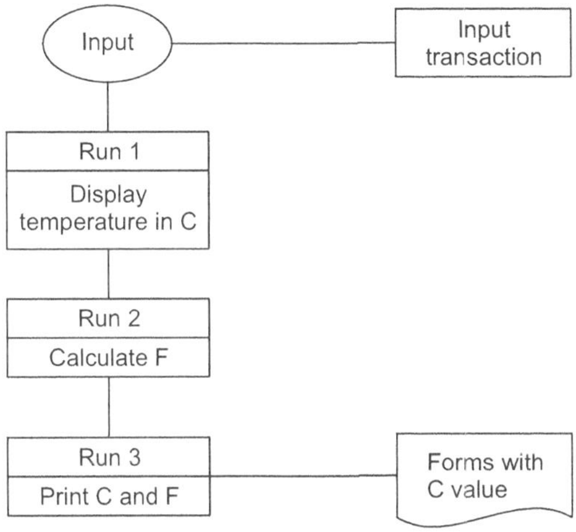

Fig. 2.5 *Run Flowchart*

(*c*) **Program flowcharts:** A program flowchart represents, in detail, the various steps to be performed within the system for transforming the input into output. The various steps are logical/ arithmetic operations, algorithms etc. It serves as the basis for discussions and communication between the system analysts and the programmers. Program flowcharts are quite helpful to programmers in organising their programming efforts. These flowcharts constitute an important component of documentation for an application.

Figure 2.6 represents a program flowchart for finding the sum of first five natural numbers (*i.e.*, 1, 2, 3, 4, 5).

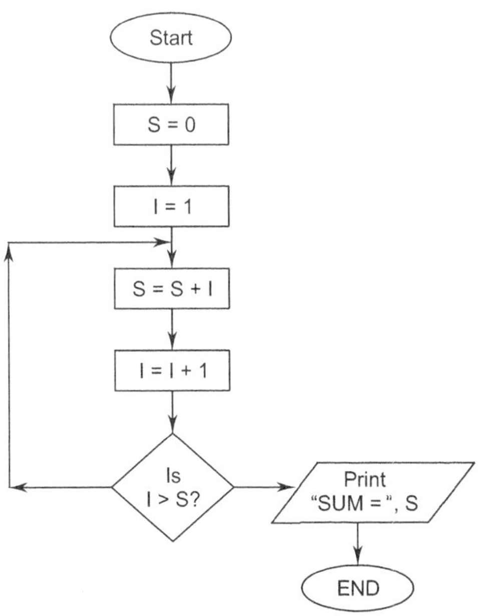

Fig. 2.6 *Program Flowchart*

(*d*) **Data flow diagram:** Data flow diagrams are the most commonly used way of documenting the process of current and required systems. As their name suggests they are a pictorial way of showing the flow of data into, around and out of a system.

(*e*) **Defining DFD:** Graphical representation of a system's data and how the processes transform the data is known as Data Flow Diagram (or DFD). Unlike, flowcharts, DFDs do not give detailed descriptions of modules but graphically describe a system's data and how the data interact with the system.

(*f*) **Components of DFD:** DFDs are constructed using four major components

- external entries
- data stores
- processes and
- data flows

(*i*) *External entities:* External entities represent the source of data as input to the system. They are also the destination of system data. External entities can be called data stores out side the system. These are represented by squares.

(*ii*) *Data stores:* Data stores represent stores of data within the system. Examples, computer files or databases. An open-ended box represents a data/store — data at rest or a temporary repository of data.

(*iii*) *Process:* Process represents activities in which data is manipulated by being stored or retrieved or transferred in some way. In other words we can say that process transforms the input data into output data. Circles stand for a process that converts data into information.

(*iv*) *Data flows:* Data flows represents the movement of data from one component to the other. An arrow identifies data flow — data in motion. It is a pipeline through which information flows. Data flows are generally shown as one-way only. Data flows between external entities are shown as dotted lines.

(*g*) **Physical and Logical DFD:** Consider the figure 2.7. It is clear from the figure that orders are placed, orders are received, the location of ordered parts is determined and delivery notes are dispatched along with the order.

Fig. 2.7

It does not however tell us how these things are done or who does them. Are they done by computers or manually and if manually who does them ? A logical DFD of any information system is one that models what occurs without showing how it occurs.

A physical DFD shows, how the various functions are performed? Who does them? Consider the following figure:

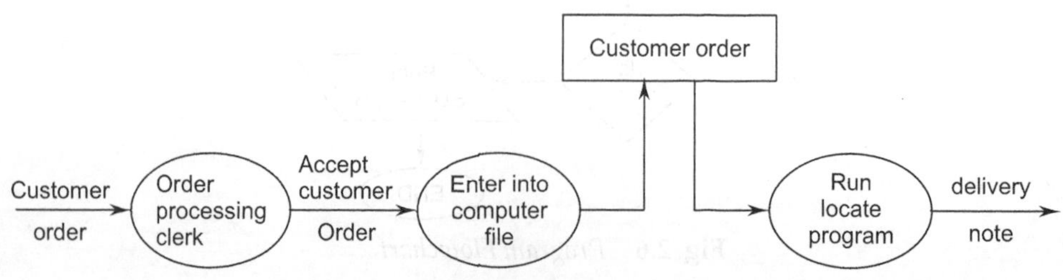

Fig. 2.8

The figure 2.7 is opposite, it shows the actual devices that perform the functions. Thus there is an "order processing clerk", an "entry into computer file" process and a "run locate program" process to locate the parts ordered. DFD(s) that shows how things happen, or the physical components are called physical DFD(s).

Typical processes that appear in physical DFDs are methods of data entry, specific data transfer or processing methods.

(*h*) **Difference between flowcharts and DFD:** The program flowchart describes boxes that describe computations, decisions, interactions and loops. It is an important to keep in mind that data flow diagrams are not program flowcharts and should not include control elements. A good DFD should

- have no data flows that split up into a number of other data flows
- have no crossing lines
- not include flowchart loops of control elements
- not include data flows that act as signals to activate processes.

2.8.2 Decision Tables and Decision Trees

Decision tables and trees were developed long before the widespread use of computers. They not only isolate many conditions and possible actions but they help ensure that nothing has been overlooked.

(*a*) **Decision tables:** The decision table is a chart with four sections listing all the logical conditions and actions. In addition the top section allows space for title, date, author, system and comment as shown in the table 1.1.

Table 1.1 Decision Table

TITLE : **Author :** **Comments :**	**DATE :** **System :**
Condition Stub	Condition Entry
Action Stub	Action Entry

The **condition stub** contains a list of all the necessary tests in a decision table. In the lower left-hand corner of the decision table we find the action stub where one may note all the processes desired in a given module. Thus **Action Stub** contains a list of all the processes involved in a decision table.

The upper right corner provides the space for the **condition entry** — all possible permutations of yes and no responses related to the condition stub. The yes and no possibilities are arranged as a vertical column called rules. Rules are numbered 1, 2, 3 and so on. We can determine the rules in a decision table by the formula:

Number of rules = 2^N = 2^N where N represents the number of condition and ^ means exponentiate. Thus a decision table with four conditions has 16 ($2^4 = 2 \times 2 \times 2 \times 2 = 16$) rules one with six conditions has 64 rules and eight conditions yield 256 rules.

The **Condition entry** contains a list of all the yes/no permutations in a decision table. The lower right corner holds the action entry. X's or dots indicate whether an action should occur as a consequence of the yes/no entries under condition entry. X's indicate action; dots indicate no action.

Thus Action entry indicates via dot or X whether something should happen in a decision table. Let us consider the following example of book order illustrated by table 2.2.

If order is from book store
And if order is for 6 copies
Then discount is 25%
Else (if order is for less then 6 copies)
No discount is allowed
Else (if order is from libraries)
If order is for 50 copies or more
Then discount is 15%
Else if order is for 20 to 49 copies
Then discount is 10%
Else if order is for 6 to 19 copies
Then discount is 5%
Else (order is for less then 6 copies)
No discount is allowed

A decision table for the above process is illustrated below:

Table 2.2 Decision Table

Title: **Author:** **Comments:**		**Date:** **System:**					
Condition Sub		**Condition Entry**					
		1	**2**	**3**	**4**	**5**	**6**
IF	Customer is bookstore	Y	Y	N	N	N	N
	Order size is 6 or more	Y	N	N	N	N	N
	Customer is library	N	N	Y	Y	Y	Y
	Order size is 50 or more	N	N	Y	N	N	N
	Order size is 20–49	N	N	N	Y	N	N
	Order size is 6–19	N	N	N	N	Y	N
Then	Allow 25% discount	X	·	·	·	·	·
	Allow 15% discount	·	·	X	·	·	·
	Allow 10% discount	·	·	·	X	·	·
	Allow 5% discount	·	·	·	·	X	·
	No discount	·	X	·	·	·	X
	Action Stub	Action Entry					

(*b*) **Decision tree:** The decision tree defines the conditions as a sequence of left to right tests. A decision tree helps to show the paths that are possible in a design following an action or decision by the user. Figure 2.9 illustrates the concept of decision tree.

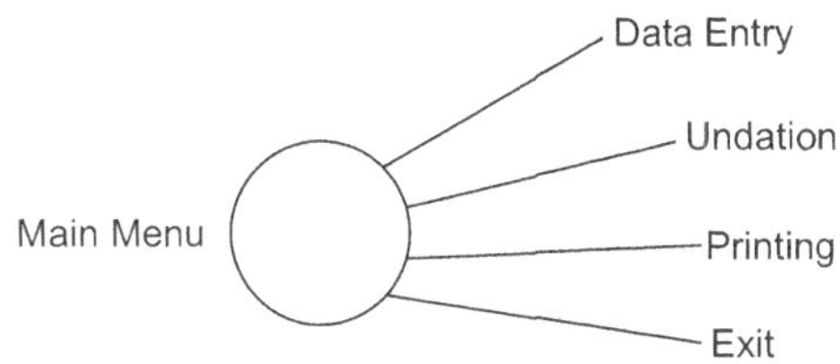

Fig. 2.9 *Decision Tree*

Decision tree turns a decision table into a diagram. This tool is read from left to right, decision results in a fork, and all branches end with an outcome. Figure 2.10 illustrates the decision tree for the book order decision table we saw earlier.

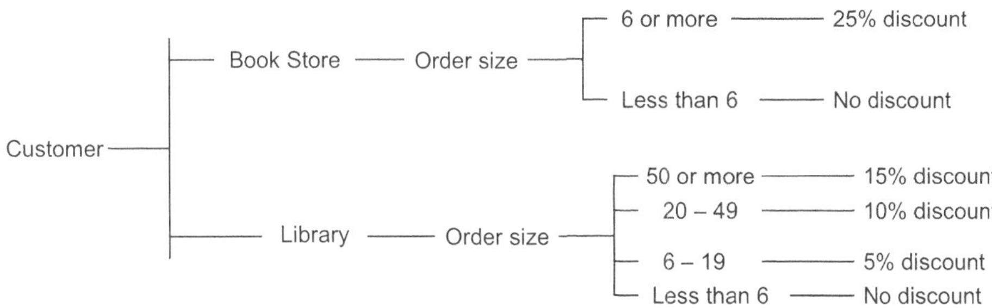

Fig. 2.10 *Decision Tree for Book Order*

EXERCISE

1. What is the main activities involved Software Development Life Cycle Model?
2. Describe Preliminary Investigation.
3. Describe coding.
4. Describe System Testing.
5. Describe Error Distribution with Phases.
6. Describe Waterfall Software Development Life Cycle Model.
7. Describe Prototyping Software Development Life Cycle Model.
8. Describe Iterative Enhancement Model.
9. Describe The Spiral Model.
10. Describe Object Oriented Methodology.
11. Describe Dynamic System Development Method.
12. Describe CASE Tools.
13. Can 'CASE' do Everthing?
14. Describe System Description Techniques.
15. Describe Flowcharts.
16. Difference between flowcharts and DFD.
17. Describe Decision Tables and Decision Trees.

MULTIPLE CHOICE QUESTIONS

1. The major goal of requirement determination phase of information system development is
   (*a*) determine whether information is needed by an organization
   (*b*) determine what information is needed by an organization

(*c*) determine how information needed by an organization can be provided
(*d*) determine when information is to be given.

2. Information requirements of an organization can be determined by
(*a*) interviewing managers and users and arriving at the requirements based on consensus
(*b*) finding out what similar organizations do
(*c*) telling organization what they need based on your experience
(*d*) sending a questionnaire to all employees of the organization.

3. It is necessary to prioritize information requirements of an organization at the requirements determination phase as
(*a*) it is always good to prioritize
(*b*) there are conflicting demands from users
(*c*) there are constraints on budgets, available time, human resource and requirement
(*d*) all good organization do it.

4. Requirement specification is carried out
(*a*) after requirements are determined
(*b*) before requirements are determined
(*c*) simultaneously with requirements determination
(*d*) independent of requirements determination.

5. The role of a system analyst drawing up a requirements specification is similar to
(*a*) architect designing a building
(*b*) a structural engineer designing a building
(*c*) a contractor constructing a building
(*d*) the workers who construct a building.

6. It is necessary to consult the following while drawing up requirement specification
(*a*) only top managers
(*b*) only top and middle management
(*c*) only top, middle and operational managers
(*d*) top, middle and operational managers and also all who will use the system.

7. In order to understand the working of an organization for which a computer based system is being designed, an analyst must
(*a*) look at only current work and document flow in the organization
(*b*) discuss with top level and middle level management only
(*c*) interview top, middle, line managers and also clerks who will enter data and use the system
(*d*) only clerical and middle level staff who have long experience in the organization and will be users of the system.

8. A feasibility study is carried out
(*a*) after final requirements specifications are drawn up
(*b*) during the period when requirements specifications are drawn up
(*c*) before the final requirements specifications are drawn up
(*d*) at any time.

9. The main objective of feasibility study is
(*a*) to assess whether it is possible to meet the requirements specifications
(*b*) to assess if it is possible to meet the requirements specified subject to constraints of budget, human resource and hardware

(*c*) to assist the management in implementing the desired system
(*d*) to remove bottlenecks in implementing the desired system.

10. It is necessary to carry out a feasibility study as
(*a*) top management can not ensure that a project is feasible before calling a system analyst
(*b*) top management is not sure what they want from the system
(*c*) even though top management is in favor of the system, technology may not be mature for implementation
(*d*) all organizations do it.

11. Feasibility study is carried out by
(*a*) managers of the organization
(*b*) system analyst in consultation with managers of the organization
(*c*) users of the proposed system
(*d*) systems designers in consultation with the prospective users of the system.

12. Initial requirements specification is
(*a*) not changed till the end of the project
(*b*) continuously changed during project implementation
(*c*) only a rough indication of the requirement
(*d*) changed and finalized after feasibility study.

13. Final specifications are drawn up by
(*a*) system analyst in consultation with the management of the organization
(*b*) the managers of user organization
(*c*) system analyst in consultation with programmers
(*d*) system designers along with users.

14. The main goal of arriving at a final specification is
(*a*) to tell the organization's managers how the system will function
(*b*) to tell the organization's managers what the proposed system will achieve in a language understood by them
(*c*) to compute the cost of implementing the system
(*d*) to assist in designing the system.

15. The final specifications are arrived at
(*a*) after feasibility study
(*b*) during feasibility study
(*c*) just before implementation phase
(*d*) when the system is being designed.

16. System approval criteria are specified
(*a*) when the final specifications are drawn up
(*b*) during feasibility study
(*c*) during the requirements specifications stage
(*d*) during system study stage.

17. System test plan is specified
(*a*) when the final specifications are drawn up
(*b*) during feasibility study

(*c*) during the requirements specifications stage
(*d*) during system study stage.

18. Hardware study is required
(*a*) to find out cost of computer system needed
(*b*) to determine the type of computer system and software tools needed to meet the final system specification
(*c*) to make sure that the system does not become obsolete
(*d*) to find how to implement the system.

19. Hardware study is carried out
(*a*) after the final system is specified
(*b*) at the requirements specification stage
(*c*) before the requirements are specified
(*d*) whenever management decides it is necessary.

20. System design is carried out
(*a*) as soon as system requirements are determined
(*b*) whenever a system analyst feels it is urgent
(*c*) after final system specifications are approved by the organization
(*d*) whenever the user management feels it should be done.

21. The primary objective of system design is to
(*a*) design the programs, databases and test plan
(*b*) design only user interfaces
(*c*) implement the system
(*d*) find out how the system will perform.

22. The primary objective of system implementation is
(*i*) to build a system prototype
(*ii*) to train users to operate the system
(*iii*) to implement designed system using computers
(*iv*) write programs, create databases and test with live data
(*a*) *i, iii*
(*b*) *i, ii, iii*
(*c*) *ii, iii*
(*d*) *ii, iv*.

23. During system implementation the following are done
(*i*) programs are written and tested with operational data
(*ii*) user documentation is created and users trained
(*iii*) programmers are recruited and trained
(*iv*) the system is tested with operational data
(*a*) *i* and *iii*
(*b*) *ii* and *iii*
(*c*) *ii* and *iv*
(*d*) *i*, *ii* and *iv*.

24. System evaluation is carried out
- (*a*) after the system has been operational for a reasonable time
- (*b*) during system implementation
- (*c*) whenever managers of user organization want it
- (*d*) whenever operational staff want it.

25. The main objective of system evaluation is
- (*a*) to see whether the system met specification
- (*b*) to improve the system based on operational experience for a period
- (*c*) to remove bugs in the programs
- (*d*) to asses the efficiency of the system.

26. Systems are modified whenever
- (*a*) user's requirements change
- (*b*) new computers are introduced in the market
- (*c*) new software tools become available in the market
- (*d*) other similar organization modify these system.

27. The main objective of system modification is
- (*a*) to use the latest software tools
- (*b*) to meet the user's new/changed needs
- (*c*) to use the latest hardware
- (*d*) to have the most modern system.

28. To easily modify the existing system it is necessary to
- (*a*) use good software tools
- (*b*) use the best hardware available
- (*c*) design the system which can be changed at low cost
- (*d*) keep the programming team happy.

29. It is necessary to design an information system to easily accommodate change, because
- (*a*) new computers are introduced every year
- (*b*) new computer languages become popular every year
- (*c*) organizations' requirements change over a period of time
- (*d*) systems need continuous debugging.

30. Changing an operational information system is
- (*a*) impossible
- (*b*) expensive and done selectively
- (*c*) never required
- (*d*) usually done.

31. System analysts have to interact with
- (*i*) managers of organizations
- (*ii*) users in the organization
- (*iii*) programming team
- (*iv*) data entry operator
    - (*a*) *iii* and *iv*
    - (*b*) *i*, *ii* and *iii*

(*c*) *ii, iii* and *iv*

(*d*) *ii* and *iii*.

32. The primary responsibility of a systems analyst is to

(*a*) specify an information system which meets the requirements of an organization

(*b*) write programs to meet specifications

(*c*) maintain the system

(*d*) meet managers of the organization regularly.

33. The responsibilities of a system analyst include

(*i*) defining and prioritizing information requirement of an organization

(*ii*) gathering data, facts and opinions of users in an organization

(*iii*) drawing up specifications of the system for an organization

(*iv*) designing and evaluating the system

(*a*) *i* and *ii*

(*b*) *i, ii* and *iv*

(*c*) *i, ii, iii* and *iv*

(*d*) *i, ii* and *iii*.

34. The most important attribute of a systems analyst is

(*a*) excellent programming skills

(*b*) very good hardware designing skills

(*c*) very good technical management skills

(*d*) very good writing skills.

35. Among the attributes of a good systems analyst the following are essential

(*i*) knowledge of organization

(*ii*) analytical mind

(*iii*) ability to communicate orally

(*iv*) excellent mathematical abilities

(*a*) *i* and *ii*

(*b*) *i, ii* and *iii*

(*c*) *i, ii* and *iv*

(*d*) *i, iii* and *iv*.

36. Among the attributes of a systems analyst the following are most important

(*i*) knowledge of computer systems and currently available hardware

(*ii*) good interpersonal relations

(*iii*) broad knowledge about various organizations

(*iv*) very good accountancy knowledge

(*a*) *i, iii* and *iv*

(*b*) *i* and *iii*

(*c*) *i, ii* and *iv*

(*d*) *i, ii* and *iii*.

37. Managers in organizations should not design their own systems as

(*a*) systems have to interact with other systems

(*b*) they do not have the special skills necessary to design systems (*c*) it is not their job

(*d*) they are always very busy.

38. Systems analyst should use software tools in their work as

(*a*) all analysts use them

(*b*) they assist in systematic design of systems

(*c*) they are inexpensive

(*d*) they are easily available.

Key to Objective Questions

1. (*b*)	**2.** (*a*)	**3.** (*c*)	**4.** (*a*)	**5.** (*a*)
6. (*d*)	**7.** (*c*)	**8.** (*c*)	**9.** (*b*)	**10.** (*c*)
11. (*b*)	**12.** (*c*)	**13.** (*a*)	**14.** (*b*)	**15.** (*a*)
16. (*a*)	**17.** (*a*)	**18.** (*b*)	**19.** (*a*)	**20.** (*c*)
21. (*a*)	**22.** (*d*)	**23.** (*d*)	**24.** (*a*)	**25.** (*b*)
26. (*a*)	**27.** (*b*)	**28.** (*c*)	**29.** (*c*)	**30.** (*b*)
31. (*b*)	**32.** (*a*)	**33.** (*d*)	**34.** (*c*)	**35.** (*b*)
36. (*d*)	**37.** (*b*)	**38.** (*b*).		

3

INTRODUCTION TO MIS

3.0 INTRODUCTION

The system provides information on the past, present and project future and on relevant events inside and outside the organization. It may be defined as a planned and integrated system for gathering relevant data, converting it in to right information and supplying the same to the concerned executives. The main purpose of MIS is to provide the right information to the right people at the right time.

The Concept of management information systems originated in the 1960s and become the byword of almost all attempts to relate computer technology and systems to data processing in business . During the early 1960s , it became evident that the computer was being applied to the solution of business problem in a piecemeal fashion, focusing almost entirely on the computerization of clerical and record—keeping tasks. The concepts of management information systems was developed to counteract such in efficient development and in effective use of the computer. The MIS concepts is vital to efficient and effective computer use in business of two major reasons:

- It serves as a systems framework for organizing business computer applications. Business applications of computers should be viewed as interrelated and integrated computer—based information systems and not as independent data processing job.
- In emphasizes the management orientation of electronics information processing in business. The primary goal of computer based information systems should be the processing of data generated by business operations.

  A management information system is an integrated man—machine systems that provides information to support the planning and control function of manager in an organization.
- The out put of an MIS is information that sub serves managerial functions. When a system provides information to persons who are not managers, then it will not be considered as part of an MIS . For .example , an organization often process a lot of data which it is required by law to furnish to various government regulatory agencies. Such a system, while it may have interfaces with an MIS, would not be a part of it, Instances

of such systems are salary disclosures and excise duty statements. By the same token to sophisticated computer — aided design system for engineering purposes would also not be a part of an MIS.

- Generally, MIS deals with information that is systematically and routinely collected in accordance with a well-defined set of rules. Thus, and MIS is a part of the formal information network in an organization. Information that has major managerial planning significance is sometimes collected at golf courses. Such information is not part of MIS, how ever, one—shot market research data collected to gauge the potential of a new product does not come with in the scope of an MIS by our definition because although such information may be very systematically collected it is not collected on a regular basis.
- Normally, the information provided by an MIS helps the managers to make planning and control decisions. Now, we will see, what is planning and control. Every organization in order to function must perform, certain operations. For Example, a car manufacturer has to perform certain manufacturing activities, a wholesaler has to provide water to its area of jurisdiction. All these are operations that need to be done. Besides, these operations, an organization must make plans for them. In other words it must decide on how many and what type of cars to make next month or what commissions to offer retailers or what pumping stations to install in the next five years.

  Also an organization must control the operations in the light of the plans and targets developed in the planning process. The car manufacturer must know if manufacturing operations are in line with the targets and if not, he must make decisions to correct the deviation or revise his plans. Similarly the wholesaler will want to know the impacts that his commissions have had on sales and make decisions to correct adverse trends. The municipal corporation will need to control the tendering process and contractors who will execute the pumping station plans.

  Generally, MIS is concerned with planning and control. Often there are elaborate systems for information that assists operations. For example, the car manufacturer will have a system for providing information to the workers on the shop floor about the job that needs to be done on a particular batch of material. There may be route sheets, which accompany the rate materials and components in their movement through various machines. This system per se provides only information to support operation. It has no managerial decision—making significance. It I not part of an MIS. If, however, the system does provided information on productivity, machine utilization or rejection rates, then we would say that the system is part of an MIS.
- Generally MIS has all the ingredients that are employed in providing information support to manager to making planning and control decisions. Managers often use historical data on an organization's activities as well as current status data make planning and control decisions. Such data comes from a data base which is contained in files maintained by the organization. This data base is an essential component of an MIS. Manual procedures that are used to collect and process information and computer hardware are obvious ingredients of an MIS. These also form part of the MIS. In summary, when we say that " an MIS is an integrated man—machine systems that provided information to supports the planning and control function of managers in an origination . It does the following function.

- sub serves managerial function
- collects stores, evaluates information systematically and routinely
- supports planning and control decisions
- Includes files, hardware, software, software and operations research models.

Effective management information systems are needed by all business organization because of the increased complexity and rate of change of today's business environment. For Example, Marketing manager need information about sales performance and trends, financial manger returns, production managers needs information analyzing resources requirement and worker productivity and personnel manager require information concerning employee compensation and professional development. Thus, effective management information systems must be developed to provide modern managers with the specific marketing, financial, production and personnel information products they required to support their decision making responsibilities.

3.1 WHAT IS MANAGEMENT INFORMATION SYSTEM

Management Information system is sets of inter — related procedures using IT infrastructure in a business enterprise to generate and disseminate desired information. Such systems are designed to support decision—making by the people associated with the enterprise in the process of attainment of its objectives. The business information system gets data and other resources of It infrastructure as input from the environment and process them to satisfy the information needs of different entities associated with the business enterprise. There are systems of control over the use of IT resources and feedback system offers useful clues for increasing the benefits of information system to business. The business information system is sub systems of business system and themselves serve the function of feedback and control in business system.

3.2 NATURE/FEATURE/CHARACTERISTICS OF MANAGEMENT INFORMATION SYSTEM

The basic characteristics of MIS are as follows:

1. The Management Information systems are subject to the dynamics of business environment and need to be flexible enough to absorb the inevitable changes in the information of business. They have to be efficient to satisfy the demanding and hard task matters.
2. Management Information system needs to be proactive. They should anticipate changes in information needs of users and accordingly adapt themselves to suit their needs. This has become important because of the fact that the mangers get involved in the runtime activities to the extent that the decision making becomes a matter of imitating what competitors are doing or planning to do, rather than making an informed choice.
3. The purpose of Management Information system is to cater to the information needs for decision-making in business.
4. The Management Information systems have to design keeping in view the availability of financial and human resources to the business enterprise.
5. The cost effectiveness is a matter of prime concern in the development and maintenance of Business Information system. Economic justification for investment in IT infrastructure for Management Information system is a pre condition for its existence and sustenance.

3.3 KEY COMPONENTS OF MANAGEMENT INFORMATION SYSTEM

Management Information systems can be described by four key components; they are as follows:

1. Decision
2. Transaction and processing
3. Information and flow
4. Individuals or functions involved.
5. Types of Information systems.

It is difficult to observe the decision process through which we can see and review the results of a decision. Transactions are usually more visible, though many current systems use computer programs, principles, an observer can see information and its flows. Individuals can be observed too.

3.4 ADVANTAGES OF MIS

1. **It Facilitates Planning :** MIS improves the quality of plants by providing relevant information for sound decision—making. Due to increase in the size and complexity of organizations, managers have lost personal contact with the scene of operations.
2. **In Minimizes Information Overload :** MIS change the larger amount of data in to summarized form and there by avoids the confusion which may arise when managers are flooded with detailed facts.
3. **MIS Encourages Decentralization :** Decentralization of authority is possibly when there is a system for monitoring operations at lower levels. MIS is successfully used for measuring performance and making necessary change in the organizational plans and procedures.
4. **It Brings Co-ordination :** MIS facilities integration of specialized activities by keeping each department aware of the problem and requirements of other departments. It connects all decision centers in the organization .
5. **It Makes Control Easier :** MIS serves as a link between managerial planning and control. It improves the ability of management to evaluate and improve performance. The used computers has increased the data processing and storage capabilities and reduced the cost.
6. **MIS assembles**, process , stores , Retrieves , evaluates and Disseminates the information.

3.5 LIMITATIONS OF MIS

The following are the main hindering factors to the development of MIS:

1. ***Lack of proper objectives and goals for many MIS projects.*** Too many MIS projects are embarked upon by organizations without clear objectives and goals, which leads them into not being able to design and implement a good MIS. With a lack of objectives many organizations have failed to coordinate their information systems, which is essential for the proper working of MIS. The result is that the uncoordinated efforts of the different departments end up being wasted.
2. ***Lack of management participation and development.*** There has been a general lack of top management participation and involvement in many MIS projects. Too many MIS projects are left to project leaders who neither have the authority nor know much about the management process. Some managers, in order to appear that they are involved,

delegate the participation to one of their assistants. The thing these managers fail to realize is that they are the ones going to use the information, and not the assistants. The main reason for this lack of management participation is basically the fact that many of the managers find themselves in a dilemma. On the one hand there are those enthusiasts who believe an MIS can do everything, while there are those who think that MIS should be abandoned. Most managers are then caught in the middle of these views and they find it difficult to make a decision one way or the other. As a result they either do not commit themselves or they delegate the work to a junior person who predictably fails to attain the expected results.

3. ***Control measures and evaluative criteria are inadequate or absent.*** Lack of control is a direct result of lack of management involvement and results in a lack of proper MIS objectives. Many organizations that have control measures have found them dysfunctional to the MIS development. For example, tight controls have put pressure on MIS executives, forcing them only to seek short cuts.
4. ***False assumptions are used in designing MIS.*** MIS information analysts must make many assumptions, some of which hold while others do not. False assumptions often lead to improperly defined system objectives.
5. ***Inability of many system designers to identify information needs for managers.*** It is very difficult to determine the information needs for managers. Because managers, by the nature of some of their decisions, cannot determine their own information needs. System designers, not being sure what information the managers actually require, go ahead and design systems they hope will satisfy the managers. Sometimes systems designers are able to determine the information needs of the operating management and they try to apply those needs to all the other management levels, which is of little use.
6. ***Lack of flexibility in many MIS.*** Some MISs fail the test of time when the environment they were designed for changes. Any MIS requires a degree of flexibility to meet changing and diverse information needs of managers.
7. ***Poor implementation program.*** Just as a good MIS design program is required, a good implementation program is also of high priority. Many well—designed MISs have failed because of lack of proper implementation programs. When considering implementation, a number of issues are involved, such as how should MIS be implemented? Also connected with the implementation program is the fact that there is a tendency for many organizations to try to implement MIS through the same techniques and people as used for data processing.
8. ***Too much emphasis is placed on technical aspects while placing relatively little emphasis on human factors.*** Many MISs have been designed around only technical factors giving little or no consideration at all to the humans who will use the system. Many good technically designed systems have failed to work because the designers have failed to recognize this important man/machine relationship.

3.6 MANAGEMENT INFORMATION SYSTEM VERSUS DATA PROCESSING SYSTEM

A management information system, or MIS, is a computer—based system that optimizes the collection, transfer, and presentation of information throughout an organization by using an integrated structure of databases and information flow. An MIS has been called a method, a function, an approach, a process, an organization, a system, and a subsystem.

Data processing systems, or DP systems, are concerned with transaction handling and record—keeping, usually for a particular functional area. Here are a few differences between an MIS and a DP system:

1. The integrated database of an MIS enables greater flexibility in meeting the information needs of management.
2. An MIS integrates the information flow between functional areas (accounting, marketing, inventory management, etc.), whereas DP systems tend to support a single functional area.
3. An MIS caters to the information needs of all levels of management, whereas DP systems focus on the clerical and operational levels.
4. Management's information needs are supported on a timelier basis with an MIS than they are with a DP system. An MIS, for example, has online inquiry capability for the immediate generation of reports, whereas a DP system usually produces only scheduled reports.

3.7 MANAGEMENT INFORMATION SYSTEM VERSUS DECISION PROCESSING SYSTEM

The terms MIS and DSS stand for Management Information Systems and Decision Support Systems respectively. There has been a lot of talk regarding these two, whether they are actually the same thing or if there are any significant differences between the two.

MIS is basically a kind of link to facilitate communication between managers across different areas in a business organization. MIS plays a pivotal role in enabling communications across the floor of an organization, between various entities therein.

DSS, many consider, is advancement from the original MIS. However, this is not the sole difference between the two. While there may not be too much separating the two, the difference is still there, as is apparent when we say DSS is an advancement over MIS.

The essential difference between the two is in focus. DSS, as the term indicates, is about leadership and senior management in an organization providing good, reliable judgment as well as vision. MIS, on the other hand, is about focusing on the actual flow of information itself.

Characteristics of MIS are

- Structured decision—making
- Monitoring and Controlling Operations
- Routine decision—making
- Present and Past—tense
- Periodic and Exception reports
- Measuring progress towards goals
- Limited solution set
- Rigid design
- Traditional SDLC—design "freezing"

Characteristics of DSS are

- Semi to Un—structured decision—making
- Tactical decision—making (resource allocation)
- Ad hoc, or problem resolution decision—making
- Future tense (based on historical models)
- Ad hoc reports
- Determining tactics to meet goals
- "Unlimited" solution set
- Flexible design
- Iterative design approaches — not frozen

3.8 DECISION MAKING AND INFORMATION SYSTEMS FOR AN ORGANIZATION

Since MIS is concerned largely with managerial applications, an appreciation of the theory of organization is a necessary prerequisite for successful application of MIS. Some professionals in the MIS area bring forth this point in the cryptic definition of MIS as "the supply of right information, in right time, at right level". Before discussing the use of MIS in decision-making we will first discuss the basic structure of any organization *i.e.* what is the hierarchy followed in any organization. The level of management in the context of MIS refers to a classification of management, originally developed by Anthony.

The different levels of management are generally referred to as a Pyramid in a pictorial form to emphasize the fact that in any organization there are a few top positions, a large number of supervisory staff and a much large number of operational staff. Placing these three staff positions in order from top to bottom would lead to a structure loosely resembling the historic Egyptian pyramid.

We will now discuss how this pyramid represents the three categories of employees working in an organization. Anthony classified the three levels as strategic, tactical and operational. The strategic management is concerned with long term policy decisions like new plant location, new products, diversification, etc.; they typically need a summary of plant/ organizational level information, but need lots of unstructured and even vague information pertaining to the environment — the competitors, fiscal policy changes of the Government, emerging technologies etc. the tactical management comprising functional managers would need some external information but a lot of organization-wide information to exercise control like budgeting, quality level, service level, inventory level etc. The operational management is only concerned with plant/organizational level information but in a far detailed manner like individual operator specific, machine specific and shift specific performance measures. As we have already discussed the three attributes of Data or Information. Let's see how they are applicable to the three levels, which we have discussed above. To be successful, MIS is an organization must explicitly take into account this classification of management. Since the summary information to be provided to the tactical and strategic management must be culled out of operational information, the accuracy and timeliness of information collection and dissemination is important at the operational level. However at the tactical and operational level, relevance is the watch-word. A relevant but slightly inaccurate-data is better than irrelevant but accurate data. The context decides the tradeoffs, particularly when cost early generation data processing are involved, historically the failures of early generation data processing departments are attributes to the lack of appreciation of this point. Some professionals call this process as the provision of information Filter meaning that only filtered information called out of operational data must be presented to the middle and top management. Some others put it more effectively in the form of emphasizing efficiency at the operational level and effectiveness at the tactical and strategic level. We are talking in the section above we talked about the use of MIS in an Organization. Now let us discuss the hierarchical structure of an organization and type of Information System required at various levels of an Organization.

Successful development of information systems call for a deep understanding of the organizational structure and dynamics of the enterprise. Some organization are goal oriented, the analyst must be clear as to what information exactly need to be collected, stored and analyzed. Since every information must have a context, only operational information that ultimately has some decision-making contribution must be collected. Second the information collected and processed must be consistent with the level of the organization to which it is to be presented. Any organization consists of three levels, we will now take in to account the differences in the nature of decisions made by the middle level and upper level as lower level is not responsible for making any type of decisions. According to Anthony's classification, there are basically three levels of management, independent of the size of the enterprise: operational level, middle level and top level management. Operational decisions that call for large volumes of internal data (local to the enterprise). The middle management is concerned with medium range (tactical) decisions that call for much less information. The top management being concerned with long term (strategic) decisions calling for just a few vital internal information but a lot of external information as well. Any successful information system should take into account such a pattern of information needs by the management.

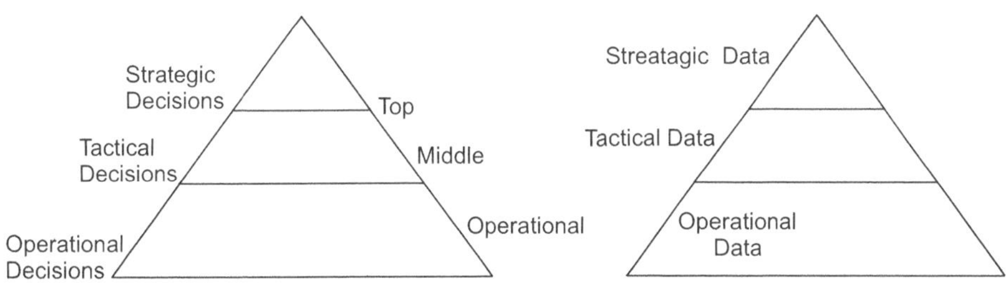

This is generally pictorially displayed in the form of management vs. Information pyramid. You might all agree with us that management basically involves decision-making activities. The importance of information to management is further emphasized by the fact that much of management is primarily decision making. While there are several views of what constitute management, the generally accepted planning, organizing, coordinating, directing and control are all concerned with decision making. In this text we take such a view of management and we perceive management information systems to support such managerial decision-making. We also would like to emphasize that information systems should address clearly the situations of programmed decisions and non- pro grammed decisions by properly structuring the appropriate information. Failure to recognize intrinsic difference may lead to a failure of the information system. All of us know that there are several functional areas or management viz. personnel, marking, production, finance and services will be significantly influenced by the information systems that are to be implemented in the organization. Care must also be taken to recognize the fact that in every functional area the mapping of the informational pyramid must be carefully worked out. Typical example of the three levels of information among the functional areas of management are as follows:

	Production	**Finance**	**Personnel**	**Marketing**
Strategic	New plant Location	Alternative Financing	Welfare policy	Competitor Survey
Tactical	Production Bottleneck	Variance Analysis	Performance Appraisal	Advertising
Operational	Daily Scheduling	Payroll	Leave records	Sales analysis

Example of tvoical MIS system

3.9 ORGANIZATION INFORMATION STRATEGY

A number of organizations have started to implement an organizational information strategy. These companies recognize that information is an organizational asset and should be maintained as such. They also recognize the lack of a central strategy has created major problems across the organization.

One of these problems is the inability of the people in the organization to find accurate and qualified information. According to a recent research 15-to-30 percent of a knowledge-worker's time is spent seeking specific information and that fruitless information searches cost the Fortune 500 alone as much as $8.5 billion a year in lost productivity. Such major losses could be rectified by making the needed information available as needed.

What Is Information Strategy

Information strategy can be defined as an organization's unified blueprint for capturing, integrating, processing, delivery, and presentation of information in a clean, consistent, and timely manner. All information in an organization should meet a certain standard for quality.

It should be delivered consistently across the organization, *i.e.*, asking for the same information in different divisions should yield the same result, and users and applications shouldn't have to wait long to get their requested information.

As an analogy, one could compare information in an organization to water in a typical metropolis. In the old days, as people built a house, they'd also dig a well in their backyard to reach water needed for drinking, cooking or cleaning. This water was hardly shared and was not necessarily clean.

If the building next door needed water and did not have a well people had to grab a bucket, go next door, take water from the well, and carry it to their own building.

As people matured in the art of city planning, we learned to think of water as a common utility and to integrate, clean, and distribute it from a central organization in the metropolis. You might say that we, as the residents of a metropolis, have an unsigned contract with our metropolitan water department to provide us with clean, consistent, and timely water.

Basically, regardless of where you are in the metropolis, you can trust that the water is consistent, has met certain level of quality, and if you open the faucet, it will flow.

The same applies to information in the organization. By implementing the same principles as our city planners, we'd be able to capture, integrate, and cleanse the information in a central repository, and to deliver it to our internal and external users in a clean, consistent, and timely manner.

There are several reasons for establishing a information strategy for any organization. First and foremost, information is an asset and should be treated as such. As with any other asset, it has value. The value of information is in it accessibility and accuracy. Information that is not accessible on demand, and/or is not accurate is not an asset.

Like most assets, information depreciates overtime, needs to be governed, and must be maintained. An information strategy allows an organization to manage, govern, and provide access to this asset.

The second reason for having an information strategy in the organization is the fact that, today, there is just way too much information in an organization to manage it loosely. We truly need a plan, a blueprint, a strategy on how to capture, store, govern, and deliver all information to internal and external users of this information.

The next major reason for having such a strategy is the business mandate for it. Business groups have become very savvy in accessing, manipulating, and utilizing this information and they demand it to be available, complete, and accurate.

In fact, with the new Web 2.0 technologies, they not only demand internal information, but also external information available in various websites such as myspace.com. Information available in such community sites could be used to analyze and gauge customer views, likes, and dislikes, in order to improve an organization's products, services, image, and/or marketing campaigns and, as such, is very important to an organization.

For example, one of our client organizations, right before going public, monitored the chatter on blogs, chat—rooms, and other community sites as well as other conventional channels to gauge the right IPO price for their stock

3.10 END USER COMPUTING

End User Computing (EUC) is a group of approaches to computing that aim at better integrating end users into the computing environment or that attempt to realize the potential for high—end computing to perform in a trustworthy manner in problem solving of the highest order. The **EUC Ranges** section describes two types of approaches that are at different ends of a spectrum. A simple example of these two extremes can use the SQL context. and php

The first approach would have canned queries and reports that for the most part would be invoked with buttons and/or simple commands. In this approach, a computing group would keep these canned routines up to date through the normal development/maintenance methods.

For the second approach, SQL administration would allow for end—user involvement at several levels including administration itself. Users would also define queries though the supporting mechanism may be constrained in order to reduce the likelihood of run—away conditions that would have negative influence on other users. We see this already in some business intelligence methods which build SQL, including new databases, on the fly. Rules might help dampen effects that can occur with the open—ended environment. The process would expect, and accommodate, the possibility of long run times, inconclusive results and such. These types of unknowns are undecidable 'before the fact'; the need to do 'after the fact' evaluation of results is a prime factor of many higher-order computational situations but cannot (will not) be tolerated by an end user in the normal production mode.

Between these two extremes view of **EUC** there are many combinations. Some of the factors contributing to the need for further EUC research are knowledge processing, pervasive computing, issues of ontology, interactive visualization and analysis coupling schemes and the like.

3.10.1 EUC Ranges

EUC might work by one type of approach that attempts to integrate the human interface ergonomically into a user centered design system throughout its life cycle. In this sense, EUC's goal is to allow unskilled staff to use expensive and highly skilled knowledge in their jobs, by putting the knowledge and expertise into the computer and teaching the end user how to access it. At the same time, this approach is used when highly critical tasks are supported by computational systems (commercial flight, nuclear plant, and the like).

Another approach to EUC allows end users (SMEs, domain experts) to control and even perform software engineering and development. In this case, it can be argued that this type of approach results mainly from deficiencies in computing that could be overcome with better tools and environments. But, high-end roles for the computer in non-trivial domains necessitate (at least, for now) a more full interchange (bandwidth for conversation) that is situational and subject to near exhaustive scrutiny (there are limits influencing how far we can go (bringing up, the necessity for a behavioral (also, see black box below) framework)). Such cannot be filled by a pre—defined system in today's world. In a sense, the computer needs to have the same credentials as does a cohort (scientific method of peer review) in the discipline. This type of computing falls on the more 'open' side of the fence where scientific knowledge is not wrapped within the cloak of IP.

In the first type of approach of EUC described above, it appears easier to teach factory workers, for example, how to read dials, push buttons, pull levers, and log results than to teach them the manufacturing process and mathematical models. The current computing trend is to simulate a console with similar dials, sliders, levers, and switches, which the end user is taught to use. To further reduce end user training, computer consoles all contain components which are shaped, labeled, coloured, and function similarly. EUC developers assume that once the end user knows what and how a particular lever works, they will quickly identify it when it appears in a new console. This means that once staff learns one console, they will be able to operate all consoles. Admittedly each console will have new components, but training is limited to those, not the whole console. This approach requires more than just Pavlovian responses as the console content will have meaning that is of use and power to the particular computing domain. That is, there may be training that reduces the time between sensor reading and action (such as the situation for a pilot of a commercial plane) however, the meaning behind the reading will include other sensor settings as well as whole context that may be fairly involved.

Computing of this type can be labelled black box where trust will be an essential part, behavioral analysis is the name of the game ,and there is a disparate (and very, very wide) gap between the domain and the computer—support ontologies.

In the other type of EUC described above, it has been argued that **a** (teaching programming and computing concepts to a domain expert (say, one of the sciences or engineering disciplines) and letting the expert develop rules (this type of action can be subsumed under the topic of business rules)) is easier than **b** (teaching the intricacies of a complex discipline to a computer worker). **b** is the normal approach of the IT—driven situation. **a** has been the reality since day one of computing in many disciplines. One may further argue that resolving issues of **a** and **b** is not unlike the interplay between distributed and centralized processing (which is an age—old concern in computing). In this sense of EUC, there may be computer scientists supporting decisions about architecture, process, and GUI. However, in many cases, the end user owns the software components. One thrust related to this sense of EUC is a focus on providing better languages to the user. ICAD was an example in the KBE context. Of late, this discipline has moved to a co—joint architecture that features advanced interactive domain visualization coupled with a complicated API accessed via VBA, C++, and the like. This type of co—jointness is an example of a domain tool augmented with non—trivial extensibility.

3.10.2 Trend

The historical view regarding end users is being eroded by the internet and wireless communication, where the traditional end user is able to actively contribute and add value to the computer system. wikis are one example where end users provide the content and free the webmaster to manage the site. Another example within the computer field is free software, where end users can engage in all aspects of software development, from feature requests, through testing and reviews, to usability, documentation, and distribution. Music, pictures, and documents are remixed and edited to satisfy personal taste and demand. The consequence is that many countries and industries have been slow or unwilling to adjust to this emerging society, but some have seen the potential and are exploring economic possibilities.

Another trend is where users specify, and even develop, rules that may be fairly normal relationships (SQL) or be hard—core numerical processes that may require attention being given to serious computational characteristics, such as ill-conditioning, parallelisms. and similar issues of an ongoing nature.

3.10.3 Research

The human interface receives continuous attention as emerging interfaces reveal more possibilities and risks. The quest to both internationalize (i18n) and localize (L10n) software is hampered by computers designed for the English alphabet, but other major languages, such as Chinese, Japanese, and Arabic, have different requirements.

Other studies range from website accessibility to pervasive computing, with the focus ranging from the human to the computer. The issue centres around how much the human can safely and reliably adjust to the computer's I/O devices on the one hand, and how unobtrusively the computer can detect the human's needs on the other.

Furthermore, issues related to computing ontologies (example: the Language/Action perspective has found success in CRM, *etc.*) continue to be of interest to EUC.

3.10.4 Analysis

The concepts related to the end user cover a wide range (novice user to intellectual borg—see Slogan 2), hence **End User Computing** can have a range of forms and values. Most early computer systems were tightly controlled by an IT department; 'users' were just that. However, at any point in the evolution of computer systems through time, there was serious work in several domains that required user development. The dynamics of the power struggles between centralized and decentralized computing have been a fact; this was partially due to the emergence of the mid—sized computers (VAX, etc.). Then, the advent of the personal workstation opened up the door, so to speak, since it allowed a more pervasive type of computation to emerge. The recent advent of 'web' services has extended the issues to a more broad scope.

In the sense of serious domain computing and given the intertwining of computation into all advanced disciplines, any tool (inclusive of any type of capability related to a domain/discipline) that is provided by a computer becomes part of the discipline (methodology, *etc.*).

As such, the issue arises about how open the tool is to scrutiny. Some disciplines require more understanding of the tool set than do others. That is, tools that are operational in scope require less understanding than those that are ontological. As an example of the latter type of influence on disciplines, consider the impact that the computer has had on the scientific method.

Some of the issues related to End User Computing concern architecture (iconic versus language interface, open versus closed, and others). These continue to be studied. Other issues relate to IP, configuration, maintenance, ... End User Computing allows more user input into system affairs that can range from personalization to full—fledged ownership of the system.

Examples of End User Computing are systems built using the 4GLs, such as MAPPER or SQL, or one of the 5GLs, such as ICAD. ICAD (in the KBE domain) stands as a prime example since it is associated with the pervasive use of Lisp (one of the 3GLs) by Engineers to accomplish remarkable effects through a long economic cycle.

EXERCISE

1. What is Management Information SYSTEM?
2. Discuss Characteristics of Management Information system.
3. Describe Key Components of Management Information system.
4. Describe Advantages of MIS.
5. Describe Limitations of MIS.
6. Describe Management Information System versus Data Processing System.
7. Describe Management Information System versus Decision Processing System.
8. Describe Decision Making & Information Systems for an organization.
9. Describe Organization Information Strategy.
10. What Is Information Strategy?
11. Describe End User Computing.

4

CONCEPT OF PLANNING AND CONTROL

4.0 ORGANIZATIONAL PLANNING

An organizational plan is basically a "to do" list for an organization. It lists out the plan of work, programs, and organizational growth over a period of time — six months, a year, a five years. They can be pretty simple to create and use. Writing a plan can just mean getting a clear list of the types of work that need to be done, the tasks involved, who is responsible for them, and when they'll be done. Below is an outline of the steps for creating an organizational plan.

Decide on Categories: First, think about all the work that your organization does, and list out the general categories—for example, Fundraising, Community Outreach, Website, and so on. Some big categories might be split up—for example, dividing Fundraising into 'Foundation Grants' and 'Grassroots Fundraising.'

Set Goals: Second, make sure the goals for your work in each category are clear. Ask yourselves, "Where do we want to be with this work in a year?" Example: *Fundraising: Raise $8000.*

Set Tasks: Next, discuss each goal and talk about all the tasks that need to be done to achieve that goal. At this point, they don't have to be in order. Some will be more specific than others; the more specific the better, in general. You may not know how to reach some goals, yet; it's fine to have a task list that looks like "Get fundraising training. Create fundraising plan and schedule. Carry out plan."

Plan a Schedule: When all the tasks are listed, number them to show a general order—what comes first, what should happen at the same time, what comes last? Then draft a schedule for the tasks—either when they will be completed, or (for ongoing tasks) when they will begin. The goal is to set a schedule that is challenging but realistic.

Choose Responsibilities: Assign responsibilities by asking people to volunteer to be responsible for goals or tasks. A person's name next to a task doesn't mean that they'll do it—just that they take responsibility for making sure it gets done. The goal here is to make sure everyone has enough responsibility to challenge them, without so much work that they will burn out. If nobody is willing to volunteer for a particular task, ask the group if it is really necessary to do it. If the group decides that it is, try to break it down into smaller tasks that might be easier to take on.

Support: Brainstorm other individuals and organizations that can provide support, assistance or advice in helping you carry out particular tasks or achieve general goals.

Follow Through: Come up with a plan to check in, support and encourage people as they carry out their tasks. This may mean choosing one person to regularly check on the status of different tasks, or it may be part of reporting back at meetings.

Plan Evaluation: Finally, set a time to revisit the whole plan as a group to evaluate how things are going and revise assignments and schedules. This may be a few months or half a year in the future.

4.1 THE PLANNING PROCESS

Planning is a process. It takes time. When done correctly, it provides a product an outline of organizational goals with a blueprint to determine how to achieve these goals. The process of planning itself is a key to its success. The process needs to involve key stakeholders, including the board and staff; it needs prioritization and consensus on goals; it needs strategies developed to meet these goals, and it needs regular review and monitoring to determine how the plan is working. Planning should be an ongoing and regular process and the agenda of each board meeting should include some aspect of the plan. As for the operating plan — it was understood more as the sum of reports on programs and finances developed in committee and monitored at regular board meetings throughout the year, than a product of active planning. Below are descriptions with distinctions about the various types of planning.

4.2 TYPES OF PLANS

Business Plan

A business plan is used when one is starting a new business or a new process or product within a business. It includes not only a description of the new business, process or product, but also a discussion of how one plans on managing the marketing, development, production, and financing of this new venture.

Organizational Plan

Organizational planning, when it does occur, too often is spurred by crisis, focused on the short term, and not well thought out. To create healthy futures, organizations must construct processes for creating their futures that are not fueled by crisis and turmoil. It can be done.

One of the most confusing aspects for those who want to plan is the variety of terms that are used in conjunction with planning. How do you differentiate between a business plan, a financial plan, a marketing plan, a human resources plan, an operations plan, a strategic plan, a long-range plan and just plain general planning? The simple answer is that each area of your business needs planning so each area should have its own grocery list of what it wishes to accomplish in the future.

Strategic Plan

A strategic plan usually refers to the overall direction you wish your business to take over the longer term. Consequently, a long-range plan and a strategic plan are often used synonymously.

Within that overall strategy a business will have shorter term financial goals, marketing goals, production goals, and human resource goals that will each need some type of plan if they are to be achieved.

Just because a strategic plan is longer term does not mean it is never changed, however. One of the most serious mistakes businesses make is not revising their strategic plan regularly. The environment the business is operating in is changing constantly. The plan must be revisited at regular intervals to reflect the impact on the business of these external factors.

There are some universal principles that are true across all types of planning. Before tackling more specific planning models, it is wise to gain an understanding of the basic principles of general planning.

4.3 PLANNING PRINCIPLES

Any plan should include who, what, when, where, how, and why.

- Who is needed to accomplish this task?
- What needs to be done?
- When does it start and end?
- Where will it take place?
- How will it happen?
- Why must we do it?

Along with the answers to these questions there needs to be some operational scheme to organize the tasks needed to achieve the goal.

A helpful approach is to work backward from the goal to decide what must be done to reach it. The backward approach is a way of looking at the big picture first, and then planning all tasks, conditions, and details in a logical sequence to make the big picture happen. From this a to-do list can easily be made. This list will become a checklist to ensure everything is progressing as planned. Adjustments can be made based on changing circumstances. The plan (list) should be referenced often as a set of signposts on the journey towards the goals.

For many of us who left corporate America in favour of a smaller work environment, the idea of drafting a plan may seem offensive. After all, isn't frustration with all that busywork one of the reasons we left in the first place? We all have an aversion to doing anything on our job that doesn't immediately help the situation we are now experiencing. However, isn't it also true that a little foresight and action before the fact can help eliminate many of the problems we face each day. Wouldn't it be nice to anticipate something like a price cut by your major competitor or a rise in the interest rate on your credit line? Of course it would. And with that anticipation comes an organized and effective response. That is what planning is really about.

4.4 CHARACTERISTICS OF CONTROL PROCESS

The control process is cyclical which means it is never finished. Controlling leads to identification of new problems that in turn need to be addressed through establishment of performance standards, measuring performance etc.

Employees often view controlling negatively. By its very nature, controlling often leads to management expecting employee behaviour to change. No matter how positive the changes may be for the organization, employees may still view them negatively.

Control is both anticipatory and retrospective. The process anticipates problems and takes preventive action. With corrective action, the process also follows up on problems.

Ideally, each person in the business views control as his or her responsibility. The organizational culture should prevent a person walking away from a small, easily solvable problem because "that isn't my responsibility." In customer driven businesses, each employee cares about each customer. In quality driven dairy farms, for example, each employee cares about the welfare of each animal and the wear and tear on each piece of equipment.

4.5 ELEMENTS OF AN ORGANIZATION PLANNING PROCESS

- Review of organization's mission statement.
- Review of organization's vision, values.
- Evaluation of progress toward it's goals.
- Self-evaluation of the Board.
- Examination of the external and internal environments of the nonprofit.
- Gathering of input from staff, committees and constituents.
- Assignment of responsibilities to committees by the Board.
- Adoption of an annual budget.
- Assignment of responsibilities to committees by the Board.
- Development of work plans in pursuit of the objectives.
- Norms for how work gets done and decisions get made by the Board.
- Reporting on goals and accomplishments to the nonprofit's constituencie.

4.6 YOUR ORGANIZATION THREE YEARS FROM NOW...

Daydream about your organization and what you want it to look like three years from now. What do you want for the nonprofit? Work through the following topics to get a clearer picture of where you want to be.

Constituency — Whom will you be serving? Will that population be different from today's? How? Who will be your members and supporters? How will they be different from your present constituency? Why?

Program/Services — What activities, services and programs will you be carrying out three years from now? What will the mix of those services look like? Why?

Workforce — What kind of staff will the organization have, both paid and volunteer? What will they be doing? What kind of qualifications and training will they have? How much will they be paid?

Financial Resources — What will your budget be? Where will the money come from? Describe the organization's financial situation.

Physical Resources — What will your office be like? Where will you be located? What equipment will you have? Will you own property?

Community Collaboration — Describe the relationship you will have with other organizations. With whom will you be working? How do you want to be working with them? What networks will you be connected to?

Governance — Describe the board of directors you want for the organization. What will be the composition? How will your constituency be involved? Who will have a part in decision making? How will the board be working together? Is it different from today? Why?

Marketing/Public Relations — How will you be getting your message across in the community? Who will you be targeting with that message?

Management — Describe how the organization will be managed? What will you be expecting of your executive director?

4.7 MISSION STATEMENT

Does your mission statement — your reason for existence — meet the following criteria?

- Is it results-oriented and not activity oriented?
- Does it clearly state the business your organization is in and wants to be in the future?
- Is it realistic — is the scope of the statement appropriate to your organization, its goals and objectives?
- Is it excelsior for which the organization exists, allowing for techniques or programs to change as circumstances vary?
- Is it outward or client-oriented, as opposed to organizationally or inwardly bound?
- Will the statement provide boundaries or a focus for organizational planning?
- If the statement were printed in the newspaper, would everyone in the community understand the nature of the organization?

4.8 CONSIDERATIONS IN MAKING A PLANNING CALENDAR

A well organized and thorough annual planning calendar must include the following:

- When the fiscal year begins.
- When the regular Board meetings are scheduled. If special accommodations are required, these should be arranged for well in advance of the actual meeting, and the requisite tasks should be included in the calendar.
- When major funding proposals are due. A flow sheet so progress can be tracked will help reduce deadline stresses.
- When Board members are elected.
- When the annual meeting takes place. Be sure to include and schedule event planning details as thoroughly as possible.
- When other special events or activities are scheduled.
- Who will be responsible for making sure the calendar is revised as necessary and the schedule deadlines are being met?

4.9 DEVELOPING GOALS AND OBJECTIVES

People and organizations often get bogged down in semantics over what a goal is supposed to look like, what an objective is, and how to distinguish the two. Goals say what you want to accomplish. Objectives say how you intend to go about accomplishing your goals. Work plans say who will do what, by when, using what resources, to meet objectives and accomplish goals. What really matters is simply that the planning group agrees on what criteria goals and objectives should meet for your organization at this time. The following are a list of characteristics of good goals and objectives:

Good goals should...

- Be a statement of **end**, not of means.
- Reflect what you **want**, not what you're doing.
- Be **realistic** enough to be implemented within the organization's resources.
- Show some **"stretch."**
- Describe achievement that is **measurable**.
- Be **qualitative** as well as measurable.

Good objectives specify...

- A particular intended **outcome**.
- A **time frame** in which the outcome will be reached.
- **Methods** by which the outcome will be pursued.
- A minimum of **acceptability**.

4.10 ORGANIZATION CONTROL

Organization Control includes any process designed to assure that organization plans are carried out the way they were designed. Traditionally, control processes were primarily quantitative in nature. *i.e.*, budgets, standard cost systems, market quotas. Thus, the duty for establishment and analysis of control system results developed primarily as an accounting function. During the past decade, control systems have moved from strictly quantitative in nature to both quantitative and qualitative in nature. *i.e.*, From performance bonuses based on bottom-line net income to efforts that generate increased satisfaction of customers with the quality of products or services

The contemporary attitude of control and control systems is that such control efforts should motivate people toward desired organizational behavior and not promote dysfunctional behaviour.

	Traditional Outlook	**1990s Through 21st Century**
What is measured	Meeting Budget	Customer Satisfaction
	Production Efficiency	New Product Development
	Inputs	Outcomes
	Quantitative Performance	Quantitative and Qualitative Performance
Who is measured	Individuals	Teams (Groups)
	Functions	Cross-Functional Efforts
	Responsibility Centers	

How rewarded	Efficiency Profits ROI	Quality Innovation Creativity Overall Company Performance
Focus	Internal	Macro-Environment Industry Environment Internal

Organizational control refers to control internal activities of an organization in response to the environment in which it operates. Organizational control procedures consist of three functions:

- Maintaining sustainability of the organization through goal achievement;
- Coordinating and integrating of differentiated parts of the organization;
- Promoting adaptation to both internal and external change.

Planning procedures of an organization is an important part of organizational control, because planning procedures can be used to serve each of the three functions of organizational control as:

- Much planning is concerned with goal setting with a view to subsequent monitoring and control, *e.g.*, budgetary planning and control.
- Some planning activity is concerned with ensuring adequate coordination between different departments engaged on parts of a larger task, *e.g.*, project planning.
- Some planning is specially oriented towards modifying the stance of the organization toward its environment, *e.g.*, corporate strategic planning.

4.11 NATURE OF CONTROL IN ORGANIZATION

- The domination of one individual or group by another through exercise of power. (Most common idea)
- The idea of regulation and the monitoring of activities. (Second Strand)
- Application of policies and procedures for directing, regulating and co-coordinating production, administration and other business activities in a way to achieve the objectives of the enterprise. (Webster's dictionary definition)
- Monitoring activities and then taking action in order to ensure that desired ends are attained. (Cybernetic sense of control)

4.12 RELATIONSHIP BETWEEN CONTROL AND ORGANIZATION

Organization and Control are closely interrelated; because:

- Control is a central and inescapable feature of all human organizations.
- There is a practically universal agreement that organization implies control.
- Organization without some form of control is impossible.

- Organization can be viewed as a control process, occurring when groups of people feel the need to co-operate in order to achieve purposes which require their joint action.
- Control can be viewed as the process of ensuring that the organization is adapted to its environment and is pursuing courses of action that will enable it to achieve its purposes.

EXERCISE

1. What is Organizational Planning?
2. Describe the Planning Process.
3. Describe Types of Plans.
4. Describe Planning Principles.
5. Describe Characteristics of Control Process.
6. Describe Elements of an Organization Planning Process.
7. Describe Mission Statement.
8. Describe Considerations in Making a Planning Calendar.
9. Describe Developing Goals and Objectives.
10. Describe Organization Control.
11. Describe Nature of Control in Organization.
12. Describe Relationship between Control and Organization.

5

INTRODUCTION TO VALUE CHAIN

5.0 PORTER'S VALUE CHAIN MODEL

Value Chain Analysis describes the activities that take place in a business and relates them to an analysis of the competitive strength of the business. The value chain is a systematic approach to examine the development of competitive advantage. M. E. Porter created it in his book, Competitive Advantage (1980). The chain consists of a series of activities that create and build value. They culminate in the total value delivered by an organisation. The 'margin' depicted in the diagram is the same as added value. The organisation is split into 'primary activities' and 'support activities.' To better understand the activities through which a firm develops a competitive advantage and creates shareholder value, it is useful to separate the business system into a series of value-generating activities referred the value chain.

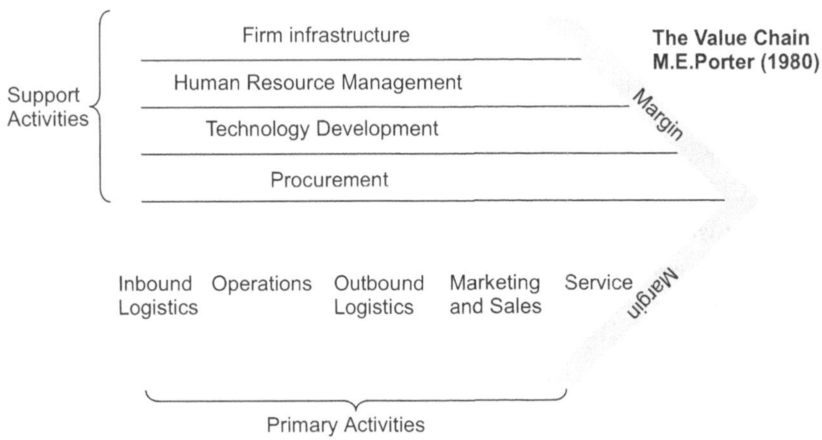

Influential work by Michael Porter suggested that the activities of a business could be grouped under two headings:

1. **Primary Activities** — Those that are directly concerned with creating and delivering a product (*e.g.*, component assembly).

Inbound Logistics

Here goods are received from a company's suppliers. They are stored until they are needed on the production/assembly line. Goods are moved around the organisation.

Operations

This is where goods are manufactured or assembled. Individual operations could include room service in an hotel, packing of books/videos/games by an online retailer, or the final tune for a new car's engine.

Outbound Logistics

The goods are now finished, and they need to be sent along the supply chain to wholesalers, retailers or the final consumer.

Marketing and Sales

In true customer orientated fashion, at this stage the organisation prepares the offering to meet the needs of targeted customers. This area focuses strongly upon marketing communications and the promotions mix.

Service

This includes all areas of service such as installation, after-sales service, complaints handling, training and so on.

2. **Support Activities**, which whilst they are not directly involved in production, may increase effectiveness or efficiency (*e.g.*, human resource management). It is rare for a business to undertake all primary and support activities.

Procurement

This function is responsible for all purchasing of goods, services and materials. The aim is to secure the lowest possible price for purchases of the highest possible quality. They will be responsible for outsourcing (components or operations that would normally be done in-house are done by other organisations), and ePurchasing (using IT and web-based technologies to achieve procurement aims).

Technology Development

Technology is an important source of competitive advantage. Companies need to innovate to reduce costs and to protect and sustain competitive advantage. This could include production technology, Internet marketing activities, lean manufacturing, Customer Relationship Management (CRM), and many other technological developments.

Human Resource Management (HRM)

Employees are an expensive and vital resource. An organisation would manage recruitment and selection, training and development, and rewards and remuneration. The mission and objectives of the organisation would be driving force behind the HRM strategy.

Firm Infrastructure

This activity includes and is driven by corporate or strategic planning. It includes the Management Information System (MIS), and other mechanisms for planning and control such as the accounting department.

Value Chain Analysis is one way of identifying which activities are best undertaken by a business and which are best provided by others ("out sourced").

5.1 LINKING VALUE CHAIN ANALYSIS TO COMPETITIVE ADVANTAGE

What activities a business undertakes is directly linked to achieving competitive advantage. For example, a business which wishes to outperform its competitors through **differentiating** itself through higher quality will have to perform its value chain activities better than the opposition. By contrast, a strategy based on seeking **cost leadership** will require a reduction in the costs associated with the value chain activities, or a reduction in the total amount of resources used.

Primary Activities

Primary value chain activities include:

Primary Activity	Description
Inbound logistics	All those activities concerned with receiving and storing externally sourced materials
Operations	The manufacture of products and services — the way in which resource **inputs** (*e.g.*, materials) are converted to **outputs** (*e.g.*, products)
Outbound logistics	All those activities associated with getting finished goods and services to buyers
Marketing and sales	Essentially an information activity — informing buyers and consumers about products and services (benefits, use, price etc.)
Service	All those activities associated with maintaining product performance after the product has been sold

Support Activities

Support activities include:

Secondary Activity	Description
Procurement	This concerns how resources are acquired for a business (*e.g.*, sourcing and negotiating with materials suppliers)
Human Resource Management	Those activities concerned with recruiting, developing, motivating and rewarding the workforce of a business
Technology Development	Activities concerned with managing information processing and the development and protection of "knowledge" in a business
Infrastructure	Concerned with a wide range of support systems and functions such as finance, planning, quality control and general senior management

5.2 STEPS IN VALUE CHAIN ANALYSIS

Value chain analysis can be broken down into a three sequential steps:

1. Break down a market/organisation into its key activities under each of the major headings in the model;
2. Assess the potential for adding value via cost advantage or differentiation, or identify current activities where a business appears to be at a competitive disadvantage;
3. Determine strategies built around focusing on activities where competitive advantage can be sustained.

5.3 USES OF VALUE CHAIN MODEL

The value chain model is a useful analysis tool for defining a firm's core competencies and the activities in which it can pursue a competitive advantage as follows:

- **Cost advantage**: by better understanding costs and squeezing them out of the value-adding activities.
- **Differentiation**: by focusing on those activities associated with core competencies and capabilities in order to perform them better than do competitors.

Cost Advantage and the Value Chain

A firm may create a cost advantage either by reducing the cost of individual value chain activities or by reconfiguring the value chain.

Once the value chain is defined, a cost analysis can be performed by assigning costs to the value chain activities. The costs obtained from the accounting report may need to be modified in order to allocate them properly to the value creating activities.

Porter identified 10 cost drivers related to value chain activities:

- Economies of scale
- Learning
- Capacity utilization
- Linkages among activities
- Interrelationships among business units
- Degree of vertical integration
- Timing of market entry
- Firm's policy of cost or differentiation
- Geographic location
- Institutional factors (regulation, union activity, taxes, etc.)

A firm develops a cost advantage by controlling these drivers better than do the competitors.

A cost advantage also can be pursued by reconfiguring the value chain. Reconfiguration means structural changes such a new production process, new distribution channels, or a different sales approach. For example, FedEx structurally redefined express freight service by acquiring its own planes and implementing a hub and spoke system.

Differentiation and the Value Chain

A differentiation advantage can arise from any part of the value chain. For example, procurement of inputs that are unique and not widely available to competitors can create differentiation, as can distribution channels that offer high service levels.

Differentiation stems from uniqueness. A differentiation advantage may be achieved either by changing individual value chain activities to increase uniqueness in the final product or by reconfiguring the value chain.

Porter identified several drivers of uniqueness:

- Policies and decisions
- Linkages among activities
- Timing
- Location
- Interrelationships
- Learning
- Integration
- Scale (*e.g.*, better service as a result of large scale)
- Institutional factors

Many of these also serve as cost drivers. Differentiation often results in greater costs, resulting in tradeoffs between cost and differentiation.

There are several ways in which a firm can reconfigure its value chain in order to create uniqueness. It can forward integrate in order to perform functions that once were performed by its customers. It can backward integrate in order to have more control over its inputs. It may implement new process technologies or utilize new distribution channels. Ultimately, the firm may need to be creative in order to develop a novel value chain configuration that increases product differentiation.

5.4 TECHNOLOGY AND THE VALUE CHAIN

Because technology is employed to some degree in every value creating activity, changes in technology can impact competitive advantage by incrementally changing the activities themselves or by making possible new configurations of the value chain.

Various technologies are used in both primary value activities and support activities:

- **Inbound Logistics Technologies**
    - Transportation
    - Material handling
    - Material storage
    - Communications
    - Testing
    - Information systems
- **Operations Technologies**
    - Process
    - Materials
    - Machine tools
    - Material handling
    - Packaging
    - Maintenance
    - Testing
    - Building design and operation
    - Information systems

- **Outbound Logistics Technologies**
  - Transportation
  - Material handling
  - Packaging
  - Communications
  - Information systems
- **Marketing and Sales Technologies**
  - Media
  - Audio/video
  - Communications
  - Information systems
- **Service Technologies**
  - Testing
  - Communications
  - Information systems

Note that many of these technologies are used across the value chain. For example, information systems are seen in every activity. Similar technologies are used in support activities. In addition, technologies related to training, computer-aided design, and software development frequently are employed in support activities.

To the extent that these technologies affect cost drivers or uniqueness, they can lead to a competitive advantage.

5.5 LINKAGES BETWEEN VALUE CHAIN ACTIVITIES

Value chain activities are not isolated from one another. Rather, one value chain activity often affects the cost or performance of other ones. Linkages may exist between primary activities and also between primary and support activities.

Consider the case in which the design of a product is changed in order to reduce manufacturing costs. Suppose that inadvertantly the new product design results in increased service costs; the cost reduction could be less than anticipated and even worse, there could be a net cost increase.

Sometimes however, the firm may be able to reduce cost in one activity and consequently enjoy a cost reduction in another, such as when a design change simultaneously reduces manufacturing costs and improves reliability so that the service costs also are reduced. Through such improvements the firm has the potential to develop a competitive advantage.

5.6 ANALYZING BUSINESS UNIT INTERRELATIONSHIPS

Interrelationships among business units form the basis for a horizontal strategy. Such business unit interrelationships can be identified by a value chain analysis.

Tangible interrelationships offer direct opportunities to create a synergy among business units. For example, if multiple business units require a particular raw material, the procurement of that material can be shared among the business units. This sharing of the procurement activity can result in cost reduction. Such interrelationships may exist simultaneously in multiple value chain activities.

Unfortunately, attempts to achieve synergy from the interrelationships among different business units often fall short of expectations due to unanticipated drawbacks. The cost of coordination, the cost of reduced flexibility, and organizational practicalities should be analyzed when devising a strategy to reap the benefits of the synergies.

5.7 OUTSOURCING VALUE CHAIN ACTIVITIES

A firm may specialize in one or more value chain activities and outsource the rest. The extent to which a firm performs upstream and downstream activities is described by its degree of vertical integration.

A thorough value chain analysis can illuminate the business system to facilitate outsourcing decisions. To decide which activities to outsource, managers must understand the firm's strengths and weaknesses in each activity, both in terms of cost and ability to differentiate. Managers may consider the following when selecting activities to outsource:

- Whether the activity can be performed cheaper or better by suppliers.
- Whether the activity is one of the firm's core competencies from which stems a cost advantage or product differentiation.
- The risk of performing the activity in-house. If the activity relies on fast-changing technology or the product is sold in a rapidly-changing market, it may be advantageous to outsource the activity in order to maintain flexibility and avoid the risk of investing in specialized assets.
- Whether the outsourcing of an activity can result in business process improvements such as reduced lead time, higher flexibility, reduced inventory, etc.

5.8 THE VALUE CHAIN SYSTEM

A firm's value chain is part of a larger system that includes the value chains of upstream suppliers and downstream channels and customers. Porter calls this series of value chains the *value system*, shown conceptually below:

The Value System

Linkages exist not only in a firm's value chain, but also between value chains. While a firm exhibiting a high degree of vertical integration is poised to better coordinate upstream and downstream activities, a firm having a lesser degree of vertical integration nonetheless can forge agreements with suppliers and channel partners to achieve better coordination. For example, an auto manufacturer may have its suppliers set up facilities in close proximity in order to minimize transport costs and reduce parts inventories. Clearly, a firm's success in developing and sustaining a competitive advantage depends not only on its own value chain, but on its ability to manage the value system of which it is a part.

EXERCISE

1. Describe Porter's Value Chain Model.
2. Describe linking Value Chain Analysis to Competitive Advantage.
3. Describe Steps in Value Chain Analysis.
4. Describe Uses of Value Chain Model.
5. Discuss Cost Advantage and the Value Chain.
6. Discuss Differentiation and the Value Chain.
7. Discuss Technology and the Value Chain.
8. Discuss Linkages between Value Chain Activities.
9. Discuss Analyzing Business Unit Interrelationships.
10. Discuss Outsourcing Value Chain Activities.
11. Discuss the Value Chain System.

6

MANAGING KNOWLEDGE IN INFORMATION SYSTEM

6.0 INTRODUCTION

A 'system approach' is followed while managing organizations and that information, at the right time and place, plays a pivotal role in today's corporate functions/activities. Information has come to play a pivotal role and is regarded as a critical resource in view of the contemporary, fiercely competitive business environment, both local and global. It is, therefore, imperative that organizations develop and continue to have 'current' and appropriate information system to ensure organizational effectiveness, efficiency and competitiveness.

Information systems have, therefore, to be developed in the peculiar and specific organizational context. These activities related to/with development of information system are generally referred to as System Development.

System Development encompasses all the activities, which go into producing/providing information systems solution to an organization's problems or opportunities. It is a structured problem-solving endeavor consisting of distinct activities, which generally takes place in sequential and chronological order. As the system is organization/activity-specific, systems development necessitates interaction with the organization's members, units, departments, division etc.

6.1 SYSTEM AS PLANNED ORGANIZATIONAL CHANGE

A fundamental change in the manner in which business it's conducted is frequently referred to as reorganization or business process reengineering. Information technology is usually the major enabler of such reorganization. Organizations are managed today by asset of principles that have evolved since the beginning of the industrial revolution. This revolution started with the concept of division of labor, conceived by Adam Smith in 1776. According to this concept, instead of one craftsman making an entire product, several people would make the product, each specializing in one task. Each task would be relatively simple, so it would be easy to learn. This would reduce the long apprenticeship periods. In addition, when people specialize in this simple task, output van increase.

This situation led to cheaper products and consequently higher demand. Since the tasks were simple, they were easy to automate when machines were introduced. Automation reduced the price of products further and further and factories became larger and larger. Instead of producing for customer after an order was placed, products were produced in large quantities and then sold in the market place. Several principles and methods were created over the years that enhanced the development of the industrial revolution. The most important ones are:

- Specialization of labor.
- Mass Production.
- Hierarchical organization structure following functional specializations with top down lines of authority.
- Assembly lines that bring the work to the worker whenever possible.
- Complex support systems for planning and budgeting, resource allocation, coordination and control.

These principles and methods were successful in developing world—class organizations, moving nations to a developed status and significantly increasing standards of living.

The need of Integration

Besides creating inefficient redundancies, the vertical structure with its functional information systems causes difficulties in the integration of information that is required for decision-making. For example, account numbers in an information system developed along departmental lines may not be logically related and so cannot be used for cross—referencing a customer's account. This seriously limits reporting capabilities. A loan officer, for instance may want to check information pertaining to a loan applicant's saving accounts. However, there may be even have to ask the loan applicant if he/she has a saving account with the bank and what the account number is.

Consider a case where the management of the bank wants to increase the offering of mortgage loans. Management decides to send letters encouraging specific customers to consider buying homes, using convenient financing available through the bank. Management also decides that the best customer to which to send such letter are the following:

1. Customer who do not currently have mortgage loans or who have loans for a very small percentage of the value of their homes.
2. Customers who have good checking account records.
3. Customers with sufficient funds in their saving accounts to make a down payments on a home.
4. Customers who have good payment records on any installment loads with the bank.

Because the data necessary to identify such customers may be available in different files of different databases, there may be no convenient or economic way to integrate them. Using innovations such as data warehouses special integrated software can be helpful but expensive. Management is understandably disappointed and unable to function effectively. For optimum use of information, integration should cross not only departmental boundaries, but also organizational ones, reaching suppliers and customers.

All too often, however, organizations have failed to integrate information systems. Nonintegrated information systems and the conflict between the horizontal nature of business processes and the vertical (functional) structure of businesses are the primary reasons for organizational problems that necessitate business process reengineering.

6.2 BUSINESS PROCESS REENGINEERING AND PROCESS IMPROVEMENT

Business Process Reengineering (BPR) is a holistic process that can lead to complete organizational transformation and stabilization. An organization's business processes are the activities that use various kinds of inputs to create an output of value to the customer. For example, accepting an application for a loan, processing it, and approving or rejecting it is a business process in a bank. An organization operates numerous business processes to attain its goals. In the process of business reengineering (BPR), an organization fundamentally rethink and radically redesigns its business processes to achieve dramatic improvements in measures of performance such as quality, cost, speed, and services. BPR can be introduced in one, several or all-organizational processes. Information technology makes possible most BPR projects.

6.2.1 Principles of BPR

Certain common principles exist in Business Process Reengineering; most of them ate facilitated by IT. The major principles are as follows:

- Several jobs are combined into one.
- Employees make decisions. Decision-making becomes part of the job.
- Steps in the business processes are performed in a natural order, and several jobs get done simultaneously.
- Processes may have multiple versions. This make possible the economics of scale that result from mass production, yet allows customization of products and services.
- Work is performed where it makes the most sense, including at the customer or supplier's site. Thus, work is shifted, if necessary, across organizational and even international boundaries.
- Reconciliation is minimized by cutting back the number of external contact points and by creating business alliances.
- A hybrid centralized/ decentralized operations is used.
- A single point of contact is provided to customers.

6.2.2 IT Tools for BPR

A large variety of IT tools can be used to support BPR. These support tools can be divided into the following categories:

1. **Simulation and visual simulation tools:** Simulation is essential to support the modeling activities. In addition to conventional simulation and visual simulation tools there are simulation tools that are specifically oriented for BPR such as SIMPROCESS, ProMode4l and BPSimulatior.
2. **Flow diagrams:** Flow diagrams can be made with CASE tools or other system development charting tools. They can also be made by specialized BPR tools that are usually integrated other tools.

3. **Work analysis:** Analyzing both existing processes and proposed solutions can be accomplished with tools that conduct forecasting, risk analysis and optimization, such as I—think and BizCase and Turbo SPR.
4. **Other tools:** Several special tools plan and manage the BPR process and the organization transformation. Information tools and technologies can also be part of the BPR solution itself. For example CAD/CAM and imaging technologies contribute to cycle time reduction, EDI support virtual cooperations and other inter-organizational systems and expert systems support case managers and mass customization.
5. **Integrated tool kits:** Several integrated tools kits are available to support-to-support BPR. The most well tool is SAP R/3.
6. **Internet and intranet infrastructure:** The role of IT in business process reengineering is increasing due to new application based on Internet and intranet infrastructure.

6.2.3 Major Reengineering Activities

Reengineering efforts involve many activities; major activities are:

- Redesign of process
- From mass production to mass customization.
- Cycle time reduction.

Reconstructing Entire Organizations

- The networked organization.
- Empowerment
- Empowerment's relationship of information technology.
- Empowerment of customers, suppliers and business partners.
- Teams.

6.3 TQM AND SIX SIGMA

6.3.1 Total Quality Management

Total Quality Management id a composition of three words:

Total + Quality + Management

Total : Involving the entire organization, supply chain, and/or product life cycle

Quality : With its usual definitions, with all its complexities.

Management : The system of managing with steps like Plan, Organize, Control, Lead, Staff, provisioning and organizing.

As defined by the International Organization for Standardization (ISO):

"TQM is a management approach for an organization, centered on quality, based on the participation of all its members and aiming at long-term success through customer satisfaction, and benefits to all members of the organization and to society."

Total Quality Management is an approach to the art of management that originated in Japanese industry in the 1950's and has become steadily more popular in the West since the early 1980's.

Total Quality is a description of the culture, attitude and organization of a company that aims to provide, and continue to provide, its customers with products and services that satisfy their needs. The culture requires quality in all aspects of the company's operations, with things being done right first time, and defects and waste eradicated from operations.

Many companies have difficulties in implementing TQM. Surveys by consulting firms have found that only 20–36% of companies that have undertaken TQM have achieved either significant or even tangible improvements in quality, productivity, competitiveness or financial return. As a result many people are sceptical about TQM. However, when you look at successful companies you find a much higher percentage of successful TQM implementation.

Some useful messages from results of TQM implementations:

- if you want to be a first—rate company, don't focus on the second-rate companies who can't handle TQM, look at the world—class companies that have adopted it
- the most effective way to spend TQM introduction funds is by training top management, people involved in new product development, and people involved with customers
- it's much easier to introduce EDM/PDM in a company with a TQM culture than in one without TQM. People in companies that have implemented TQM are more likely to have the basic understanding necessary for implementing EDM/PDM. For example, they are more likely to view EDM/PDM as an information and workflow management system supporting the entire product life cycle then as a departmental solution for the management of CAD data

Important aspects of TQM include customer-driven quality, top management leadership and commitment, continuous improvement, fast response, actions based on facts, employee participation, and a TQM culture.

Customer—driven quality

TQM has a customer-first orientation. The customer, not internal activities and constraints, comes first. Customer satisfaction is seen as the company's highest priority. The company believes it will only be successful if customers are satisfied. The TQM company is sensitive to customer requirements and responds rapidly to them. In the TQM context, 'being sensitive to customer requirements' goes beyond defect and error reduction, and merely meeting specifications or reducing customer complaints. The concept of requirements is expanded to take in not only product and service attributes that meet basic requirements, but also those that enhance and differentiate them for competitive advantage.

Each part of the company is involved in Total Quality, operating as a customer to some functions and as a supplier to others. The Engineering Department is a supplier to downstream functions such as Manufacturing and Field Service, and has to treat these internal customers with the same sensitivity and responsiveness as it would external customers.

TQM leadership from top management

TQM is a way of life for a company. It has to be introduced and led by top management. This is a key point. Attempts to implement TQM often fail because top management doesn't lead and get committed — instead it delegates and pays lip service. Commitment and personal involvement is required from top management in creating and deploying clear quality values and goals consistent with the objectives of the company, and in creating and deploying well defined systems, methods and performance measures for achieving those goals. These systems and methods guide all quality activities and encourage participation by all employees. The development and use of performance indicators is linked, directly or indirectly, to customer requirements and satisfaction, and to management and employee remuneration.

Continuous improvement

Continuous improvement of all operations and activities is at the heart of TQM. Once it is recognized that customer satisfaction can only be obtained by providing a high-quality product, continuous improvement of the quality of the product is seen as the only way to maintain a high level of customer satisfaction. As well as recognizing the link between product quality and customer satisfaction, TQM also recognizes that product quality is the result of process quality. As a result, there is a focus on continuous improvement of the company's processes. This will lead to an improvement in process quality. In turn this will lead to an improvement in product quality, and to an increase in customer satisfaction. Improvement cycles are encouraged for all the company's activities such as product development, use of EDM/PDM, and the way customer relationships are managed. This implies that all activities include measurement and monitoring of cycle time and responsiveness as a basis for seeking opportunities for improvement.

Elimination of waste is a major component of the continuous improvement approach. There is also a strong emphasis on prevention rather than detection, and an emphasis on quality at the design stage. The customer—driven approach helps to prevent errors and achieve defect—free production. When problems do occur within the product development process, they are generally discovered and resolved before they can get to the next internal customer.

Fast response

To achieve customer satisfaction, the company has to respond rapidly to customer needs. This implies short product and service introduction cycles. These can be achieved with customer—driven and process-oriented product development because the resulting simplicity and efficiency greatly reduce the time involved. Simplicity is gained through concurrent product and process development. Efficiencies are realized from the elimination of non-value-adding effort such as re-design. The result is a dramatic improvement in the elapsed time from product concept to first shipment.

Actions based on facts

The statistical analysis of engineering and manufacturing facts is an important part of TQM. Facts and analysis provide the basis for planning, review and performance tracking, improvement of operations, and comparison of performance with competitors. The TQM approach is based on the use of objective data, and provides a rational rather than an emotional basis for decision making. The statistical approach to process management in both engineering and manufacturing recognizes that most problems are system-related, and are not caused by particular employees. In practice, data is collected and put in the hands of the people who are in the best position to analyze it and then take the appropriate action to reduce costs and prevent non-conformance. Usually these people are not managers but workers in the process. If the right information is not available, then the analysis, whether it be of shop floor data, or engineering test results, can't take place, errors can't be identified, and so errors can't be corrected.

Employee participation

A successful TQM environment requires a committed and well-trained work force that participates fully in quality improvement activities. Such participation is reinforced by reward and recognition systems which emphasize the achievement of quality objectives. On-going education and training of all employees supports the drive for quality. Employees are encouraged to take more responsibility, communicate more effectively, act creatively, and innovate. As people behave the way they are measured and remunerated, TQM links remuneration to customer satisfaction metrics.

A TQM culture

It's not easy to introduce TQM. An open, cooperative culture has to be created by management. Employees have to be made to feel that they are responsible for customer satisfaction. They are not going to feel this if they are excluded from the development of visions, strategies, and plans. It's important they participate in these activities. They are unlikely to behave in a responsible way if they see management behaving irresponsibly saying one thing and doing the opposite.

Product development in a TQM environment

Product development in a TQM environment is very different to product development in a non—TQM environment. Without a TQM approach, product development is usually carried on in a conflictual atmosphere where each department acts independently. Short-term results drive behavior so scrap, changes, work-arounds, waste, and rework are normal practice. Management focuses on supervising individuals, and fire—fighting is necessary and rewarded.

Product development in a TQM environment is customer-driven and focused on quality. Teams are process-oriented, and interact with their internal customers to deliver the required results. Management's focus is on controlling the overall process, and rewarding teamwork.

Awards for Quality achievement

The Deming Prize has been awarded annually since 1951 by the Japanese Union of Scientists and Engineers in recognition of outstanding achievement in quality strategy, management and execution. Since 1988 a similar award (the Malcolm Baldrige National Quality Award) has been awarded in the US. Early winners of the Baldrige Award include AT&T (1992), IBM (1990), Milliken (1989), Motorola (1988), Texas Instruments (1992) and Xerox (1989).

6.3.2 What is Six Sigma?

Six sigma is a customer based approach realizing that defects are expensive. Fewer defects mean lower costs and improved customer loyalty. The lowest cost, high value producer is the most competitive provider of goods and services. Six sigma is a way to achieve strategic business results.

Six sigma processes will produce less than 3.4 defects or mistakes per million opportunities. Many successful six sigma projects do not achieve a 3.4 ppm or less defect rate. That just indicates that there is still opportunity.

Six sigma is the application of the tools on selected important projects at the appropriate time.

Six Sigma is a quality methodology that can produce significant benefit to businesses and organizations. Not much text, however, has been written about the structure needed to successfully implement Six Sigma quality within your business or organization. Now I will focus on roles and responsibilities, as well as required rewards and recognition for a successful Six Sigma quality program.

6.3.3 Roles and Responsibilities

Quality Leader/Manager (QL/QM) — The quality leader's responsibility is to represent the needs of the customer and to improve the operational effectiveness of the organization. The Quality function is typically separated from the manufacturing or transactional processing functions in order to maintain impartiality. The quality manager sits on the CEO/President's staff, and has equal authority to all other direct reports.

Master Black Belt (MBB) — Master Black Belts are typically assigned to a specific area or function of a business or organization. It may be a functional area such as human resources or legal, or process specific area such as billing or tube rolling. MBBs work with the owners of the process to ensure that quality objectives and targets are set, plans are determined, progress is tracked, and education is provided. In the best Six Sigma organizations, process owners and MBBs work very closely and share information daily.

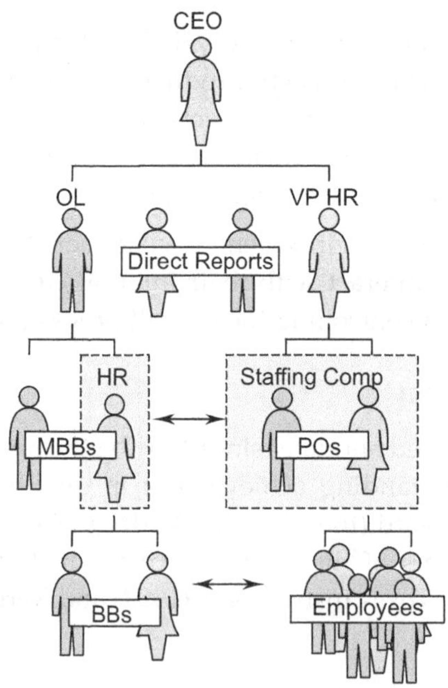

Process Owner (PO) — Process owners are exactly as the name sounds — they are the responsible individuals for a specific process. For instance, in the legal department there is usually one person in charge — maybe the VP of Legal — that's the process owner. There may be a chief marketing officer for your business — that's the process owner for marketing. Depending on the size of your business and core activities, you may have process owners at lower levels of your organizational structure. If you are a credit card company with processes around billing, accounts receivable, audit, billing fraud, etc., you wouldn't just have the process owner be the chief financial officer, you would want to go much deeper into the organization where the work is being accomplished and you can make a big difference.

Black Belt (BB) — Black Belts are the heart and soul of the Six Sigma quality initiative. Their main purpose is to lead quality projects and work full time until they are complete. Black Belts can typically complete four to six projects per year with savings of approximately $230,000 per project. Black Belts also coach Green Belts on their projects, and while coaching may seem innocuous, it can require a significant amount of time and energy.

Green Belt (GB) — Green Belts are employees trained in Six Sigma who spend a portion of their time completing projects, but maintain their regular work role and responsibilities. Depending on their workload, they can spend anywhere from 10% to 50% of their time on their project(s). As your Six Sigma quality program evolves, employees will begin to include the Six Sigma methodology in their daily activities and it will no longer become a percentage of their time — it will be the way their work is accomplished 100% of the time.

Now we know how some companies have organizationally structured their Six Sigma quality program. But how do you ensure that everyone's doing their job? How do you keep your employees motivated when fires are burning all over the corporate landscape?

6.3.4 Six Sigma Organizational Architecture — Rewards and Recognition

Six Sigma is a quality methodology that can produce significant benefit to businesses and organizations. Not much text, however, has been written about the structure needed to successfully implement Six Sigma quality within your business or organization.

Six Sigma Architecture focused on roles and responsibilities of a successful Six Sigma quality program. This page focuses on the rewards and recognition associated with a successsful Six Sigma quality program.

Rewards and Recognition

We all know that roles assignment is not enough to start and maintain a successful Six Sigma quality program. Rewards and recognition must be part of the equation. So how do we reward the different roles within the organization? Let's start with the Green Belts and work our way back up the organization.

Green Belts — Depending on the size of the project and the resulting benefits, gift certificates, cash and stock options are all motivating factors. But don't underestimate the motivating power of a public congratulations in front of peers — it is many times even more effective than a monetary amount. Depending on the progress of your program, you may want to tie their salary action to the results of the project(s) they completed during the past year.

Black Belts and Master Black Belts — Their salary and bonus structure should be tied to the number of projects and benefit of those projects to the business bottom line. Metrics including productivity, loss reduction, improved quality, reduced overhead, etc. should all be factors in determining the proper payout for performance. For under performing BBs and MBBs, the performance appraisal meeting should serve as a fulcrum in modifying their behaviors and actions.

Process Owners — Here's one of the key roles that needs to be defined properly. The Process Owner's compensation (salary and bonus) must be tied directly to quality efforts within their organization. It's not enough to allow Quality to 'work with us,' but their metrics and efforts need to be utilizing all of the quality tools appropriately. Why not make 25% of their bonus tied to meeting their quality initiative goals and objectives? Then have them report on how they did before you determine the bonus payout.

Quality Leader – Performance based compensation (salary and bonus). Leadership capabilities are critical to this position, so not only should the quantitative aspects (savings, projects, training, etc.) be measured, but so should the qualitative. The difficulty arises in defining and clearly identifying the required behaviors.

CEO – The buck stops here. If the CEO is fully on board with the Quality initiative, He/She will have no problem tying the compensation of her/his direct reports to Quality deliverables.

6.3.5 TQM Vs Six Sigma

Six Sigma and TQM

Six Sigma is a relatively new concept as compared to Total Quality Management (TQM). However, when it was conceptualized, it was not intended to be a replacement for TQM. Both Six Sigma and TQM have many similarities and are compatible in varied business environments, including manufacturing and service industries. While TQM has helped many companies in improving the quality of manufactured goods or services rendered, Six Sigma has the potential of delivering even sharper results.

Total Quality Management

Total Quality Management is often associated with the development, deployment, and maintenance of organizational systems that are required for various business processes. It is based on a strategic approach that focuses on maintaining existing quality standards as well as making incremental quality improvements. It can also be described as a cultural initiative as the focus is on establishing a culture of collaboration among various functional departments within an organization for improving overall quality.

Comparison to Six Sigma

In comparison, Six Sigma is more than just a process improvement program as it is based on concepts that focus on continuous quality improvements for achieving near perfection by restricting the number of possible defects to less than 3.4 defects per million. It is complementary to Statistical Process Control (SPC), which uses statistical methods for monitoring and controlling business processes. Although both SPC and TQM help in improving quality, they often reach a stage after which no further quality improvements can be made. Six Sigma, on the other hand, is different as it focuses on taking quality improvement processes to the next level.

The basic difference between Six Sigma and TQM is the approach. While TQM views quality as conformance to internal requirements, Six Sigma focuses on improving quality by reducing the number of defects. The end result may be the same in both the concepts (*i.e.*, producing better quality products). Six Sigma helps organizations in reducing operational costs by focusing on defect reduction, cycle time reduction, and cost savings. It is different from conventional cost cutting measures that may reduce value and quality. It focuses on identifying and eliminating costs that provide no value to customers such as costs incurred due to waste.

TQM initiatives focus on improving individual operations within unrelated business processes whereas Six Sigma programs focus on improving all the operations within a single business process. Six Sigma projects require the skills of professionals that are certified as 'black belts' whereas TQM initiatives are usually a part-time activity that can be managed by non-dedicated managers.

Applications Where Six Sigma is Better

Six Sigma initiatives are based on a preplanned project charter that outlines the scale of a project, financial targets, anticipated benefits and milestones. In comparison, organizations that have implemented TQM, work without fully knowing what the financial gains might be. Six Sigma is based on DMAIC (Define—Measure—Analyze—Improve—Control) that helps in making precise measurements, identifying exact problems, and providing solutions that can be measured.

TQM is a quality control approach that is usually thought of along with the development, implementation, and continual control of different organizational systems that are used with a number of different processes. TQM is based on a particular organizational approach, an approach that zones in on how to keep already existing quality standards at a high while simultaneously improving quality. Essentially, TQM is meant to focus on the culture of a business. What TQM strives to do is to get different departments in your business-whether manufacturing, service, or something else-to work together so that you can all help improve the quality of processes and products.

Six Sigma is also an approach that seeks to correct and improve the quality of your processes. So how is Six Sigma different from TQM? Well, let's look at how it's obviously different. TQM strives for general improvements based on a collaborative cultural approach to the problem. Six Sigma also requires the efforts of numerous departments. However, Six Sigma is a statistical and data driven approach that measures and analyzes data in an effort to discover how variations and defects can be reduced to the level where when you are running a process, there are less than 3.4 defects per million cycles or million products. Six Sigma is used along with Statistical Process Control, and together the two of them use statistics in order to monitor and maintain your processes. Six Sigma is a lot of TQM taken to another level.

So now that we've gone over what the general differences are between TQM and Six Sigma, let's talk about the most fundamental difference between the two approaches. The fundamental difference between Six Sigma and TQM is the way that each one approaches quality control. First, let's look at TQM. TQM defines quality as the level to which a process or a product meets standards produced inside the company. Six Sigma shifts the definition of quality to a relational one, emphasizing that quality is based on the fewest number of defects, which must be removed as much as possible. However, Six Sigma's quality is also defined in large part by the customer, who determines the value of the process or the product. Six Sigma takes a more holistic approach to quality improvement, working to improve the entire business instead of focusing on individual processes and operations within segregated departments. Another difference between TQM and Six Sigma is that if you want to implement Six Sigma's approach, you need professionals who are certified in Six Sigma techniques. TQM does not require this type of complete, full-time dedication to the quality management system chosen by your company. Once again, while there are many fundamental and superficial differences between Six Sigma and TQM, the two can work in tandem and support each other in all situations.

6.4 KNOWLEDGE MANAGEMENT IN THE ORGANIZATION

Knowledge management is an emerging field. A recent US study by Omni Tech Consulting Group indicated that KM is in the early stages of development, having at most only a moderate effect on today's organizations. However, over 80 percent of top executives expect KM will have a significant and major impact on their organizations. Executives recognize KM as a trump card with which they can distance themselves from competition. Many executives have called KM as the most significant strategic progress developing in the past 25 years.

6.4.1 Understanding Knowledge

Knowledge Management means different things to different people and because it is still a developing field, there is no settled definition as yet. However, a good working definition of knowledge management is: "the process of accumulating and creating knowledge efficiently, managing a knowledge base and facilitating the sharing of knowledge so that it can be applied efficiently throughout the organization".

- **Knowledge** can be defined as the *"understanding obtained through the process of experience or appropriate study."*
- Knowledge can also be an accumulation of facts, procedural rules, or heuristics.
    - A **fact** is generally a statement representing truth about a subject matter or domain.
    - A **procedural rule** is a rule that describes a sequence of actions.
    - A **heuristic** is a rule of thumb based on years of experience.
- **Intelligence** implies the capability to acquire and apply appropriate knowledge.
    - **Memory** indicates the ability to store and retrieve relevant experience according to will.
    - **Learning** represents the skill of acquiring knowledge using the method of instruction/ study.
- **Experience** relates to the understanding that we develop through our past actions.
- Knowledge can develop over time through successful experience, and experience can lead to expertise.
- **Common sense** refers to the natural and mostly unreflective opinions of humans.

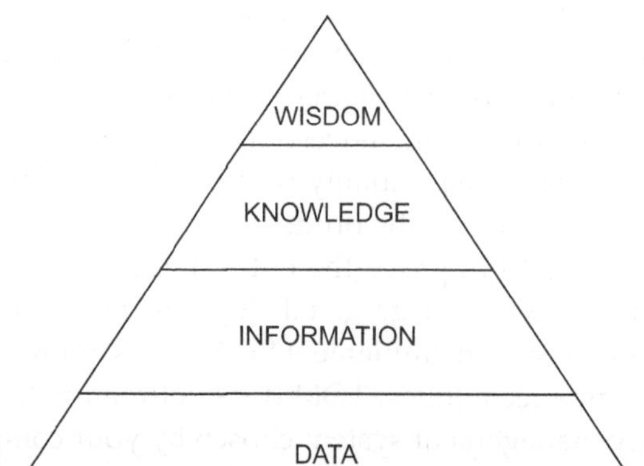

Knowledge Management and its Characteristics

The challenge of Knowledge Management is to determine what information within an organization qualifies as"valuable."All information is not knowledge, and all knowledge is not valuable. The key is to find the worthwhile knowledge within a vast sea of information.

1. **Knowledge Management is about people.** It is directly linked to what people know, and how what they know can support business and organizational objectives. It draws on human competency, intuition, ideas, and motivations. It is not a technology-based concept. Although technology can support a Knowledge Management effort, it shouldn't begin there.
2. **Knowledge Management is orderly and goal—directed.** It is inextricably tied to the strategic objectives of the organization. It uses only the information that is the most meaningful, practical, and purposeful.
3. **Knowledge Management is ever—changing.** There is no such thing as an immutable law in Knowledge Management. Knowledge is constantly tested, updated, revised, and sometimes even"obsoleted"when it is no longer practicable. It is a fluid, ongoing process.
4. **Knowledge Management is value-added.** It draws upon pooled expertise, relationships, and alliances. Organizations can further the two—way exchange of ideas by bringing in experts from the field to advise or educate managers on recent trends and developments. Forums, councils, and boards can be instrumental in creating common ground and organizational cohesiveness.
5. **Knowledge Management is visionary.** This vision is expressed in strategic business terms rather than technical terms, and in a manner that generates enthusiasm, buy—in, and motivates managers to work together toward reaching common goals.
6. **Knowledge Management is complementary.** It can be integrated with other organizational learning initiatives such as Total Quality Management (TQM). It is important for knowledge managers to show interim successes along with progress made on more protracted efforts such as multiyear systems developments infrastructure, or enterprise architecture projects.

6.4.2 Cognitive Psychology

- **Cognitive psychology** tries to identify the cognitive structures and processes that closely relates to skilled performance within an area of operation.
- It provides a strong background for understanding knowledge and expertise.
- In general, it is the interdisciplinary study of human intelligence.
- The two major components of cognitive psychology are:
  - **Experimental Psychology:** This studies the cognitive processes that constitutes human intelligence.
  - **Artificial Intelligence(AI):** This studies the cognition of Computer-based intelligent systems.
- The process of eliciting and representing experts knowledge usually involves a *knowledge developer* and some *human experts* (domain experts).
- In order to gather the knowledge from human experts, the developer usually interviews the experts and asks for information regarding a specific area of expertise.

- It is almost impossible for humans to provide the completely accurate reports of their mental processes.
- The research in the area of cognitive psychology helps to a better understanding of what constitutes knowledge, how knowledge is elicited, and how it should be represented in a corporate knowledge base.
- Hence, cognitive psychology contributes a great deal to the area of knowledge management.

6.4.3 Data, Information and Knowledge

- **Data** represents unorganized and unprocessed facts.
  - Usually data is static in nature.
  - It can represent a set of discrete facts about events.
  - Data is a prerequisite to information.
  - An organization sometimes has to decide on the nature and volume of data that is required for creating the necessary information.
- **Information**
  - Information can be considered as an aggregation of data (processed data) which makes decision making easier.
  - Information has usually got some meaning and purpose.
- **Knowledge**
  - By knowledge we mean *human understanding of a subject matter that has been acquired through proper study and experience.*
  - Knowledge is usually based on learning, thinking, and proper understanding of the problem area.
  - Knowledge is not information and information is not data.
  - Knowledge is derived from information in the same way information is derived from data.
  - We can view it as an understanding of information based on its perceived importance or relevance to a problem area.
  - It can be considered as the integration of human perceptive processes that helps them to draw meaningful conclusions.

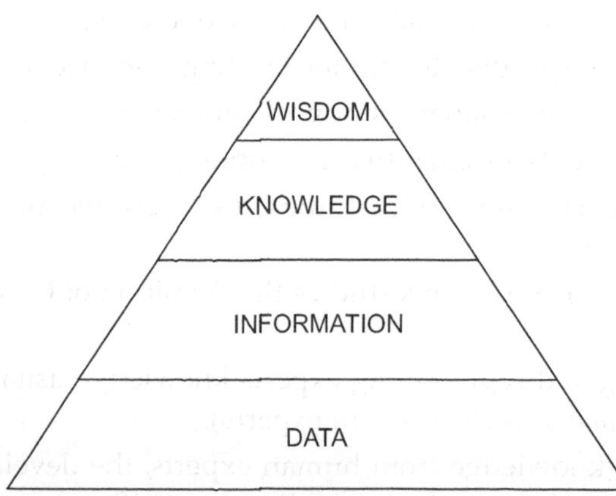

Fig. 6.1 *Data, Information, Knowledge and Wisdom*

6.4.4 Related Concepts

Several valuable concepts are closely related to knowledge management

- **Knowledge Assets:** The knowledge regarding markets, products, technologies and organizations that a business owns or need to owns, and that enables its business process to generate profit.
- **Best Practice:** A collection of most of the successful solutions and /or case studies related to a specific problem or simulation in a particular industry or in business world generally.
- **Intellectual Capital:** The collection of the knowledge, documents, research and internal discussion amassed by an organization over the years.
- **Knowledge System:** A comprehensive cooperate wide system that collects knowledge, stores it in a database, maintains the database, and disseminates the knowledge to users.
- **Competitive Intelligence:** The various activities conducted by companies, usually with IT tools, to collect competitive information about the competitors, product, and markets.

6.4.5 IT Support of Knowledge Management Activities

The new challenges of KM requires that information systems departments begin providing systems that support KM. The major KM activities that must be supported are as follows:

- **Knowledge Identification:** determines what knowledge (information) is critical to decision making.
- **Knowledge Discovery and Analysis:** Using search engines, databases and data mining, the proper knowledge must be found, analyzed and put in to proper context.
- **Establishment of Organizational Knowledge Bases**: Organizational knowledge and best practice need to be stored in a knowledge base, which is indexed and properly maintained. An organizational knowledge base should not be confused with knowledge used for solving a very specific problem.
- **Knowledge Distribution and Use:** Target audiences are defined and technologies are put into place to enable knowledge delivery when needed.

6.4.6 Implementing Knowledge Management

Because of potential for big-offs from KM, companies are considering not only creating organization Knowledge Management bases, but also completely themselves as based organizations. Even a new position, chief Knowledge Management officer has been created, whose role is to capture and leverage structured Knowledge Management using IT.

Sharing Knowledge Management also means facilitating, organizational learning. Organizational learning is an important approach that advocates that organizations must learn from their experiences in order to survive. Learning failures can be fatal for organizations. Because Knowledge Management bases enable companies to learn faster than their competitors, they give those who use them a suitable competitive advantage. People can learn from the experience of others when this experience is documented in a Knowledge Management base.

6.4.7 Kinds of Knowledge

- Deep Knowledge: Knowledge acquired through years of proper experience.
- Shallow Knowledge: Minimal understanding of the problem area.

- Knowledge as Know—How: Accumulated lessons of practical experience.
- Reasoning and Heuristics: Some of the ways in which humans reason are as follows:
    - Reasoning by analogy: This indicates relating one concept to another.
    - Formal Reasoning: This indicates reasoning by using *deductive* (exact) or *inductive* reasoning.
        - Deduction uses major and minor premises.
        - In case of deductive reasoning, new knowledge is generated by using previously specified knowledge.
        - Inductive reasoning implies reasoning from a set of facts to a general conclusion.
        - Inductive reasoning is the basis of scientific discovery.
        - A *case* is knowledge associated with an operational level.
- Common Sense: This implies a type of knowledge that almost every human being possess in varying forms/amounts.
- We can also classify knowledge on the basis of whether it is *procedural, declarative, semantic,* or *episodic.*
    - *Procedural knowledge* represents the understanding of how to carry out a specific procedure.
    - *Declarative knowledge* is routine knowledge about which the expert is conscious. It is shallow knowledge that can be readily recalled since it consists of simple and uncomplicated information. This type of knowledge often resides in short-term memory.
    - *Semantic knowledge* is highly organized, "chunked" knowledge that resides mainly in long—term memory. Semantic knowledge can include major concepts, vocabulary, facts, and relationships.
    - *Episodic knowledge* represents the knowledge based on episodes (experimental information). Each episode is usually "chunked" in long—term memory.
- Another way of classifying knowledge is to find whether it is *tacit* or *explicit*
    - *Tacit knowledge* usually gets embedded in human mind through experience.
    - *Explicit knowledge* is that which is codified and digitized in documents, books, reports, spreadsheets, memos etc.

6.4.8 Expert Knowledge

It is the information woven inside the mind of an expert for accurately and quickly solving complex problems.

- Knowledge Chunking
    - Knowledge is usually stored in experts long—range memory as *chunks*.
    - Knowledge chunking helps experts to optimize their memory capacity and enables them to process the information quickly.
    - Chunks are groups of ideas that are stored and recalled together as an unit.
- Knowledge as an Attribute of Expertise
    - In most areas of specialization, insight and knowledge accumulate quickly, and the criteria for expert performance usually undergo continuous change.
    - In order to become an expert in a particular area, one is expected to master the necessary knowledge and make significant contributions to the concerned field.

- The unique performance of a true expert can be easily noticed in the quality of decision making.
- The true experts (knowledgeable) are usually found to be more selective about the information they acquire, and also they are better able in acquiring information in a less structured situation.
- They can quantify soft information, and can categorize problems on the basis of solution procedures that are embedded in the experts long range memory and readily available on recall.
- Hence, they tend to use knowledge—based decision strategies starting with known quantities to deduce unknowns.
- If a first-cut solution path fails, then the expert can trace back a few steps and then proceed again.
- Nonexperts use means-end decision strategies to approach the problem scenario.
- Nonexperts usually focus on goals rather than focusing on essential features of the task which makes the task more time consuming and sometimes unreliable.
- Specific individuals are found to consistently perform at higher levels than others and they are labeled as experts.

6.4.9 Thinking and Learning in Humans

- Research in the area of artificial intelligence has introduced more structure into human thinking about thinking.
- Humans do not necessarily receive and process information in exactly the same way as the machines do.
- Humans can receive information via seeing, smelling, touching, hearing (sensing) etc., which promotes a way of thinking and learning that is unique to humans.
- On macro level, humans and computers can receive inputs from a multitude of sources.
- Computers can receive inputs from keyboards, touch screens etc.
- On micro level, both human brain and CPU of a computer receive information as electrical impulses.
- The point to note here is that the computers must be programmed to do specific tasks. Performing one task does not necessarily transcend onto other tasks as it may do with humans.
- Human learning: Humans learn new facts, integrate them in some way which they think is relevant and organize the result to produce necessary solution, advice and decision. Human learning can occur in the following ways:
    - Learning through Experience.
    - Learning by Example.
    - Learning by Discovery.

6.4.10 Challenges in KM Systems Development

- Changing Organizational Culture:
    - Involves changing people's attitudes and behaviours.

- Knowledge Evaluation:
  - Involves assessing the worth of information.
- Knowledge Processing:
  - Involves the identification of techniques to acquire, store, process and distribute information.
  - Sometimes it is necessary to document how certain decisions were reached.
- Knowledge Implementation:
  - An organization should commit to change, learn, and innovate.
  - It is important to extract meaning from information that may have an impact on specific missions.
  - Lessons learned from feedback can be stored for future to help others facing the similar problem(s).

6.5 CREATING A VIRTUAL COMPANY

A virtual company needs a virtual meeting room. In the past, we have been experimenting with a couple of systems. In short: none of the systems we tested worked without problems.

Ideally, we would like to have a system that includes the following features:

- voice—over—IP
- video
- whiteboards and writeboards
- sharing documents and collaborating in real time
- sharing desktops

Our default system is Skpye. In its current version, Skype allows up to 25 participants in a telephone conference. If somebody doesn't have access to a computer, we can connect them by calling their land line or mobile telephone, using Skype Out credits. By the way — this is a strange notion in our modern world — who wouldn't be further away more than 500 yards from the next Internet connected computer? If you are not in the Amazon. And if you are in the Amazon, it is either a holiday and you wouldn't participate in a conference, or you are on an expedition, and then you would have a satellite Internet connection with you. In essence, we have learned that Skype is the easiest possibility of connecting the voices of team members. Skype is free or cheap respectively if you use Skype Out. Technology works pretty well although sometimes one has to be patient to get 5–6 peoples' audio equipments working. Also, people drop out from time to time and the conference manager has to reconnect them, which distracts the conference participants. Skype doesn't have a real writeboard but one can use the Skype chat to take notes.

The other option is WebEx. I have only participated in 2 WebEx conferences and I liked them. WebEx has voice—over—IP, whiteboards, chat, and some other nice features. I also like the nice desing and its structure. So, I wanted to test it more and subscribed to a free trial. The first time, the free trial worked (but I had only one more person connected). After that, the system refused further login attempts. A series of telephone and email conversations with hotlines and service staff did not help. At the end, the WebEx staff obvioulsy lost interest in me because they stopped contacting me although I filed a strong complaint. Here I am — I would like to test WebEx further but don't know how. Not a good start. The fees for a WebEx conference seem to be pretty high, but

I haven't really gotten into price negotiations (like other similar software providers, they do not publish their entire price list but want you to negotiate with their sales persons).

In the past, we had used hot conference quite successfully, and sometimes I consider going back to it. I even did Webinars through the system. Hotconference includes voice-over-IP, video, whiteboards, chat, desktop sharing. The technology problems are the same like in other software platforms. Obviously there is a generic problem which is related to the audio systems of computers - these are the only problems we have faced in all applications. Some audio equipment just refuses to work, and even worse, sometimes it works and sometimes it doesn't. Bandwidth is another inhibitive factor in most of the systems. The advantage of Hotconference is its price - much more affordable than other systems. However, when we stopped using it, I had the feeling that they didn't put much effort into further development. For a long time, the system wouldn't work on Macs, and I don't know whether they have introduced this option later on. The CEO of the company, Joel Therien is a viral marketer. He continues to send you emails even if you have told him 5 times that you don't want them. Fortunately they now go into my spam folder right away.

Then, there is Adobe Acrobat Connect Pro (which used to be Macromedia Breeze). I am excited about the possibilities and the flexibility of that software. It has voice-over-IP, video, white and writeboards, chat, presentation and desktop sharing and you can arrange the parts as you like. Additionally, it is programmed in Flash so you don't need to download software to your computer (which many organizations wouldn't allow). However, the problems of audio equipment are the same like described before. And it is pricy, too.

The technical problems of voice-over-IP solutions reduce the efficiency of virtual conferences quite dramatically. We usually spend 15–20 minutes at the beginning of each larger conference to adjust all our machines; and in long conferences, people drop out and have to be reconnected.

An alternative to the described platforms is the use of classical telephone conferences combined with a software that does everything except connecting voices and videos, such as GoToMeeting and others. I will write about these possibilities at another occasion.

6.6 BECOMING AN ANGLE COMPANY

An angle is driven by its employees, who all care about the way we live our lives, the way we interact with people throughout our lives and the need to do our bit for the community and the environment. An-angle specializes in projects which embrace those values and helps to communicate them through the way we work.

At an angle we try to balance our ideals with practical and profitable business. It is a misconception that combining ideals with profitability creates an inferior product. This can be demonstrated by looking at one of n-angle's main drivers, appropriate application.

The idea of appropriate application works on many levels and is derived from a thorough understanding of the problem (whether that be data analysis, multimedia or web page design). Only when you understand how the problem interacts with each area of the business, now and in the future, can you make informed decisions. Similarly, this applies to understanding the real needs of the business rather than using the latest technology to create unnecessary complexity and risk. Appropriate application is the consideration of this.

When applied, appropriate application allows decisions to be made with a full understanding of the impact on resources both now and in the future.

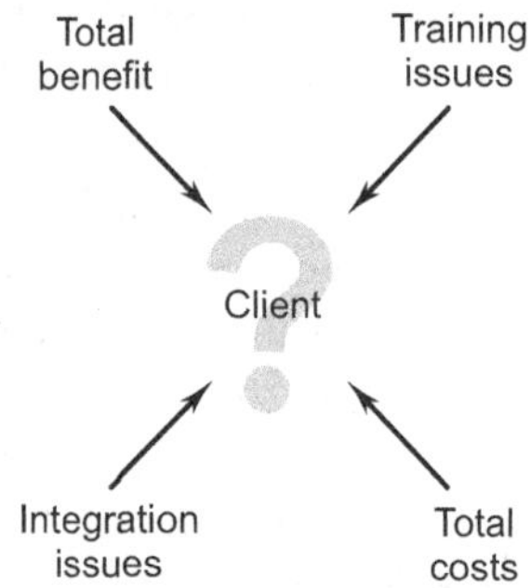

This can be demonstrated by considering the following. In modern business there is a tendency to tackle problems with more advanced technology rather than first going back to basics and really understanding the problem. The effect of this can be:

- the total cost of the solution is initially higher,
- the new technology needs to be tested with all other systems in the business to check its robustness
- there are training issues for the new processes
- when staff with specific knowledge leave, how is the information passed on?

6.7 BUILDING A KNOWLEDGE CREATING COMPANY

In the currently emerging knowledge society, knowledge is seen as the most important success factor. Similar to the significance of technologies and mechanical machines during the industrial revolution, knowledge creation, knowledge management, and organizational innovations will play the pivotal role in the future's businesses. The creation and acquisition of knowledge as well as its efficient utilization will be the most decisive factors for maintaining or achieving the leading edge in successful markets. Under these circumstances, it makes perfect sense to talk about successful products as being the coordinated and reified knowledge of some business enterprise.

Despite of the very substantial successes of information technology in modern industry, this technology has not increased the productivity of modern businesses in the expected magnitude. The disappointment about the overall benefits of current information technology in industry is clearly expressed by the catchy phrase that "information systems would show up everywhere in the world except in productivity statistics". And it is indeed true that the very practical problems of managing knowledge in some enterprise is not yet solved satisfactorily. Even the most innovative approaches primarily deal with knowledge conservation, distribution, and sharing, whereas knowledge-creation is mostly neglected.

Recently, (Choo, 1996) concisely summarized Nonaka & Takeuchi's comprehensive model of organizational knowledge creation:

"Knowledge creation is achieved through a recognition of the synergistic relationship between tacit and explicit knowledge in the organization, and through the design of social processes that create new knowledge by converting tacit knowledge into explicit knowledge. Tacit knowledge is personal knowledge that is hard to formalize or communicate to others. It consists of subjective know-how, insights, and intuitions that come to a person from having been immersed in an activity for an extended period of time. Explicit knowledge is formal knowledge that is easy to transmit between individuals and groups. It is frequently articulated in the form of mathematical formulas, rules, specifications, and so on. The two categories of knowledge are complementary. Tacit knowledge, while it remains closely held as personal know-how, is of limited value to the organization. Explicit knowledge does not appear spontaneously, but must be nurtured and cultivated from the seeds of tacit knowledge. Organizations need to become skilled at converting personal, tacit knowledge into explicit knowledge that can push innovation and new product development. Whereas Western organizations tend to concentrate on explicit knowledge, Japanese firms differentiate between tacit and explicit knowledge, and recognize that tacit knowledge is a source of competitive advantage."

The model comprises the following steps: (1) sharing of tacit knowledge, (2) creating concepts, (3) justifying concepts, (4) building an archetype, and (5) cross-leveling of knowledge. The several phases are explained as follows (Nonaka and Takeuchi, 1995):

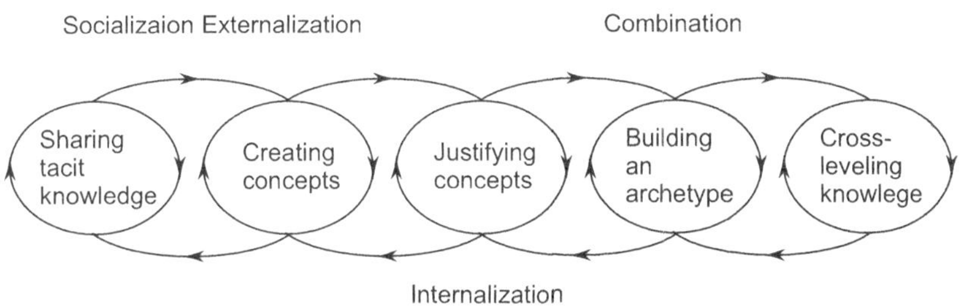

Five-phase Model of the Organizational Knowledge-Creation Process

"... The organizational knowledge-creation process starts with the sharing of tacit knowledge, which corresponds roughly to socialization, since the rich and untapped knowledge that resides in individuals must first be amplified within the organization. In the second phase, tacit knowledge shared by, for example, a self-organizing team is converted to explicit knowledge in the form of a new concept, a process similar to externalization. The created concept has to be justified in the third phase, in which the organization determines if the new concept is truly worthy of pursuit. Receiving the go-ahead, the concepts are converted in the fourth phase into an archetype, which can take the form of a prototype in the case of "hard" product development or an operating mechanism in the case of "soft" innovations, such as a new corporate value, a novel managerial system, or an innovative organizational structure. The last phase extends the knowledge created in, for example, a division to others in the division, across to other *divisions, or even to outside constituents in what we term cross-leveling of knowledge. ...*"

EXERCISE

Short Answer Questions

1. List various Principles of BPR.
2. What are the IT tools for BPR?
3. List Major Reengineering Activities.
4. Define Total Quality Management.
5. What is Customer-driven quality?

6. Describe TQM leadership from top management.
7. What do you mean by Continuous improvement?
8. Describe Employee participation in TQM.
9. Describe TQM as culture.
10. Define Knowledge.
11. Compare Data, Information and Knowledge.
12. How we implement Knowledge Management?
13. Describe Kinds of Knowledge.
14. Describe Expert Knowledge.
15. Describe Thinking and Learning in Humans.
16. What are the Challenges in KM Systems Development?

Long Answer Questions

1. Describe System as Planned Organizational Change.
2. Describe Business Processing Reengineering in detail.
3. Describe roles and responsibilities, as well as required rewards and recognition for a successful Six Sigma quality program.
4. Describe TQM in detail.
5. Describe Six Sigma Organizational Architecture — Rewards and Recognition.
6. Compare TQM and six sigma.
7. Describe Knowledge Management in the organization.
8. Describe Cognitive Psychology.
9. What are major activities supported by knowledge management?

FURTHER READING AND REFERENCES

1. Management Information Systems: Davis Olson, Mc. Graw Hill.
2. Management Information Systems: W.S. Jawadekar, TMH
3. Management Information Systems: Laudon $ Laudon, Pearson Education, Asia
4. Management Information Systems: James a O'Brien

7

Business Applications of IT

7.0 INTERNET AND ELECTRONIC COMMERCE

The Internet provides an opportunity to create markets, and serve customers in ways hitherto unimaginable. A couple of years ago many viewed electronic commerce as simply trading using online networks and EDI (Electronic Data Interchange). For them, the Internet was "totally irrelevant and unsuitable for electronic commerce". Their views have changed! Many large companies and retailers are now flocking to the Internet. Many have suffered set-backs through rishing into this new medium carrying over baggage from established practices, This briefing sets out the scope of Internet commerce, indicates the opportunities and challenges, and gives insights into the strategies of the entrepreneurs who are succeeding.

7.0.1 Benefits of the Internet for Electronic Commerce

1. **Ease of access and global reach:** World Wide Web (www) is an ideal mechanism for providing relevant information to the public globally. It allows organizations an opportunity for publicizing their products and services at minimal cost. By putting information on routinely asked questions on the home pages, organizations are saving costs by reducing the number of customer service representatives. Customers can place orders through the Internet once security issues are worked out. The WWW holds the potential to increase the market share and helps expand new markets by virtue of its global reach. Additionally, easy access to information through the Internet gives the opportunity to compare the costs and characteristics of product and services.
2. **Low-cost advertising medium:** There is no doubt that Internet has become an inexpensive advertising medium for organizations and is being effectively used by some firms for commerce. The comments made by the vice-president of IT of a large multinational firm allude to this issue: "The purpose of the Internet offerings are to open our products and services to a new customer base who prefer to use the internet for their shipping needs and to maintain a leading-edge technology position and image in the market place and against our competitors".
3. **Low barriers to entry:** Small and large firms alike have the opportunity to be on the WWW and conduct business on the internet. The barriers to entry to the Internet are

minuscule. This point was noted by the President of a consulting and staffing agency who was interviewed: "home pages give equal footing to small organizations with large national firms".

4. **Perceived image enhancer:** Several executives mentioned that they have to have presence on the Internet as their competitors are already on the Internet. Without it their reputation can be tarnished and they will be perceived as laggards in employing stat-of-art technologies. Many executives admitted that on the issue of determining the value and direct benefits of Internet to their bottom line, the 'jury is still out' but they must keeping moving forward for the reasons above. ternet Commerce stands at a critical juncture. After an exhilarating start-up, further development hinges on bridging the chasm between early adopter and a true mass market. We envision Eco System ad the foundation of that bridge.

7.0.2 Types of Electronic Commerce

There are five categories of electronic commerce according to their applications.

- Business to Consumer electronic Commerce
- Business to Business Applications (inter-organizational EC)
- Internal Business Processes (intra-organizational EC)
- Consumer to business EC
- B2G/G2B EC

7.0.2.1 Business to Consumer Commerce

Formerly whatever was sold in the market, consumers had to buy but the scenario has changed. Today the customers give their specifications and the manufacturers try and supply it. In fact it is because of choosy customers, more and more variety has to be offered therefore business houses have to set up attractive electronic market places to entice the consumers since business houses may be remotely located geographically but they have to have the ability to retain customers therefore they have to optimize on factors like performance service efficiency, personalization, socialization and offering of incentives. Some key factors which lead to the success of Electronic Marketing are :

1. **Price Attractiveness:** Overpricing will not help an EC as only advertising can be done on EC but can't force a customer to buy a particular product therefore offering discounts and value added products are easier to trade using EC.
2. **Attractive Web Sites:** No consumer would like to wait while transactions are performed. The Web site should be attractive enough to hold the attention of the consumer by providing quick and easy access and user friendly ordering processes with instant acknowledgment.
3. **Electronic Payments:** Since EC does not rely on money and local cheques, there are many services introduced which makes payment easy.
   (*i*) **Smart Card and Credit Card Services:** On-line credit card services have made payment procedures easy. Large amount of security standards have been improvised so as to make the system fool proof.
   (*ii*) **Electronic Cheques:** This is an electronic version of paper cheques which ensures that instant clearing of cheques takes place so that no 'bouncing back' possibility occurs.

(*iii*) **Micro Payments:** This is a service designed to support small payments/micro payments for information products over WWW *e.g.*, Electronic coins of Cyber coin supports payment from ($.25 to $10).

4. **Personalization:** Some web sites keep a track of the path followed by a customer in his former trip so when he returns, he is welcomed and guided on to those parts of the site he is attracted to, therefore making a customer more comfortable thus encouraging return visits. Also a list of priorities can be made so that casual visitors, industrial customers and domestic consumers can be dealt with separately and in a different way.
5. **Socialising:** There are Chat and discussion groups available which let the customer know of the views of people already using a specific product thus enabling him to have a feeling of belongingness to a unique group of like minded individuals thus helping to build up customer loyalty.
6. **Global Marketing:** Setting up physical global distribution networks and service centres will aid electronic commerce because E-commerce can only provide information and transmit messages but physical delivery is in the hands of business houses only.
7. **New Technology Products:** Since awareness rate is high on EC, product life cycles become short with the arrival of new technology products. Launching of new products is faster using EC as advertising is instant and immediate success or failure is known quickly.
8. **Electronic Catalogues:** Help in providing more information or simple ways to find products.

   A brief comparison between traditional & E-Catalogues is given below.

Description	E-Catalogue	Traditional Catalogue
Interactivity	Two way communication between consumers and businesses can occur in real time.	One way *i.e.*, from the business house to consumers. Infect printed catalogs are not at all interactive.
Dynamic updating of catalogues	Changes in prices, repackaging, re-channeling and other minor adjustments are easily performed.	This facility is not available until the printed catalog is edited and re-printed.
Hyper Text Linking	You can go from one part of catalog to another directly and any term requiring clarification can directly be dealt with first and then you can proceed sequentially.	Here information is provided sequentially one after the other *i.e.*, the way the catalog is designed.
Global Presence Linking	Global presence of small organisations is felt at minimal cost on Internet and other online services.	For small organisations to show their presence widely, is not possible as high costs have to be incurred.

Hyper text

9. **Convenience:** Shopping can be done from anywhere and at anytime.
10. **Time Saving:** Time lost in traveling to and from the stores is saved. In fact if a consumer knows his requirements the entire process of ordering and payment takes a few seconds.
11. **Easy Navigation :** There is no use spending time at a web site if you can't find what you're looking for. On its opening page, www.etoys.com lets you tailor a search for toys by a child's age, by brand name, or by price.

Cons of On-line Shopping

(*i*) **Visualization Only:** The web site may display the product but the user can't feel, taste or try the product.

(*ii*) **Time Lag:** It is difficult to find out the actual time of the arrival of the product.

(*iii*) **Internet Connectivity:** Having a slow modem, or a dial up connection, or technical delays caused due to heavy Internet traffic may cause lots of delay.

(*iv*) **Slow Web Sites**: Web Sites using a lot of graphics and images take a lot of time to download and is frustrating for the consumer as a lot of time is consumed.

(*v*) **Search Methods:** Not all search methods may be known to cyber shoppers therefore a lot of time may be wasted before the actual location is reached.

(*vi*) **Shipping and Handling Costs:** Sometimes shipping and handling costs may be higher than the cost of item purchased. Again if shipping costs are not known in advance then may be heavy amounts may have to be shelled out at the time of delivery.

7.0.2.2 Internal Business Processes or Intra-organizational EC

The purpose behind Intra-organizational EC is to help a company maintain relationships which are critical to delivering superior customer services. Many inter—networked enterprises are customer driven and market driven therefore constant monitoring and evaluation of customers, suppliers, competitors data should be compiled from their web sites and discussion groups. The feedback got is used to shape the organization's strategies in term of product design, advertising, customer services etc. EC facilitates managers to communicate using video conferencing, E-mail and bulletin boards so that information is better disseminated and right decisions can be made.

Today large corporate Intranets have been installed so that information can be assessed and published. On line publishing helps to reduce costs as printing and distributing and faster there is a better co-ordination between the various departments. In fact all efforts are being made to convert organization into a paperless office. From this perspective the main applications of electronic commerce are:

- Supplier management
- Inventory management
- Distribution management
- Channel management
- payment management

7.0.2.3 Business to Business (Inter-organizational EC)

Organizations use EC not only to interact better with their customers, for better co-ordination within the organization but also for inter-organization relationships. A few of these business applications are:

(*i*) Supplier management: Here the main objective is to provide purchase managers with better control over purchasing habits. The number of suppliers is reduced and business relationships are strengthened thus making strong virtual teams leading to reduce processing costs and cycle time.

(*ii*) Inventory Management: The purpose of EC is to lower the inventory levels by reducing out of stock circumstances and over stuffing of inventory. Again lead times are reduced so that the order-ship-bill cycle is reduced.

(*iii*) Channel Management: The use of open networks has enhanced inter business communication. No time, labour costs have to occur to obtain accurate information. Communication on the internet is multi point to multipoint therefore participants can limit themselves to their field of interest.

(*iv*) Distribution Management: As a result of EDI (Electronic Data Interchange) purchase orders, bills, shipping notices all contain accurate and sufficient data are thus transmitted as shipping documents

(*v*) Payment Management: Electronic payments ensure that payments can be made between suppliers and organizations quickly thus reducing insecurities and lower processing costs.

(*vi*) Financial management: EC has enabled global companies to manage their money in various foreign exchange accounts.

(*vii*) Sales force management: Communication and flow of information among the sales, customer service, and production functions have improved.

7.0.2.4 Consumer to Business Electronic Commerce

From consumer to business perspective EC provides the following economic transactions:

- **Social interaction:** Electronic commerce enables consumer to communicate with each other through e-mail, videoconferencing, and news groups.
- **Personal finance management:** Electronic applications like quicken enable consumer to manage investments and personal finances using online banking tools.
- **Purchasing products and information:** Electronic applications enable consumer to find online information about existing and new products and services.

7.0.2.5 B2G/G2B (Business to Government / Government to Business)

Some authors identify a separate category of B2G. In some cases, it is used to refer to **sales** by business enterprises to government. There are some differences between this and other variants of B2B (*e.g.*, more formality in RFT/RFP/RFQ processes, more emphasis on probity, and contracts entered into with the relevant body politic rather than with the purchasing organisation itself); but there are not necessarily enough differences to warrant significantly different treatment from B2B generally.

In other cases, B2G refers to **service delivery** by government to business enterprises (for which 'G2B' would make more sense), or is concerned with **regulation** by government of business enterprises. This may be a more worthwhile distinction from B2B, because it commonly involves different goods and services, different approaches to the transaction, and different requirements of technology (*e.g.*, payment systems, and aspects of security).

Government is frequently presumed to be homogeneous (despite the rarity with which two agencies in the same jurisdiction perform the same function). In practice, there are two particularly important dimensions across which government agencies commonly need to be differentiated:

- by **the function of the agency**:
  - service delivery:
    - insourced;
    - outsourced (including 'purchaser/provider');
  - regulatory;
  - policy;
- by **the level of government** to which it belongs:
  - supra-national (*e.g.*, EU, OECD, NAFTA);
  - national;
  - regional / state / province / land / canton / etc.; and
  - local.

7.0.3 Business Applications of Electronic Commerce

Some common applications related to electronic commerce are the following:

- Email
- Enterprise content management
- Instant messaging
- Newsgroups
- Online shopping and order tracking
- Online banking
- Online office suites
- Domestic and international payment systems
- Shopping cart software
- Teleconferencing
- Electronic tickets

7.0.4 Electronic Business Infrastructure

E-Commerce infrastructure is the share of total economic infrastructure used to support electronic business processes and conduct electronic commerce transactions. It includes hardware, software, telecommunication networks, support services, and human capital used in electronic business and commerce. Examples of *e*-business infrastructure are:

- Computers, routers, and other hardware
- Satellite, wire, and optical communications and network channels
- System and applications software
- Support services, such as web site development and hosting, consulting, electronic payment, and certification services.
- Human capital, such as programmers.

7.0.5 Electronic Commerce Processes

Processes that a business organization conducts over a computer-mediated network. Business organizations include any for-profit, governmental, or nonprofit entity. Examples of on-line e-business processes include the following:

- Purchasing
- Selling
- Vendor-managed inventory
- Production management
- Logistics
- Communication and Support Services such as on-line training and recruiting.

7.1 INTRANETS AND EXTRANET

Intranet/Extranet form a major part of the information systems of many corporates. A lot of companies use intranets/extranets as a powerful tool to manage their resources and work in a systematic manner. One of our most valued services is helping companies enhance their business and communication channels by using Intranet and Extranet technology. An Intranet is a use of Net and Web technology that happens inside your own organization. An Extranet is an Intranet that people outside your formal organization have access to.

What could you use an intranet for in a business environment? Some ideas include

- document distribution—reducing cost improving timeliness of distributed information
- provide a secure medium for the distribution of confidential information
- interactive services—surveys, etc.,
- training
- database access
- inter-company communication
- customer support.

7.1.1 What is an Intranet?

An intranet is a private computer network based on the communication standards of the Internet. It is smaller version of the Internet that only the members of an organization can see. Companies can create, within their walls, a manageable, secure version of the World Wide Web. Using Intranets (and extranets) will change the culture of an organisation. By making a lot of information easily available, you empower staff to make informed decisions. Intranets allow an organization to spend less time on things that bring no value such as chasing down the right information to solve a problem. Productivity increases as corporate knowledge is more accessible and the data is more accurate.

- Flexibility in time of delivery of knowledge is gained as information is always a click away
- Intranets allow for a place where boundaries are lowered and information exchange is encouraged. This leads to more informed employees with the ability to make better, faster decisions. This in turn leads to better productivity and more time for revenue generation.

7.1.2 Extranets

Having all of your key business information easily and quickly accessible will help your business to prosper. Providing those on your supply chain, including your customers, with all the information they need to improve their business relationship with you will help your business to grow and develop. Intranets and extranets make use of all the technology of the internet to supply these things through secure managed channels so helping you to monitor and control your business in a cost-effective way. If used properly they can drastically speed up the pace with which you can communicate within a geographically dispersed community.

Just as there are many internal uses for web technology, companies often need to find better ways to communicate with external customers and suppliers. Extranets can improve your sales, marketing, supplier and customer service channels by allowing these groups of users to access your extranet and obtain the information they need.

Extranet application areas for customers, partners, and dealers include:

- product brochures and specifications
- product pricing
- frequently asked questions
- ordering information
- distributor/sales contact list
- customer support contact numbers
- details of warranties/support documents
- employee recruitment.

Benefits of Riva Intranet/ Extranet Solutions:

» Well planned Intranet roadmap
» Flexible, Scalable, robust and user friendly
» Quick time to market and implement
» Customizable for any industry verticals
» Assures very good ROI
» Scalable architecture to integrate into KM and CRM systems.

7.1.3 Difference between Intranet, Extranet and Internet

The term "intranet" is somewhat misleading conceptually, because it invites a contrast to the term "Internet." The real contrast is with the World Wide Web—an important distinction, because "Internet" focuses on physical and technical networks, while the Web focuses on the set of content accessible on that physical and technical infrastructure.

When I coined the term "IntraNet" at Amdahl Corp. in the summer of 1994, it did have the connotation of an internal Web rather than just an internal Internet. In fact, the term we used internally before this was the too-cumbersome "Enterprise-Wide Web". So, while the ambiguity of "intranet" was apparent even back then, for lack of a better alternative, it caught on.

In the early days, I defined an intranet as "An infrastructure based on Internet standards and technologies that supports sharing of content within a limited and well-defined group". The "infrastructure" referred to the organizational and management infrastructure that created, managed, and shared the content. The only technical constraint was that the physical network be based on the Internetworking Protocol (IP).

You might notice that this definition encompasses what we call extranets today, because the defining factor is a "limited and well-defined group", and does not specify any official organizational affiliation. The Web, in contrast, is an unlimited group.

Today I think of intranets, extranets, and the Web as collections of content. An intranet is a set of content shared by a well-defined group within a single organization. An extranet is a set of content shared by a well-defined group, but one that crosses enterprise boundaries.

These access distinctions are important, because Web-based content uses the same technical infrastructure regardless of access decisions. This means it is much easier to change access to specific content than it was in the old proprietary world, where making something more widely available often entailed a major conversion effort.

As technical infrastructure becomes less of a barrier to accessing specific content, it becomes important to pay attention to how, or if, we want to restrict access. The terms "intranet" and "extranet", as imperfect as they are provide us with conceptual and pragmatic tools for discussing to whom we want to make specific content available.

These terms may continue to evolve in meaning. For now, a set of content accessed by members of a single organization is an intranet, even if the information travels across the public Internet infrastructure.

7.2 FUNDAMENTALS OF STRATEGIC ADVANTAGE

Information technology can change the way businesses compete. For this reason, you should view information systems strategically, that is, as vital competitive networks, as a means of organizational renewal, and as a necessary investment in technologies that help an enterprise achieve its strategic objectives.

7.2.1 Competitive Strategy Concepts

The strategic role of information systems involves using information technology to develop products, services, and capabilities that give a company strategic advantages over the competitive forces it faces in the global marketplace. This creates strategic information systems, information systems that support or shape the competitive position and strategies of an enterprise. So a strategic information system can be any kind of information system (TPS, MIS, DSS, etc.) that helps an organization:

1. Gain a competitive advantage
2. Reduce a competitive disadvantage
3. Meet other strategic enterprise objectives

According to Michael Porter, a firm can survive and succeed in the long run if it successfully develops strategies to confront five competitive forces that shape the structure of competition in its industry. These include:

1. Rivalry of competitors within its industry
2. Threat of new entrants
3. Threat of substitutes
4. Bargaining power of customers
5. Bargaining power of suppliers

A variety of competitive strategies can be developed to help a firm confront these competitive forces. These include:

- **Cost Leadership Strategy**
    - Become a low cost producer of products and services
    - Find ways to help suppliers or customers reduce their costs
    - Increase the costs of competitors.
- **Differentiation Strategy**
    - Develop ways to differentiate products and services from competitors.
    - Reduce the differentiation advantages of competitors.
- **Innovation Strategy - Find new ways of doing business**
    - Develop new products and services
    - Enter new markets or marketing segments
    - Establish new business alliances
    - Find new ways of producing products/services
    - Find new ways of distributing products/services
- **Growth Strategies**
    - Significantly expand the company's capacity to produce goods and services
    - Expand into global markets
    - Diversify into new products and services
    - Integrate into related products and services.
- **Alliance Strategies**
    - Establish new business linkages and alliances with customers, suppliers, competitors, consultants and other companies (mergers, acquisitions, joint ventures, forming virtual companies, etc.).

7.2.2 Strategic Roles for Information Systems

How can the preceding competitive strategy concepts be applied to the *strategic role of information systems*? Information technology can be used to implement a variety of competitive strategies. These include the five basic competitive strategies (differentiation, cost, innovation, growth, alliance), as well as other ways that companies can use information systems strategically to gain a competitive edge. For example:

1. Lower Costs
2. Differentiate
3. Innovate
4. Promote Growth
5. Develop Alliances
6. Improve quality and efficiency
7. Build an IT platform
8. Other strategies
    - Use inter-organizational information systems to create switching costs that lock in customers and suppliers.

- Use investments in IT to build barriers to entry against industry outsiders.
- Use IT components to make substitution of competing products unattractive.

7.2.3 Improving Business Processes

Investments in information technology can help make a firm's operational processes substantially more efficient, and its managerial processes much more effective. By making such improvements to its business processes a firm may be able to:

1. Dramatically cut costs
2. Improve the quality and customer service
3. Develop innovative products for new markets.

7.2.4 Promoting Business Innovation

Investments in information systems technology can result in the development of new products, services, and processes. This can:

1. Create new business opportunities
2. Enable a firm to enter new markets
3. Enable a firm to enter into new market segments of existing markets.

7.2.5 Lock In Customers and Suppliers

Investments in information technology can also allow a business to *lock in customers and suppliers* (and lock out competitors) by building valuable new relationships with them. This can be accomplished by:

1. Deters both customers and suppliers from abandoning a firm for its competitors or intimidating a firm into accepting less profitable relationships.
2. Offer better-quality service to customers allows a company to differentiate themselves from their competitors.
3. Create *inter-organizational information systems* in which telecommunications networks electronically link the terminals and computers of businesses with their customers and suppliers, resulting in new business alliances and partnerships.

7.2.6 Creating Switching Costs

A major emphasis in strategic information systems is to build *switching costs* into the relationships between a firm and its customers or suppliers. That is, investments in information systems technology can make customers or suppliers dependent on the continued use of innovative, mutually beneficial inter-organizational information systems. Then, they become reluctant to pay the cost in time, money, effort, and inconvenience that it would take to change to a firm's competitors. Example: APOLLO (USA) airline reservation system, and GEMNI (CAN) airline reservation system.

7.2.7 Raising Barriers to Entry

Investment in information technologies that increase operational efficiency can erect *barriers to entry* for new players in the industry, and can discourage firms already in the market. This can be accomplished by:

1. Increasing the amount of investment or the complexity of the technology required to compete in a market segment.
2. Discourage firms already in the industry and deter external firms from entering the industry.

7.2.8 Leveraging a Strategic IT Platform

Information technology enables a firm to build a strategic IT platform that allows it to take advantage of strategic opportunities. Typically, this means acquiring hardware and software, developing telecommunications networks, hiring information system specialists, and training end users. A firm can then leverage investment in information technology by developing new products and services.

7.2.9 Developing a Strategic Information Base

Information systems allow a firm to develop a *strategic information base* that can provide information to support the firm's competitive strategies. A firm's database is considered a strategic resource that is used to support strategic planning, marketing, and other strategic initiatives. These resources are being used by firms in such areas as:

1. Strategic planning
2. Marketing campaigns
3. Erecting barriers to entry for competitors
4. Finding better ways to lock in customers and suppliers.

7.2.10 Breaking Business Barriers

Several vital capabilities of information technology that break traditional barriers to strategic business success include:

1. Break time barriers.
2. Break geographic barriers.
3. Break cost barriers.
4. Break structural barriers.

7.2.10.1 Breaking Time Barriers

Information technology is used to shorten the intervals between the various critical steps in a business process. Telecommunications is a lot faster than most other forms of communications, thus, it provides information to remote locations immediately after it is requested.

7.2.10.2 Breaking Geographic Barriers

Telecommunications networks enable you to communicate with people almost anywhere in the world. Telecommunications and computing technologies make it possible to distribute key business activities to where they are needed, where they are best performed, or where they best support the competitive advantage of a business.

7.2.10.3 Breaking Cost Barriers

Computers and telecommunications can often significantly reduce the cost of business operations when compared with other means of information processing and communications. For example, they can reduce costs in such areas as production, inventory, distribution, or communications. Information technologies have also helped companies cut labor costs, minimize inventory levels, reduce the number of distribution centers, and lower communications costs.

The New Economies of Information

The internetworking of businesses and consumers via the Internet, intranets, and extranets is breaking the cost barriers raised by traditional economic trade-offs in information content and delivery. In communicating with each other and consumers, businesses have had to make trade-offs between:

Reach: The number of people receiving or exchanging information.

Richness: The bandwidth, customization, and interactivity of information.

Bandwidth: Amount of information content delivered within a given time period.

Customization: Degree to which information content is customized for its recipient.

Interactivity Amount of dialogue between the information provider and the recipient.

7.2.10.4 Breaking Structural Barriers

Computers and telecommunications networks can help a business develop strategic relationships by establishing new electronic linkages with customers, suppliers, and other business entities. For example, telecommunications networks can support innovations in the delivery of services, increase the scope and penetration of markets, and create strategic alliances with customers, suppliers, and even a firm's competitors.

7.2.11 The Value Chain and Strategic IS

An important concept that can help a manager identify opportunities for strategic information systems is the *value chain* concept as developed by Michael Porter. This concept:

1. Views a firm as a series or "chain", of basic activities that add value to its products and services and thus, add a margin of value to the firm.
2. Some business activities are viewed as primary activities, and others are support activities. This framework can highlight where competitive strategies can best be applied in a business.
3. Managerial end users should try to develop strategic information systems for those activities that add the most value to a company's product or services, and thus to the overall business value of the firm.

7.3 STRATEGIC APPLICATIONS AND ISSUES IN INFORMATION TECHNOLOGY

There are various ways in which organizations view and use information technology. These include:

1. Strategic
2. Offensive
3. Defensive
4. Cost-justified
5. Controlled.

7.3.1 Reengineering Business Processes

One of the most popular competitive strategies today is *business process reengineering* (BPR), most often simply called reengineering. Reengineering is the fundamental rethinking and radical redesign of business processes to achieve dramatic improvements in cost, quality, speed, and service. BPR combines a strategy of promoting business innovation with a strategy of making major improvements to business processes so that a company can become a much stronger and more successful competitor in the marketplace.The potential payback of reengineering is high, but also is its level of risk and disruption to the organizational environment.

The Role of Information Technology

Information technology plays a major role in reengineering business processes. The speed, information processing power, and ease-of-use of modern computer hardware, software, and networks can dramatically increase the efficiency of business processes, and communications and collaboration among the people responsible for their operation and management.

7.3.2 Improving Business Quality

No single approach to organizational change is appropriate for all circumstances. One important strategic thrust is continuous quality improvement, popularly called total quality management (TQM). Previous to TQM, quality was defined as meeting established standards or specifications for a product or service. Statistical quality control programs were used to measure and correct any deviations from standards.

7.3.3 Total Quality Management

Quality is defined as meeting or exceeding the requirements and expectations of customers for a product or service. This may involve many features and attributes such as:

1. Performance
2. Reliability
3. Durability
4. Responsiveness
5. Aesthetics
6. Reputation

Total quality management uses a variety of tools and methods to seek continuous improvement of quality, productivity, flexibility, timeliness, and customer responsiveness.

7.3.4 Becoming an Agile Competitor

Agility in competitive performance is the ability of a business to prosper in rapidly changing, continually fragmenting global markets for high-quality, high-performance, customer-configured products and services. An agile company can:

1. Make a profit in markets with broad product ranges and short model lifetimes
2. Process orders in arbitrary lot sizes
3. Offer individualized products while maintaining high volumes of production.

Agile companies depend heavily on information technology to:

1. Enriched its customers with customized solutions to their needs.
2. Cooperate with other businesses to bring products to market as rapidly and cost-efficient as possible.

3. Combine the flexible, multiple organizational structures it uses.
4. Leverage the competitive impact of its people and information resources.

The Role of Information Technology

IT is a strategic requirement for agile product development and delivery. Information systems provide the information people need to support agile operations, as well as the information built into products and services.

7.3.5 Creating a Virtual Company

A *virtual company* is an organization that uses information technology to link people, assets, and ideas. Six basic characteristics of successful virtual companies include:

1. Adaptability
2. Opportunism (opportunity-exploiting organization)
3. Excellence
4. Technology
5. Borderless
6. Trust-based

7.3.5.1 Virtual Company Strategies

Forming virtual companies have become an important competitive strategy in today's dynamic global markets. Information technology plays an important role in providing computing and telecommunications resources to support the communications, coordination, and information flows needed. Managers of a virtual company depend on IT to help them manage a network of people, knowledge, financial and physical resources provided by many business partners to quickly take advantage of rapidly changing model opportunities.

Business strategies of virtual companies include:

1. Share infrastructure and risk
2. Link complementary core competencies
3. Reduce concept to cash time through sharing
4. Increase facilities and market coverage.
5. Gain access to new markets and share market or customer loyalty
6. Migrate from selling products to selling solutions.

7.3.5.2 Building the Knowledge-Creating Company

To many companies today, lasting competitive advantage can only be theirs if they become *knowledge-creating companies* or *learning organizations.* That means consistently creating new business knowledge, disseminating it widely throughout the company, and quickly building the new knowledge into their products and services. Knowledge-creating companies exploit two kinds of technology:

1. Explicit Knowledge: Data, documents, things written down or stored on computers.
2. Tacit Knowledge: "How-tos" of knowledge, which reside in workers.

Successful *knowledge management* creates techniques, technologies, and rewards for getting employees to share what they know and to make better use of accumulated workplace knowledge.

7.3.6 Knowledge Management Systems

Knowledge management has become one of the major strategic uses of information technology. Many companies are building *knowledge management systems* to manage organizational learning and business know-how. The goal of KMS is to help knowledge workers create, organize, and make available important business knowledge, wherever and whenever it's needed in an organization. This includes processes, procedures, patterns, reference works, formulas, "best practices", forecasts, and fixes. Internet and intranet web sites, groupware, data mining, knowledge bases, discussion forums, and videoconferencing are some of the key information technologies for gathering, storing, and distributing this knowledge.

Characteristics of KMS

1. KMS are information systems that facilitate organizational learning and knowledge creation.
2. KMS use a variety of information technologies to collect and edit information, assess its value, disseminate it within the organization, and apply it as knowledge to the processes of a business.
3. KMS are sometimes called *adaptive learning* systems. That's because they create cycles of organizational learning called *learning loops*, where the creation, dissemination, and application of knowledge produces an adaptive learning process within a company.
4. KMS can provide rapid feedback to knowledge workers, encourage behavior changes by employees, and significantly improve business performance.
5. As an organizational learning process continues and its knowledge base expands, the knowledge-creating company integrates its knowledge into its business processes, products, and services. This makes it a highly innovative and agile provider of high quality products and customer services, and a formidable competitor in the marketplace.

7.3.7 Using the Internet Strategically

In the past the Internet has been used as a marketing channel for companies who want to publish information about themselves and their products. Recently, this has given way to more innovative uses of the Internet. Organizations have realized that the Internet can be used strategically for competitive advantage. However, in order to optimize this strategic impact, a company must continually assess the strategic position of its Internet-based applications. A *strategic position matrix* can help a company identify where to concentrate its use of the Internet to gain competitive advantage. These strategies include:

- **Cost and Efficiency Improvements:** This quadrant represents a low amount of internal company, customer, and competitor connectivity and use of IT via the Internet and other networks.

Strategy: Focus on improving efficiency and lowering costs by using the Internet and the World Wide Web as a fast, low cost way to communicate with customers, suppliers, and business partners.

Example: The use of E-mail and a company Web site.

- **Performance Improvement in Business Effectiveness:** Here a company has a high degree of internal connectivity and pressures to substantially improve its business processes, but external connectivity by customers and competitors is still low.

Strategy: Make major improvements in business effectiveness.

Example: Widespread internal use of Internet-based technologies like intranets can substantially improve information sharing and collaboration within the business.

- **Global Market Penetration:** A company that enters this quadrant of the matrix must capitalize on a high degree of customer and competitor connectivity and use of IT.

Strategy: Develop Internet-based applications to optimize interaction with customers and build market share.

Example: Outstanding Web sites with value-added information services and online customer support.

- **Product and Service Transformation:** Here a company and its customers, suppliers, and competitors are extensively networked. Internet-based technologies, including Web sites, intranets, and extranets, must now be implemented throughout the company's operations and business relationships.

Strategy: Develop strategic electronic commerce applications to develop and deploy new Internet-based products and services that strategically reposition it in the marketplace.

Example: Use the Internet for online transaction processing of sales of products and services at company Web sites, and electronic document interchange (EDI) with suppliers.

7.3.8 Internet Value Chains

The value chain concept helps a company evaluate how to use information technology strategically. Value chains can also be used to strategically position a company's Internet-based applications to gain competitive advantage. The value chain model can be used to outline several ways that a:

1. Company's Internet connections with its customers could provide business benefits and opportunities for competitive advantage.
2. Company's Internet connections with its suppliers could be used for competitive advantage.
3. Company's internal operations can benefit strategically from Internet-based applications.

7.3.9 The Challenges of Strategic IS

The IS function can help managers develop competitive weapons that use information technology to implement a variety of competitive strategies to meet the challenges of the competitive forces that confront any organization. Successful strategic information systems are not easy to develop and implement. They may require major changes in the way a business operates, and in their relationships with customers, suppliers, competitors, internal and external stakeholders, and others.

7.3.10 Sustaining Strategic Success

Success and sustain ability depends on many environmental and fundamental business factors, and especially on the actions and strategies of a company's management team. Sustained success in using information technology strategically seems to depend on three sets of factors:

- **The Environment:** A major environmental factor is the structure of an industry.
- **Foundation Factors:** Unique industry position, alliance, assets, technological resources, and expertise are foundation factors that give a company a competitive edge in the market.

- **Management Actions and Strategies:** A company's management must develop and initiate successful actions and strategies that shape how information technology is actually applied in the marketplace. Examples include:
  (*a*) Preempting the market by being first and way ahead of competitors in a strategic business use of IT.
  (*b*) Creating switching costs and barriers to entry
  (*c*) Developing strategies to respond to the catch-up moves of competitors
  (*d*) Managing the business risks inherent in any strategic IT initiatives.

7.4 KEY TERMS AND CONCEPTS

Agile Competitor

Agile competitor is the ability of a company to profitably operate in a competitive environment of continual and unpredictable changes in customer opportunities.

Breaking Business Barriers

Several vital capabilities of information technology that break traditional barriers to strategic business success include breaking time barriers, geographic barriers, cost barriers, and structural barriers.

Breaking Business Barriers: Cost Barriers

Telecommunications and computing technologies make it possible to break cost barriers by significantly increasing the efficiency of business operations.

Breaking Business Barriers: Geographic Barriers

Telecommunications and computing technologies make it possible to distribute key business activities to where they are needed, where they are best performed, or where they best support the competitive advantage of a business.

Breaking Business Barriers: Structural Barriers

Computers and telecommunications networks can help a business develop strategic relationships by establishing new electronic linkages with customers, suppliers, and other business entities.

Breaking Business Barriers: Time Barriers

Information technology is used to shorten the intervals between the various critical steps in a business process. Telecommunications is a lot faster than most other forms of communications, thus, it provides information to remote locations immediately after it is requested.

Building a Strategic IT Platform

Building strategic IT platforms enables a firm to take advantage of strategic opportunities. Typically, this means acquiring hardware and software, developing telecommunications networks, hiring IS specialists, and training end users.

Business Process Reengineering

Reengineering is the fundamental rethinking and radical redesign of business processes to achieve dramatic improvements in cost, quality, speed, and service.

Competitive Forces

A firm must confront (1) rivalry of competitors within its industry, (2) threats of new entrants, (3) threats of substitutes, (4) the bargaining power of customers, and (5) the bargaining power of suppliers.

Competitive Strategies

A firm can develop cost leadership, product differentiation, and business innovation strategies to confront its competitive forces.

Creating Switching Costs

The cost in time, money, effort, and inconvenience that it would take a customer or supplier to switch its business to a firm's competitors.

Developing a Strategic Information Base

A firms database is considered a strategic resource which is used to support strategic planning, marketing, and other strategic initiatives.

Improving Business Processes

By improving operational efficiency, a firm may be able to: cut costs, improve the quality and delivery of its products and services, improve operational efficiency through reengineering, adopt a low cost leadership strategy, and increase quality and service by choosing a product differentiation strategy.

Interorganizational IS

Information systems that interconnect an organization with other organizations such as a business and its customers and suppliers.

Knowledge-Creating Company

That means consistently creating new business knowledge, disseminating it widely throughout the company, and quickly building the new knowledge into their products and services.

Knowledge Management System

The goal of KMS is to help knowledge workers create, organize, and make available important business knowledge, wherever and whenever it's needed in an organization.

Leveraging Investment in IT

A firm can then leverage investment in information technology by developing new products and services.

Locking in Customers and Suppliers

Building valuable relationships with customers, and suppliers which deter them from abandoning a firm for its competitors or intimidating it into accepting less profitable relationships.

New Economics of Information

The internetworking of businesses and consumers via the intranets, and extranets is breaking the cost barriers raided by traditional economic trade-offs in information content and delivery.

Promoting Business Innovation

Investments in information systems technology can result in the development of new products, services, and processes. This can create new business opportunities, allow a firm to enter new markets or to enter new market segments of existing markets.

Raising Barriers to Entry

Technological, financial, or legal requirements which deter firms from entering an industry.

Strategic Business use of the Internet Technologies

The Internet promises to be an attractive and cost-efficient way for many companies to develop strategic collaboration, operations, marketing, and alliances needed to solve and succeed in today's fast-changing global markets.

Strategic Information System

Information systems that provide a firm with competitive products and services which give it a strategic advantage over its competitors in the marketplace.

Strategic Roles of Information Systems

Information systems that promote business innovation, improve operational efficiency, and build strategic information resources for a firm.

Sustaining Competitive Advantage

Sustained success in using information technology strategically seems to depend on three sets of factors: The environment, foundation factors, and management actions and strategies.

Total Quality Management

Total quality management uses a variety of tools and methods to seek continuous improvement of quality, productivity, flexibility, timeliness, and customer responsiveness.

Value Chain

Viewing a firm as a series or chain of basic activities that add value to its products and services and thus add a margin of value to the firm.

Virtual Company

A virtual company is an organization that uses information technology to link people, assets, and ideas.

EXERCISE

1. Describe Internet and Electronic Commerce.
2. What are the benefits of the Internet for Electronic Commerce?
3. Describe types of Electronic Commerce.
4. Describe business applications of Electronic Commerce.
5. Describe Electronic Business Infrastructure.
6. Describe Electronic Commerce Processes.
7. Describe Intranets and Extranet.
8. What is an intranet?
9. What is the difference between Intranet, Extranet and Internet?
10. Describe fundamentals of Strategic Advantage.
11. Describe Competitive Strategy Concepts.
12. Describe Strategic Roles for Information Systems.
13. Describe Improving Business Processes.
14. Describe Promoting Business Innovation.
15. Describe Lock In Customers and Suppliers.
16. Describe Creating Switching Costs.
17. Describe Raising Barriers to Entry.
18. Describe Leveraging a Strategic IT Platform.
19. Describe Developing a Strategic Information Base.
20. Describe Breaking Business Barriers.
21. Describe Breaking Structural Barriers.
22. Describe the Value Chain and Strategic IS.
23. Strategic applications and issues in Information Technology.
24. Describe Reengineering Business Processes.
25. Describe Total Quality Management.
26. Describe becoming an Agile Competitor.
27. Describe creating a Virtual Company.
28. Describe Knowledge Management Systems.
29. Describe Internet Value Chains.
30. Describe the challenges of Strategic IS.
31. Describe Sustaining Strategic Success.

8

Introduction to Enterprise Resource Planning

8.0 INTRODUCTION

Enterprise Resource Planning (ERP) integrates core business areas such as manufacturing, distribution, financials and human resources. ERP is often implemented in companies together with process-oriented organization or Supply Chain Management (SCM). In order to manage the information-flow of such structures new IT-systems are generated — known as ERP-systems. IT-systems of this kind allow managers from all departments to look vertically and horizontally across the organization to see what others are accomplishing or not. It attempts to integrate all departments and functions across a company onto a single computer system that can serve all those different department's particular needs. ERP-systems also implement and automate business processes, putting them into a useful format that is standardized across the corporation and between their suppliers and customers. ERP-systems capture data about historical activity, current operations and future plans and organize it into information people can use to help develop business strategies.

In the ERP industry, the systems are often referred to as the 4M's. Man, Money, Materials and Machines. This type of system brings all four aspects of business together, giving them a synergistic value. ERP is an enabling technology that can give corporations a strong competitive edge. In addition, this technology is as close to virtual enterprises as business today has ever seen.

8.1 HISTORY

The history of ERP can be traced back to the 1960's, when the focus of systems was mainly towards inventory control. Most of the systems software were designed to handle inventory based in traditional inventory concepts. The 1970's witnessed a shift of focus towards MRP (Material Requirement Planning). This system helped in translating the master production schedule into requirements for individual units like sub assemblies, components and other raw material planning and procurement. This system was involved mainly in planning the raw material requirements.

Then, in 1980's came the concept of MRP-II (Manufacturing Resource Planning), which involved optimizing the entire plant production process. Though MRP-II, in the beginning was an extension of MRP to include shop floor and distribution management activities, during later years, MRP-II was further extended to include areas like Finance, Human Resource, Engineering, Project Management etc. This gave birth to ERP (Enterprise Resource Planning) which covered the cross-functional coordination and integration in support of the production process. The ERP as compared to its ancestors included the entire range of a company's activities.

However, it has been within the last five years that ERP has really taken off and seen record revenues by the software companies. In the past, ERP software was used to numbercrunch and schedule manufacturing processes. Management was not using ERP to its full potential. Today, ERP is the foundation of businesses domestically and globally. It is used as a management tool and gives organizations a great competitive advantage.

But the consulting firm that created the term a decade ago Gartner, claimed ERP was dead.

They also recognized that the need for an information backbone for an enterprise hasn't gone away. As e-business becomes business as usual, sharing accurate real-time information about orders and inventory is critical to success. And not just across an enterprise. Now, business needs to move that information across a supply chain.

1960s Enterprise Resource Planning (ERP) is born in the early 1960s from a joint effort between J.I. Case, the manufacturer of tractors and other construction machinery, and partner IBM. Material Requirements Planning or MRP is the initial effort. This application software serves as the method for planning and scheduling materials for complex manufactured products.

1970s Initial MRP solutions are big, clumsy and expensive. They require a large technical staff to support the mainframe computers on which they run.

1972 **Five engineers in Mannheim, Germany begin the company, SAP (Systemanalyse und Programmentwicklung). The purpose in creating SAP is to produce and market standard software for integrated business solutions.**

1975 Richard Lawson, Bill Lawson, and business partner, John Cerullo begin Lawson Software. The founders see the need for pre-packaged enterprise technology solutions as an alternative to customized business software applications.

1976 In the manufacturing industry, MRP (Material Requirements Planning) becomes the fundamental concept used in production management and control.

1977 Jack Thompson, Dan Gregory, and Ed McVaney form JD Edwards. Each founder takes part of their name to create the company moniker. Larry Ellison begins Oracle Corporation.

1978 Jan Baan begins The Baan Corporation to provide financial and administrative consulting services.

1979 Oracle offers the first commercial SQL relational database management system.

1980 JD Edwards begins focusing on the IBM System/38 in the early 1980s. MRP (Manufacturing Resources Planning) evolves into MRP-II as a more accessible extension to shop floor and distribution management activities.

1981	Baan begins to use Unix as their main operating system.
1982	Baan delivers its first software product. JD Edwards focuses on the IBM System/38.
1983	Oracle offers both a VAX mode database as well as a database written entirely in C (for portability).
1984	Baan shifts the focus of their development to manufacturing.
1985	JD Edwards is recognized as an industry-leading supplier of applications software for the highly successful IBM AS/400 computer, a direct descendant of the System/38.
1987	PeopleSoft is founded by Dave Duffield and Ken Morris in 1987.
1988	PeopleSoft's Human Resource Management System (HRMS) is developed.
1990	Baan software is rolled out to 35 countries through indirect sales channels. The term ERP (Enterprise Resource Planning) is coined in the early 1990's when MRP-II is extended to cover areas like Engineering, Finance, Human Resources, and Project Management.
1991	PeopleSoft sets up offices in Canada. This leads the way to their presence in Europe, Asia, Africa, Central and South America, and the Pacific Rim.
1995	Baan grows to more than 1,800 customers worldwide and over 1,000 employees.
1999	JD Edwards has more than 4,700 customers with sites in over 100 countries. Oracle has 41,000 customers worldwide (16,000 U.S.). PeopleSoft software is used by more than 50 percent of the human resources market. **SAP is the world's largest inter-enterprise software company and the world's fourth largest independent software supplier overall. SAP employs over 20,500 people in more than 50 countries.** To date, more than 2,800 of Baan's enterprise systems have been implemented at approximately 4,800 sites around the world.
2000 and Beyond	Most ERP systems are enhancing their products to become "Internet Enabled" so that customers worldwide can have direct access to the supplier's ERP system.

Need of ERP

ERP Systems are growing very fast. ERP had growth very fast because of the following reasons.

- To enable improved business performance.
  - Cycle time reduction
  - Increased business agility
  - Inventory reduction
  - Order fulfillment improvement
- To support business growth requirements.
  - New products/product lines, new customers
  - Global requirements including multiple languages and currencies
- To provide flexible, integrated, real time decision time decision support.
  - Improve responsiveness across the organization
- To eliminate limitation in legacy systems.
  - Century dating issues
  - Fragmentation of data and processing

  - Inflexibility to change
  - Insupportable technologies.
- To take advantage of the unstamped mid-market.
  - Increased functionality at a reasonable cost
  - Client/Server open system technology
  - Vertical Market Solutions.

8.2 DEFINITION OF ERP

ERP is the acronym of Enterprise Resource Planning. ERP utilizes ERP software applications to improve the performance of organizations' resource planning, management control and operational control. ERP software is multi-module application software that integrates activities across functional departments, from product planning, parts purchasing, inventory control, product distribution, to order tracking. ERP software may include application modules for the finance, accounting and human resources aspects of a business.

8.3 ERP AS SYSTEM PERSPECTIVE

ERP, often like other IT and business concepts, are defined in many different ways. A sound definition should several purposes:

1. It answers the question of "what is ..."?
2. It provides a base for defining more detailed concepts in the field—ERP software, ERP systems, ERP implementation etc.
3. It provides a common ground for comparison with related concepts—CRM, SCM etc.
4. It helps answer the basic questions in the field—benefits of ERP, the causes of ERP failure etc.

A definition of ERP based on **Systems Theory** can server those purposes.

ERP is a system which has its goal, components, and boundary.

The Goal of an ERP System — The goal of ERP is to improve and streamline internal business processes, which typically requires reengineering of current business processes.

The Components of an ERP System — The components of an ERP system are the common components of a Management Information System (MIS).

- **ERP Software** — Module based ERP software is the core of an ERP system. Each software module automates business activities of a functional area within an organization. Common ERP software modules include product planning, parts purchasing, inventory control, product distribution, order tracking, finance, accounting and human resources aspects of an organization.
- **Business Processes** — Business processes within an organization falls into three levels — strategic planning, management control and operational control. ERP has been promoted as solutions for supporting or streamlining business processes at all levels. Much of ERP success, however, has been limited to the integration of various functional departments.
- **ERP Users** — The users of ERP systems are employees of the organization at all levels, from workers, supervisors, mid-level managers to executives.

- **Hardware and Operating Systems** — Many large ERP systems are UNIX based. Windows NT and Linux are other popular operating systems to run ERP software. Legacy ERP systems may use other operating systems.

The Boundary of an ERP System — The boundary of an ERP system is usually small than the boundary of the organization that implements the ERP system. In contrast, the boundary of supply chain systems and ecommerce systems extends to the organization's suppliers, distributors, partners and customers. In practice, however, many ERP implementations involve the integration of ERP with external information systems.

8.4 ERP SOFTWARE

Features of ERP Software

The general features which ERP software should have are:

- planning for investment protection
- guarantee of easy upgrade to new releases
- personalisable with its own tools
- compatible with future versions
- provision of a recovery method
- parameters for behavioural models
- maintenance contract

8.5 FUNCTIONAL MODULES OF ERP SOFTWARE

ERP software is made up of many software modules. Each ERP software module mimics a major functional area of an organization. Common ERP modules include modules for product planning, parts and material purchasing, inventory control, product distribution, order tracking, finance, accounting, marketing, and HR. Organizations often selectively implement the ERP modules that are both economically and technically feasible.

ERP Production Planning Module

In the process of evolution of manufacturing requirements planning (MRP) II into ERP, while vendors have developed more robust software for production planning, consulting firms have accumulated vast knowledge of implementing production planning module. Production planning optimizes the utilization of manufacturing capacity, parts, components and material resources using historical production data and sales forecasting.

ERP Purchasing Module

Purchase module streamline procurement of required raw materials. It automates the processes of identifying potential suppliers, negotiating price, awarding purchase order to the supplier, and billing processes. Purchase module is tightly integrated with the inventory control and production planning modules. Purchasing module is often integrated with supply chain management software.

ERP Inventory Control Module

Inventory module facilitates processes of maintaining the appropriate level of stock in a warehouse. The activities of inventory control involves in identifying inventory requirements, setting targets, providing replenishment techniques and options, monitoring item usages, reconciling the inventory balances, and reporting inventory status. Integration of inventory control module with sales, purchase, finance modules allows ERP systems to generate vigilant executive level reports.

ERP Sales Module

Revenues from sales are live blood for commercial organizations. Sales module implements functions of order placement, order scheduling, shipping and invoicing. Sales module is closely integrated with organizations' ecommerce websites. Many ERP vendors offer online storefront as part of the sales module.

ERP Market in Module

ERP marketing module supports lead generation, direct mailing campaign and more.

ERP Financial Module

Both for-profit organizations and non-profit organizations benefit from the implementation of ERP financial module. The financial module is the core of many ERP software systems. It can gather financial data from various functional departments, and generates valuable financial reports such balance sheet, general ledger, trail balance, and quarterly financial statements.

ERP HR Module

HR (Human Resources) is another widely implemented ERP module. HR module streamlines the management of human resources and human capitals. HR modules routinely maintain a complete employee database including contact information, salary details, attendance, performance evaluation and promotion of all employees. Advanced HR module is integrated with knowledge management systems to optimally utilize the expertise of all employees.

8.6 ERP SYSTEMS

ERP Systems - ERP Software, Business Processes, Users and Hardware from a systems perspective, the components of an ERP system are the common components of Management Information Systems (MIS) — software, business processes, users and hardware. AN ERP system is more than sum of its parts or components. Those components interact together to achieve a common goal — streamline and improve organizations' business processes.

ERP Software

ERP software applications are module-based. Each software module automates business processes within a functional department. ERP applications can be implemented and deployed module-by-module. Major ERP software modules cover the major functional areas of organizations. Common ERP modules include product planning module, parts and material purchasing module, inventory control module, product distribution module, order tracking module, finance module, accounting module, marketing module, and HR module. Organizations often selectively implement the ERP modules that match their business needs.

Reengineering of Business Processes

Anthony, R. A classifies organizational processes into three levels — strategic planning, management control and operational control. The driving force behind the acceptance of ERP was to streamline and automate enterprise-wide resource planning at strategic planning level. In reality, much of ERP success has been in facilitating operational coordination across departments. The success of ERP at strategic planning, management control calls for the integration of ERP with other enterprise applications and demand long term management commitment.

ERP Users

Following Anthony, R. A's classification of organizational processes, workers can be classified into 1) those who execute strategic planning, 2) those who perform managerial control, and 3) those who do operational control. Even though ERP applications have been mostly beneficial to the operational control, the users of a ERP system include workers from all levels of an organization.

Operating Systems for ERP

ERP software runs on various operating systems and hardware, from UNIX, Linux, Windows to mainframe. Since one organization may acquire ERP and other enterprise software from many different vendors, the requirements for running ERP applications are common — security, stability, scalability and open standards.

8.7 ERP SYSTEMS AND BUSINESS CONTINUITY MANAGEMENT

An ERP (Enterprise Resource Planning) system is a multi-module computer application which is designed to support all of the key activities of an enterprise in an integrated fashion. This includes managing the key elements of the supply chain operation — product planning, purchasing, production control, inventory control, interaction with suppliers and customers, delivery of customer service and keeping track of orders. It may also include HR modules which maintain a central database of the organisation's people, which is critical to production and staff scheduling functions, and to staff payments.

An ERP is regarded as central to an organisation's ambition to survive and prosper in today's business environment. It often replaces a myriad of individual systems including accounting systems, and production planning and inventory control systems. Its predecessor systems were often a mix of custom-built systems and package software. They frequently were based on a variety of computer hardware and software platforms and database management systems where significant work had been put into developing and managing the interfaces between them.

The use of ERP allows for greater efficiencies in many ways. It can be a much more effective way of providing computer support to the business functions. It is particularly relevant in the case of large complex businesses or where it is necessary to rationalise and integrate systems and operations in situations where mergers and acquisitions have given rise to a mixed bag of systems and computer platforms. It also allows for significantly greater efficiencies in managing the supply chain. Customers have become more dependent on faster delivery of product and tighter lead times. Safety stocks can almost disappear and JIT (just-in-time) philosophies dominate. In effect ERP has the effect of making an enterprise more time-sensitive and consequently more vulnerable to the impact of time delays.

While there are undoubted benefits, an ERP also poses significant challenges in the areas of information security and business continuity planning. For most businesses the implementation of an ERP is a major, complex project. As such it is not without its risks and this in itself is a business continuity issue. There are many examples of ERP projects that have gone wrong — failed, finished well over budget, or simply failed to achieve the benefits which were anticipated.

Prior to ERP a business tended to have multiple points of failure of computer-based systems and facilities. There were potential breakdowns with individual systems and with the many interfaces between systems. However there tended to be workarounds available and in some cases it was even possible to revert to manual procedures. With ERP there are fewer points of failure but if there is a failure the impact can be very significant. One of the major advantages of ERP is that it allows an organisation to totally redesign its operations rather than just computerise further the existing ways of doing things. This means that there is no real alternative available if problems arise. If it takes time to recover the implications can be very serious and business may grind to a halt. Production may stop, selling, inventory management and other key functions may find it impossible to continue. Time and production records may be unavailable and it may not even be possible to pay staff on schedule.

In the systems environment that tended to exist before ERP, a company's IT disaster recovery plan might allow for the recovery of different systems and databases at different times. Some could be recovered in parallel using different teams of computer support personnel but there would almost always be a priority sequence which aimed to restore the key systems and computer platforms first. With ERP the usual approach to recovery is to restore the environment as a whole and to have all systems modules available simultaneously.

Another factor which can impact on the recovery of ERP systems is the lack of sufficient in-house knowledge of the intricacies of the ERP. Because of the range of facilities available, and the resultant complexity inherent in an ERP, the detailed knowledge frequently resides with supplier personnel, consultants and freelance experts in the product who were involved in implementation and then moved on. Sometimes the knowledge transfer to in-house staff may be insufficient to provide adequate expertise when problems arise. In theory anyone should be able to effect a recovery from a business recovery plan regardless of who customised, built and implemented the system. With systems as complex and as integrated with the business processes as an ERP this may not always be the case. This should be considered early in the process of implementing an ERP and adequate time must be allowed in the implementation plan for documenting these aspects comprehensively.

Consider Business Continuity at the ERP Planning Stage

ERP implementation is an expensive exercise. Apart from the cost of the application and the hardware and software platforms a considerable amount of expensive input will be required from the suppliers and consultants in design, build, data loading, implementation and training activities. Despite the benefits that will be expected to accrue, the cost of installing such a system will be such that there may be a temptation to trim costs by omitting expenditure required to address the business continuity issues. It may be difficult to get board approval anyway without adding further to the bill. The attitude may be 'let's get it up and running and we can address the business continuity issues in the next phase'. The history of ERP implementations indicates that the budgets for this initial phase are often exceeded. Consequently it becomes more difficult to get money allocated to continuity aspects during subsequent phases.

Considering the vulnerability of the enterprise in the event of problems this is false economy. If left till the 'next phase' it will probably never happen. If planned and provided for from the start the costs are likely to be considerably less than when the facilities are provided later on.

There should be active involvement of the business continuity function from the planning stage onwards. Some of the benefits of this approach and the issues to be addressed in these phases of the project include:

- Potential outages can be considered and thought given to what alternative processes can be designed in at the same time.
- Resilience can be considered more realistically at the point when keeping the costs to a minimum is not the overriding viewpoint.
- How does the planned infrastructure meet the recovery requirements? For example if a SAN (storage area network) is involved have the recovery and resilience aspects been fully thought through?
- Will all of the eggs be in the one basket? Should the computer facilities be split over multiple sites? If this is done does it overcome the need to have arrangements for access to a business recovery site from a recovery facilities vendor?
- Sometimes the funding for recovery sites comes from a designated business continuity budget. This means that the project does not have to carry the costs but it can result in a greater overall cost. Like any other project the overall costs should include the cost of the continuity aspects.
- If there is only a single-site computer system how is it proposed to test and implement subsequent upgrades to the systems? Moving to new releases of an ERP system with significant new facilities can be a major issue.

The implementation of an ERP is usually associated with very tight and often immovable deadlines. For example it may be related to key activities happening during the holiday period or at a slack time of the year. It may be a question of having to have certain aspects of it live from the start of the financial year. In the headlong rush forward BCM issues can be sacrificed to more immediate and, at the time, more urgent tasks.

8.8 FORCE FUELLING ERP

There are three major forces behind ERP

1. **To integrate financial data.** As the CEO tries to understand the companies overall performance, he or she may find many different versions of the truth. Finance has its own set of revenue numbers, sales has another version, and the different business units may each have their own versions of how much they contributed to revenues. ERP creates a single version of the truth that cannot be questioned because everyone is using the same system.

   Instruments for Finance

   General ledger Keeps centralized charts of accounts and coorporate financial balances.

   Accounts receivable Tracks payments due to a company from its customers.

   Accounts payable Schedules bill payments to suppliers and distributors.

   Fixed assets Manages depreciation and other costs associated with tangible assets such as buildings, property and equipment.

   Treasury management Monitors and analyzes cash holdings, financial deals and investment risks.

Cost control Analyses coorporate costs related to overhead, products and manufacturing orders.

2. **To standardize manufacturing processes.** Manufacturing companies - especially those with an appetite for mergers and acquisitions - often find that multiple business units across the company make the same widget using different methods and computer systems. Standardizing those processes and using a single, integrated computer system can save time, increase productivity and reduce head count.
3. **To standardize Human Resource (HR) information.** Especially in companies with multiple business units, HR may not have a unified, simple method for tracking employee time and communicating with them about benefits and services. ERP can fix that. In the race to fix these problems, companies often lose sight of the fact that ERP packages are nothing more than generic representations of the ways a typical company does business. While most packages are exhaustively comprehensive, each industry has its quirks that make it unique. Most ERP systems were designed to be used by discrete manufacturing companies (who make physical things that can be counted), which immediately left all the process manufacturers (oil, chemical and utility companies that measure their products by flow rather than individual units) out in the cold. Each of these industries has struggled with the different ERP vendors to modify core ERP programs to their needs.

The important thing is not to focus on how long it will take, real transformational ERP efforts usually run between one to three years, on average - but rather to understand why you need it and how to use it to improve your business.

Instruments for Manufacturing and Logistics

Production planning Performs capacity planning and creates a daily production schedule for a company's manufacturing plants.

Materials management Controls purchasing of raw materials needed to build products. Manages inventory stocks.

Order entry and processing Automates the data entry process of customer orders and keeps track of the status of orders.

Warehouse management Maintains records of warehoused goods and processes movement of products through warehouses.

Transportation management Arranges, schedules and monitors delivery of products to customers via trucks, trains and other vehicles.

Project management Monitors costs and work schedules on a project-by-project basis.

Plant maintenance Sets plans and oversees upkeep of internal facilities. Customer

Service management Administers installed-base service agreements and checks contracts and warranties when customers call for help.

Instruments for Human Resources

Human resources administration Automates personnel management processes including recruitment, business travel and vacation allotments.

Payroll Handles accounting and preparation of checks related to employee, salaries, wages and bonuses.

Self-service HR Lets workers change their personal information and benefit allocations online without having to send forms to human resources.

8.9 THE COST OF ERP

Meta Group recently did a study looking at the Total Cost of Ownership (TCO) of ERP, including hardware, software, professional services, and internal staff costs. The TCO numbers include getting the software installed and the two years afterward, which is when the real costs of maintaining, upgrading and optimizing the system for your business are felt. Among the 63 companies surveyed — including small, medium and large companies in a range of industries – the average TCO was $15 million (the highest was $300 million and lowest was $400,000). While it's hard to draw a solid number from that kind of a range of companies and ERP efforts, Meta came up with one statistic that proves that ERP is expensive no matter what kind of company is using it. The TCO for a "heads-down" user over that period was a staggering $53,320. If you are willing to wait for it you will have pretty good payback — the Meta Group study found that it took eight months after the new system was in (31 months total) to see any benefits. But the median annual savings from the new ERP system was $1.6 million per year.

The challenge for ERP II is 2-fold. First it is to aggregate and manage the data surrounding all the transactions of an enterprise as accurately as possible in real time. Then it is to open up the system to make that information available to trading partners. ERP is all about sharing information and collaboration. Management is under constant pressure to improve competitiveness by lowering operating cost and improving logistics. Organizations therefore have to be more responsive to the customer and competition.

8.10 ADVANTAGES OF ERP

Faster inventory turnover	Without ERP, a business may turn over its inventory once or twice a year. With ERP to automate processes such as production planning and procurement, many manufacturers and distributors increase inventory turns by tenfold and reduce inventory costs by 10% to 40%. The result is significant reduction in inventory expense, as well as associated transportation, storage and warehousing costs. This, in turn, leads to better cash flow.
Improved customer service	To remain competitive, manufacturers are looking to improve their customer-order fulfillment rates. In many cases, an ERP system can increase fill rates to 80% or 90% by providing the information that allows the company to have the right product in the right place at the right time. The result is higher customer satisfaction and retention. Although it's hard to put a price on lost business, customers will take their business elsewhere if the products they want are not available when they need them.
Better inventory accuracy, fewer audits	Some manufacturers physically count inventory each month-in some cases, each weekend often have an inventory accuracy rate as low as 20%. An ERP system can increase inventory accuracy to more than 90%, while reducing the need for frequent physical audits. For many, a comprehensive physical inventory is not only costly in itself, but requires a temporary shutdown of business to count, tag and check stock.
Reduced setup times	Manufacturers often spend anywhere from one to three shifts setting up major pieces of production machinery. An ERP system can improve setup time by 25% to 80%-from days to a few hours by grouping similar production jobs together, ensuring coordination of people, tools and machinery, and planning for maximum equipment use and efficient machine maintenance to minimize downtime. Optimizing production in this manner translates into increased capacity, which means you can make more products with the same amount of machinery and people, thus increasing revenue and ROI without having to increase capital expenses.

Higher quality, less re-work	In some plants, re-work rates, because of unacceptable quality, may fall between 15% and 40% of production output. The production staff may not realize there is a problem until after the product has been manufactured. ERP software with a strong manufacturing component proactively pinpoints quality issues, providing the information needed to increase production efficiency and reduce or eliminate re-work.
Timely revenue collection, improved cash flow	Some companies take up to 90 days to collect on customer invoices. An ERP system can automatically generate a list of late paying customers, send notifications as needed, and "redflag" customers whose credit should be put on hold before more products are manufactured or shipped. ERP systems give manufacturers the power to proactively examine accounts receivable before significant problems occur, instead of merely reacting. Timely receivable equates to better cash flow, freeing up funds for the business to invest in revenue generating assets.

Need of ERP

ERP Systems are growing very fast. ERP had growth very fast because of the following reasons.

- To enable improved business performance.
  - Cycle time reduction
  - Increased business agility
  - Inventory reduction
  - Order fulfillment improvement
- To support business growth requirements.
  - New products/product lines, new customers
  - Global requirements including multiple languages and currencies
- To provide flexible, integrated, real time decision time decision support.
  - Improve responsiveness across the organization
- To eliminate limitation in legacy systems.
  - Century dating issues
  - Fragmentation of data and processing
  - Inflexibility to change
  - Insupportable technologies
- To take advantage of the unstamped mid — market.
  - Increased functionality at a reasonable cost
  - Client/Server open system technology
  - Vertical Market Solutions.

8.11 DISADVANTAGES OF ERP

When an ERP project fails, the finger pointing often begins with the software. But in many cases a lack of planing prior to implementation and unrealistic expectations are the real points behind an unsuccessful ERP execution. "We find companies are buying the software but they really don't know what there doing with it" says Barry Levine, practice leader at Toronto-based Richter Consulting Group.

The companies install their ERP projects like:

The Big Bang: In this, the most ambitious and difficult of approaches to ERP implementation, companies cast off all their legacy systems at once and implement a single ERP system across the entire company.

Franchising strategy: This approach suits large or diverse companies that do not share many common processes across business units. Independent ERP systems are installed in each unit, while linking common processes, such as financial book keeping, across the enterprise.

This has emerged as the most common way of implementing ERP.

Slam-dunk: ERP dictates the process design in this method, where the focus is on just a few key processes, such as those contained in an ERP system's financials module. The slam-dunk is generally for smaller companies expecting to grow into ERP.

The goal here is to get ERP up and running quickly and to ditch the fancy reengineering in favor of the ERP system's "canned" processes.

8.12 COMMON MYTHS OF ERP

The first myth is that ERP is a computer system. Yes, computers and IT are integral part of an ERP system; but ERP is primarily an enterprise — wide system, which encompasses cooperate mission, objectives, attributes, beliefs, values, operating style, and people who makes the organization.

The second myth is that ERP is for manufacturing organizations alone. This assumption is basically due to the way in which ERP was historically developed from the methods of Material Requirement Planning (MRP) and Manufacturing Resource Planning (MRP II). But now ERP is not limited to any particular segment of Industry, it is a integration of many modules like Strategic and operational planning, manufacturing, material management, quality management, sales and distribution, maintenance management, logistics management, human resources, finance.

EXERCISE

1. What is ERP?
2. Write a note on history of ERP.
3. Describe need of ERP.
4. Describe ERP as System Perspective.
5. What are the Features of Erp Software?
6. Describe Functional Modules of ERP Software.
7. Describe Reengineering of Business Processes.
8. Describe ERP Users.
9. Describe Operating Systems for ERP.
10. Describe ERP systems and business continuity management.
11. What are the Forces Fuelling ERP?
12. Describe the Cost of ERP.
13. What are the advantages of ERP?
14. What are the disadvantages of ERP?
15. What are the Common myths of ERP?

9

Customer Relationship Management

Every company wants to secure long term, mutually beneficial relationships with its customers. This is the goal of Customer Relationship Management, or CRM. Technology, in the form of networked collaboration, communication, knowledge management and automated electronic processes can enable different groups within the company to work seamlessly as one unit to fulfil the CRM vision. The accepted definition of CRM technology is generally accepted to apply to "front office" processes - but the true philosophy of CRM applies to everyone in the company.

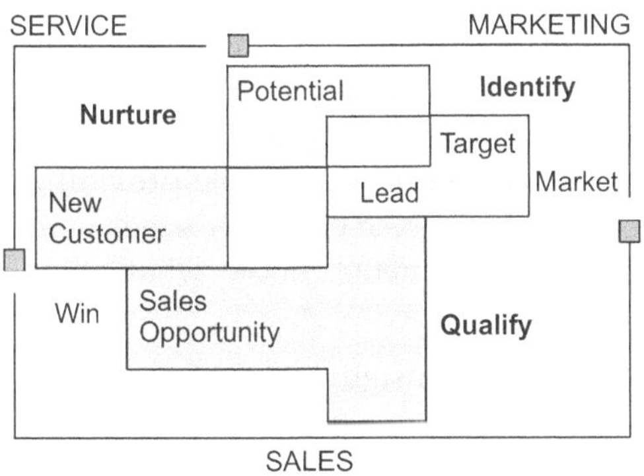

The diagram shows how business processes flow between the three core "customer facing" functions of marketing, sales and after sales service. The complete cycle of locating potential customers, selling them your product, and ensuring their satisfaction throughout the lifetime of the product can be referred to as the "customer acquisition and retention loop".

9.0 INTRODUCTION

Customer Relationship Management (CRM) solutions provide customer-oriented services for planning, developing, maintaining, and expanding customer relationships, with special attention paid to the new possibilities offered by the Internet, mobile devices, and multi-channel interaction. CRM enables a company to capture a consolidated customer view through multi-channel interactions in a data warehouse solution.

Sophisticated analytical techniques are then applied to this customer information to better understand and predict customer behaviour. CRM can then be used to strategically implement acquired customer knowledge in every area of the company, from the highest management level to all employees who come into direct contact with customers. CRM thus enables an organisation to address its customers' preferences and priorities much more effectively and efficiently. CRM is a tool that can help organisations to profitably meet the lifetime needs of customers better than their competitors.

9.1 DEFINITIONS

Customer Relationship Management (CRM) is the practice of using information gathered through customer interaction to strengthen the relationship a company has with that customer. First and foremost, CRM should be thought of as a business process and long-term strategy of maintaining product or service value. **Ryan Mayberry, Metrex Internet Solutions**

Customer relationship management (CRM) creates a comprehensive picture of customer needs, expectations and behaviors by analyzing information from every customer transaction. CRM creates the customer intelligence necessary to develop customer relationships. (**www.bettermanagement.com**)

CRM stands for **Customer Relationship Management**. It is a process or methodology used to learn more about customers' needs and behaviors in order to develop stronger relationships with them. There are many technological components to CRM, but thinking about CRM in primarily technological terms is a mistake. The more useful way to think about CRM is as a process that will help bring together lots of pieces of information about customers, sales, marketing effectiveness, responsiveness and market trends.

CRM (customer relationship management) is an information industry term for methodologies, software, and usually Internet capabilities that help an enterprise manage customer relationships in an organized way. For example, an enterprise might build a database about its customers that described relationships in sufficient detail so that management, salespeople, people providing service, and perhaps the customer directly could access information, match customer needs with product plans and offerings, remind customers of service requirements, know what other products a customer had purchased, and so forth.

CRM helps businesses use technology and human resources to gain insight into the behavior of customers and the value of those customers.

CRM is short for Customer Relationship Management, the industry term for the set of methodologies and tools that help an enterprise manage customer relationships in an organized way.

Thus, CRM Involves:

- Automating processes in sales, marketing, and service functions.
- Increasing the efficiency of these processes to improve customer satisfaction.
- Conducting interactions with customers on a more informed basis.
- Individually tailoring interactions to suit the specific customer's needs.
- Compiling information that increases understanding of customer behaviour and then analysing the acquired information to generate customer intelligence that can be used by the marketing function to find brand new customers, retain existing customers, and cultivate a deeper share of wallet from all customers.

The ability of a CRM solution to measure, predict, and optimise customer relationships is directly proportional to the quality and comprehensiveness of the information provided to the analytical solutions. Hence, the integrated enterprise application software solutions of today incorporate a data warehouse to bring together data from enterprise resource planning (ERP), supply chain management (SCM), product lifecycle management (PLM), and customer relationship management (CRM) systems. This also enables the companies to improve on their key performance indicators (KPIs) for the entire supply chain.

Basic Objectives

The basic objectives of customer relationship management are:

- Extending/widening customer relationships—This involves acquiring new and profitable customers, which, in turn, requires the company to determine the following:
- Products and services of interest to the potential customers that can be supplied by the company.
- Type of customers that will contribute to the profitability and long-term growth of the company.
- Lengthening relationships with existing customers—This involves focusing on profitable customers to retain them. Recently, companies have shifted their focus from individual transactions to designing their market offerings and prices to make a profit over the customer's lifetime. This means that company will sometimes underprice to gain new customers and it will be generous in its pricing and services to existing customers with an eye toward retaining them for the long run. This requires the company to determine the following:
- Customers that make significant contribution to profits and hence should be retained.
- Customers that might leave (churn out) because they are not satisfied with the company's products and/or services or, because they have started to find the competitors' products and services more attractive.

The emphasis traditionally has been on pre-selling and selling rather than caring for the customer afterward. A highly satisfied customer stays loyal longer, buys more new products and upgrades, talks favourably about the company to the prospects, is less sensitive to price, offers ideas for new product and service to the company, and costs less to serve than new customers.

- Deepening customer relationships—This involves transforming unimportant (less profitable, short-term) customers into highly profitable, long-term business partners. This, in turn, requires the company to determine the following:
- Customers whose share of wallet can be and should be increased. Share of wallet is the ratio of the expenditure of a customer on a specific product group with a specific supplier to the total expenditure of that customer on that specific product group.
- The opportunities for up-selling and/or cross-selling additional products and services that would be of interest to customers.

CRM also enables a company to keep customer information consistent throughout the organisation and makes it available across all touch-points where the company interacts with the customer.

CRM can be described as a Web-enabled sales and marketing tool that synergistically combines the functionalities of database marketing, one-to-one marketing, and sales force automation (SFA). CRM enables companies to provide excellent real-time customer service by developing a relationship with each valued customer through the effective use of individual account information. CRM holds that a major driver of company profitability is the aggregate lifetime value of the company's customer base.

How CRM Works

CRM employs the following steps of database and one-to-one marketing:

- Identify prospects and customers: One of the ways companies can generate sales leads is by advertising their products or services through advertisements that include a response feature, such as a business reply card or toll-free phone number. The database is built from these responses. The database can be sorted to identify the best prospects, who can then be contacted by mail, phone, or personal call in an attempt to convert them into customers.
- Differentiate customers in terms of their requirements and their lifetime value to the company. Lifetime value can be used to decide how much the company can invest to build relationships with a particular customer. The company might decide to invest in the customer to retain him and thus reduce the rate of customer defection (churn) or to turn low-profit customers into more profitable ones by increasing the longevity of the customer relationship and/or by enhancing the growth potential of each customer through cross-selling, up-selling, and increased share of wallet.
- Interact with individual customers to improve learning about their individual needs and to build stronger relationships.
- Customise products and services and personalise all communications with each individual customer

Potential benefits and cost of CRM to an organization and customers

	To the Organization	To the Customer
CRM benefits	• Increased revenue through acquisition of new customers, retaining existing customers, and increased share of wallet through up-selling, cross-selling, etc. • Reduced costs—The ability to differentiate between customers on the basis of their long-term profitability helps the organization to plan better, cost-effective marketing strategies to derive better returns on marketing investments. Automation of many services and ability to provide many services as self-services further reduces the cost.	• The continuity derived from a relationship with the same seller results in a simplified buying process and reduction in customer's perceived risk. This, in turn, increases the feeling of safety and comfort. • CRM provides more avenues for customers to communicate and explain their needs to the organization through numerous contact points. • Customers get increased satisfaction and a feeling of being special and important because of the increased personalization of services and customization of goods offered to them.
CRM costs	• CRM requires the organization to make significant investments in IT infrastructure. • The organization has to incur the cost of process change arising out of alteration in the habitual pattern of accomplishing tasks. Employees find it far easier to carry on traditional transaction marketing. The company might need to spend significant amount of efforts to make employees adapt to CRM.	• Possible or inevitable loss of privacy. Many customers don't want a company to collect and store information about them. Online companies must disclose their privacy policies to the customers and give them the right not to have their information stored in a database. • Opportunity cost associated with ignoring other offers from competitive sources-once a habit is formed most customers would refrain from exerting the effort to assess the options and prices offered by others.

9.2 CRM SOFTWARE

Sales Force Automation

- **Contact management:** Contact management software stores, tracks and manages contacts, leads of an enterprise.
- **Lead management:** Enterprise lead management software enables an organization to manage, track and forecast sales leads. Also helps understand and improve conversion rates.

9.3 ECRM OR WEB BASED CRM

The Internet Revolution is over. Revolutions are gateways that take us through a gauntlet of change — from old world to the new — often in an accelerated and brutal manner. When a revolution is over, its survivors face not only the challenging task of building and sustaining the new world, but also a vast array of new opportunities.

The new economy has begun. Today, the Internet is a given, the web is a significant economic and social force, and e-mail is the predominant form of written business communication. The new economy has brought more than just technological change to the business world. The Internet revolution was really about people — customers — and the fundamental shift of market power from the seller to buyer. In the new economy, customer's expectations are very different than before. A company's understanding of this difference and its ability to capitalize on it will be the key to its success.

The first paradigm shift from Old Economy to New Economy primarily addressed the mechanics of business operations and supporting technologies. The second paradigm shift - and the one that many businesses fail to make — addresses the relationship between businesses and the customers they serve; that is the shift from customer relationship management to eCRM. This article discusses this new paradigm — eCRM.

What is eCRM?

eCRM uses the electronic media to integrate and simplify customer-related business processes, drastically reducing costs of customer-facing operations while achieving CRM's primary goal: to enhance the customer experience. It ensures that a company's various divisions share a single view of the customer, and that the customers get a single view of the company.

eCRM derives from CRM techniques, which leveraged call center and direct marketing technology to market mass-produced goods and services to small market sub-segments. eCRM expands on this technology by using next generation segmentation and analysis technologies, comprehensive customer interaction data, multi-channel communications and one-to-one interactions to market customized products and services to ever-more precise segments.

Why eCRM?

More competitors. Shorter product life cycles. An explosion of new technologies. New distribution channels. These are some of the primary factors that are driving companies to focus on customer relationship strategies.

Shorter product life cycles have robbed companies from enjoying the sustained financial benefits of being product innovators. Not only can competitors bring copycat products to market quicker, new generations of products are introduced much more quickly.

New technologies have changed the way organizations operate and produce, enabling new competitors to emerge virtually overnight. Technology has also led to "pink pill" syndrome. Technology vendors have been over promising and under delivering; organizations have taken their fill of pink pills and now need to determine how to create effective solutions.

There has also been an explosion of new technology-driven channels to reach the customer. Organizations must figure out how to effectively integrate the telephone, the Internet, branch offices, mobile sales, kiosks, ATMs, interactive TV, wireless and related options with conventional outreach methods to build customer loyalty.

In a cost cutting model, organizations could trim the expense side without growing the revenue side to achieve financial goals. But this can only work short-term until all the fat has been cut. Eventually, profitability objectives must be met by growing revenues. Another challenge facing firms is how to grow the business and generate revenue, while maintaining a reasonable expense model. This is no simple task. These factors are driving companies to focus on Customer Relationship Management.

Traditionally, companies have focused on winning, rather than retaining, customers. A dominating market share typically translated into production economies of scale and the ability to become a low cost producer. The goal was to continually feed the funnel with additional customers, grow market share, and replace those customers who defected to competitors. Many researchers have established that it can cost four to ten times more to replace current customers than it does to keep one. This again highlights the importance of eCRM. A study published in Harvard Business Review by Reicheld & Sasser concluded:

Some companies can boost profits by almost

100% by retaining just 5% more of their customers.

Why is there so much customer turnover anyway?

In most industries product differentiation is disappearing. Technological innovations can be quickly copied. Customer ties to products are weaker because many substitutes are available. However, service differentiation is one area where it is possible to lock in a customer, and a competitive advantage.

Industry analysts have reported that 70% of repeat purchases are made out of indifference, not out of loyalty. The implications are profound. A significant portion of customers may be vulnerable to competitive marketing programs and underscores the need to strengthen customer loyalty. Today, customer-focused companies are beginning to tie traditional product— based strategies with new customer relationship—based strategies to impact customer loyalty.

eLoyalty Matrix

The eLoyalty Matrix, an economic model developed at eLoyalty, shows that turnover is greatest with customers who are dissatisfied with the relationship they have with the company. By coupling relationship and product strategies, organizations can effectively create customer loyalty.

The key is to focus on the customer's relationship with the company. Even though Customers C and D both had poor product experiences, Customer D's willingness to continue a relationship with the company dramatically differs from the behavior of the Saboteur.

By combining the notions of Customer Value with Customer Loyalty, it is possible to enhance relationship equity, leading to greater customer referencability and customer forgiveness. Also, it lays the foundation for a market segment where it is easier to introduce new products and services.

The five engines of eCRM

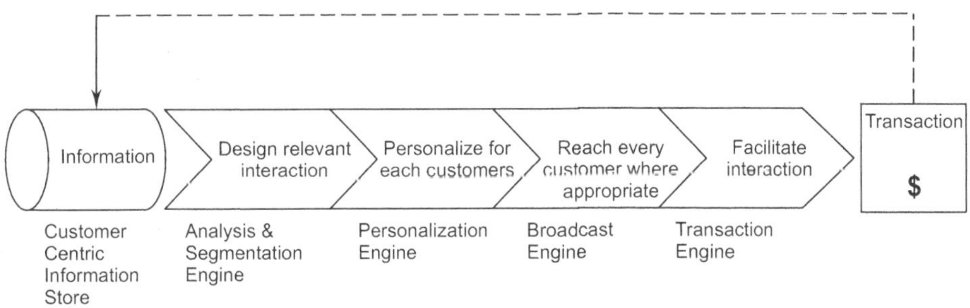

Fig. 9.2. *Five engines together provide the platform for an eCRM business process. Without these five engines, eCRM is not a scalable, defensible business proposal practice for a company.*

The Customer Centric Information Store

A unified view of every customer

eCRM initiatives depend on a 360-degree customer view. A Customer-centric Information Store integrates data from disparate information sources such as web sites, transactional systems, and operational databases, call centers, enterprise resource planning systems and third party data. This engine enables companies to recognize and respond accurately to customers, whether they purchase products through a physical store; telephone a call center, or browse a web site. Consequences of an incomplete customer view are often harsh. Presenting customers with inappropriate offers, diluting loyalty and trust, stall eCRM efforts.

Such an Information Store should be scalable, flexible and give high performance. Effectively applied, the Customer-centric Information store decreases customer attrition rates and improves retention. Over time, the Customer-centric Information Store forms an inventory of customer trust and loyalty, becoming a valuable corporate asset and giving an enterprise, a source of competitive advantage.

The Analysis and Segmentation Engine

Building trusted customer relationships depends on accurate customer segmentation. The Analysis and Segmentation Engine performs business analysis, segmentation and prediction so that customer interactions take place in an appropriate and personalized manner. Without this engine, eCRM lacks the intelligence to be effective - even if it has massive volumes of customer-centric information.

The Personalization Engine

A Personalization Engine makes it possible to personalize products and services for customers in a cost-effective manner, by lowering the marginal cost of personalization. Until now, personalized attention and service were labor intensive and not scalable to serve a large customer base without high costs. Most companies provide personalized attention to a small group of clients who are "worth it". Today, every Amazon.com customer gets personal recommendations for books due to Amazon's personalization technology. The addition of thousands of customers to Amazon's base has a minimal effect on their cost to sustain this high level of service. This "scalable" personalization is unprecedented in business history — personalization that relies on static information about customer transactions.

The Broadcast Engine

The Broadcast Engine—enabling 24/7 customer interactions

Continuous customer interaction and value exchange require 24/7 access to customers. While the web is becoming increasingly pervasive, few customers are on line all day. However, they are increasingly reachable through other communication devices. A recent META Group study projects that the average number of communication devices per consumer will quadruple in the next three years. This is not just a consumer phenomenon but a business shift as well. Corporate use of wireless technology will quadruple in the next three years. Successful eCRM requires an engine that reaches mil-lions of customers wherever they are: at home, via phone or TV set-top box, at work - via email, or on the road via WAP phone or pager. A scalable Broadcast Engine that is built on an open architecture and supports all communication devices enables this level of customer interaction.

The Transaction Engine

Interactions lead to trusted relationships

An effective Transaction Engine promotes information exchange between every customer and the enterprise. Like the small town shopkeeper who often conversed with his customers, the

Transaction Engine maintains customer contact and transmits information to the Customer-centric Information Store for later use. Leveraging the other four eCRM Engines, the Transaction Engine develops informed life-long customer relationships.

What does it all mean?

Achieving eCRM is not an end in itself — it is a means to success. The vehicle for the journey being the Internet.

As the competition for customer loyalty has grown more intense, the need for a comprehensive Analytical eCRM solution has increased. Businesses are allocating millions of dollars to eCRM software solutions, but the ROI on such packaged applications varies widely. The investment in such solutions is more than financial. Technology is never a substitute for a sound business model and a real market opportunity. The smart businesspersons know that it's the understanding of customer needs; the satisfaction of those needs, and the relationship that ensues that makes business successful. The principles of eCRM are not very different from that that your great-grandfather might have followed when he ran his shop or office in 1900. The infrastructure may have changed but the relationship between the business and the customers has not changed a lot.

- **Self Service CRM:** Self service CRM (eCRM) software Enables web based customer interaction, automation of email, call logs, web site analytics, campaign management.
- **Survey Management Software:** Survey Software automates an enterprise's Electronic Surveys, Polls, Questionnaires and enables understand customer preferences.

Customer Service

- Call Center Software
- Help Desk Software

Partner Relationship Management

- Contract Management Software

  Contract Management Software enables an enterprise to create, track and manage partnerships, contracts, agreements.

  Example: Upside Software, Accruent Software, diCarta, I-Many.
- Distribution Management Software

Who uses it? From small enterprises to multinational corporations, any business that maintains regular interaction with customers benefits from a well organized CRM system.

9.4 KEY FEATURES OF CRM TOOLS

CRM includes all business processes in sales, marketing, and service that touch the customer. With CRM software tools, an enterprise might build a database about its customers that describes relationships in sufficient detail so that management, salespeople, people providing service, and even the customer can access information, match customer needs with product plans and offerings, remind customers of service requirements, check payment histories, and so on.

9.5 ISSUES IN CUSTOMER RELATION MANAGEMENT

Anyone evaluating a CRM technology must consider the same 10 points to make it successful. In determining an approach on the first — Company Goals and Strategy — the others may no longer apply, but if questions remain, considering these 10 points will remove any doubts:

1. Company Goals and Strategy
2. Web-based, Client side/ Hosted or on premise
3. Budget and Total Cost of Ownership
4. Scalability and Room to Grow
5. Rapid Deployment
6. Customized for your Business Needs
7. Works with Existing Systems
8. Vendor Reputation, Product Reliability
9. User Interface Meets User Needs - Usability
10. Functionality

Company Goals and Strategy — First and Foremost

In choosing a CRM solution that meets the individual needs of a company, there are multiple factors to be considered. CRM solutions are not all created equal, and the challenges facing a small to medium business (SMB) in meeting their customer's demands are sure to be very different than those a multi-billion dollar enterprise encounters. A telecommunications company with offices in hundreds of cities will likely not have the same requirements a small retailer from the mid-west has. However, many people fail to consider the business objective as the first thought that should go into choosing a CRM technology.

As the most important factor to take into consideration when evaluating a CRM solution, business objectives are sometimes overlooked as the technology's capabilities become a primary focus. The challenge is not in defining your company's IT strategy but in clearly defining the business objectives and then mapping the IT strategy to these goals.

Are the company's growth objectives clearly defined? What is the company's primary objective? To increase revenue, then how? Does access to real-time analytics impact decisions that could drive the business? Do customers interact mainly with customer service reps via phone or email? Is self service an important feature that needs to be manged via the Internet? Is there a corporate goal to integrate your applications across the organization to use information from varied programs to drive revenue opportunites? Is the ability to integrate with mobile phones to provide salespeople with the necessary tool they need when they're on the road critical to your business needs?

The decision to choose a CRM solution needs to be a business decision first and foremost. Once the business goals are defined other aspects — primarliy the capabilities of the technology - can be considered, if there is more than one solution that might fit the business objectives.

Web-based, Client Side/ Hosted or on Premise

In-house or hosted solutions each offer advantages. Hosted CRM solutions are typically thought of as easy to implement, secure and accessible. However, if your employees will not have regular internet access, online CRM software may not be feasible.

If you are looking for a solution that easily integrates with your back-office and third-party applications as part of a strategy to integrate your applications across the organization, you might consider an in-house solution.

A large business that already has an on-premise CRM solution may decide that a hosted solution is the perfect way to rapidly extend their CRM capabilities to a remote division. Or, a small but fast-growing organization may choose a hosted CRM solution that allows it to gain quick access to market-leading CRM features and functionality without having to invest up front in hardware or software.

If you have an internal IT department that can suppport the solution, an on-premise solution allows for customized features and other advantages. The benefits each of these alternatives brings to the company should map to your business goals and strategy.

Budget and TCO

If the business goals have been defined appropraitely, another consideration is in attributing a budget to the solution. The lowest initial cost should not be the only factor in a decision as the upfront costs only make up a portion of the overall investment. Only an estimated 30 percent of a CRM solution's costs can be attributed to the initial software purchase; the remaining 70 percent goes to:

- Customization
- Integration
- Maintenance
- Deployment
- Training
- Upgrades

Unless these costs are accounted for in advance, the company opting for a 'bargain' application is very likely to be shocked with a higher than anticipated total cost of ownership. The result is often a failed deployment. Budget and TCO often play a large part of the decision making process.

Scalability and Room to Grow without Repeated Upgrades

Pending your growth strategy, planning for future growth with a scalable product can be critical. SMB's in particular do not want to spend time developing and deploying software; they want to use it. Choosing a vendor that will make the enhancement process painless can help while selecting a system with a consistent and readily upgradeable architecture, should also factor into your decision. A well-defined, well-documented and proven roadmap to accommodate growth is a minimum requirement. Vendors that stand by their products never abandon their legacy customers, and depending on your objectives, the ability to add more employees may impact a decision.

Rapid Deployment

The average deployment of an in-house CRM solution is between three to six months, whereas the average deployment of a hosted CRM solution is a few weeks (in some cases users can start using the service in real-time as soon as they sign up). The speed of deployment of a hosted CRM solution often speaks to the midmarket company, which is concerned with keeping costs down, while making the best technological investments for its business needs, but the solution they get will most likely not be "robust". Deployment may halt the company's direction for time and for a smaller business this could be critical. Determining if the length of deployment will impact the business can determine of a solution is right for you.

Customized for your Business Needs

Varied industries have solutions that are customized for the specific vertical initially, and then some are able to be easily adapted further for minimal cost. If there is a specific need that is critical to the overall company objectives, a tailored solution might be the answer.

Works with Existing Systems

Rather than pulling out existing systems or requiring employees to adopt multiple new technologies at one time and threatening the success of the CRM implementation, choosing a system that work with your existing infrastructure can be critical. Choosing a CRM tool that pulls data from legacy programs or allows back office information to be used in better servicing the customer are something else to consider in your choice.

Vendor Reputation, Product Reliability

Choosing a reputable vendor with a reliable product is a factor for consideration as well. Consolidation in the market has been active in the past few years and promises to continue as does the struggle some smaller less stable companies have as they continue to fold. Choosing a vendor that will continue to be viable years from now and provide continued service can impact your decision as well.

User Interface Meets User Needs

Find out if your employees can learn the software, use it efficiently, and whether or not it adds to productivity. If the CRM solution is too complicated or is deployed without proper training, users tend to not use the solution because they don't know how to use it. Don't be afraid to evaluate multiple vendors and CRM solutions until you find the best fit. Any CRM software vendor who really wants your business will offer a free trial or evaluation. This lets you integrate the software, test its features and determine if a solution will be used.

Functionality

If the decision is not apparent at this stage, the extra features and functionalities can help a final choice. Generation of usable graphs and charts from the analytics the program provides might be a few steps easier with one product or the steps to click through a function make be quicker with one vendor. However, it's likely that additional functionality decisions may not be necessary after a company's business objectives are clearly defined and an appropriate solution mapped to fit.

9.6 GOALS OF CRM

Every company wants to secure long term, mutually beneficial relationships with its customers. This is the goal of Customer Relationship Management, or CRM. Technology, in the form of networked collaboration, communication, knowledge management and automated electronic processes can enable different groups within the company to work seamlessly as one unit to fulfil the CRM vision. The accepted definition of CRM technology is generally accepted to apply to "front office" processes - but the true philosophy of CRM applies to everyone in the company.

The diagram shows how business processes flow between the three core "customer facing" functions of marketing, sales and after sales service. The complete cycle of locating potential customers, selling them your product, and ensuring their satisfaction throughout the lifetime of the product can be referred to as the "customer acquisition and retention loop".

Apart from processes, the CRM technology mandates that all interactions between the customer and the company are recorded and stored in a central information database, which can be shared with anyone in the company who contributes to processing the customer's transaction. The three core functions of marketing, sales and service seamlessly contribute to and use the same database of information.

In summary, the two principle ways that technology fulfils the vision of CRM are through the streamlining of processes and the acquisition of information to form knowledge about the customer.

The business process flow from marketing to sales to service follows this pattern:

Marketing — campaigns to search out possible new purchasers for the company's product or service (these could be totally new or even repeat customers). After identifying contacts with serious requirements, marketing hands over these "sales opportunities" to the sales department. Technology assists the marketing process by assisting in marketing plans, automating marketing campaigns, measuring the results and much, much more.

Sales — is responsible to turn the sales opportunity into a won order against the competition. Here the complete scope of selling strategy and tactics will come into play. Technology assists in the sales process by freeing the salesperson from much of the burden of administration and also by assisting in the strategies of the sales process itself. Once a sale is won, the new customer is passed to the group responsible for after-sales service.

After-Sales Service — Customers won't rush to buy from you again unless they were thoroughly satisfied the first time around. It is the job of after-sales service to ensure that the customer is happy — does the product do what it is supposed to? - if not, fix it. Did we meet our commitment of performance? Dependent on the industry, service can take many forms. Therefore the technology solution to automating the service function has to be flexible enough to handle many differing requirements. Overall, service automation contributes to the recording and resolution of all customer issues, together with measuring the company's performance at fixing problems in a timely fashion. The lessons learned are invaluable in determining new strategies that can lead to improvement and further customer satisfaction.

EXERCISE

1. Define Customer Relationship Management.
2. What are the basic objectives of customer relationship management?
3. Describe CRM Software.
4. What is eCRM?
5. Describe Key Features of CRM Tools.
6. Describe Issues in Customer relation Management.
7. What are the Goals of CRM?

10

INTRODUCTION TO SUPPLY CHAIN MANAGEMENT

10.0 INTRANET AND SUPPLY CHAIN MANAGEMENT

One of the most exciting trends today is the use of World Wide Web and Intranets in managing the supply chains. Supply chain management—the means by which firms engaged in creating, distributing, and selling products could join forces to establish a supply network with an unbeatable competitive advantage-has emerged as one of the most powerful business-improvement tools around. Companies all over the world are pursuing supply chain as the latest methodology to reduce costs, increase customer satisfaction, better utilize assets, and build new revenues. In this fiercely competitive environment, the gap between firms that are succeeding and those that aren't is rapidly expanding. In Advanced Supply Chain Management, leading expert Charles Poirier presents the four levels of accomplishment that separate the successful firms from the "wannabes." He details these four levels, from the beginning stages to the most advanced techniques and processes. Each level is described in detail so a firm can calibrate itself and determine what work remains to be done to close the gap.

A *supply chain* is a network of facilities and distribution options that performs the functions of procurement of materials, transformation of these materials into intermediate and finished products, and the distribution of these finished products to customers. Supply chains exist in both service and manufacturing organizations, although the complexity of the chain may vary greatly from industry to industry and firm to firm.

Supply chain management has emerged as the new key to productivity and competitiveness of manufacturing and service enterprises. The importance of this area is shown by a significant spurt in research in the last five years and also proliferation of supply chain solutions and supply chain companies (*e.g.*, i2, Manugistics, etc.). All major ERP companies are now offering supply chain solutions as a major extended feature of their ERP packages.

Supply chain management is a major application area for Internet Technologies and Electronic Commerce (ITEC). In fact, advances in ITEC have contributed to growing importance of supply chain management and SCM in turn has contributed to many advances in ITEC.

10.1 FUNDAMENTALS OF SUPPLY CHAIN MANAGEMENT

10.1.1 History of Supply Chain Management

The concept of SCM is not new; it has evolved over the past thirty-five years. In the 1970s, business focused on very specific functions in the supply chain. They wanted to improve manufacturing, or they were focused on sales and marketing or on distribution. With the advent of the 1980s, business realized that integrating all facts of their enterprise could increase productivity and margins. In the 1990s, business realized that product excellence alone fails to guarantee success. In fact, customers except many services including the prompt delivery of products to precise locations, with near – perfect on-time delivery and physical quantity.

10.1.2 Definitions of Supply Chain Management

A Supply Chain is a network of supplier, manufacturing, assembly, distribution, and logistics facilities that perform the functions of procurement of materials, transformation of these materials into intermediate and finished products, and the distribution of these products to customers. Supply chains arise in both manufacturing and service organizations. Supply Chain Management (SCM) is a systems approach to managing the entire flow of information, materials, and services from raw materials suppliers through factories and warehouses to the end customer. SCM is different from SUPPLY MANAGEMENT, which emphasizes only the buyer-supplier relationship.

10.1.3 Pull Versus Push Supply Chain Management

The consumer need based business model is given in the below given figure, which shows the push versus pull models of SCM in a retail environment. In the more traditional "push" model, the merchandise is pushed into the customer's hands. In the pull model, the customer actually initiates the supply chain. This is also called a demand – driven model. As the consumer moves through the supermarket checkout, the scanner picks up the exact detail of his/her purchases. These transactions are used to trigger product deliveries from the distribution depots. Further data aggregations at the distribution depots are signed back to the manufacturers preparing their next deliveries to replenish the depot. The manufacturer's production programs are simultaneously updated to take account of the delivery schedules and their purchasing schedules are adjusted accordingly, so that the raw material suppliers alter their own delivery plans. Often, all this happens before the customer has signed his/her credit card slip and left the store.

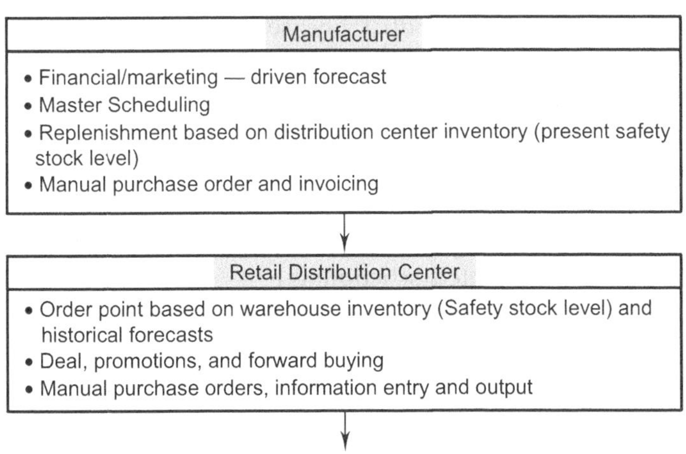

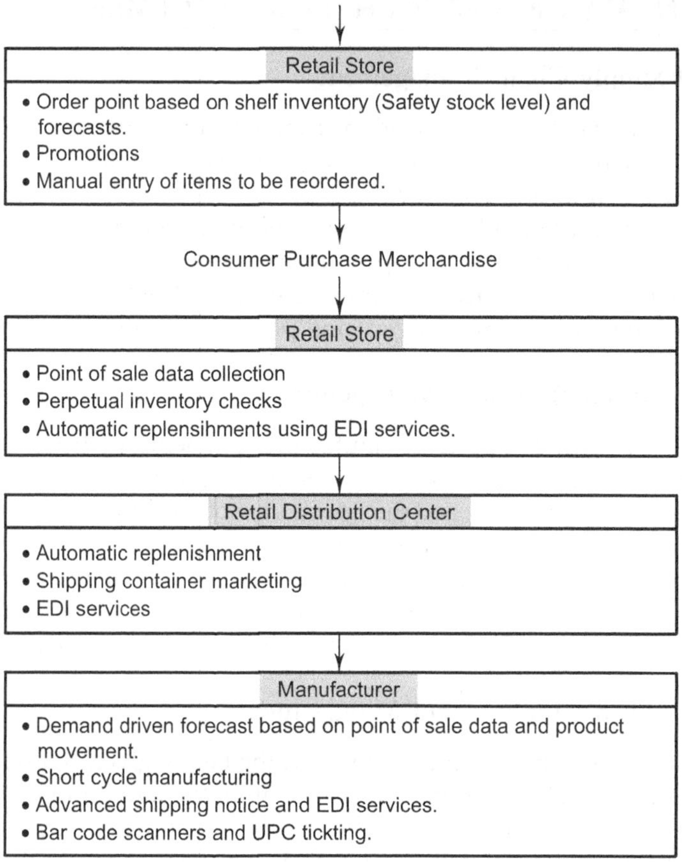

10.1.4 Faces of Supply Chain Management

SCM has two major faces to it. The first can be called loosely as the back-end and comprises the physical building blocks such as the supply facilities, production facilities, warehouses, distributors, retailers, and logistics facilities. The back-end essentially involves production, assembly, and physical movement. Major decisions here include:

1. **Procurement** (supplier selection, optimal procurement policies, etc.)
2. **Manufacturing** (plant location, product line selection, capacity planning, production scheduling, etc.)
3. **Distribution** (warehouse location, customer allocation, demand forecasting, inventory management, etc.)
4. **Logistics** (selection of logistics mode, selection of ports, direct delivery, vehicle scheduling, etc.)
5. **Global Decisions** (product and process selection, planning under uncertainty, real-time monitoring and control, integrated scheduling.)

Stochastic models (Markov chains, queueing networks), optimization models (LP, ILP, MILP, heuristics), and simulation provide the basis for the above decisions.

The second face (which can be called the front-end) is where IT and ITEC play a key role. This face involves processing and use of information to facilitate and optimize the back-end operations.

Key technologies here include: EDI (for exchange for information across different players in the supply chain); Electronic payment protocols; Internet auctions (for selecting suppliers, distributors, demand forecasting, etc.); Electronic Business Process Optimization; E-logistics; Continuous tracking of customer orders through the Internet; Internet-based shared services manufacturing; etc.

10.1.5 Basic Components of Supply Chain Management

Supply chain management (SCM) is the combination of art and science that goes into improving the way your company finds the raw components it needs to make a product or service and deliver it to customers. The following are five basic components of SCM.

1. **Plan** – This is the strategic portion of SCM. You need a strategy for managing all the resources that go toward meeting customer demand for your product or service. A big piece of planning is developing a set of metrics to monitor the supply chain so that it is efficient, costs less and delivers high quality and value to customers.
2. **Source** – Choose the suppliers that will deliver the goods and services you need to create your product. Develop a set of pricing, delivery and payment processes with suppliers and create metrics for monitoring and improving the relationships. And put together processes for managing the inventory of goods and services you receive from suppliers, including receiving shipments, verifying them, transferring them to your manufacturing facilities and authorizing supplier payments.
3. **Make** – This is the manufacturing step. Schedule the activities necessary for production, testing, packaging and preparation for delivery. As the most metric-intensive portion of the supply chain, measure quality levels, production output and worker productivity.
4. **Deliver** – This is the part that many insiders refer to as logistics. Coordinate the receipt of orders from customers, develop a network of warehouses, pick carriers to get products to customers and set up an invoicing system to receive payments.
5. **Return** – The problem part of the supply chain. Create a network for receiving defective and excess products back from customers and supporting customers who have problems with delivered products.

10.2 MANAGING RETAIL SUPPLY CHAINS

As Competitive pressures within the industry have intensified, retailers have focused Increasingly on the importance of efficient merchandise management to improve their financial performance. There are two axioms by which retailers take any decision: Merchandise has to be 'on trend' and it must be in stock. Failure to manage merchandise to meet customer demand results in lost sales and ultimately leads to obsolescence and bankruptcy.

Managing the retail supply chain is crucial to the success of all retailers. First we see the definition of retail supply chain. A retail supply chain is a number of independent activities which, working together, transfer goods from their point of origin to the final customer. Although the SCM concept is common for all retailers, each retailer will implement this in a different way. Variations are the result of retailers specific needs and the demands placed on them by the marketplace and their customers.

10.3 SUPPLY CHAIN DECISIONS

We classify the decisions for supply chain management into two broad categories – strategic and operational. As the term implies, strategic decisions are made typically over a longer time horizon. These are closely linked to the corporate strategy (they sometimes {\it are} the corporate strategy), and guide supply chain policies from a design perspective. On the other hand, operational decisions are short term, and focus on activities over a day-to-day basis. The effort in these type of decisions is to effectively and efficiently manage the product flow in the "strategically" planned supply chain.

There are four major decision areas in supply chain management: 1) location, 2) production, 3) inventory, and 4) transportation (distribution), and there are both strategic and operational elements in each of these decision areas.

10.3.1 Location Decisions

The geographic placement of production facilities, stocking points, and sourcing points is the natural first step in creating a supply chain. The location of facilities involves a commitment of resources to a long-term plan. Once the size, number, and location of these are determined, so are the possible paths by which the product flows through to the final customer. These decisions are of great significance to a firm since they represent the basic strategy for accessing customer markets, and will have a considerable impact on revenue, cost, and level of service. These decisions should be determined by an optimization routine that considers production costs, taxes, duties and duty drawback, tariffs, local content, distribution costs, production limitations, etc. (See Arntzen, Brown, Harrison and Trafton [1995] for a thorough discussion of these aspects.) Although location decisions are primarily strategic, they also have implications on an operational level.

10.3.2 Production Decisions

The strategic decisions include what products to produce, and which plants to produce them in, allocation of suppliers to plants, plants to DC's, and DC's to customer markets. As before, these decisions have a big impact on the revenues, costs and customer service levels of the firm. These decisions assume the existence of the facilities, but determine the exact path(s) through which a product flows to and from these facilities. Another critical issue is the capacity of the manufacturing facilities—and this largely depends the degree of vertical integration within the firm. Operational decisions focus on detailed production scheduling. These decisions include the construction of the master production schedules, scheduling production on machines, and equipment maintenance. Other considerations include workload balancing, and quality control measures at a production facility.

10.3.3 Inventory Decisions

These refer to means by which inventories are managed. Inventories exist at every stage of the supply chain as either raw materials, semi-finished or finished goods. They can also be in-process between locations. Their primary purpose to buffer against any uncertainty that might exist in the supply chain. Since holding of inventories can cost anywhere between 20 to 40 percent of their value, their efficient management is critical in supply chain operations. It is strategic in the sense that top management sets goals. However, most researchers have approached the management of inventory from an operational perspective. These include deployment strategies (push versus pull), control policies — the determination of the optimal levels of order quantities and reorder points, and setting safety stock levels, at each stocking location. These levels are critical, since they are primary determinants of customer service levels.

10.3.4 Transportation Decisions

The mode choice aspect of these decisions are the more strategic ones. These are closely linked to the inventory decisions, since the best choice of mode is often found by trading-off the cost of using the particular mode of transport with the indirect cost of inventory associated with that mode. While air shipments may be fast, reliable, and warrant lesser safety stocks, they are expensive. Meanwhile shipping by sea or rail may be much cheaper, but they necessitate holding relatively large amounts of inventory to buffer against the inherent uncertainty associated with them. Therefore customer service levels, and geographic location play vital roles in such decisions. Since transportation is more than 30 percent of the logistics costs, operating efficiently makes good economic sense. Shipment sizes (consolidated bulk shipments versus Lot-for-Lot), routing and scheduling of equipment are key in effective management of the firm's transport strategy.

10.4 SUPPLY CHAIN MODELING APPROACHES

Clearly, each of the above two levels of decisions require a different perspective. The strategic decisions are, for the most part, global or "all encompassing" in that they try to integrate various aspects of the supply chain. Consequently, the models that describe these decisions are huge, and require a considerable amount of data. Often due to the enormity of data requirements, and the broad scope of decisions, these models provide approximate solutions to the decisions they describe. The operational decisions, meanwhile, address the day-to-day operation of the supply chain. Therefore the models that describe them are often very specific in nature. Due to their narrow perspective, these models often consider great detail and provide very good, if not optimal, solutions to the operational decisions.

To facilitate a concise review of the literature, and at the same time attempting to accommodate the above polarity in modeling, we divide the modeling approaches into many areas — Network Design, "Rough Cut" methods, simulation based methods and hub — spokes model. The network design methods, for the most part, provide normative models for the more strategic decisions. These models typically cover the four major decision areas described earlier, and focus more on the design aspect of the supply chain; the establishment of the network and the associated flows on them. "Rough cut" methods, on the other hand, give guiding policies for the operational decisions. These models typically assume a "single site" (*i.e.*, ignore the network) and add supply chain characteristics to it, such as explicitly considering the site's relation to the others in the network. Simulation methods are a method by which a comprehensive supply chain model can be analyzed, considering both strategic and operational elements. However, as with all simulation models, one can only evaluate the effectiveness of a pre-specified policy rather than develop new ones. It is the traditional question of "What If?" versus "What's Best?". Hub — spokes is a combination of network design and rough cut method, which identifies some core functional areas and supporting subordinate function. This assist in optimization of supply chain performance.

10.4.1 Network Design Methods

As the very name suggests, these methods determine the location of production, stocking, and sourcing facilities, and paths the product(s) take through them. Such methods tend to be large scale, and used generally at the inception of the supply chain. The earliest work in this area, although the term "supply chain" was not in vogue, was by Geoffrion and Graves [1974]. They introduce a multicommodity logistics network design model for optimizing annualized finished product flows from plants to the DC's to the final customers. Geoffrion and Powers [1993] later give a review of the evolution of distribution strategies over the past twenty years, describing how the descendants of the above model can accommodate more echelons and cross commodity detail.

Breitman and Lucas [1987] attempt to provide a framework for a comprehensive model of a production-distribution system, "PLANETS", that is used to decide what products to produce, where and how to produce it, which markets to pursue and what resources to use. Parts of this ambitious project were successfully implemented at General Motors.

Cohen and Lee [1985] develop a conceptual framework for manufacturing strategy analysis, where they describe a series of stochastic sub- models, that considers annualized product flows from raw material vendors via intermediate plants and distribution echelons to the final customers. They use heuristic methods to link and optimize these sub- models. They later give an integrated and readable exposition of their models and methods in Cohen and Lee [1988].

Cohen and Lee [1989] present a normative model for resource deployment in a global manufacturing and distribution network. Global after-tax profit (profit-local taxes) is maximized through the design of facility network and control of material flows within the network. The cost structure consists of variable and fixed costs for material procurement, production, distribution and transportation. They validate the model by applying it to analyze the global manufacturing strategies of a personal computer manufacturer.

Finally, Arntzen, Brown, Harrison, and Trafton [1995] provide the most comprehensive deterministic model for supply chain management. The objective function minimizes a combination of cost and time elements. Examples of cost elements include purchasing, manufacturing, pipeline inventory, transportation costs between various sites, duties, and taxes. Time elements include manufacturing lead times and transit times. Unique to this model was the explicit consideration of duty and their recovery as the product flowed through different countries. Implementation of this model at the Digital Equipment Corporation has produced spectacular results — savings in the order of $100 million dollars.

Clearly, these network-design based methods add value to the firm in that they lay down the manufacturing and distribution strategies far into the future. It is imperative that firms at one time or another make such integrated decisions, encompassing production, location, inventory, and transportation, and such models are therefore indispensable. Although the above review shows considerable potential for these models as strategic determinants in the future, they are not without their shortcomings. Their very nature forces these problems to be of a very large scale. They are often difficult to solve to optimality. Furthermore, most of the models in this category are largely deterministic and static in nature. Additionally, those that consider stochastic elements are very restrictive in nature. In sum, there does not seem to yet be a comprehensive model that is representative of the true nature of material flows in the supply chain.

10.4.2 Rough Cut Methods

These models form the bulk of the supply chain literature, and typically deal with the more operational or tactical decisions. Most of the integrative research (from a supply chain context) in the literature seem to take on an inventory management perspective. In fact, the term "Supply Chain" first appears in the literature as an inventory management approach. The thrust of the rough cut models is the development of inventory control policies, considering several levels or echelons together. These models have come to be known as "multi-level" or "multi-echelon" inventory control models. For a review the reader is directed to Vollman et al. [1992].

Multi-echelon inventory theory has been very successfully used in industry. Cohen et al. [1990] describe "OPTIMIZER", one of the most complex models to date — to manage IBM's spare parts inventory. They develop efficient algorithms and sophisticated data structures to achieve large scale systems integration.

Although current research in multi-echelon based supply chain inventory problems shows considerable promise in reducing inventories with increased customer service, the studies have several notable limitations. First, these studies largely ignore the production side of the supply chain. Their starting point in most cases is a finished goods stockpile, and policies are given to manage these effectively. Since production is a natural part of the supply chain, there seems to be a need with models that include the production component in them. Second, even on the distribution side, almost all published research assumes an arborescence structure, i. e. each site receives re-supply from only one higher level site but can distribute to several lower levels. Third, researchers have largely focused on the inventory system only. In logistics-system theory, transportation and inventory are primary components of the order fulfillment process in terms of cost and service levels. Therefore, companies must consider important interrelationships among transportation, inventory and customer service in determining their policies. Fourth, most of the models under the "inventory theoretic" paradigm are very restrictive in nature, i.e., mostly they restrict themselves to certain well known forms of demand or lead time or both, often quite contrary to what is observed.

10.5 SUPPLY CHAIN APPLICATION SOFTWARE'S

Supply chain application effectiveness is dependent on access to data from multiple systems inside and out of the enterprise, but integration is still so costly and complex that only critical function and partners are connected. The high cost of software maintenance and development is forcing companies to deny their operating units the capabilities they require to prosper and differentiate from the competition. If indeed companies compete with their supply chains, many are doing it with their technology arm tied behind their backs.

Supply chain management software is possibly the most fractured group of software applications on the planet. Each of the five major supply chain steps previously outlined composes dozens of specific tasks, many of which have their own specific software. Some vendors have assembled many of these different chunks of software together under a single roof, but no one has a complete package that is right for every company. For example, most companies need to track demand, supply, manufacturing status, logistics (*i.e.* where things are in the supply chain), and distribution. They also need to share data with supply chain partners at an ever increasing rate. While products from large ERP vendors like SAP's Advanced Planner and Optimizer (APO) can perform many or all of these tasks, because each industry's supply chain has a unique set of challenges, many companies decide to go with targeted best of breed products instead, even if some integration is an inevitable consequence.

It's worth mentioning that the old adage about systems only being as good as the information that they contain applies doubly to SCM. If the information entered into a demand forecasting application is not accurate then you will get an inaccurate forecast. Similarly, if employees bypass the supply chain systems and try to manage things manually, then even the most expensive systems will provide an incomplete picture of what is happening in a company's supply chain.

10.5.1 Relationship between ERP and SCM

Many SCM applications are reliant upon the kind of information that is stored in the most quantity inside ERP software. Theoretically you could assemble the information you need to feed the SCM applications from legacy systems (for most companies this means Excel spreadsheets spread out all over the place), but it can be nightmarish to try to get that information flowing on a fast, reliable basis from all the areas of the company. ERP is the battering ram that integrates all that information together in a single application, and SCM applications benefit from having a single major source to go to for up-to-date information. Most CIOs who have tried to install SCM applications say they are glad they did ERP first. They call the ERP projects "putting your information house in order." Of course, ERP is expensive and difficult, so you may want to explore ways to feed your SCM applications the information they need without doing ERP first. These days, most ERP vendors have SCM modules so doing an ERP project may be a way to kill two birds with one stone. Companies will need to decide if these products meet their needs or if they need a more specialized system.

Applications that simply automate the logistics aspects of SCM are less dependent upon gathering information from around the company, so they tend to be independent of the ERP decision. But chances are, you'll need to have these applications communicate with ERP in some fashion. It's important to pay attention to the software's ability to integrate with the Internet and with ERP applications because the Internet will drive demand for integrated information. For example, if you want to build a private website for communicating with your customers and suppliers, you will want to pull information from ERP and supply chain applications together to present updated information about orders, payments, manufacturing status and delivery.

10.5.2 Goal of Installing Supply Chain Management Software

Before the Internet came along, the aspirations of supply chain software devotees were limited to improving their ability to predict demand from customers and make their own supply chains run more smoothly. But the cheap, ubiquitous nature of the Internet, along with its simple, universally accepted communication standards have thrown things wide open. Now, you can connect your supply chain with the supply chains of your suppliers and customers together in a single vast network that optimizes costs and opportunities for everyone involved. This was the reason for the B2B explosion; the idea that everyone you do business with could be connected together into one big happy, cooperative family.

Of course, reality isn't quite that happy and cooperative, but today most companies share at least some data with their supply chain partners. The goal of these projects is greater supply chain visibility. The supply chain in most industries is like a big card game. The players don't want to show their cards because they don't trust anyone else with the information. But if they showed their hands they could all benefit. Suppliers wouldn't have to guess how many raw materials to order, and manufacturers wouldn't have to order more than they need from suppliers to make sure they have enough on hand if demand for their products unexpectedly goes up. And retailers would have fewer empty shelves if they shared the information they had about sales of a manufacturer's product in all their stores with the manufacturer. The Internet makes showing your hand to others possible, but centuries of distrust and lack of coordination within industries make it difficult.

Over the last few years most companies have gotten over the trust issue. In many cases "gotten over" is a euphemism for "have been bullied into sharing supply chain information from a dominant industry player." Want to sell your goods in Wal-Mart? Better be prepared to share data.

The payoff of timely and accurate supply chain information is the ability to make or ship only as much of a product as there is a market for. This is the practice known as just-in-time manufacturing, and it allows companies to reduce the amount of inventory that they keep. This can cut costs substantially, since you no longer need to pay to produce and store excess goods.

10.5.3 Supply Chain Collaboration

Let's look at consumer packaged goods for an example of collaboration. If there are two companies that have made supply chain a household word, they are Wal-Mart and Procter & Gamble. Before these two companies started collaborating back in the '80s, retailers shared very little information with manufacturers. But then the two giants built a software system that hooked P&G up to Wal-Mart's distribution centers. When P&G's products run low at the distribution centers, the system sends an automatic alert to P&G to ship more products. In some cases, the system goes all the way to the individual Wal-Mart store. It lets P&G monitor the shelves through real-time satellite link-ups that send messages to the factory whenever a P&G item swoops past a scanner at the register.

With this kind of minute-to-minute information, P&G knows when to make, ship and display more products at the Wal-Mart stores. No need to keep products piled up in warehouses awaiting Wal-Mart's call. Invoicing and payments happen automatically too. The system saves P&G so much in time, reduced inventory and lower order-processing costs that it can afford to give Wal-Mart "low, everyday prices" without putting itself out of business.

10.5.4 The Roadblocks to Installing Supply Chain Software

Gaining Trust from your Suppliers and Partners

Supply chain automation is uniquely difficult because its complexity extends beyond your company's walls. Your people will need to change the way they work and so will the people from each supplier that you add to your network. Only the largest and most powerful manufacturers can force such radical changes down suppliers' throats. Most companies have to sell outsiders on the system. Moreover, your goals in installing the system may be threatening to those suppliers, to say the least. For example, Wal-Mart's collaboration with P&G meant that P&G would assume more responsibility for inventory management, something retailers have traditionally done on their own. Wal-Mart had the clout to demand this from P&G, but it also gave P&G something in return-better information about Wal-Mart's product demand, which helped P&G manufacture its products more efficiently. To get your supply chain partners to agree to collaborate with you, you have to be willing to compromise and help them achieve their own goals.

Internal Resistance to Change

If selling supply chain systems is difficult on the outside, it isn't much easier inside. Operations people are accustomed to dealing with phone calls, faxes and hunches scrawled on paper, and will most likely want to keep it that way. If you can't convince people that using the software will be worth their time, they will easily find ways to work around it. You cannot disconnect the telephones and fax machines just because you have supply chain software in place.

Many Mistakes at First

There is a diabolical twist to the quest for supply chain software acceptance among your employees. New supply chain systems process data as they are programmed to do, but the technology cannot absorb a company's history and processes in the first few months after an implementation. Forecasters and planners need to understand that the first bits of information they get from a system might need some tweaking. If they are not warned about the system's initial naiveté, they will think it is useless. In one case, just before a large automotive industry supplier installed a new supply chain forecasting application to predict demand for a product, an automaker put in an order for an unusually large number of units. The system responded by predicting huge demand for the product based largely on one unusual order. Blindly following the system's numbers could have led to inaccurate orders for materials being sent to suppliers within the chain. The company caught the problem but only after a demand forecaster threw out the system's numbers and used his own. That created another problem: Forecasters stopped trusting the system and worked strictly with their own data. The supplier had to fine-tune the system itself, then work on reestablishing employees' confidence. Once employees understood that they would be merging their expertise with the system's increasing accuracy, they began to accept and use the new technology.

10.5.5 Extended Supply Chain

The extended supply chain is a clever way of describing everyone who contributes to a product. So if you make text books, then your extended supply chain would include the factories where the books are printed and bound, but also the company that sells you the paper, the mill where that supplier buys their stock, and so on. It is important to keep track of what is happening in your extended supply chain because with a supplier or a supplier's supplier could end up having an impact on you (as the old saying goes, a chain is only a strong as its weakest link). For example, a fire in a paper mill might cause the text book manufacturer's paper supplier to run out of inventory. If the text book company knows what is happening in its extended supply chain it can find another paper vendor.

10.5.6 Impact of Globalization on the Supply Chain

The extended supply chain is a clever way of describing everyone who contributes to a product. So if you make text books, then your extended supply chain would include the factories where the books are printed and bound, but also the company that sells you the paper, the mill where that supplier buys their stock, and so on. It is important to keep track of what is happening in your extended supply chain because with a supplier or a supplier's supplier could end up having an impact on you (as the old saying goes, a chain is only a strong as its weakest link). For example, a fire in a paper mill might cause the text book manufacturer's paper supplier to run out of inventory. If the text book company knows what is happening in its extended supply chain it can find another paper vendor.

10.5.7 Some Emerging Technologies that will Affect the Supply Chain

The most notable is Radio Frequency Identification, or RFID. RFID tags are essentially barcodes on steroids. Whereas barcodes only identify the product, RFID tags can tell what the product is, where it has been, when it expires, whatever information someone wishes to program it with. RFID technology is going to generate mountains of data about the location of pallets, cases, cartons, totes and individual products in the supply chain. It's going to produce oceans of information about when and where merchandise is manufactured, picked, packed and shipped. It's going to create rivers of numbers telling retailers about the expiration dates of their perishable items—numbers that will have to be stored, transmitted in real-time and shared with warehouse management, inventory management, financial and other enterprise systems. In other words, it is going to have a really big impact.

Another benefit of RFIDs is that, unlike barcodes, RFID tags can be read automatically by electronic readers. Imagine a truck carrying a container full of widgets entering a shipping terminal in China. If the container is equipped with an RFID tag, and the terminal has an RFID sensor network, that container's whereabouts can be automatically sent to Widget Co. without the truck ever slowing down. It has the potential to add a substantial amount of visibility into the extended supply chain.

Right now the two biggest hurdles to widespread RFID adoption are the cost of building the infrastructure and the lack of agreed-upon industry standards.

10.5.8 Service Oriented Architecture of SCM Software

Identifying the Problem

For the report, 'Service Oriented Architecture in the Supply Chain', AberdeenGroup surveyed almost 300 line-of-business executives about the effectiveness of their supply chain applications in supporting their strategies for profitable growth. More than 60 percent of companies with annual revenues of more than US$1 billion say they either have, or are in the process of, standardising on common ERP platforms for supply chain management. However, our survey found that companies use a wide variety of applications and services to manage the supply chain. Only six percent of companies of any size said they use ERP exclusively for supply chain management. With the wide spectrum of applications and services used by most companies to manage the supply chain, it's no wonder that more than 60 percent of survey respondents say that even the integration of internal supply chain applications would give them a competitive advantage. Leveraging a large ERP investment is important, and there is nothing inherently wrong with standardising applications where appropriate. Even with this in mind, though, the cost and complexity of creating an integrated supply chain application portfolio using traditional methods prevents most companies from considering it.

The challenge of standardisation and integration is further compounded by the fact that most companies report using either heavily customised or internally built software that allows them to offer differentiated services and create finely tuned processes unique to themselves. Only 18 percent of companies say they manage their supply chains with commercial software that has little or no modifications from the standard package. A strategy of ripping out and replacing legacy applications to standardise on a single application platform may satisfy the need for integration, but forces the company from the beginning to recreate its intellectual property on an entirely new application. Too often, the results are disappointing and the cost staggering.

Is the enterprise faced with the Hobson's choice of either standardising on a common application platform or continuing with the application chaos that exists today? The answer is no. Service Oriented Architecture (SOA) promises to change the way business and technology vendors buy, sell, deploy and manage their application portfolios. For the first time, business users will be able to summon applications to support a business process rather that launch a business process constrained by the application.

SOA Allows Business Process to Drive Technology

SOA has been a topic of intense interest in the technology community for more than four years. The concept is based on information technology best practices in design and deployment of applications and their supporting infrastructure. It will, over time, revolutionise how software is built, sold and distributed. SOA's momentum is growing fast, and as we will see, conditions over the next five years favor ever speedier adoption.

Business users of supply chain technology must understand the capabilities and potential of SOA, both today and in the future. SOA's real advantage is conforming technology to meet business users' process demands. Without a joint relationship between IT and business, SOA will never come close to reaching its potential. Integration will be vastly simplified by the use of standards that will allow a common way to communicate and, for the first time, an enterprise will be able to free itself from the restrictions of having to manage business processes as defined by a software application. Business users will have a buffet of different services and functions they can combine at will to create the right set of automated processes to service particular customers, support with automation the one-of-a-kind processes that can distinctly differentiate themselves from competitors, and be able to integrate with partners without today's high costs and complexity.

Packaged Applications — the Next Legacy Systems

The architectural approach to SOA forces enterprises to think of using technology in an entirely different way. It's hard to conceptualise, because we have all been trained to think of technology as it's currently deployed. Once you grasp its significance, though, you'll begin to understand the flexibility in process it will afford enterprises.

In five years, the applications on which you base your business will be on the way to becoming a largely ignored set of software left to manage basic administrative tasks like finance and human resources. Applications and information on demand is the next big wave of enterprise computing. Need shipment status or the latest production updates from your offshore supplier? You can access that information in the same way: real-time, every time, directly from the source, whether within or outside your company.

The improved integration approach is far superior to what is done now. Real-time data is available on demand, easy to access, and communicated in a standard protocol that all participating applications can understand. Beyond connecting just the applications within our own enterprises, the vision of SOA promises that companies will be able to reach out to business partners, application providers, and other data sources, on-demand.

Integration is Part, but not All, of the SOA Value Proposition

As they're constructed today, supply chain applications dictate, rather than conform to, the workflow needed to satisfy business partner requirements and efficiency goals within organisations. Imagine a world where the best application functionality can be summoned to support best practice business processes. Instead of buying an entire application set, the user can choose to summon only that part of the software that best meets his needs, and combine it with slices of functionality from other applications to build a 'composite' application. From the seemingly mundane task of routing and scheduling transportation, to the strategically important task of building collaborative processes with major customers, flexibility is required. Rarely can companies afford the luxury of maintaining one process to support multiple customers, and this is particularly true when creating strategic relationships with important customers or suppliers. By definition the relationship is unique, the source of competitive advantage, and unlikely that any packaged application could support it with out of the box software.

Multiple user interfaces, data spread across separate databases, and the inflexibility of the applications themselves fail to help enterprises meet the challenge of responding to customer requirements. Only 26 percent say their software allows them to quickly adapt to customer requirements. The others are forced to make the hard tradeoff of denying customers their requests or employing expensive workarounds to satisfy them, driving customer profitability down and dissatisfaction rates up.

Service-oriented architecture's concept of a composite application challenges the rigidity found in today's technology. The SOA strategy envisions that rather than have complex applications whose functions are bound together tightly, the applications instead would be loosely coupled functions, called business services, and would be available for use for whatever process requested it. Take, for example a provider of warehouse business services. Rather than having to buy and implement an entire application, companies will be able to buy from a business service provider individual functions such as inventory control, stock locator, labeling, and the myriad other functions it offers.

The composite application would link these warehouse services with appropriate order management, inventory planning and transportation business services to create a fulfillment process that is as unique as the user designed workflow. Business services could be added to enable cross-docking, multi-channel fulfillment, and value-added services to be available when required. Data within legacy systems can also be exposed to processes, giving them new life in the SOA world.

A powerful workflow engine within the composite application controls when business services are invoked, and there can be endless variations to the workflow itself, dependent on product, customer requirement, or whatever condition causes a departure from the standard process. In the future, the owner of the business process will have control over design and implementation of processes, and not have to depend on vendor or IT resources to implement them.

Making SOA Successful

The process flexibility that SOA enables isn't something to be wary of if used and governed correctly. It points to the need for IT and business to create a close working relationship, with IT maintaining standards and the methodology for change, and the business user articulating requirements that are required to deliver differentiated services. SOA affords the organisation to improve process performance incrementally, fine tuning at a very granular level of detail.

For the first time, the enterprise has the opportunity to start weaving together processes, applications, and data in a timely and efficient manner. The technology also allows for the sharing of these processes with business partners, an inevitable challenge and opportunity in today's global, multi-channel world. The enterprise is more agile in the processes it produces, and the unique supply chain services it can bring to customers. With this flexibility comes the opportunity to differentiate itself from the competition. And, for the first time, we have technology that's not limited to a wealthy few; SOA and its technological components are available to companies of all sizes.

10.6 EXAMPLES OF SUPPLY CHAIN APPLICATION SOFTWARE'S

1. SOA Software's Service Manager™ and Partner Manager™ enable enterprises to enhance the capabilities of their Supply Chain Management (SCM) solutions using XML and Web services with the confidence that security and management challenges will be met. Enterprises can maximize existing investment in SCM technologies by extending their reach through XML and Web services

   The Service Manager™ delivers a comprehensive Web Services Management and Security infrastructure solution for XML and Web services.

   SOA Software's Management Point™ implements powerful security policy enforcement and enablement services, and provides industry-leading service and SLA management capabilities.

   SOA Software's Registry abstracts service consumers from provider end-points with comprehensive service location and versioning meta data.

   SOA Software's Gateway™ provides application and adapter developers with advanced security and management capabilities without complex programming.

   - The Service Manager Console provides a single point of control for managing multiple participants in SCM
   - The Service Manager provides a standards-based solution that functions across multiple enterprises
   - The detached Management Point provides a flexible, adaptable, budget conscious "hub and spoke" approach to integrating multiple enterprises
   - The Service Manager provides security across the multiple domains involved in SCM

   The Service Manager™ also offers powerful integration capabilities allowing it to be managed as part of existing operations management frameworks like Tivoli Enterprise Console and HP Openview, and security solutions like Tivoli Access Manager and Netegrity SiteMinder and TransactionMinder.

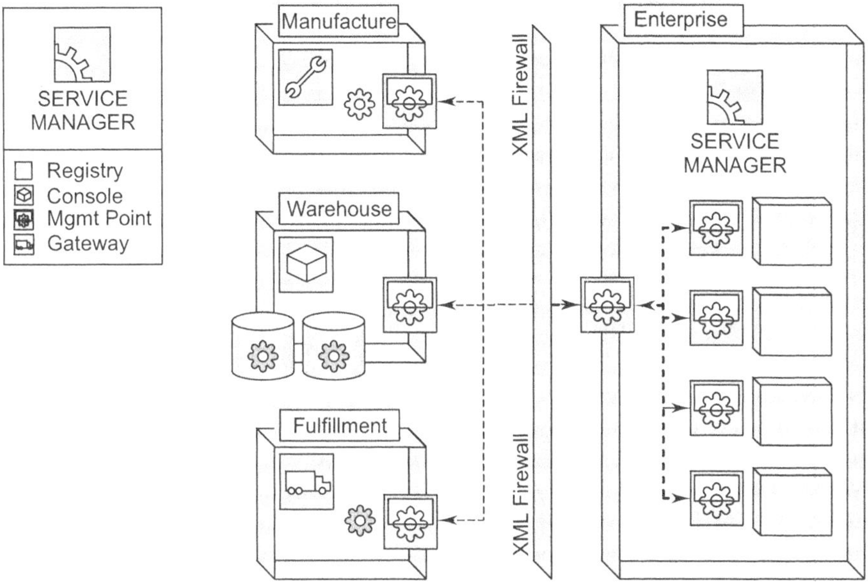

Supply Chain Management Considerations for Web Services

Crosses Enterprise Boundaries – The nature of SCM is that it requires integration and co-operation between multiple enterprises, with all the challenges inherent in doing business across enterprise boundaries. Web services offers an ideal solution to the large-scale integration problem SCM poses, however this is only true if the Web services are interoperable. Ensuring service location transparency and seamless interoperability requires a comprehensive Web Services Management solution.

Single Point of Control – SCM is essentially a complex multi-enterprise integration challenge. The business that owns the supply chain needs to ensure central control of the entire process. An effective Web Services Management fabric with powerful central policy administration and security capabilities can ensure that all parties involved in the supply chain adhere to centrally mandated rules and policy.

Multi-domain Security – Security and identity management is one of the biggest challenges facing any business initiative that crosses enterprise boundaries. Web services standards are just beginning to address the issues of federated identity authentication and authorization. Web Services Management solutions can provide the bridge between partner identity and authorization services to deliver a complete federated solution.

2. The HP Real Time Supply Chain (RTSC) solution consists of three components: the RTSC Data Manager, supply chain business applications, and supply chain consulting and integration services from HP and its partners.

   The foundation of the RTSC solution, the RTSC Data Manager, integrates, collects, cleanses, distributes and analyzes data from all supply chain applications across the enterprise—whether they number in the tens or hundreds. The system creates a single, up-to-the-second view of data and delivers it in real time to supply chain applications through publish-andsubscribe technology.

   The RTSC Data Manager exploits the continuous availability and data integrity of the HP NonStop server to guarantee the delivery of messages and data to and from other applications. The system can scale to support a virtually unlimited number of applications. NonStop SQL/MX Database enables essential, mixed workload processing for a real-time enterprise environment.

Key Benefits

- ***Reliable***-NonStop servers are designed for continuous availability. In a recent yearly survey, 96 percent of these installed systems had zero downtime.
- ***Scalable***-The modular architecture of NonStop S-series servers, which use HP ServerNet Technology, allows you to scale from a two-processor system to a configuration of more than 4,000 processors, with linear performance and no changes to the application.
- ***Manageable***-You can manage NonStop servers with industry-standard management tools in a heterogeneous environment.
- ***Affordable***-The Standish Group reports that NonStop servers deliver the lowest total cost of ownership of all enterprise-class systems, including UNIX® and Microsoft Windows based servers, Windows NT system clusters, and IBM mainframe servers.
- ***Open* NonStop**- servers have an open system that runs many industry-standard development and management tools and application environments, including Java™, CORBA, Tuxedo, Microsoft ActiveX, POSIX, Microsoft Visual Studio .NET, XML, UNIX, Simple Object Access Protocol (SOAP), Web services, HTTP, Open Database Connectivity (ODBC), C, C++, COBOL, CA-Unicenter, HP Systems Insight Manager Software, and BMC PATROL. NonStop servers can fully interoperate with Oracle databases and application servers by using Java Database Connectivity (JDBC) and Oracle Application Server software.
- ***Flexible* Applications**- can be written, tested, debugged, and compiled on a PC or workstation by development staff trained on industry-standard tools.
- ***Internet enabled***-NonStop servers are the engine behind many key Internet sites, including the world's largest Internet service provider (ISP) and many Internetenabled brokerages, travel reservation services, home banking applications, business-to-business applications, and application service providers (ASPs).

EXERCISE

1. Describe Intranet and supply chain Management.
2. Describe History of Supply Chain Management.
3. Define Supply Chain Management.
4. Describe Pull versus Push Supply Chain Management.
5. Describe Faces of Supply Chain Management.
6. Describe basic Components of Supply Chain Management.
7. Describe Managing Retail Supply Chains.
8. Describe Supply Chain Decisions.
9. Describe Inventory Decisions.
10. Describe Supply Chain Modeling Approaches.
11. Describe Supply Chain Application Software's.
12. What are the goals of installing supply chain management software?
13. Describe supply chain collaboration.
14. Describe the roadblocks to installing supply chain software.
15. Describe Extended supply chain.
16. Describe Impact of globalization on the Supply Chain.
17. Describe some emerging technologies that will affect the Supply Chain.
18. Describe Service Oriented Architecture of SCM Software.
19. Discuss Examples of Supply chain application software's.

11

PROCUREMENT MANAGEMENT

11.0 INTRODUCTION

Procurement Management is tightly integrated with Accounting, Purchasing, and Job Costing. Automated processes help ensure that materials are accurately tracked. Purchasing tools streamline the ordering of material from vendors, the issuing of subcontracts and the management of materials-related documents. Easily account for materials received, invoiced, backordered, produced, and used. Procurement Management tracks purchase commitments, quantities, pricing, and receipts (by job, work order, equipment part, or inventory). From start to finish, contractors can streamline processes and maximize profits by having the right materials on site at the right time.

With all the discussion of procurement and how it works in businesses, the biggest question is does it actually save money? After all, that's the real bottom line. One large company that had an annual purchasing expenditure of about $10 billion was able to shave over 15% off that amount annually just by leveraging the buying power of all their worldwide divisions. Those numbers clearly illustrate that, when done correctly, a procurement system can definitely save a company money, as well as provide a number of other benefits, particularly to large companies that spend a sizable chunk of their revenue on purchasing goods and services for their business.

Besides the impressive cost savings, procurement management can also save valuable time and can streamline the workforce. With procurement systems, many of the steps involved in purchasing are either not necessary or are automated so that the entire process runs smoother and faster. Also, because most corporations divide up the purchasing responsibilities among their multiple divisions, they typically have several staff members who are technically doing the exact same job in different locations. By centralizing all of a company's procurement needs into a single department or firm, these redundant job positions can be eliminated. Additionally, the excess office space and equipment can either be liquidated or used for more productive business endeavors.

In order to achieve these and the other benefits procurement management offers, companies must be willing to go through many steps. Implementation does require some changes both in technology, in personnel, and in attitude. Without these changes, the procurement system simply won't be effective.

One of the first of these changes is to adopt a positive sourcing methodology. Many corporations simply place orders; they don't form relationships with suppliers. While the distinctions may not seem great, the reality is that these sellers are critical components of a business's success, and they need to be treated that way. The overall goal of a strong sourcing methodology is to achieve a mutually satisfying agreement that will provide the buyer with the goods he needs at a reasonable price and that will secure the seller a steady customer in the future.

Another change with procurement is the workforce. Employees who will be dealing directly with vendors need to be highly trained and experienced in the industry in which the business is involved. For example, a pharmaceutical company would need to hire individuals who are familiar with the types of chemicals used in the creation of prescription drugs. By hiring individuals who are experts in their field and who are then trained in the procurement process of the company, suppliers feel more comfortable doing business with the buying firm.

With a more centralized approach to procurement, large corporations are also in the position to have their purchasing team specialize in certain areas of procurement. An automobile manufacturer may have one team responsible for purchasing machinery, another for raw materials, and a third for temporary employees. This type of specialization would be too costly if all of the purchasing was spread out across the globe but when dealing with billions of dollars in goods and services being handled in one area, specialization is almost a necessity.

Tracking suppliers, using reverse auctions, and evaluating costs are all other important parts of the procurement system. By tracking suppliers, the buyer is able to determine whether or not they continuously live up to expectations. Through reverse auctions, buyers are able to keep prices lower while selecting from a wide array of potential sellers. Plus, continually evaluating costs prevents companies from losing sight of the biggest benefit of procurement management: its cost-effectiveness.

11.1 DEFINITION OF E-PROCUREMENT

E-Procurement is more than just a system for making purchases online. A properly implemented system can connect companies and their business processes directly with suppliers while managing all interactions between them. This includes management of correspondence, bids, questions and answers, previous pricing, and multiple emails sent to multiple participants.

A good e-procurement system helps a firm organize its interactions with its most crucial suppliers. It provides those who use it with a set of built-in monitoring tools to help control costs and assure maximum supplier performance. It provides an organized way to keep an open line of communication with potential suppliers during a business process. The system allows managers to confirm pricing, and leverage previous agreements to assure each new price quote is more competitive than the last.

11.2 BENEFITS OF ADOPTING AN E-PROCUREMENT SYSTEM

E-Procurement helps with the decision-making process by keeping relevant information neatly organized and time-stamped. Most are template-driven which makes all transactions standardized and track able. Keeping track of all bids means leveraging your knowledge to obtain better pricing. Companies can focus on their most lucrative trading partners and contracts.

Well-managed e-procurement helps reduce inventory levels. Knowing product numbers, bid prices and contact points can help businesses close a deal while other suppliers are struggling to gather their relevant data.

E-Procurement systems that allow multiple access levels and permissions help managers organize administrative users by roles, groups, or tasks. Procurement managers do not need to be as highly trained or paid because such systems are standardized and easy to learn.

11.3 TYPICAL ADOPTION STRATEGIES

Some firms have discovered that many of their transactions still take place on paper, and they have run into problems ranging from content management to supplier participation in their systems. Most companies who desire to make the switch fall into two camps. The first are the slow step-by-step adopters. They implement one piece of their system at a time and slowly bring trading partners on board. The others follow the total replacement model. They build a totally parallel system, test it, then switch over to it when it works. There is usually some pain involved and some mistakes are discovered, but by and large these are absorbed and the business continues.

11.4 PITFALLS TO AVOID

Don't bite off more than you can chew. The parallel system approach should only be used if you have the time and resources to do this. If not, stick to the incremental approach.

Don't expect an immediate return on investment. A short-term gain may be noticeable, but it may be eaten up by the cost of staff training and equipment purchases. A year or two down the road, a larger ROI should be evident.

EXERCISE

1. What is Procurement Management?
2. Define E-Procurement.
3. Describe Benefits of Adopting an E-Procurement System.
4. Describe typical Adoption Strategies.

12

ENTERPRISE AND GLOBAL MANAGEMENT

12.0 INTRODUCTION

Unfortunately, businesses haven't always worked as a unit. Production created business processes separately from Accounting. Sales and Marketing had their own systems, and so on. Usually none of the systems linked into the others within the same company (application specific view). Most systems were intentionally created separately, since technology did not allow an entire organization to feed from one big, integrated system.

Now technological advances have given corporations the computing capacity and the tools to create a single system that can link all parts of the organization. With the explosion of the Internet, the ability to bring vendors and suppliers into the organization's system is now available through enterprise computing.

12.1 MANAGING IT INFRASTRUCTURE AND ARCHITECTURE: ENTERPRISE COMPUTING

Compare the difference between the following two figures, the old view of systems, and, the new way of thinking about Information Systems.

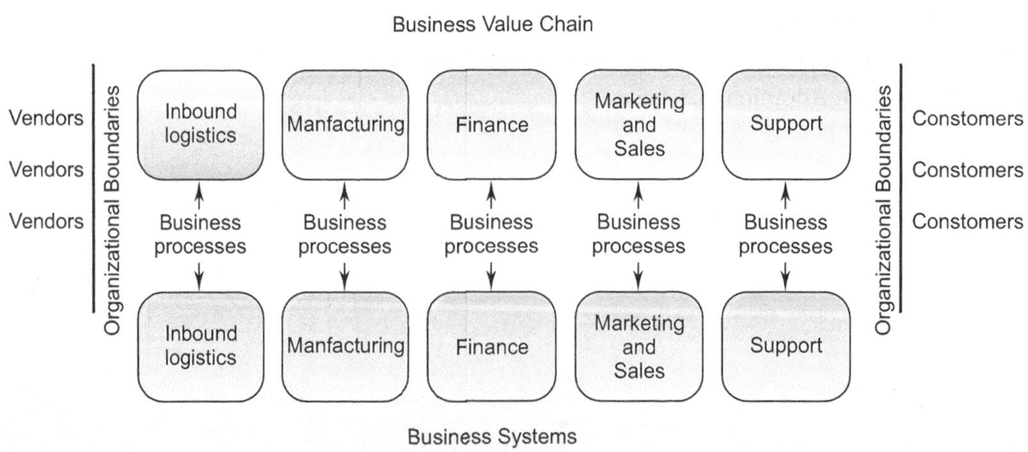

Fig. 12.1

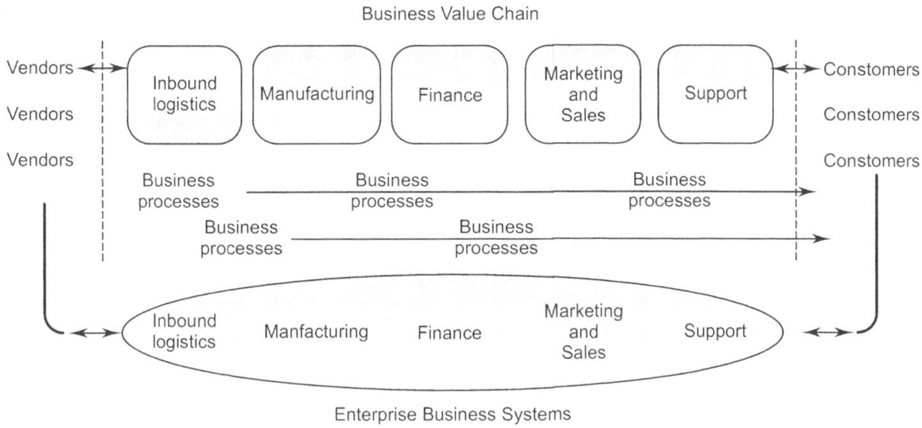

Fig. 12.2

Basic Concepts of Enterprise Computing

The four basic concepts of enterprise computing are compared in the following table.

Table 12.1 Basic Concepts of Enterprise Computing

Concept	Measure	Key Questions
IT intendment portfolio	Benchmark competitors' expenditures	Are we spending too much, or too little on IT? Are we receiving a good return on investment?
IT infrastructure	Lists of technical capabilities	Do we have she technical capability to achieve our strategic objectives?
Business logic	Descriptions of business model and processes	How do we plan to make money and what business activities and processes should we emphasize?
IT architecture	Descriptions of systems that support business model and processes	Do we have the right systems environment and applications to implement the business logic?

The information technology investment portfolio is concerned with the amount of money firms spend on Information Systems and whether the organization is receiving a fair return on its investment. With "Internet-centric" companies, this concept can be skewed or simply thrown out altogether. Many of these companies are more concerned with the strategic value of their Information Systems and don't expect a return for several years. Amazon.com loses millions of dollars every quarter but it continues to focus on brand building rather than a real dollar return on investment.

Just as every town and city in the world relies on basic facilities to function, such as roads and utilities, corporations rely on the proper amount of hardware, software, and people to create and operate their IT *infrastructures*. Firms should continually review and question whether they have the right mix of each to carry out their business plan.

How do companies intend to make money? After all, isn't that why businesses exist? When businesses answer that question, they have found their business logic. Combine the IT infrastructure with the business logic, in the right mix, and you have the information architecture necessary to make the firm a success.

When developing enterprise computing systems, there are no cookie cutter answers to the tough questions management must explore and answer. The company needs to develop a plan, complete with graphics and descriptions that spell out how the business processes will be supported by the Information System and how the company expects to excel using enterprise computing.

It's not enough to tell your suppliers they will be able to use your Information System. The real question is how the key business processes will be enhanced by allowing suppliers to tap into the information system.

How will you know if the organization is really better off with the enterprise computing system? You should measure the company's performance after implementing the new system with its performance before installation. That's the only sure way you'll know if the effort has paid off.

Industrial Networks and Trans-enterprise Systems

Selling paper towels may seem like a very simple task. Have you ever thought about the supplies that go into that roll of paper towels? Where do the raw products come from? Once the towels are made, how do they get on the shelves of your local grocery store? Many suppliers and vendors are involved in the product from start to finish: it's not produced solely by the manufacturer.

What if the maker of the paper towels was able to control the product lifecycle better and thereby reduce costs by including the suppliers and vendors in the total process? That's what industrial networks are all about.

The dilemma occurs when various manufacturers develop separate systems for their products and then expect the suppliers to join in. If a supplier deals with several different manufacturers, it could end up with several different systems that don't mesh.

Business Drivers: The Changing Business Environment

It's not your father's business environment anymore. We've seen tremendous changes in the world over the last ten years, many of them driven by technological changes and advances. The following table describes the business factors that drive change and highlights the impact of each on companies trying to keep up.

Table 12.2 Business Drivers of Enterprise Systems: Changing Environments

Business Driver	Impact
Market change	Globalization and increasing information intercity reduce margins in traditional industries
Industry change	Mergers acquisitions and consolidations in traditional industries in-crease scale economics and intensity industry competition
Firm-level change	Business process redesign efforts of the 1990s in traditional industries force jettisoning legacy systems and highlight the need for enterprise-wide systems to support the newly defined business processes
Product change	The growth of information, knowledge, and high-tech-based products shortens product cycle times: increasing information intensity of traditional products and services shortens cycle times
Management process thinking	From discrete business process focus toward a view of the firm as an integrated set of processes: from neoclassical competition firm-based views toward industry-based views of cooperation and alliance
Management strategy	Growing belief that information architecture investments could lead to unique knowledge that could not be purchased on input factor markets.

The factor associated with all the drivers of change is that businesses aren't as free to raise prices. They must cut costs in order to stay competitive and to expand their markets. The emerging global economy has put the brakes on simple price changes to enhance the bottom line. Many companies have been able to hold the line on costs by updating their IT infrastructures and reshaping their IT architectures.

Businesses also realize they cannot allow islands of information to exist in their organizations but must have a cohesive Information System that feeds information from one unit to another. Older systems didn't allow for cross-utilization of information. Companies with these older systems are now realizing the severe disadvantage they suffer if they don't use information as a key resource.

In 1999 Bill Gates, Chairman of Microsoft, Inc., published a book called *Business @ the Speed of Thought*. The tile alone speaks volumes about how companies are beginning to view information and how fast information-based products and services change. Today's innovation is tomorrow's dinosaur. Products and services that used to take months and years to develop can now be brought to market in weeks or days.

In the past businesses were judged by how well they functioned within their own business. Now they are branded by the entire industry to which they belong. Vehicle manufacturers are judged on the value chain they help create within the entire industry, from the procurement of raw products to the impact on the environment from the vehicle emissions.

Many Internet-based companies are racing to build brand awareness and improve processes and products. Charles Schwab online brokerage, for example, is far ahead of its competitors in the delivery of online stock trading. It seems reasonable to think that Schwab could take a rest, because it will be quite a while before the competition catches up to the superior infrastructure and product delivery it's built. Don't be so sure. Other brokerage firms are forging ahead and building their own systems to take advantage of new enterprises on the Internet. No company can afford to rest for even a little while lest the competition beat it at its own game.

Technology Drivers: The New Networked Environment

Just five short years ago, the term *virtual organization* didn't exist. Now, more and more companies are adopting this concept because of the technological drivers in enterprise systems and industrial networks. Virtual partnerships are possible and make sense because of advances in technology.

If a company wants to embark on a new service, it doesn't necessarily have to work alone. It doesn't have to hire the people, purchase the hardware and software, and struggle with all the development costs by itself. It can partner with another company, use networks to enhance product delivery and keep costs down. A company using enterprise computing and industrial networks can go places not possible a few short years ago.

An Ideal Model of Enterprise Computing

In an ideal world, the business drives the technology and not the technology the business. To have this happen, four conditions must exist:

- The right amount of infrastructure.
- Close coupling of the architecture and the business processes.

- Adequate strategy to cope with environmental and competitive pressures.
- An adequate governance model to align the IT infrastructure with the business strategy.

12.2 MANAGING THE NEW IT INFRASTRUCTURE

How do you get information, the right kind and the right amount, from the environment into the organization and then move it throughout the organization? Let's look at some ways to do this successfully.

Elements of the New IT Infrastructure

The old days were simple: Your organization probably had a huge mainframe sitting in the basement with dummy terminals spread throughout the company. All data were maintained on the one system and specialists were the only ones allowed to touch it.

Now you must try to mesh remnants of the old legacy systems with the newer servers which have countless clients connected to them. On top of that, employees are more mobile nowadays and need cell phones. Not just plain old cell phones: These cell phones must be connected to the company's Intranet so product data can be downloaded while the salesperson is sitting thousands of miles away in a meeting with a potential customer. The icing on the cake are all the users who want to use fourth-generation software to build their own applications using downloaded corporate data.

Each element of the new IT Infrastructure poses its own unique set of challenges not just to the IT staff, but to the organization as a whole. Sally in Marketing just can't understand why she can't develop her own set of data and store it on her desktop. Tom in Sales wants to buy the latest Palm Pilot device to use in customer meetings and can't figure out how to connect it to the enterprise computing system. The newest product supplier needs help accessing the corporate Extranet in order to get information added to its own database. The local phone company is short of help and can't get the extra T1 transmission line installed for Internet access for three more months. The outsourcing consultant company needs to know how soon the company will be ready to test the newest order-processing application. The CEO needs someone in her office right away to help her set up the latest version of the Internet browser.

Key Infrastructure Decisions

Many companies have five-year plans for their products and services. That's good; companies should have an idea of where they want to go. As the text points out, "The overarching question is 'What business capabilities are we seeking?'" To say that arriving at the answer is difficult is a drastic understatement.

Most of these technologies seem to be obsolete or outdated a few months after they are purchased. The key is to select the technologies that fit somewhere in the middle of what you are currently using and where you want to be in a few years.

If your organization is currently using WINTEL (Windows operating systems and Intel processors) technology as the basis for your system, you shouldn't purchase Apple machines. Should the organization decide to move towards technology that's not compatible with the current infrastructure, plans need to be made and funds allotted for some type of middleware that will allow compatibility for the time being.

Software development projects must be judged on whether the company adopts a policy to build its own, use a pre-written specialized program, or go with general off-the-shelf software. We've discussed the pros and cons of each of these in previous chapters. The important thing to remember is that the software must support the business processes, both current and future.

As a company decides on the type of software to use, it must decide how the software will be deployed. Management needs to take a hard look at where it intends to be five years from now when deciding this question. Will the software be an enterprise-wide program, managed regionally, in separate business units, or installed on a local basis with each geographic unit operating independently? The decision made at this point will set the stage for how easy or difficult future expansion will be.

In the old days organizations had one choice for telecommunications: AT and T. That's was it. Now the choices are as broad and varied as the globe itself. Does the company go with a local, private provider or a global, public provider, or a combination of the two? If you need the most advanced security for data transmissions you may need to build your own telecommunications network; but this is very expensive and very limiting.

Connecting Infrastructure to Strategy: Governance

How do you know that the decisions you make regarding the IT infrastructure are the right ones for the organization? By letting business goals and strategies guide you. Focusing on the goals will prevent the business from purchasing unnecessary technology just because it's there. Having the organizational strategy decide the direction of the infrastructure will curb the impulse to grab the newest toys with the neatest bells and whistles.

Four levels of the organization should govern decisions about the IT infrastructure:

- CEO, CIO, and the strategic council.
- Operational groups.
- Business units and regional units.
- Specific business functions.

Dealing with Mergers and Acquisitions

If you can't build it, buy it. If you can't beat the competition, join it. Spread your risks by expanding into other product lines. Often companies decide it's better to merge or acquire other companies than to go it alone.

When a company does decide to merge with or acquire another company, it usually makes the decision from a strategic point of view. The senior executives are more concerned with how the new company can help them win new customers, enhance current products or services, or beat the competition. Very little time is spent exploring how the IT infrastructures will mesh with each other. Yet the inability to bring divergent systems together can derail the new enterprise.

Executives should learn to consider the impact information technology will have on making the new organization a success. Which system will they keep as the predominant system? How will the data be merged? Will new applications be required? What kind of IT staff will be needed for the new system? Of course many of these same types of questions must be asked of every business unit in the combined organization. However, since the Information System plays such a critical role in the success or failure of the new company, these are very important questions to ask specifically of the IT department.

The business environment may drive the merger and/or acquisition, but information technology makes it happen -- or not happen.

12.3 ENTERPRISE SYSTEMS

Now that the company has agreed to use enterprise computing and the grand design approach to solving problems, what are the effects on the IT infrastructure?

- Experimentation with other designs is limited.
- Significant resource commitments are necessary.
- This approach is nonadaptive.
- Success depends on faithful execution of all its elements.

Enterprise Systems: The Vision

What is the scope of enterprise systems, and what are they supposed to accomplish? Here's the dream:

"No more islands" is one of the great promises of enterprise computing. A single system will serve all areas of the organization and all data and information will be managed from a single point of view—that of the total organization. will manage from a firm-wide vantage point. They won't make decisions in isolation from other business units. Whatever they do in their own department will be available to all other business units.

All for one and one for all. Data will be managed for the total organization and cross-fed to and from individual units. This holds the promise of easy expansion to accommodate new business ventures and new technologies.

The organization will truly be driven by the customer and not by traditional production and supply factors. The customer will dictate that individual units act in a more cohesive manner and provide "one face" representing the entire organization. The business is then able to respond faster and more efficiently to competitive markets and add new products and services for the customer.

Enterprise Systems: The Reality

Lofty goals indeed--and necessary ones in today's business environment. Here's the real story. Many of the systems in place today have been around for a long time—much longer than expected in many cases. The systems have created dependencies that may be difficult to break. Enterprise systems promise to replace these aging systems with new hardware and software from top to bottom. And they promise to do it quickly. Take everything you've learned in this course and ask yourself if it's truly possible to do this so quickly.

There are some things you can't put a price tag on, such as improved customer relations or better employee morale. Yet these are the very benefits enterprise systems touts as their cornerstone for success. Some benefits won't be realized for years, especially if the firm installs the enterprise system in a piecemeal fashion. But the **bean counters, bless** them, want concrete evidence of the financial payback on the investment.

Even though enterprise systems promise improvements over older legacy systems patched together over time, do they really deliver on that promise? Do you have the technical knowledge available within the firm to conquer the new hardware, software, business process changes, and persware development necessary to make the new system a success? Or are you just gaining a whole new set of problems similar to the old problems but with new names?

Building bridges between the old system and the new can be worse and cost more than continually expanding and improving the old system. The new enterprise systems offer opportunities, but you'll still be relying on the old system for some time.

Some business assets can be sold and bought: new equipment that makes the production line more efficient, streamlined customer order processes, new trucks that reduce shipping costs. But how do you buy or sell strategic advantages that come from enterprise systems? Moreover, how do you take advantage of the new opportunities offered by the newer systems? And last, if all your competitors are using the same enterprise system, how do you create differentiation for your suppliers and customers?

12.4 INDUSTRIAL NETWORKS AND EXTENDED ENTERPRISE SYSTEMS

When you're trying to imagine industrial networks, think about the automobile manufacturers. Ford, GM, and Daimler Chrysler make cars and trucks. Do they make every part of every car and do they actually sell every car? Do they make the tires? Do they make the starter assemblies? Do they own the trucks and trains that transport the cars to the dealers? Do they own the dealers?

No; when you think about it, the Big Three are assemblers of vehicles. Goodyear, Michelin, and others make the tires. Delphi Industries makes the starters. Independent truckers and the railroad lines own the transportation. Individual people own the dealerships. But they all work in concert to get your favorite car or truck to your doorstep. An industrial network links them all together in a vertical chain.

Industrial Networks: The Vision

How we'd like it to be: When you order a new vehicle, the information is passed from the dealer or Web site to the manufacturer. At the same time, information regarding the specifications of your new car are passed to the parts suppliers, the tire makers, and the truckers. Everyone along the way knows what you ordered and when you expect delivery.

If one piece of the vertical network needs help or information or improvements, all other parts of the network can help. Managers won't think of their individual companies, but will act on behalf of the entire industry.

Managers, specifically IT managers, will be required to view their information infrastructures from the vantage point of an entire industry and not their individual companies. Suppliers won't benefit from having three or four different platforms thrust on them by various manufacturers.

It may seem strange that a company can enhance its business capabilities by joining forces with competitors. Industrial networks and the promise of greater efficiencies and lower costs demand that firms do so. The example in the text of Dell and IBM working together to increase their sales is an excellent snapshot of the future of other industries.

Industrial Networks: The Reality

Landmines abound in this new paradigm. Here's the real story.

Companies have always safeguarded information to increase their competitive advantage. And now they're just going to throw open the doors and give critical information to the world? Not quite. Businesses will still control the release and flow of information in one of three ways:

- **Hierarchy :** One company decides for the rest how information will be disseminated, who gets it, and how they are allowed to use it.
- **Market interface :** Each company is on equal footing with its partners and lets the marketplace drive their participation.
- **Network interface :** A third party or a steering committee of sorts manages the network.

Who will pay for what and at what percentage? Will all partners in the industrial network share the costs equally? How will suppliers and vendors be charged for the benefits they receive? How will a company determine its return on investment, especially when the return may be in less tangible benefits?

Systems break down and require upgrades. Who will be responsible for maintenance of the system? When a firm relies solely on itself for information, that question is easily answered. It isn't so clear when a company relies on an industrial network shared by other companies and competitors. Divided loyalties between a company's own internal network and the industrial network is a very real concern.

Steps to Building and Managing ES and IN

Questions managers need to ask themselves before embarking on the long voyage:

1. Where are you now in relation to the technology and the other firms? On a piece of paper, draw a circle and write inside "You are here." Describe your company in terms of its technology knowledge and describe other firms in the same way.
2. Know who you are and where you want to be: Draw another circle and write inside "Where you belong?" Now fill in everything in between. Get input from various sources. Be honest with yourself and your company.
3. Devise a five-year plan: Sketch out ideas of what your company could look like in the next five-years.
4. Understand the necessary and fundamental changes required: Are you ready and willing to change the way you manage? Are the other managers ready and willing?
5. Recognize the need to re-educate employees: How will you retrain managers and employees to carry out the changes you described in item 4?
6. Provide incentive systems for the new environment: The carrot-and-stick approach does work.

12.5 GLOBAL ENTERPRISE SOLUTIONS

IT and Communication network is lifeline of every 21st Century Enterprise and it is important to design and implement fit for purpose IT infrastructure and networks. Equally vital task for IT leaders is to entrust the monitoring and upkeep of their IT real estate with a trusted, reliable and efficient partner.

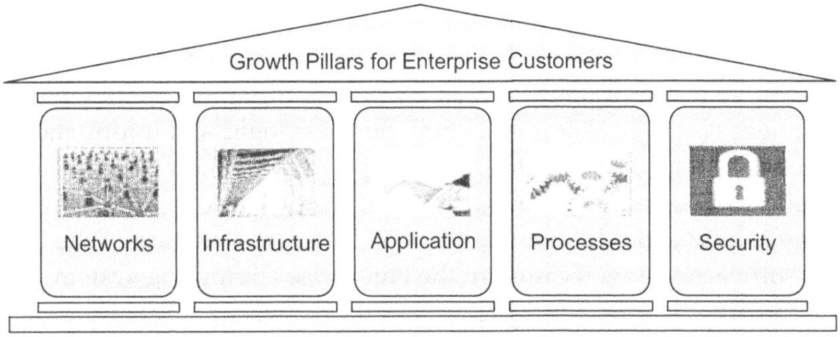

Fig. 12.3

Working as for global communications providers, a company must have gained strong experience in following aspects of business:

- High Availability, High Transaction I.T. Environment.
- Multiple customer touch points for both B2B and B2C operations.
- Cutting edge , rapidly changing technology landscape.

Global Enterprise Solutions are based on the above characteristics and their Enterprise portfolio can cater to needs of our Enterprise Customers in the following areas:

1. **Network Services**
   (*a*) Network Planning, Design and Optimisation.
   (*b*) Network and Application Performance Engineering.
   (*c*) Unified Communication and Next Generation Networks.
   (*d*) Enterprise Capacity Planning and monitoring.
2. **Infrastructure Managed Services**
   (*a*) Remote Infrastructure Management incl. L1, L2 and L3.
   (*b*) Data Centre Management Services.
   (*c*) Managed Networks Services.
   (*d*) Infrastructure Consulting *e.g.*, ITIL, Unified Window.
3. **Business process outsourcing Services across all phases of business lifecycle**
   (*a*) Customer Relationship Management - Acquisition, Retention and In-Life.
   (*b*) Finance and Accounting.
   (*c*) Human Resources.
   (*d*) Market Research and Data Analytics.
   (*e*) Business Support Services - Learning, Inventory, Procurement etc.
4. **Enterprise Platforms and Applications like ERP/CRM/ BI/ ECM**
   (*a*) Packaged Solutions - SAP, Oracle, Microsoft.
   (*b*) Platform Modernisation - SoA, Web2.0, Enterprise IP TV.
   (*c*) Enterprise Portal and Content Management - Sharepoint, Life Ray etc.
   (*d*) End to End Testing (Strategy till Execution) and Test Automation.
5. **Infrastructure and Application Security**
   (*a*) Managed Security Services and 24 × 7 Security Ops Centre.
   (*b*) Identity and Access Management.
   (*c*) Disaster Recovery and Business Continuity Planning.
   (*d*) Application and Network Security consulting and projects.

SUMMARY

Enterprise computing views an organization as a whole and not just as its separate parts. Four concepts--IT investment portfolio, IT infrastructure, business logic, and information architecture--are necessary elements for success in enterprise computing. The new IT infrastructure is more complex and complicated than ever. Choosing the right technology demands an understanding of where the company is now and where it wants to go. The core structure of the business should decide the type of software and its location in the enterprise computing system.

Industrial networks link suppliers with manufacturers from the beginning of the process to the conclusion of the transaction. Information is passed on all along the way to gain efficiencies and cut costs. Industrial networks may require a sea-change in the way a company functions. Managers must be ready and willing to accommodate the changes.

EXERCISE

1. Explain the importance of IT Infrastructure and Enterprise Computing.
2. Find out the drivers forcing organisations in a changing environment.
3. Explain how to manage the IT infrastructure effectively.
4. Write a note on Enterprise Systems and Industrial Networks.
5. Explain the difference between enterprise computing and industrial networks.

13

SECURITY AND ETHICAL CHALLENGES OF IT

13.0 INFORMATION SECURITIES AND CONTROL

We have, seen in our earlier chapter how Information Technology and Computers have brought about a paradigm shift in the way the corporate organizations operate. We have also noted the significant impact of IT and computers on the business processes, evolution of new Products/ Services, improved profits, global integration and more efficient and effective allocation and utilization of resources, among others.

I.T. and computers have indeed heralded the 'Information Age'. Resultantly, 'Information' itself has emerged as one of the most valuable and sought after 'RESOURCE', conferring competitive advantage on those organizations, which have it.

But those organizations which missed the bus, did try to regain their position by sometimes, poaching or, on other occasions, trying to encroach upon the Information Resource base of their competitors, by cracking or breaking into the Information/Computer Systems of their leading counterparts. The spread of Internet and the relative ease of access made this task of 'Information Breach' relatively easier. The cracking or breaking into the computer system by way of malicious and unauthorized access could be any one of the following or otherwise:

(*a*) Unauthorized reading of data (Theft of Information).

(*b*) Unauthorized modification of data.

(*c*) Unauthorized destruction of data.

Information resources are scattered throughout the organization. Furthermore employees travel with and take home corporate computers and data. Information is transmitted to and from the organization and among the organization's components. IT physical resources, data, software, procedures and any other information resources may therefore be vulnerable to security risk in many places at any time.

13.0.1 System Vulnerability

Information systems are made up many components that may be in several locations. Thus, each information system is vulnerable to many potential hazards. The vulnerability of information systems is increasing as we move to a world of networked computing. Theoretically there are hundreds of points in corporate information system that can be subject to some threat. These threats can be classified unintentional or intentional.

13.0.1.1 Unintentional Threats

Unintentional threats can be divided into three major categories: human errors, environmental hazards and computer system failures. Several computer problems result from human error. Errors can occur in the design of hardware or information system. They can also occur in the programming, testing, data collection, data entry, authorization and instructions. Human error contributes to the vast majority of control and security related problems in much organization. Environment hazards include earthquakes, hurricanes, serve, snow, sand, storms, floods, tornadoes, power failures or strong fluctuations, fires, defective air conditioning, explosions, radioactive fallout and water cooling system failures. Such hazards may disrupt normal computer operations and result in long waiting periods and exorbitant costs while computer programs and data files are recreated. Computer system failures can be result of poor manufacturing or defective material. Unintentional malfunctions can happen for other reasons, raging from lack of experience to incompatibility of software.

13.0.1.2 Intentional Threats

Computer systems may be damaged as a result of intentional actions. Some examples are: theft of data, inappropriate use of data, theft of mainframe computer time, theft of equipment or programs; deliberate manipulation in handling, entering, processing, transferring or programming data; labor strikes, riots or sabotage; malicious damage to computer resources; destruction from virus and similar attacks, and miscellaneous computer abuse and crimes. Most of the intentional threats are viewed, when executed as computer crimes.

13.0.2 Protecting Information Systems

The large number of potential threats to information systems has resulted in a great number of defensive strategies and tools. Defending information systems is not a simple or inexpensive task for the following reasons:

- Hundreds of potential threats exist.
- Computing resources may be situated in many locations.
- Many individual control information aspects.
- Computer networks can be outside the organization and difficult to protect.
- Rapid technological changes make some controls obsolete as soon as they are installed.
- Many computer crimes are undetected for a long period of time, so it is difficult to "learn from experience".
- People tend to violate security procedures because the procedures are inconvenient.
- Many computer criminals who are caught often go unpunished, so there is a little deterrent effect.
- The amount of computer knowledge necessary to commit computer crimes is usually minimal.
- The cost of preventing hazards can be very high. Therefore, most organizations simply cannot afford to protect against all possible hazards.
- It is difficult to conduct a cost — benefit justification for controls before an attack occurs since it is difficult to assess the cost of hypothetical attack.

13.0.3 How Do We Protect IT

Protection of IT is a accomplished by inserting controls - defense mechanism that are designed to protect all the components of an information system, specifically, data, software, hardware and networks. The following are the Major defense strategies:

- **Controls for prevention and deterrence**: Properly designed controls may prevent error from occurring, deter criminals from attacking the system, and better yet, deny access to unauthorized people. Prevention and deterrence are especially important where the potential for damage is very high.
- **Detection:** It may not be economically feasible to prevent all hazards and preventive measures may not always work. Therefore, unprotected systems are vulnerable to attack. Like a fire, the easier it is detected, the easier it is to combat and the less damage. Detection can be performed in many cases by using special diagnostic software.
- **Limitation:** This means minimizing losses once a malfunction has occurred. Users typically want their systems back in operation as quickly as possible. This can be accomplished by including a fault - tolerant system that permits operation in a degraded mode until full recovery is made.
- **Recovery:** A recovery plan explains how to fix a damaged information system as quickly as possible. Replacing rather than repairing components can be a route for fast recovery.
- **Correction:** Correcting damaged systems can prevent the problem from occurring again.

13.0.4 General Controls

The major categories of general controls are physical controls, access controls, data security controls, communication/network controls and administrative controls.

13.0.4.1 Physical Controls

Physical security refers to the physical protection of computer facilities and resources. This includes protecting physical property such as computers, data centers, software, manuals, and networks. Physical security provides protection against most natural hazards as well as against human hazards. Appropriate physical security may include several controls such as human guards and locked doors.

Access Controls: Access control is the restriction of unauthorized user access to a portion of a computer system or to the entire system. To gain access, a user must first be authorized. Then, when the user attempts to gain access, he or she must be authenticated. Access control software is commercially available for large mainframes, mini computers, personal computers, local area networks and dial in communications networks.

Biometric controls: A biometric control is an automated method of verifying the identity of a person, based on physiological or behavioral characteristics. The most common biometric controls are the following:

- **Hand geometry:** Similar to fingerprints except the verifier uses a television like camera to take a picture of the user's hand. Certain characteristics of the hand are electronically compared against the information stored in the computer.

- **Blood vessel pattern in the retina of an eye:** A match is attempted between the pattern of the blood vessels in the back-of-the-eye retina that is being scanned and a pre stored picture of the authorized individual's retina.
- **Voice:** A match is attempted between the user's voice and the voice pattern stored on templates.
- **Signature:** Signatures are matched against the pre stored authentic signature. This method can supplement a photo-card ID system.
- **Keystroke dynamics:** the person's keyboard pressure and speed it matched against pre-stored information.
- **Facial themography:** An infrared camera captures a portrait of the face and resisters the different temperatures emanating from underlying blood vessels. The picture is stored. When you use the computer another picture is taken and matched with the pre-stored one.
- **Fingerprints:** each time a user wants access, matching a fingerprint against a template containing the authorized person's fingerprint identifies him/her.

13.0.4.2 Data Security Controls

Data security is concerned with protecting data from accidental or intentional disclosure to unauthorized persons or from unauthorized modifications or destruction. Data security functions are implemented through operating systems, security access control programs, and database/data communications products, recommended backup/recovery procedures, application programs and external control procedures. Data security must address

13.0.4.3 Communication (Network) Controls

High-speed public data networks, such as AT&T's have become increasingly popular way for banks, airlines, retailers and other business to relay customer information and other data to their branch offices. Such public networks, which are about 50 percent cheaper than private lines, are called frame relay networks. The most network access control that includes authentication and passwords, encryption, cable, testers and firewalls.

13.0.4.4 Administrative Controls

Administrative controls deals with issuing guidelines and monitoring compliance with the guidelines. These controls are frequently built into the application and are usually written ad validation rules. They can be classified into three categories: input controls, processing controls and output controls.

Input controls: Input controls are designed to prevent data alteration or loss. Data are checked for accuracy, completeness and consistency.

Processing controls: Processing controls ensure that data are complete, valid and accurate when being processed and that programs have been properly executed. These programs allow only authorized users to access certain programs or facilities and they monitor the computer's use by the individuals.

Output controls: Output controls ensure that the results of computer processing are accurate, valid, complete and consistent. By studying the nature of common output errors and the causes of such errors, management can evaluate possible controls to deal with problems. Also, control ensures that outputs are sent only to authorized personnel.

13.1 WHY BREAK I.T. SYSTEM SECURITY?

There could be a number of reasons as to why people/organizations would want to crack or break into the computer systems of their competitors, in particular.

Some of the most popular reasons could be mentioned as follows:

(*a*) Revenge

(*b*) Money

(*c*) A shot at / of notoriety

(*d*) The challenge of doing "IT".

Its me, of course, did it for the sake ("hack" ?) of it and some others did it simply for the "kick". Regardless of the reasons, there is no denying the fact there continued to be a number of attempts — some successful, some failed — against the Computer / IT. Systems security. It in became apparent, indeed imperative, that the organizational "Information Resources" needed to be jealously guarded, protected and controlled against such unauthorized and desired access as, otherwise, not only the data, the networks and the information infrastructure but, ultimately, the organization itself could be at risk.

Our future is not secure if your Information is not secure became the motto.

13.2 INFORMATION SYSTEM SECURITY THREATS

Then it comes to Information System Security and Control, it must be realized that, broadly, there are two different types of threats/problems:

13.2.1 The External Threat and The Internal Threat

Of course, with the prevalence of remote access, the World Wide Web, Intranets and Extranets, - distinction/difference between the External Threats and the Internal Threats is more often hirred and hazy. It would not be out of place to say that the difference is more logical than a physical one.

Let us now discuss, in detail, these security threats and managerial responses to find a way?

The external security/control threats

The external threats would be those emanating from outside the organization. To provide security against these threats, the following issues need to be addressed:

The organization's connections to internet.

The Remote Dial-in capabilities.

Internet connections

Normally, in every organization there are relatively few, identifiable internet connections. It is, therefore, relatively easy to focus upon them and exercise control. The interconnection connection should be protected by a "Firewall".

Firewalls are hardware and software combinations that guard the border between the corporate Inter/Intranet (Private Access) and the Internet (Public Access) as illustrated in next page:

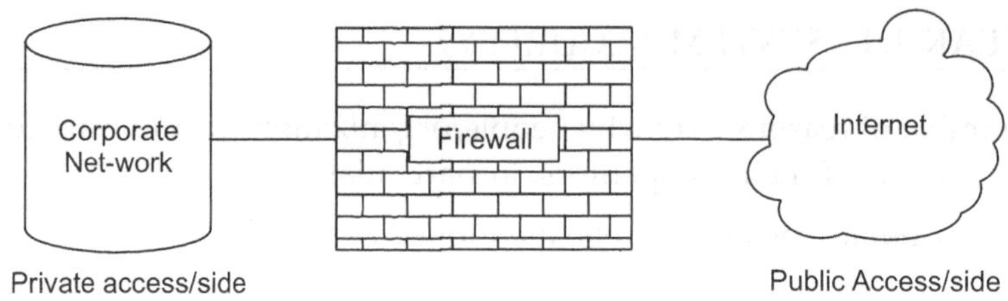

Fig. 13.1 *Firewalls*

Firewalls can control who, if anyone, can surf the Web, download files etc. Firewalls can also hide the organizational network's identity from the rest of the world on the Internet, as the corporate internal IP address(s) is/are never used.

It should be remembered that if the organization's Internet connections are not protected by Firewalls, it would be like going away on leave/vacation/holidays and leaving the door unlocked. It would be an invitation for disaster as, while there may not be any visible indication that you are vulnerable, the first person who comes knocking on the door is going to find out that the door is open and not locked, and he may not be exactly your best and trusted friend!

Remote Dial-in Capabilities

While the Internet connections are few and easy to watch/control, the threats from Dial-in are real. There might be hundreds of dial-in threats, most of which might be unknown to the security administration.

Any user in the organization with a phone line and a modem attached to his PC can be an exposure for external access.

While controlling remote dial-in capabilities, the following aspects need to be given due weight age/considerations:

(*a*) Remote Access
(*b*) Remote Access Servers (RAS)
(*c*) Server ID
(*d*) The weak points of the system environment.

Internal Security Threats

It is generally thought that the people who are employees of the company are on 'our' side and the real threat for security comes from "outside". Nothing can be more ironic then that, more often than not, the greatest security threats come from within!

It is, therefore, imperative that formal security policies/measures are carefully designed and scrupulously followed to ensure best protection and prevent security breaches.

The policies/measures need to address the following aspects:

1. Passwords
2. User Termination
3. Special Privilege IDs
4. Access Reviews
5. Authorization levels

6. User information
7. Routine maintenance
8. Software updates
9. Virus checking/checks
10. Physical considerations
11. Audit Trails

Passwords

Password should be at least five characters in length. It should be neither the same as the user's ID — nor be a common word. It should expire/change regularly and reuse of the older Password should not be permitted. Some software, with the ability to disable an ID if too many or specified failed attempts are made within a specified period of time should be installed

User Terminations

When the user ceases to be an employee, intern, temporary associate or consultant/ contractor, the user security administrator must be informed forthwith, so that the user 'ID could be determinated.

Special Privilege IDs

Certain functionaries (like Network/System Managers) are allotted special IDs and passwords called Root, Supervisor or Administrator ID/Passwords) providing 'Carte Blanche' access to the system.

These passwords too should be changed regularly and changed immediately when someone who knows them leaves the organization.

Access Review

There are generally number of users and hundreds of thousands, if not millions, of files on computer networks. Some type of user administrator review must be undertaken - twice or thrice a year — to ensure that unauthorized users are not given access.

Authorization Levels

It must be made clear as to who has authority over what. It must also be ensured that the requests for authorization — permitting access to relative database files-are received and issued in writing, usually via e-mail.

Further, the user could be assigned several forms of authorization for access to parts of database. The authorization could be:

Read authorization

Insert authorization

Update authorization

Delete authorization

Index authorization

Resource authorization
Actuation authorization
Drop authorization

User Information

The users should be made aware of the security issues.

Routine Maintenance

Routine maintenance should mainly cover activities like:

(*a*) IDs that have not been used in a predefined period of time should be disabled.
(*b*) Logs giving details about unsuccessful log-in attempts should be reviewed and investigated.
(*c*) Files that have not been accessed for quite some time should be purged, to free up space.

Software Updates

Security Administrators should regularly check with the software vendors to obtain and apply the latest software updates or patches that help close security gaps/holes.

Virus Checking

Viruses are any type of programming code that intentionally causes a system disruption, shut down or loss of data. The disruption might be harmless or even amusing — like displaying the message, "Feel like banana?" on the computer screen. The disruption could also be hostile and destructive leading to erasing of files/data on hard-drives without any intimation.

There are many types of viruses including those known as "Trojan Horses" and "Worms". Some other major viruses are "Melissa", "Chernobyl", and "Explorer Zip Worms", "I Love You", "Code Red" and "WBL SQL Slammer", among others.

Viruses, therefore, have been occupational annoyances/hazards to the IT professionals. As, however, viruses pose a very real threat to security, due, in fact, special attention has to be aid to the virus protection programmes, policies and procedures. Installation of anti-virus software is, hence, a must. Pattern files, which contain all the information that the actual anti-viruses program uses to look for virus, must be updated regularly. Further, as E-mail has become the most prevalent form for propagating viruses, anti-virus software should be installed on mail servers to scan message attachments.

Some of the anti-virus software products currently in use are Symantec's Norton Antivirus, Network Associates. Total Virus Defence Product Suit and Intel's LANDesk etc.

Physical Considerations

The physical access to the IT area needs to be controlled. Access to the computer room or data centre should be limited on 'need' basis. Other IT areas — auxiliary storages, wiring — etc. should be locked. Even printed report distribution should be controlled and apart from the door-locks and access cards, shredders should be made available to dispose of dundant output. Visitors should be personally escorted within the premises.

Audit Trails

Can/should be made mandatory to maintain an Audit Trail. An Audit Trail is a log of all changes (inserts/deletes/updates) to the database, along with information such as which were performed the change and when the change was performed.

The Audit Trails help 'Security' and 'Control' in a number of ways. To illustrate, Audit Trails help in:

(*a*) Tracing all the updates performed.

(*b*) Finding incorrect/fraudulent updates.

(*c*) Finding the person who carried out the updates.

Audit Trails could be created by defining appropriate triggers on relation updates, Audit tralls could also be based on built-in mechanisms.

13.3 ETHICAL AND SOCIAL DIMENSIONS

13.3.1 Introduction

In our earlier discussions, we have noted how I.T. has changed and is changing the rules of competition. But as the rules of competition changed and application of computers increased exponential speed, it has also given rise to a number of ethical and social dilemmas. It is proposed to discuss some of the illustrative, ethical and social dilemmas/dimensions of I.T. Information Systems Applications in the following paragraphs.

13.3.2 What is Ethics/Ethical?

While 'Ethics' means 'the system or code of morals of a particular person, religion, group or professions", "Ethical" means "having to do with ethics or morality of or conforming to moral standards conforming to the standards of conduct of given profession or group".

A person's ethics, according to Griffin(1990) are formulated through the operation of five key process in the individual's environment viz,

1. Family Influences
2. Peer Influences
3. Experiences
4. Values and Morals
5. Situational Factors

13.3.3 Ethical Issues Related to Systems

Ethics is a branch of philosophy that deals with what is considered to be right and wrong. There are many definitions of ethics, such as "codes of morals of a particular profession", "the standards of conduct of a given profession", "agreement among people to do the right and to avoid the wrong". In one of the oldest codes of ethics, the Ten Commandments, Clear specifications are given about what an individual should and should not do. Over the years, philosophers have proposed many ethical guidelines. It is important to realize that what is unethical is not necessarily illegal.

A Framework for Ethics

Many companies and professional organizations develop their own codes of ethics. A code of ethics is a collection of principles intended as a guide for members of a company or an organization. The diversity of IT application and the increased use of the technology have created a variety of ethical issues. Prof. R.O. Masson & others categories ethical issues into four types: privacy, accuracy, property and accessibility.

1. **Privacy issues:** Collection, storage and dissemination of information about individuals.
   - What information about oneself should an individual be required to revel to others?
   - What kind of surveillance can be employer use on its employees?
   - What thing can people keep to themselves and not to be forced to revel others?
   - What information about individuals should be kept in databases and how secure is the information there?
2. **Accuracy issues:** Authenticity, fidelity and accuracy of information collected and processes.
   - Who is responsible for authenticity, fidelity, and accuracy of information collected?
   - How can we ensure that errors in databases, data transmissions and data processing are accidental and not intentional?
   - Who is to be held accountable for errors in information and how should the injured party be compensated?
3. **Property issues:** Ownership and value of information.
   - **Who owns the information?**
   - What are the just and fair prices for its exchange?
   - How should one handle software privacy?
   - Under what circumstances can one use proprietary databases?
   - Can corporate computers be used for private purposes?
   - How should experts who contribute their knowledge to create expert system be compensated?
   - How should access to information channels be allocated?
4. **Accessibility issues**: Right to access information and payment of fees to access it.
   - Who is allowed to access information?
   - How much should be changed for permitting accessibility to information?
   - How can accessibility to computers be provided for employees for disabilities?
   - Who will be provided with equipment needed for accessing information?
   - What information does a person or an organization has a right or privilege to obtain and under what conditions and with what safeguards?

13.3.4 Ethical Dimensions

The Ethical Dimensions would broadly cover the following aspects :

1. Obligation to Management
2. Obligation to Society
3. Obligation to Employer
4. Obligations to Country

Ethical Dilemmas

Some of the illustrative ethical dilemmas could be summarized as follows:

1. Inappropriate use of computers technology.
2. Inappropriate use of computer resources.
3. Inefficient programming logic.
4. Inefficient processing instructions.
5. Manipulation of records.
6. Deletion/Distortion of records.

In view of the enormous power of Information Technology, and the resultant 'Nuisance Value' (Hacking, for example), it is imperative that a professional Code of Conduct and Ethics be devised and globally implemented for the I.T. Professionals.

13.4 BUSINESS ETHICS

Business ethics is the behavior that a business adheres to in its daily dealings with the world. The ethics of a particular business can be diverse. They apply not only to how the business interacts with the world at large, but also to their one-on-one dealings with a single customer.

Many businesses have gained a bad reputation just by being in business. To some people, businesses are interested in making money, and that is the bottom line. It could be called capitalism in its purest form. Making money is not wrong in itself. It is the manner in which some businesses conduct themselves that brings up the question of ethical behavior.

Good business ethics should be a part of every business. There are many factors to consider. When a company does business with another that is considered unethical, does this make the first company unethical by association? Some people would say yes, the first business has a responsibility and it is now a link in the chain of unethical businesses.

Many global businesses, including most of the major brands that the public use, can be seen not to think too highly of good business ethics. Many major brands have been fined millions for breaking ethical business laws. Money is the major deciding factor.

If a company does not adhere to business ethics and breaks the laws, they usually end up being fined. Many companies have broken anti-trust, ethical and environmental laws and received fines worth millions. The problem is that the amount of money these companies are making outweighs the fines applied. Billion dollar profits blind the companies to their lack of business ethics, and the dollar sign wins.

A business may be a multi-million seller, but does it use good business ethics and do people care? There are popular soft drinks and fast food restaurants that have been fined time and time again for unethical behavior. Business ethics should eliminate exploitation, from the sweatshop children who are making sneakers to the coffee serving staffs who is being ripped off in wages. Business ethics can be applied to everything from the trees cut down to make the paper that a business sells to the ramifications of importing coffee from certain countries.

Business ethics is a form of applied ethics that examines ethical principles and moral or ethical problems that arise in a business environment.

In the increasingly conscience-focused marketplaces of the 21st century, the demand for more ethical business processes and actions (known as ethicism) is increasing Simultaneously, pressure is applied on industry to improve business ethics through new public initiatives and laws (*e.g.*, higher UK road tax for higher-emission vehicles). Businesses can often attain short-term gains by acting in an unethical fashion; however, such antics tend to undermine the economy over time.

Business ethics can be both a normative and a descriptive discipline. As a corporate practice and a career specialization, the field is primarily normative. In academia descriptive approaches are also taken. The range and quantity of business ethical issues reflects the degree to which business is perceived to be at odds with non-economic social values. Historically, interest in business ethics accelerated dramatically during the 1980s and 1990s, both within major corporations and within academia. For example, today most major corporate websites lay emphasis on commitment to promoting non-economic social values under a variety of headings (*e.g.*, ethics codes, social responsibility charters). In some cases, corporations have redefined their core values in the light of business ethical considerations (*e.g.*, BP's "beyond petroleum" environmental tilt).

13.4.1 Overview of Issues in Business Ethics

General business ethics

- This part of business ethics overlaps with the philosophy of business, one of the aims of which is to determine the fundamental purposes of a company. If a company's main purpose is to maximize the returns to its shareholders, then it should be seen as unethical for a company to consider the interests and rights of anyone else.
- Corporate social responsibility or CSR: an umbrella term under which the ethical rights and duties existing between companies and society is debated.
- Issues regarding the moral rights and duties between a company and its shareholders: fiduciary responsibility, stakeholder concept v. shareholder concept.
- Ethical issues concerning relations between different companies: *e.g.*, hostile take-overs, industrial espionage.
- Leadership issues: corporate governance.
- Political contributions made by corporations.
- Law reform, such as the ethical debate over introducing a crime of corporate manslaughter.
- The misuse of corporate ethics policies as marketing instruments.

Ethics of accounting information

- Creative accounting, earnings management, misleading financial analysis.
- Insider trading, securities fraud, bucket shops, forex scams: concerns (criminal) manipulation of the financial markets.
- Executive compensation: concerns excessive payments made to corporate CEO's and top management.
- Bribery, kickbacks, facilitation payments: while these may be in the (short-term) interests of the company and its shareholders, these practices may be anti-competitive or offend against the values of society.

Ethics of human resource management

The ethics of human resource management (HRM) covers those ethical issues arising around the employer-employee relationship, such as the rights and duties owed between employer and employee.

- Discrimination issues include discrimination on the bases of age (ageism), gender, race, religion, disabilities, weight and attractiveness.
- Issues surrounding the representation of employees and the democratization of the workplace: union busting, strike breaking.
- Issues affecting the privacy of the employee: workplace surveillance, drug testing.
- Issues affecting the privacy of the *employer*: whistle-blowing.
- Issues relating to the fairness of the employment contract and the balance of power between employer and employee: slavery, indentured servitude, employment law.
- Occupational safety and health.

Ethics of sales and marketing

Marketing which goes beyond the mere provision of information about (and access to) a product may seek to manipulate our values and behavior. To some extent society regards this as acceptable, but where is the ethical line to be drawn? Marketing ethics overlaps strongly with media ethics, because marketing makes heavy use of media. However, media ethics is a much larger topic and extends outside business ethics.

- Pricing: price fixing, price discrimination, price skimming.
- Anti-competitive practices: these include but go beyond pricing tactics to cover issues such as manipulation of loyalty and supply chains.
- Specific marketing strategies: greenwash, bait and switch, shill, viral marketing, spam (electronic), pyramid scheme, planned obsolescence.
- Content of advertisements: attack ads, subliminal messages, sex in advertising, products regarded as immoral or harmful
- Children and marketing: marketing in schools.
- Black markets, grey markets.

Ethics of production

This area of business ethics deals with the duties of a company to ensure that products and production processes do not cause harm. Some of the more acute dilemmas in this area arise out of the fact that there is usually a degree of danger in any product or production process and it is difficult to define a degree of permissibility, or the degree of permissibility may depend on the changing state of preventative technologies or changing social perceptions of acceptable risk.

- Defective, addictive and inherently dangerous products and services (*e.g.*, tobacco, alcohol, weapons, motor vehicles, chemical manufacturing, bungee jumping).
- Ethical relations between the company and the environment: pollution, environmental ethics, carbon emissions trading
- Ethical problems arising out of new technologies: genetically modified food, mobile phone radiation and health.

- Product testing ethics: animal rights and animal testing, use of economically disadvantaged groups (such as students) as test objects.

Ethics of intellectual property, knowledge and skills

Knowledge and skills are valuable but not easily "ownable" as objects. Nor is it obvious who has the greater rights to an idea: the company who trained the employee, or the employee themselves? The country in which the plant grew, or the company which discovered and developed the plant's medicinal potential? As a result, attempts to assert ownership and ethical disputes over ownership arise.

- Patent infringement, copyright infringement, trademark infringement.
- Misuse of the intellectual property systems to stifle competition: patent misuse, copyright misuse, patent troll, submarine patent.
- Even the notion of intellectual property itself has been criticised on ethical grounds: see intellectual property.
- Employee raiding: the practice of attracting key employees away from a competitor to take unfair advantage of the knowledge or skills they may possess.
- The practice of employing all the most talented people in a specific field, regardless of need, in order to prevent any competitors employing them.
- Bioprospecting (ethical) and biopiracy (unethical).
- Business intelligence and industrial espionage.

13.4.2 International Business Ethics and Ethics of Economic Systems

The issues here are grouped together because they involve a much wider, global view on business ethical matters.

International business ethics

While business ethics emerged as a field in the 1970s, international business ethics did not emerge until the late 1990s, looking back on the international developments of that decade. Many new practical issues arose out of the international context of business. Theoretical issues such as cultural relativity of ethical values receive more emphasis in this field. Other, older issues can be grouped here as well. Issues and subfields include:

- The search for universal values as a basis for international commercial behaviour.
- Comparison of business ethical traditions in different countries.
- Comparison of business ethical traditions from various religious perspectives.
- Ethical issues arising out of international business transactions; e.g. bioprospecting and biopiracy in the pharmaceutical industry; the fair trade movement; transfer pricing.
- Issues such as globalization and cultural imperialism.
- Varying global standards - e.g. the use of child labor.
- The way in which multinationals take advantage of international differences, such as outsourcing production (e.g. clothes) and services (e.g. call centres) to low-wage countries.
- The permissibility of international commerce with pariah states.

Ethics of economic systems

This vaguely defined area, perhaps not part of but only related to business ethics is where business ethicists venture into the fields of political economy and political philosophy, focusing on the rights and wrongs of various systems for the distribution of economic benefits. The work of John Rawls and Robert Nozick are both notable contributors.

13.5.3 Theoretical Issues in Business Ethics

Conflicting interests

Business ethics can be examined from various perspectives, including the perspective of the employee, the commercial enterprise, and society as a whole. Very often, situations arise in which there is conflict between one or more of the parties, such that serving the interest of one party is a detriment to the other(s). For example, a particular outcome might be good for the employee, whereas, it would be bad for the company, society, or vice versa. Some ethicists (e.g., Henry Sidgwick) see the principal role of ethics as the harmonization and reconciliation of conflicting interests.

Ethical issues and approaches

Philosophers and others disagree about the purpose of a business ethic in society. For example, some suggest that the principal purpose of a business is to maximize returns to its owners, or in the case of a publicly-traded concern, its shareholders. Thus, under this view, only those activities that increase profitability and shareholder value should be encouraged, because any others function as a tax on profits. Some believe that the only companies that are likely to survive in a competitive marketplace are those that place profit maximization above everything else. However, some point out that self-interest would still require a business to obey the law and adhere to basic moral rules, because the consequences of failing to do so could be very costly in fines, loss of licensure, or company reputation. The noted economist Milton Friedman was a leading proponent of this view.

Some take the position that organizations are not capable of moral agency. Under this, ethical behavior is required of individual human beings, but not of the business or corporation.

Other theorists contend that a business has moral duties that extend well beyond serving the interests of its owners or stockholders, and that these duties consist of more than simply obeying the law. They believe a business has moral responsibilities to so-called stakeholders, people who have an interest in the conduct of the business, which might include employees, customers, vendors, the local community, or even society as a whole. They would say that stakeholders have certain rights with regard to how the business operates, and some would suggest that this includes even rights of governance.

Some theorists have adapted social contract theory to business, whereby companies become quasi-democratic associations, and employees and other stakeholders are given voice over a company's operations. This approach has become especially popular subsequent to the revival of contract theory in political philosophy, which is largely due to John Rawls' *A Theory of Justice*, and the advent of the consensus-oriented approach to solving business problems, an aspect of the "quality movement" that emerged in the 1980s. Professors Thomas Donaldson and Thomas Dunfee proposed a version of contract theory for business, which they call Integrative Social Contracts Theory. They posit that conflicting interests are best resolved by formulating a "fair agreement" between the parties, using a combination of i) macro-principles that all rational people would agree upon as universal principles, and, ii) micro-principles formulated by actual agreements among the interested parties. Critics say the proponents of contract theories miss a central point, namely, that a business is someone's property and not a mini-state or a means of distributing social justice.

Ethical issues can arise when companies must comply with multiple and sometimes conflicting legal or cultural standards, as in the case of multinational companies that operate in countries with varying practices. The question arises, for example, ought a company to obey the laws of its home country, or should it follow the less stringent laws of the developing country in which it does business? To illustrate, United States law forbids companies from paying bribes either domestically or overseas; however, in other parts of the world, bribery is a customary, accepted way of doing business. Similar problems can occur with regard to child labor, employee safety, work hours, wages, discrimination, and environmental protection laws.

It is sometimes claimed that a Gresham's law of ethics applies in which bad ethical practices drive out good ethical practices. It is claimed that in a competitive business environment, those companies that survive are the ones that recognize that their only role is to maximize profits.

13.4.4 Business Ethics in the Field

Corporate ethics policies

As part of more comprehensive compliance and ethics programs, many companies have formulated internal policies pertaining to the ethical conduct of employees. These policies can be simple exhor-tations in broad, highly-generalized language (typically called a corporate ethics statement), or they can be more detailed policies, containing specific behavioral requirements (typically called corporate ethics codes). They are generally meant to identify the company's expectations of workers and to offer guidance on handling some of the more common ethical problems that might arise in the course of doing business. It is hoped that having such a policy will lead to greater ethical awareness, consistency in application, and the avoidance of ethical disasters.

An increasing number of companies also requires employees to attend seminars regarding business conduct, which often include discussion of the company's policies, specific case studies, and legal requirements. Some companies even require their employees to sign agreements stating that they will abide by the company's rules of conduct.

Many companies are assessing the environmental factors that can lead employees to engage in unethical conduct.

Not everyone supports corporate policies that govern ethical conduct. Some claim that ethical problems are better dealt with by depending upon employees to use their own judgment.

Others believe that corporate ethics policies are primarily rooted in utilitarian concerns, and that they are mainly to limit the company's legal liability, or to curry public favor by giving the appearance of being a good corporate citizen. Ideally, the company will avoid a lawsuit because its employees will follow the rules. Should a lawsuit occur, the company can claim that the problem would not have arisen if the employee had only followed the code properly.

Sometimes there is disconnection between the company's code of ethics and the company's actual practices. Thus, whether or not such conduct is explicitly sanctioned by management, at worst, this makes the policy duplicitous, and, at best, it is merely a marketing tool.

To be successful, most ethicists would suggest that an ethics policy should be:

- Given the unequivocal support of top management, by both word and example.
- Explained in writing and orally, with periodic reinforcement.
- Doable....something employees can both understand and perform.
- Monitored by top management, with routine inspections for compliance and improvement.
- Backed up by clearly stated consequences in the case of disobedience.
- Remain neutral and nonsexist.

Ethics officers

Ethics officers (sometimes called "compliance" or "business conduct officers") have been appointed formally by organizations since the mid-1980s. One of the catalysts for the creation of this new role was a series of fraud, corruption and abuse scandals that afflicted the U.S. defense industry at that time. This led to the creation of the Defense Industry Initiative (DII), a pan-industry initiative to promote and ensure ethical business practices. The DII set an early benchmark for ethics management in corporations. In 1991, the Ethics & Compliance Officer Association (ECOA) — originally the Ethics Officer Association (EOA)— was founded at the Center for Business Ethics(at Bentley College, Waltham, MA) as a professional association for those responsible for managing organizations' efforts to achieve ethical best practices. The membership grew rapidly (the ECOA now has over 1,100 members) and was soon established as an independent organization.

Another critical factor in the decisions of companies to appoint ethics/compliance officers was the passing of the Federal Sentencing Guidelines for Organizations in 1991, which set standards that organizations (large or small, commercial and non-commercial) had to follow to obtain a reduction in sentence if they should be convicted of a federal offense. Although intended to assist judges with sentencing, the influence in helping to establish best practices has been far-reaching.

In the wake of numerous corporate scandals between 2001-04 (affecting large corporations like Enron, WorldCom and Tyco), even small and medium-sized companies have begun to appoint ethics officers. They often report to the Chief Executive Officer and are responsible for assessing the ethical implications of the company's activities, making recommendations regarding the company's ethical policies, and disseminating information to employees. They are particularly interested in uncovering or preventing unethical and illegal actions. This trend is partly due to the Sarbanes-Oxley Act in the United States, which was enacted in reaction to the above scandals. A related trend is the introduction of risk assessment officers that monitor how shareholders' investments might be affected by the company's decisions.

The effectiveness of ethics officers in the marketplace is not clear. If the appointment is made primarily as a reaction to legislative requirements, one might expect the efficacy to be minimal, at least, over the short term. In part, this is because ethical business practices result from a corporate culture that consistently places value on ethical behavior, a culture and climate that usually emanates from the top of the organization. The mere establishment of a position to oversee ethics will most likely be insufficient to inculcate ethical behaviour: a more systemic programme with consistent support from general management will be necessary.

The foundation for ethical behavior goes well beyond corporate culture and the policies of any given company, for it also depends greatly upon an individual's early moral training, the other institutions that affect an individual, the competitive business environment the company is in and, indeed, society as a whole.

13.4.5 Religious Views on Business Ethics

The historical and global importance of religious views on business ethics is sometimes underestimated in standard introductions to business ethics. Particularly in Asia and the Middle East, religious and cultural perspectives have a strong influence on the conduct of business and the creation of business values.

Examples include:

- Islamic banking, associated with the avoidance of charging interest on loans.
- Traditional Confucian disapproval of the profit-seeking motive.
- Quaker testimony on fair dealing

13.4.6 Related Disciplines

Business ethics should be distinguished from the philosophy of business, the branch of philosophy that deals with the philosophical, political, and ethical underpinnings of business and economics. Business ethics operates on the premise, for example, that the ethical operation of a private business is possible — those who dispute that premise, such as libertarian socialists, (who contend that "business ethics" is an oxymoron) do so by definition outside of the domain of business ethics proper.

The philosophy of business also deals with questions such as what, if any, are the social responsibilities of a business; business management theory; theories of individualism vs. collectivism; free will among participants in the marketplace; the role of self_interest; invisible hand theories; the requirements of social justice; and natural_rights, especially property_rights, in relation to the business enterprise.

Business ethics is also related to **political economy,** which is economic analysis from political and historical perspectives. Political economy deals with the distributive consequences of economic actions. It asks who gains and who loses from economic_activity, and is the resultant distribution fair or just, which are central ethical issues.

EXERCISE

1. Describe Information Securities and Control.
2. What is System Vulnerability?
3. Describe Unintentional Threats.
4. Describe Intentional Threats
5. Describe Protecting Information Systems.
6. How Do We Protect IT?
7. Describe Physical Controls.
8. Describe Data security controls.
9. Describe Communication (network) controls.

10. Describe Administrative controls.
11. Why Break I.T. System Security?
12. Describe Information System Security Threats.
13. What is Ethics/Ethical?
14. Describe Ethical Issues related to systems.
15. Describe Ethical Dimensions.
16. Describe Business Ethics.
17. Describe General business ethics.
18. Describe Ethics of accounting information.
19. Describe Ethics of human resource management.
20. Describe Ethics of sales and marketing.
21. Describe Ethics of production.
22. Describe Ethics of intellectual property, knowledge and skills.
23. Describe International business ethics and ethics of economic systems.
24. Describe Theoretical issues in business ethics.
25. Describe Religious views on business ethics.

14

QUALITY ASSURANCE AND TESTING

14.0 INTRODUCTION

Information quality and quality of software, which is used for analyzing information, is major concerned in any computerized organization. In this unit we will discuss the meaning of quality assurance, Why software quality assurance is needed, the software quality, software quality assurance, Management Role in Software Quality Assurance, Formal Quality Assurance Measures/Structure and the ETHICAL AND SOCIAL DIMENSIONS in quality assurance.

14.1 QUALITY ASSURANCE

14.1.1 Introduction

Historically speaking, application of Information Technology was initially confined to scientific and research-related activities, where time was not considered to be a constraint. However, as the I.T. capabilities and their impact on organizational functioning became apparent, I.T. emerged as a new, powerful tool to out-perform business rivals and gain competitive advantage by improving product quality, adding value to quality, facilitating product delivery and changing the very processes in an organization.

I.T. applications and, of course, the I.T. software then became a 'HOT thing, the end-user, surprisingly, being at the 'receiving end' and the software developer in the 'driver's seat.' No wonder then that the development of software, application software in particular, used to put an over-emphasis on schedule and cost, to the detriment of quality.

It is now being realized that the development of Information Systems requires a constant trade-off of Schedule and Cost Vs. Quality. With operational snags emerging after the installation of the systems and with the soaring maintenance costs, it is also being realised that there is an urgent need that software products, like any other product in the market, should also be evaluated carefully before they are delivered and implemented.

There is yet another dimension to Software Quality Assurance.

Software is ubiquitous and people often behave as if they had complete confidence in it.

For example: The ATMs or Computerized Railway Bookings or the Telephone Network. People do not expect them to fail!

Software failures can now impact upon many areas of the people's lives and are much less likely to be tolerated than in the past when software was used only by a small number of people who understood that they were using an inherently unreliable system.

Software failures can now affect people who were unaware of the fact that they were using software.

It is, therefore, the responsibility of the software developers and providers to develop and provide a software of a "Fail-safe" quality which justifies this level of public confidence.

Hence, the expectation and demand for the most stringent Software Quality Assurance Progamme to provide the required degree of confidence.

14.1.2 Why Software Quality Assurance?

Apart from the factors discussed earlier, Software Quality Assurance is also required for the following reasons:

(*a*) Avoiding legal liability if the software fails.

(*b*) Proving, with due documentation, that the software was developed using the best practices techniques embodied in various standards.

(*c*) Convincing the users or prospective clients that the developer has a satisfactory Software Quality Assurance Programme in place.

(*d*) Being able to develop/deliver a good quality product which, in turn, may enable the developer to offer guarantees with software as a part of marketing strategy.

(*e*) Making software development more cost-effective.

(*f*) Taking advantage of a rigorous Quality Assurance Programme as a marketing 'USP'.

(*g*) Taking the user/client from "Customer Satisfaction"to "Customer Delight" to "Customer LUV" and ensure "Customer Loyalty".

14.1.3 What is Software Quality?

Let us first discuss the two terms separately, before discussing Software Quality.

14.1.3.1 Software

Generally, software is defined as a set of instructions. In the context of Software Quality Assurance, let us now view the software as—

All instructions and data which are input into a computer to cause it to function in any code".

Includes "operating systems, supervisory systems, compilers and test routines as well as application programmes. It also includes the documents used to define and describe the Programme, including flow charts, network diagrams and programme listings — as well as specifications, test plans, test data, test results and user instructions".

14.1.3.2 Quality

"Quality indicates the degree of excellence of a product or service".

According to DoD 1985, Quality means the degree to which the attributes of the software enable it to perform its specified end item use.

According to ISO 1986, Quality means the totality of features and characteristics of a product or service that bear on its ability to satisfy stated or implied needs.

As could be observed, the ISO definition clearly reflects the desire to define quality in a way which captures the current concept of quality as customer satisfaction in the broadest possible context.

Now that we have noted the definitions of 'Software' and 'Quality', let us now move over to Software Quality.

14.1.3.3 What is Software Quality?

- Software Quality is the inherent ability of a software to be used for a specified purpose as the software possesses certain features and characteristics and which enable it to be used for that purpose.
- Software Quality is the ability of a software to be fit for its purpose and capability to ensure that:
  (*a*) It is reliable.
  (*b*) It is doing what it is supposed to do.
  (*c*) It is performing according to its specifications.
  (*d*) It is doing efficiently.
  (*e*) It is working efficiently for the time for which it is predicted to work.
- Software Quality would also imply
  (*a*) Quality of Conformance, reflecting the extent to which the developer has succeeded in producing software which implemented the design, and
  (*b*) Quality of Design, which reflects the extent to which a given software product meets a customer's expectations.

After having noted the definitions of software quality, let us now broadly summarise the attributes of quality known as **Quality Factors**.

- Aesthetics
- Conformance
- Correctness
- Durability
- Efficiency
- Extendability
- Integrity
- Inter-operability
- Maintainability
- Openness
- Perception/Perceived quality
- Portability
- Reliability

- Reusability
- Security
- Serviceability
- Survivability
- Testability
- Understandability(Comprehensibility)
- Usability
- User-friendliness

14.1.4 Software Quality Assurance

14.1.4.1 Quality Assurance

Quality Assurance is, "a planned and systematic pattern of all actions necessary to provide equate confidence that the item or project conforms to established technical requirements."

14.1.4.2 Software Quality Assurance

Software Quality Assurance, accordingly, lays considerable stress on getting the design it, prior to coding, although the increasing use of prototyping in systems development is producing the differences between the production stages of Hardware and Software.

Software Quality Assurance must also:

(*a*) Provide for exhaustive testing.

(*b*) Obtain a mathematical proof of correctness.

(*c*) Convince oneself that the output from each phase of the development process, which will be a different representation of the software, is functionally equivalent to its predecessor.

14.1.5 Management Role in Software Quality Assurance

The failure of the Management to properly plan and control the software development process is now felt to have been responsible for much of the poor quality software developed/ produced in the past. In fact, one of the major roadblock in software quality was the belief/ attitude that problems can be sorted out at the end of the development process.

It is now generally recognised that—Management has a key role to play in the production/ development of Quality Software, as the Software Quality Assurance, like any other form of quality assurance, is highly dependent upon management attitudes. While the organisational structures could be created and put in place any time, the real change required is the change in managerial attitudes.

The management must manifest and transmit a greater desire to produce high quality product. The Management must also commit 'commensurate resources' to ensure this. In turn, the software developers must plan and implement software development projects with the objective of "building in" quality.

Towards this end, they must—

(*a*) Establish and maintain the requirement specifications.

(*b*) Establish and implement a process for developing the software.

(*c*) Establish and maintain an evaluation process.

Further, the "Discipline Triangle" must be applied to produce quality software successfully. "The Discipline Triangle" would contain Management, Software Development and Product Assurance Discipline.

The 'Management Discipline' would include both Project Management and General Management.

The 'Software Development Discipline' would involve such activities like analysis, design, testing etc.

The 'Product Assurance Discipline' would include quality assurance, test and evaluation and configuration management.

14.1.6 The Formal Quality Assurance Measures/Structure

The formal Quality Assurance structure would need to be woven around the

ISO-9000 Standard. ISO-9001 defines a minimum set of requirements for Quality Management. It includes Quality Assurance, Quality Control, Process Control, Change Management and Formal Review.

ISO-9001 is acknowledged as requiring additional features for software development.

ISO-9001 Standard with the IEEE-1298 Standards and the ISO-9000.

3 Guidelines would be required to be considered for Software Quality Assurance.

14.1.7 Additional Considerations

In addition to the standards mentioned earlier, due attention should also be given to the following:

14.1.7.1 Quality Profile Model

To ensure quality assurance, it is imperative to keep in view the quality profile of software. A Quality Profile Model, proposed by Kaposi and Kitchenham as a way of structuring the analysis of the quality of a piece of software is presented below:

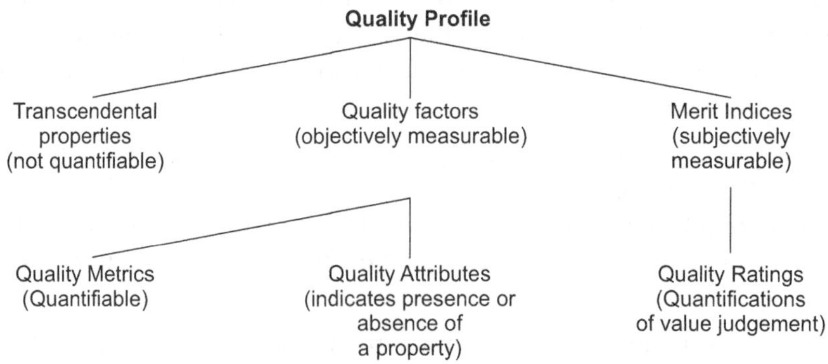

Fig. 14.1 *Quality Profile Model*

14.1.7.2 Constructive Quality Model

Kitchenham has also discussed the development of a Constructive Quality Model, known as COQUAMO'.

The Model attempts to make explicit the dependence of the achievement of a quality factor upon activities undertaken throughout the life cycle. In each stage of the life cycle, checklists can be used to monitor progress towards the achievement of the quality factor.

The Model would involve measuring three types of values: -

(*a*) Quality Factor Metrics

(*b*) Quality Indicators

(*c*) Measures of Quality Drivers

The COQUAMO Model is illustrated hereunder:

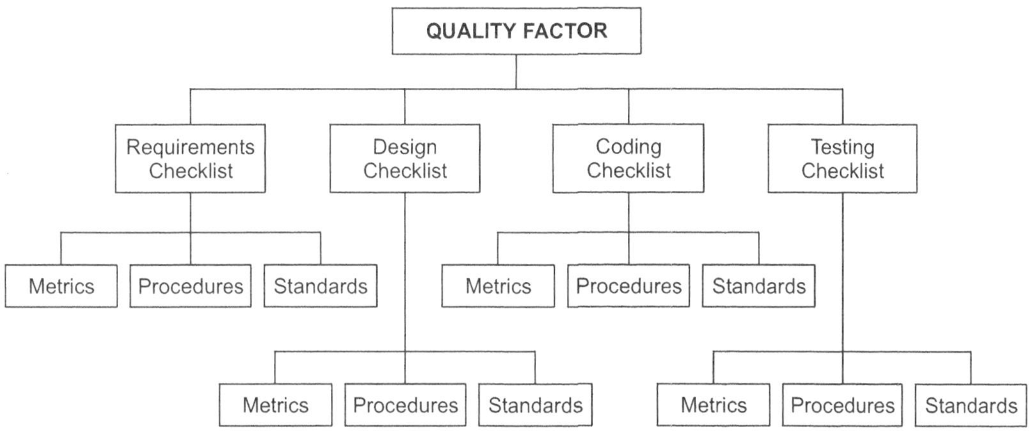

Fig. 14.2 *Constructive Quality Model*

14.1.7.3 "TickIT" Initiative

TickIT focuses on software development, as this is the component that gives an Information System its power and flexibility. Yet unfortunately, it is also the source of many of the problems.

The fundamental objective of the TickIT Initiative is to ensure that developers can deliver quality. The TickIT guide contains structured guidance for the application of ISO 9001. It also includes the ISO-9000.3 document which explains how ISO-9001 can be applied to software.

The TickIT Initiative has two components:

(*a*) A Quality Management Certification Scheme for the Software and IT industries.

(*b*) An Awareness Programme to raise the level of understanding of what quality is and how it may be achieved among the professionals within the industry.

The TickIT is about the certification of a Quality Management System within the context of an organisational commitment to Total Quality Management. Certification should result from delivering quality.

(*c*) TickIT Certification Scheme is a sector scheme.

(*d*) TickIT promotes certification within the context of Total Quality Management (TQM).

TickIT TQM Model, continuous improvement of the Quality Management System results from three long term driving components which work on the Quality Management System, the three Driving Components are:

1. Management Commitment for improvement.
2. Motivation for improvement.
3. Measurement for improvement.

14.2 GROWTH OF INTERNATIONAL INFORMATION SYSTEMS

Multinational companies, international companies and virtual global cooperation's need international information system.

- **Multinational Companies:** Multinational Companies are those that operate in several countries. Example would be Microsoft, IBM Coca-Cola and SAP/AG. Multinational organizations may have sales offices in several countries or may conduct operations in location where factory workers are plenty and inexpensive where highly skilled employees are available at low salaries, or where there is a need to be close to the market.
- **International Companies:** International companies are those that do business with other companies in different companies. For example, Toyota Motors Company, Japan works with many suppliers in the United States.
- **Virtual Global Corporations:** Virtual global corporations are joint ventures whose business partners ate located in different countries. The partners from a company for the specific purpose producing a product or service. Such companies can be temporary, with a one-time mission or they can be permanent.

Benefits of International Information systems

Regardless of its structure a company with global operations relies heavily on IT. Major benefits of international information system are as follows:

Effective communication at a reasonable cost is necessary. The partners are far from each other, yet they need to work together, make decisions, monitor transactions and provide controls. Business partners communicate through email, EDI, and extranets. Communication is even more critical if the partners speak different languages. Intelligent IT system can provide automatic translation.

Effective collaboration is needed to overcome differences in distance, time, language and culture. Collaboration can be enabled with groupware software, group decision support system, and extranets and teleconferencing devices.

Organizations accesses each other's databases and frequently work on the same projects while their members are in different locations. Information technologies such as video teleconferencing and screen sharing are useful for this purpose.

14.3 ETHICAL AND SOCIAL DIMENSIONS

14.3.1 Introduction

In our earlier discussions, we have noted how I.T. has changed and is changing the rules of competition. But as the rules of competition changed and application of computers increased exponential speed, it has also given rise to a number of ethical and social dilemmas. It is proposed to discuss some of the illustrative, ethical and social dilemmas/dimensions of I.T. Information Systems Applications in the following paragraphs.

14.3.2 What is Ethics/Ethical?

While 'Ethics' means 'the system or code of morals of a particular person, religion, group or professions", "Ethical" means "having to do with ethics or morality of or conforming to moral standards conforming to the standards of conduct of given profession or group".

A person's ethics, according to Griffin(1990) are formulated through the operation of five key process in the individual's environment viz,

1. Family Influences
2. Peer Influences
3. Experiences
4. Values and Morals
5. Situational Factors

14.3.3 Ethical Issues Related to Systems

Ethics is a branch of philosophy that deals with what is considered to be right and wrong. There are many definitions of ethics, such as "codes of morals of a particular profession", "the standards of conduct of a given profession", "agreement among people to do the right and to avoid the wrong". In one of the oldest codes of ethics, the Ten Commandments, Clear specifications are given about what an individual should and should not do. Over the years, philosophers have proposed many ethical guidelines. It is important to realize that what is unethical is not necessarily illegal.

A framework for Ethics

Many companies and professional organizations develop their own codes of ethics. A code of ethics is a collection of principles intended as a guide for members of a company or an organization. The diversity of IT application and the increased use of the technology have created a variety of ethical issues. Prof. R.O. Masson and others categories ethical issues into four types: privacy, accuracy, property and accessibility.

1. **Privacy issues:** Collection, storage and dissemination of information about individuals.
    - What information about oneself should an individual be required to revel to others?
    - What kind of surveillance can be employer use on its employees?
    - What thing can people keep to themselves and not to be forced to revel others?
    - What information about individuals should be kept in databases and how secure is the information there?
2. **Accuracy issues:** Authenticity, fidelity and accuracy of information collected and processes.
    - Who is responsible for authenticity, fidelity, and accuracy of information collected?
    - How can we ensure that errors in databases, data transmissions and data processing are accidental and not intentional?
    - Who is to be held accountable for errors in information and how should the injured party be compensated?
3. **Property issues:** Ownership and value of information.
    - Who owns the information?
    - What are the just and fair prices for its exchange?
    - How should one handle software privacy?
    - Under what circumstances can one use proprietary databases?
    - Can corporate computers be used for private purposes?
    - How should experts who contribute their knowledge to create expert system be compensated?
    - How should access to information channels be allocated?

4. **Accessibility issues:** Right to access information and payment of fees to access it.
   - Who is allowed to access information?
   - How much should be changed for permitting accessibility to information?
   - How can accessibility to computers be provided for employees for disabilities?
   - Who will be provided with equipment needed for accessing information?
   - What information does a person or an organization has a right or privilege to obtain and under what conditions and with what safeguards?

14.3.4 Ethical Dimensions

The Ethical Dimensions would broadly cover the following aspects :

1. Obligation to Management
2. Obligation to Society
3. Obligation to Employer
4. Obligations to Country

Ethical Dilemmas:

Some of the illustrative ethical dilemmas could be summarized as follows:

1. Inappropriate use of computers technology.
2. Inappropriate use of computer resources.
3. Inefficient programming logic.
4. Inefficient processing instructions.
5. Manipulation of records.
6. Deletion/Distortion of records.

In view of the enormous power of Information Technology, and the resultant 'Nuisance Value' (Hacking, for example), it is imperative that a professional Code of Conduct and Ethics be devised and globally implemented for the I.T. Professionals.

SUMMARY

In this unit we have completed meaning of quality assurance, Why software quality assurance is needed, the software quality, software quality assurance, Management Role in Software Quality Assurance, Formal Quality Assurance Measures/Structure and the ETHICAL AND SOCIAL DIMENSIONS in quality assurance.

EXERCISE

Short Answer Questions

1. What is quality assurance? Describe with the help of an example.
2. Describe Growth of International Information systems.
3. Describe various Ethical Issues related to systems.
4. Describe constrictive quality model.
5. What is the role of management in assurance of software quality?
6. Describe formal quality assurance measures.

Long Answer Questions

1. Describe Multinational Companies.
2. What do you mean by International Companies?
3. Define Data security controls.
4. What are the Benefits of International Information systems?
5. What is ethics?
6. What are ethical dimensions?
7. Why software assurance is needed?

FURTHER READING

1. Management Information Systems: Davis Olson, Mc. Graw Hill.
2. Management Information Systems: W.S. Jawadekar, TMH.
3. Management Information Systems: Laudon $ Laudon, Pearson Education, Asia.
4. Management Information Systems: James a O'Brien.

15

Cyber Crimes and Privacy Issues

15.0 INTRODUCTION

In the today's era of rapid growth, Information technology is encompassing all walks of life all over the world. These technological developments have made the transition from paper to paperless transactions possible. We are now creating new standards of speed, efficiency, and accuracy in communication, which has become key tools for boosting innovations, creativity and increasing overall productivity. Computers are extensively used to store confidential data of political, social, economic or personal nature bringing immense benefit to the society.

The rapid development of Internet and Computer technology globally has led to the growth of new forms of transnational crime especially Internet related. These crimes have virtually no boundaries and may affect any country across the globe. Thus, there is a need for awareness and enactment of necessary legislation in all countries for the prevention of computer related crime.

Globally Internet and Computer based commerce and communications cut across territorial boundaries, thereby creating a new realm of human activity and undermining the feasibility and legitimacy of applying laws based on geographic boundaries. This new boundary, which is made up of the screens and passwords, separate the "Cyber world" from the "real world" of atoms. Territorially based law-making and law-enforcing authorities find this new environment deeply threatening.

15.1 WHY CYBER LAWS AT ALL

We may ask why is there a need for a separate law to govern the Cyber World?

This may also assume significance looking to the fact that the phenomenal spread of Internet has been enabled mainly due to the absence of a centralised regulating agency.

Anyone who has access to a computer and a telephone network is free to get hooked to the Internet. This uncontrollable growth of the Internet makes the need for regulation even more badly felt.

Systems across the globe have many different rules governing the behavior of users. These users in most of the countries are completely free to join/ leave any system whose rules they find comfortable/ not comfortable to them. This extra flexibility may at times lead to improper user conduct. Also, in the absence of any suitable legal framework, it may be difficult for System.

Administrators to have a check on Frauds, Vandalism or Abuses, which may make the life of many online users miserable.

This situation is alarming as any element of distrust for Internet may lead to people avoiding doing transactions with online sites thereby directly affecting e-Commerce growth. The (Mis)Use of Internet as an excellent medium of communication may in some situations lead to direct damage to physical societies. Non-imposition of taxes on online transactions may have its destructive effect on the physical businesses and also government revenues. Terrorists may also make use of web to create conspiracies and make violence in the society.

Therefore, all of us whether we directly use Internet or not, will like to have some form of regulation or external control for monitoring online transactions and the cyber world for preventing any instability.

15.2 CYBER CRIMES

"Computer or Cyber crimes are considered as illegal, unethical or unauthorised behaviour of people relating to the automatic processing and transmission of data, use of Computer Systems and Networks".

Common types of Cyber Crimes may be broadly classified in the following groups:-

1. Against Individuals:
   - (*a*) Against Person:
     - (*i*) Harassment through e-mails.
     - (*ii*) Cyber-stalking.
     - (*iii*) Dissemination of obscene material on the Internet.
     - (*iv*) Defamation.
     - (*v*) Hacking/cracking.
     - (*vi*) Indecent exposure.
   - (*b*) Against property of an individual:
     - (*i*) Computer vandalism.
     - (*ii*) Transmitting virus.
     - (*iii*) Internet intrusion.
     - (*iv*) Unauthorised control over computer system.
     - (*v*) Hacking /cracking.
2. Against Organisations:
   - (*a*) Against Government, Private Firm, Company, Group of Individuals:
     - (*i*) Hacking & Cracking.
     - (*ii*) Possession of unauthorised information.
     - (*iii*) Cyber terrorism against the government organisation.
     - (*iv*) Distribution of pirated software etc.

3. Against Society at large:
   (*i*) Pornography (specially child pornography).
   (*ii*) Polluting the youth through indecent exposure.
   (*iii*) Trafficking.

15.3 BASIC APPROACHES FOR CREATION OF CYBER LAWS

Following are the basic approaches for creation of Cyber Laws, which will ensure the smooth governance of Internet globally:

(*a*) Formulation of new laws and amendment of existing laws by nations within their present territorial boundaries thereby attempting to regulate all actions on the Internet that have any impact on their own population.

(*b*) Nations may enter into multi-lateral international agreements to establish new and uniform rules specifically applicable to conduct on the Internet.

(*c*) Creation of an entirely new international organisation, which can establish new rules and new means of enforcing those rules.

(*d*) Guidelines and rules may naturally emerge from individual decisions like domain name and IP address registrations and by websites and users deciding about whom will they patronize.

All of these approaches have their own merits and demerits and we shall not go into those details here.

15.4 ESTABLISHING A SUITABLE FRAMEWORK

There is a dire need for the emergence of a well-defined framework of Cyber Laws, which should be able to do the following:

1. Create and implement a minimum set of guiding rules of conduct that would facilitate efficient Communications and reliable Commerce through the use of Electronic medium.
2. Define, punish and prevent wrongful actions that attack the electronic medium or harm others. One of the greatest concerns of the field of Cyber Laws has been the absence (or rather delay) of a well-defined and comprehensive framework of law across the globe. Today's *Internet* was born in the early 1960's while the initial efforts for its regulation could only surface in the late 1990's. This problem has been further aggravated by the steep rise in usage of Internet in the recent years all over the world and that too in the absence of any appropriate legal framework. *Surely, the Cyber Law scenario is globally more complicated than traditional laws owing to the reason that the range of activities which are to be governed by these laws are largely technology driven, an area which is dynamically changing and is beyond anyone's control. However enactment of these laws pose opportunities for nations to carve model Cyber Societies for the future thereby taking a lead in becoming Global IT Powers.*

Effective Implementation of any law is as critical an exercise as its enactment. A law implementing agency has to focus on the following major areas to be effective:

1. Creating a suitable climate thereby Inducing Self Compliance by the Society.
2. Regular monitoring of the scenario for reliable feedback.

3. Offering Openness and Flexibility to accept and incorporate necessary modifications at appropriate times.
4. Distinctly establishing the Authority-Responsibility guidelines for the Implementing Agency.

In order to be effective, it has to be ensured that the Law is Simple, fair and full of clarity. Failing this, the law may be misused to harass individuals resulting in its defiance. The implementing agency will then be compelled to take corrective actions to ensure implementation. This whole process may result in spread of corruption and polluting of the overall sentiments in society making the job of law implementing agencies more difficult.

15.5 CYBER LEGISLATIONS WORLDWIDE

To meet the challenge posed by new kinds of crime made possible by computer technology including telecommunication, many countries have also reviewed their respective domestic criminal laws so as to prevent computer related crimes. Some of these countries are USA, Austria, Denmark, France Germany, Greece, Finland, Italy, Turkey, Sweden, Switzerland, Australia, Canada, India, Japan, Spain, Portugal, UK, Malaysia and Singapore.

However, no country has fully resolved all the issues such as legal, enforcement and prevention of crime. The legislations enacted by different countries cover only few of the classified computer-related offences. However, looking to the dynamic and fast changing technology, new types of offences may pop-up frequently.

Some of the major types of offences against which many countries across the globe have enacted various Acts (mostly at preliminary levels) are as follows:

1. Unlawful access to data in computers,
2. Damaging data in computer etc.
3. Possession of device to obtain unauthorised telephone facilities,
4. Unauthorised access to computer and computer material
5. Committing mischief with data.
6. Data spying,
7. Computer fraud,
8. Forgery of prohibitive data,
9. Alteration of data,
10. Computer sabotage.
11. False entry in an authentic deed
12. False entry in permit licence or passport
13. Electronic record made wrongfully
14. Electronic record made wrongfully by public servant
15. Interferences with business by destruction or damage of computer
16. Interferences with computer
17. Destruction of public document
18. Destruction of private document
19. Unauthorised access with intention to commit offences/computer crimes

20. Unauthorised use and interception of computer services
21. Knowingly access of computer without authorisation related to national defence or foreign relation
22. Intentional access of computer without authorisation to obtain financial information
23. Unauthorised access of computer of a Govt. Deptt. Or agency
24. Knowingly causing transmission of data/program to damage a computer network, data or program or withhold or deny use of computer, network etc.
25. Knowingly causing transmission of data/program with risk that transmission will damage a computer network, data or program or withhold or deny use of computer, network etc, an unauthorised access of computer with intent to defraud.

15.6 DEFINING CYBER LAWS

Cyber law encompasses a wide variety of legal issues related to use of communications technology. It includes use of Internet as well as any other form of Computer or Digital Processing Devices. It includes intellectual property, privacy, freedom of expression, and jurisdiction.

As the law of Cyber Space, as envisioned by William Gibson in his novel Neuromancer , Cyber Law addresses the issues of Virtual Property and Virtual Persons. It covers rights of Netizens who are the citizens of Cyber Space and regulation of the Cyber Space for a peaceful and harmonious existence of Netizens.

The biggest challenge before Cyber Law is its integration with the legacy system of laws applicable to the physical world.

Since **Cyber Space** has no geographical boundaries, nor the **Netizens** have physical characteristics of **Sex**, **Age** etc, several conflicts surface when the rights of Netizens are viewed in the eyes of Citizens of a physical space. This is well reflected in the conflict between the Trade mark Laws and system of Domain Names.

There are several countries which have enacted special laws for regulating Cyber Space Transactions of Citizens within their Physical Jurisdiction and these are recognized as the Cyber Laws of the Physical Jurisdiction.

15.7 THE LEGAL ISSUES

In its recent Communication on Electronic Commerce, the European Commission stressed that "in order to allow for electronic commerce operators to reap the full benefits of the Single Market, it is essential to avoid regulatory inconsistencies and to ensure a coherent legal and regulatory framework for electronic commerce". The types of pitfalls that are facing any company or person wanting to set up a distance selling activity on the Internet, offering goods or services to consumers and businesses located world wide are numerous, they vary according to the type of relation you are considering entering (consumer, business), and according to the legal framework you are accustomed to operating in. To make things even more difficult, the answers are often unclear, non existent, contradictory and constitute real obstacles to conducting a commercial activity on the network .As governments continue to consider how best to enforce their interests in electronic transactions, technical standards and traditional contract principles will provide a private source of law to govern online transactions. Conceptual, operational and intellectual property issues are raised by electronic commerce, and organizations actively involved in intelligent transactions must conduct legal risk assessment in order to document their information policies.

When the World Wide Web Consortium (W3C) officially adopted the eXtensible Markup Language (XML) in mid-February 1998, the Internet finally came to what users of SGML have been enjoying for years, a meta-grammatical modeling language. The difference is, these newcomers brought millions and millions of dollars and users with them. At a time when Microsoft and Sun Microsystems fought each other in a courtroom over the future of Java, the two companies co-sponsored the 1998 XML Conference in Seattle, Washington. Wait a minute. What's going on here? and why?

Electronic commerce is what is going on, and there appears to be enough for everyone. [ELGIN1] Companies like Microsoft, Sun Microsystems and Adobe are finally working with SGML veterans like SoftQuad, ArborText and Inso because the information needs generated by electronic commerce are powerfully addressed with the modeling tools of SGML. The whole global information infrastructure could benefit from this fact, as first commercial transactions and then non-commercial transactions are transformed into a rich, rapid and accurate intelligent information stream, and structural innovation becomes a competitive market instead of a birthright of the next business cycle.

As the mechanism for mediating the exchange of value between intelligent information systems, meta-grammatical standards like XML and SGML play the same role that the law plays in mediating the exchange of value in the real world. As such, these technical standards act as a source of law for online transactions and therefore must be reliable, detailed and accurate enough for real jurisdictions to rely upon them in addressing the multitude of legal issues generated by electronic transactions.

With the passage of only one statute, digital signature laws, the way humans do business will never be the same. For as secure digital commerce evolves, the sheer number of transactions possible predicts that entities will be party to dramatically more contracts. Where there are contracts, there is litigation. Whether, when and how legal institutions will give legal effect to online transactions is the greatest challenge confronting both the legal and technological communities. Even though there are no clear answers, there are some important questions that need to be asked. This paper will attempt to spot the important legal issues generated by electronic commerce, detail the benefit of an international, content-neutral regulatory structure and suggest a semantic framework for understanding and distributing the risks of electronic transactions.

Most importantly, it is my desire to generate a dialogue among participants regarding these issues before the next generation of innovation for the global information infrastructure moots many of these questions. There is a tension between governmental bodies and the private sector over the development of a legally-sufficient electronic infrastructure, and so far, governments are waiting to see what the private sector does first. SGML/XML and the standards-based content interchange industry have an opportunity to provide that infrastructure in a vendor-neutral way, while at the same time creating a whole new and level market for semantic information tools. The Internet is a new economic environment with tremendous potential. But if the economic infrastructure of the Internet only mimics current markets, then much of that potential will be lost, and in the end, your PC will look more like the soda machine down the hall then the intelligent access point it can be.

The legal framework we are operating in is increasingly becoming complex and burdensome in one single jurisdiction alone, let alone when you are faced simultaneously with hundreds of potentially applicable legislations because you are entering agreements with customers located anywhere in the world. Besides, a number of companies and consumers are still unaware of the legal constraints they may encounter by entering electronic transactions. The objective of this present draft is to fill this gap by providing an overview of relevant legal issues raised by the development of electronic commerce.

Taxation Law

- What criteria may be used to associate on line transactions with the territory of a country?
- How can double taxation be prevented?
- How do the direct taxes rules apply in an electronic environment, both for businesses and for individuals?
- Do general taxation, VAT and custom duties regimes apply to electronic transactions?
- What is the nature of supplies on the Internet? Are the products delivered electronically goods or services?
- How can digital documents comply with existing administrative requirements to keep written evidence of commercial operation and registration in accountancy?
- How can the place and the time of the supply be determined?
- Are electronic transactions exports or imports pursuant the European VAT directives?

Electronic Payments

- What are the existing advantages and obstacles to introducing technical systems that enable electronic payments in an electronic transaction?
- Are banking regulations applicable to issuers of cybercash and cyber credit cards? Does such electronic cash constitute legal tender?
- How can credit cards and other electronic payments satisfy the legal requirements in electronic environments?
- How can privacy, consumer protection and bank secrecy be fulfilled in an electronic banking relationship?
- What is the situation concerning the use of electronic negotiable documents?

Contract Law and Evidence

- Which are the nature, parties and subject matter of the contracts?
- How to enter contracts electronically?
- What is the value of an electronic document and a digital signature?
- Where and when does the offer take place?
- What are the terms and conditions governing the contract?

Liability

- What type of liability could the various actors (service provider, access provider, TTP, seller, banking institution,) involved in the offering of goods or services face?

- What type of damages are covered?
- What are the causes of liability?

Intellectual Property Rights

- How to protect a web site, a domain name, a trade mark or any other type of intellectual property right against illegal misappropriation?
- How to control the use of protected material on the global infrastructure?
- Which rights are concerned when downloading, viewing or printing a protected work? Is there a exhaustion of rights?
- How can the rightholder expect to obtain remuneration?
- How can his moral rights be ensured?
- How should licence agreements be drafted?
- What is the legal protection of the integrity of ECMS?
- Is it possible to detect illegal use?
- Who can be considered as liable in case of copyright or trade mark infringement?

Consumer Protection

- What general or specific rules must be respected when entering a contract with a consumer or when advertising a product?
- What is the regulation of offers and marketing practices?
- What are the abusive terms of a contract?
- What type of information has to be included in a web site?
- How are the distance selling contracts regulated?
- What is the regulation of product and services liability and of products labelling and packaging?
- How can consumers have easy access to jurisdiction and which are the possibilities for consumer associations to defend consumers interests?

Privacy Issues

- What are the applicable general and specific legislations?
- Can personal data be transferred?
- What are the technical developments currently undertaken to improve the protection of privacy on the Internet? How do they comply with privacy provisions?

International Private Law

- What are the competent jurisdictions and the applicable law in the following matters: Contracts, Liability, Intellectual property Rights, Marketing and competition law, electronic payments and banking issues
- What are the specific mandatory criteria in the context of consumer protection?
- How can a jurisdictional decision be enforced in another country?
- Is on-line litigation and arbitration in commercial cases relevant?

Legislative developments are facing a new challenge brought on by the rapid development of the on-line technology and by the newly created difficulty of applying existing regulations in a networked environment. Simultaneously, technology provides more and more solutions to the threats created by the emergence of this new technology. Lawyers and technicians can no longer consider each other as enemies but have to collaborate. Technology and law must develop along each other's progress and integrate mutual input. Such connections between both already exist in a number of fields. Many examples may be mentioned such as TTPs, Privacy Enhancing Technology, ECMS, etc. Systems as PICS can also be applied to a growing number of fields, such as protection of copyright, protection of minors, consumers, etc.

Forthcoming legislative initiatives will necessarily have to encounter these technical solutions in order to address regulatory responses to the growth of electronic commerce.

EXERCISE

1. Why Cyber Laws At All?
2. Define Cyber Crimes.
3. What are the Common types of Cyber Crimes?
4. Describe Basic approaches for creation of Cyber Laws.
5. Describe Establishing a Suitable framework.
6. Describe Cyber Legislations Worldwide.
7. Define Cyber Laws.
8. Describe Legal Issues.

APPENDIX I

BASICS OF MANAGEMENT

INTRODUCTION

There's no doubt that the world has changed, is changing, and continues to change. The dynamic nature of today's organizations means both rewards and challenges for those individual who will be managing those organizations. Management is a dynamic discipline and a course pack on the subject must undergo significant changes to prepare you to manage under these conditions. Management is the organizational process that aids us in creating a service or product from the raw materials we have at hand. It is the sum of the input processes that allow us to mold something useful from what otherwise is a disarray of human resources and raw components. The output of this controlled processing creates a valuable product or service, which someone (a customer) is generally willing to pay for. Simply stated, the manager's job is to help all these processes run smoothly, and to address the roadblocks to successful output.

Management is universal in the modern industrial world and there is no substitute for good management. It makes human efforts more productive and brings better technology, products and services to our society. It is a crucial economic resource and a life-giving element in business. Without proper management, the resources of production (men, machines and materials) cannot be converted into production. Thus management is a vital function concerned with all aspects of the working of an organization. Management is a must to accomplish desired goals through group action. It is essential to convert the disorganized resources of men, machines, materials, and methods into a useful and effective enterprise. Thus management is the function of getting things done through people and directing the efforts of individuals towards a common objective

MEANING OF MANAGEMENT

Management is relatively a new discipline. Being a new discipline, it has drawn concepts and principles from economics, sociology, philosophy, psychology, statistics, and so on. The result is that each group has defined management differently. For example, economists see management as a factor of production; sociologists see it as a class or group of persons; practitioners of management treat it as a process. In spite of no clear unanimity, it is not difficult to identify the following meanings of the term management.

(*i*) Management is an art or technique of getting things done.
(*ii*) Management is a process of planning, organizing, staffing, directing and controlling.,
(*iii*) Management is a distinct activity of any organization.
(*iv*) Management is a discipline, which represents a body of knowledge.
(*v*) Management denotes a group of people.

Lets start with the basic definition of management. Management is the process of designing and maintaining an environment in which individual working together in groups efficiently accomplish the selected arm. The following points explain this definition.

1. **Management functions:** As Manager, person carry out the managerial function of planning, organizing, staffing, leading and controlling
2. **Role of Mgmt:** Mgmt is an essential for any kind of organization. Manager are charged with the responsibility taking actions that will make it possible for individuals to make their best contribution to the group objective. Mgmt thus applies to small and large organization, to profit and non-profit organization to manufacturing as well as service industry.
   (*i*) Small organization - shop (organizer will be owner itself) Large organization - hierarchy is maintained separate depts. Like HRD, Account Department
   (*ii*) Non-profitable society- charitable trust (used for welfare).
   (*iii*) Profit making organization - Escorts industry.
   (*iv*) Service industry- Banks, life insurance, Courier, Hotel.
   (*v*) Manufacturing - Automobile (Escorts), Refrigeration industry (whirlpool).
3. **Levels of Management:** Management applies to managers at all organizational levels. All managers carry out managerial function. However the time spent for each function may differ.

   Planning - Top level more involved lower level less involvement.

   Organizing - Little bit higher in top.

   Span of control - No. of persons reporting a manager.

   Leading - more in top mgmt.

   Top-level managers spent more time on planning and organizing their lower level managers. Leading on the other hand takes at great deal of time for lower level managers. The difference in the amt of time spent on controlling varies only slightly for the manager at various levels.
4. **Management Concerned:** Management is concerned with productivity *i.e.*, the effectiveness and efficiency. Successful company creates a surplus three productive open.

   Productivity can be measured as the Output to Input ratios within a time period with due consideration for quality.

$$\text{Productivity} = \frac{\text{P/O}}{\text{I/P}}$$

   (Within time period and considered) Productivity can be improved by
   (*a*) By increasing O/P with same I/P.
   (*b*) By decreasing I/P but maintaining same O/P.
   (*c*) By Increasing O/P and decreasing I/P to change the ratio favorably.

The I/P can be labors, material capital etc .In the past productivity improvement program were mostly aimed at workers level but now it is for the management also.

Managerial Skills and the Organization Hierarchy Technical Skills

It is the knowledge of and proficiency in activities involving methods, process and procedures. Thus it involves working with tools and specific work. E.g. supervisor should have the ability to teach, how to use the tools for mechanical work.

Human Skills: It is the ability to work with the people. It is the creation of an environment in which person feels secure and free to express their opinion.

Conceptual Skills: Ability to recognize the element in a situation and to understand the relationship among the elements.

Design Skills: It is the ability to solve the problem in such a way that it will benefit the organization. The importance of these skills may differ at various levels in the organization hierarchy.

1. **Lower level management:** For lower level managers technical skill is of greatest importance, human skills are also helpful in interaction with subordinate but conceptual skills are normally not critical for them.
2. **Middle management:** For middle management the need for technical skills decreases, human skills are still essential and the conceptual skills gain in importance.
3. **Top management:** For top management conceptual and human skills are very valuable but there is very less need for technical abilities. This is true for large companies but in small organization technical skills may still be quite important.

Management is an Art of Getting Things Done Through and With People

This definition emphasizes the accomplishment of tasks through the efforts of people. It makes a distinction between managers and non-managers. Whereas managers guide and coordinate the efforts of others towards certain specified goals, the non-managers actually perform the task. A manager, whatever may be his level in the organization, has to get things done through his subordinates. At higher levels, the subordinates are themselves mostly managers. It means 'management of managers'. At supervisory levels, the subordinates are non-managerial 'white-collar' or 'blue-collar' workers. 'Getting things done' means to get tasks and activities performed. Management gets things done through people both as individuals and as members of the work group. Getting things done through people is really an art. It comprises a range of skills acquired and refined in the course of practice. The skills which are required to get things done through people consist of conceptual skills, technical skills, administrative skills, social skills, and so on. With a view to getting things done through people, management has to first plan the things, which are to be done. The plans to be performed to attain the objectives are determined and assigned to individuals and work units. Besides planning and organizing tasks, management has to devise the techniques and methods of getting things done. These are effective leadership, team spirit, peoples' participation, appropriate system of cash and non-cash incentives, and so on.

Further, the obstacles, the problems and the distortions in the work environment have to be removed or minimized. This art of management is increasingly based on the *Science of management*.

Professor Harold Koontz agrees with this concept of management. In the words of Harold Koontz *Management is the art of getting things done through and with people in formally organized groups. It is the art of creating the environment in which people can perform as individuals and yet cooperate towards attainment of group's goals. It is the art of removing blocks to such performance, a way of optimizing efficiency in reaching goals.*

However, there is danger in defining management in terms of getting things done through people. This definition is subject to the following criticism.

(*i*) The workers are merely treated as means of getting results. It completely ignores the needs of the workers and does not offer them human treatment.

(*ii*) The definition is quite vague. It fails to define the functions, which a manager has to carry out to get results from others.

(*iii*) This gives the impression of the manipulative character of the practice of management.

(*iv*) Management is treated as an art. But today, it has satisfied the basic characteristics of science too. Thus management is both an art and a science.

To conclude, let us point out that the techniques of getting things done through and by the people may work for sometime but people cannot be oppressed or befooled all the time. Hence, management may be viewed as a technique of getting things done through others by satisfying their needs. It is not merely getting things done through others.

NATURE OF MANAGEMENT

The following are the important features or characteristics of management.

1. **Management is getting things done:** A manager does not do any operating work himself but gets it done through others. He must motivate the subordinates for the accomplishment of the task assigned to them.
2. **Management is an activity:** Management is a process of organized activity. It is concerned with the efficient use of resources like men, money and materials in the organization.
3. **Management is a group activity:** Management cannot exist independent of the group or organization it manages. It is a cardinal part of any group activity and inspires workers to put forth their best efforts.
4. **Management is a universal activity:** Management is a universal phenomenon. However, management principles are not universally applicable but are modified to suit the given situation and the type of organization.
5. **Management is purposeful:** Management is a goal-oriented activity. It is concerned with the accomplishment of goals through its various functions like planning, organizing, staffing, directing, and controlling.
6. **Management is a process:** Management is a process, which involves planning, organizing, directing and controlling the efforts of human resources in the use of material resources. These are the basic functions, which every manager performs for the accomplishment of certain goals.
7. **Management is an integrating process:** Management integrates men, machines and materials for performing various operations and accomplishing the stated goals. Thus, management acts as a catalytic agent in getting maximum productivity from all the resources.

8. **Management is intangible:** Management is abstract and cannot be seen with the eyes. It is evidenced by the quality of the organization and the results. Thus, feeling of management is result-oriented.
9. **Management is a profession:** Management is a profession because some of its established principles are being applied in practice.
10. **Management is a science and an art:** Management has developed certain principles and laws, which have wide applications. So it is treated as a science. It is also an art, because it is concerned with the application of knowledge for the solution of organizational problems.
11. **Management is dynamic:** Management is dynamic because it adapts itself to the social changes and introduces innovation in methodology.
12. **Management involves decision-making:** Management process involves decision-making at various levels for getting things done by others. It involves selecting the most appropriate alternative out of the several.
13. **Management applies economic principles:** Management is the art of applying the economic principles that underline the control of men and materials in the organization.
14. **Management is concerned with direction and control:** Management is concerned with the direction and control of the various activities. It deals particularly with the active direction of the human effort.

FUNCTIONS OF MANAGEMENT

Management is creative problem solving. This creative problem solving is accomplished through four functions of management: planning, organizing, leading and controlling. The intended result is the use of an organization's resources in a way that accomplishes its mission and objectives. The different functions of Management are as follows:

Planning is the ongoing process of developing the business' mission and objectives and determining how they will be accomplished. Planning includes both the broadest view of the organization, e.g., its mission, and the narrowest, e.g., a tactic for accomplishing a specific goal.

Organizing is establishing the internal organizational structure of the organization. The focus is on division, coordination, and control of tasks and the flow of information within the organization. It is in this function that managers distribute authority to job holders.

Staffing is filling and keeping filled with qualified people all positions in the business. Recruiting, hiring, training, evaluating and compensating are the specific activities included in the function. In the family business, staffing includes all paid and unpaid positions held by family members including the owner/operators.

Directing is influencing people's behavior through motivation, communication, group dynamics, leadership and discipline. The purpose of directing is to channel the behavior of all personnel to accomplish the organization's mission and objectives while simultaneously helping them accomplish their own career objectives.

Controlling is a four-step process of establishing performance standards based on the firm's objectives, measuring and reporting actual performance, comparing the two, and taking corrective or preventive action as necessary.

Each of these functions involves creative problem solving. Creative problem solving is broader than problem finding, choice making or decision making. It extends from analysis of the environment within which the business is functioning to evaluation of the outcomes from the alternative implemented.

BRIEF OVERVIEW OF CONTEMPORARY THEORIES IN MANAGEMENT

Contemporary theories of management tend to account for and help interpret the rapidly changing nature of today's organizational environments. As before in management history, these theories are prevalent in other sciences as well.

Contingency Theory

Basically, contingency theory asserts that when managers make a decision, they must take into account all aspects of the current situation and act on those aspects that are key to the situation at hand. Basically, it's the approach that "it depends." For example, the continuing effort to identify the best leadership or management style might now conclude that the best style depends on the situation. If one is leading troops in the Persian Gulf, an autocratic style is probably best (of course, many might argue here, too). If one is leading a hospital or university, a more participative and facilitative leadership style is probably best.

Systems Theory

Systems theory has had a significant effect on management science and understanding organizations. First, let's look at "what is a system?" A system is a collection of part unified to accomplish an overall goal. If one part of the system is removed, the nature of the system is changed as well. For example, a pile of sand is not a system. If one removes a sand particle, you've still got a pile of sand. However, a functioning car is a system. Remove the carburetor and you've no longer got a working car. A system can be looked at as having inputs, processes, outputs and outcomes. Systems share feedback among each of these four aspects of the systems.

Let's look at an organization. Inputs would include resources such as raw materials, money, technologies and people. These inputs go through a process where they're planned, organized, motivated and controlled, ultimately to meet the organization's goals. Outputs would be products or services to a market. Outcomes would be, e.g., enhanced quality of life or productivity for customers/clients, productivity. Feedback would be information from human resources carrying out the process, customers/clients using the products, etc. Feedback also comes from the larger environment of the organization, e.g., influences from government, society, economics, and technologies. This overall system framework applies to any system, including subsystems (departments, programs, etc.) in the overall organization.

Systems theory may seem quite basic. Yet, decades of management training and practices in the workplace have not followed this theory. Only recently, with tremendous changes facing organizations and how they operate, have educators and managers come to face this new way of looking at things. This interpretation has brought about a significant change (or paradigm shift) in the way management studies and approaches organizations.

The effect of systems theory in management is that writers, educators, consultants, etc. are helping managers to look at the organization from a broader perspective. Systems theory has brought a new perspective for managers to interpret patterns and events in the workplace. They recognize the various parts of the organization, and, in particular, the interrelations of the parts, e.g., the coordination of central administration with its programs, engineering with manufacturing, supervisors with workers, etc. This is a major development. In the past, managers typically took one part and focused on that. Then they moved all attention to another part. The problem was that an organization could, e.g., have a wonderful central administration and wonderful set of teachers, but the departments didn't synchronize at all.

Chaos Theory

As chaotic and random as world events seem today, they seem as chaotic in organizations, too. Yet for decades, managers have acted on the basis that organizational events can always be controlled. A new theory (or some say "science"), chaos theory, recognizes that events indeed are rarely controlled. Many chaos theorists (as do systems theorists) refer to biological systems when explaining their theory. They suggest that systems naturally go to more complexity, and as they do so, these systems become more volatile (or susceptible to cataclysmic events) and must expend more energy to maintain that complexity. As they expend more energy, they seek more structure to maintain stability. This trend continues until the system splits, combines with another complex system or falls apart entirely. Sound familiar? This trend is what many see as the trend in life, in organizations and the world in general.

MANAGEMENT LEVELS

Managers are organizational members who are responsible for the work performance of other organizational members. Managers have formal authority to use organizational resources and to make decisions. In organizations, there are typically three levels of management: top-level, middle-level, and first-level. These three main levels of managers form a hierarchy, in which they are ranked in order of importance. In most organizations, the number of managers at each level is such that the hierarchy resembles a pyramid, with many more first-level managers, fewer middle managers, and the fewest managers at the top level. Each of these management levels is described below in terms of their possible job titles and their primary responsibilities and the paths taken to hold these positions. Additionally, there are differences across the management levels as to what types of management tasks each does and the roles that they take in their jobs. Finally, there are a number of changes that are occurring in many organizations that are changing the management hierarchies in them, such as the increasing use of teams, the prevalence of outsourcing, and the flattening of organizational structures.

Top-Level Managers

Top-level managers, or top managers, are also called senior management or executives. These individuals are at the top one or two levels in an organization, and hold titles such as: Chief Executive Officer (CEO), Chief Financial Officer (CFO), Chief Operational Officer (COO), Chief Information Officer (CIO), Chairperson of the Board, President, Vice president, Corporate head.

Often, a set of these managers will constitute the top management team, which is composed of the CEO, the COO, and other department heads. Top-level managers make decisions affecting the entirety of the firm. Top managers do not direct the day-to-day activities of the firm; rather, they set goals for the organization and direct the company to achieve them. Top managers are ultimately responsible for the performance of the organization, and often, these managers have very visible jobs.

Top managers in most organizations have a great deal of managerial experience and have moved up through the ranks of management within the company or in another firm. An exception to this is a top manager who is also an entrepreneur; such an individual may start a small company and manage it until it grows enough to support several levels of management. Many top managers possess an advanced degree, such as a Masters in Business Administration, but such a degree is not required.

Some CEOs are hired in from other top management positions in other companies. Conversely, they may be promoted from within and groomed for top management with management development activities, coaching, and mentoring. They may be tagged for promotion through succession planning, which identifies high potential managers.

Middle-Level Managers

Middle-level managers, or middle managers, are those in the levels below top managers. Middle managers' job titles include: General manager, Plant manager, Regional manager, and Divisional manager.

Middle-level managers are responsible for carrying out the goals set by top management. They do so by setting goals for their departments and other business units. Middle managers can motivate and assist first-line managers to achieve business objectives. Middle managers may also communicate upward, by offering suggestions and feedback to top managers. Because middle managers are more involved in the day-to-day workings of a company, they may provide valuable information to top managers to help improve the organization's bottom line.

Jobs in middle management vary widely in terms of responsibility and salary. Depending on the size of the company and the number of middle-level managers in the firm, middle managers may supervise only a small group of employees, or they may manage very large groups, such as an entire business location. Middle managers may be employees who were promoted from first-level manager positions within the organization, or they may have been hired from outside the firm. Some middle managers may have aspirations to hold positions in top management in the future.

First-Level Managers

First-level managers are also called first-line managers or supervisors. These managers have job titles such as: Office manager, Shift supervisor, Department manager, Foreperson, Crew leader, Store manager.

First-line managers are responsible for the daily management of line workers-the employees who actually produce the product or offer the service. There are first-line managers in every work unit in the organization. Although first-level managers typically do not set goals for the organization, they have a very strong influence on the company. These are the managers that most employees interact with on a daily basis, and if the managers perform poorly, employees may also perform poorly, may lack motivation, or may leave the company.

In the past, most first-line managers were employees who were promoted from line positions (such as production or clerical jobs). Rarely did these employees have formal education beyond the high school level. However, many first-line managers are now graduates of a trade school, or have a two-year associates or a four-year bachelor's degree from college.

Management Levels and the Four Managerial Functions

Managers at different levels of the organization engage in different amounts of time on the four managerial functions of planning, organizing, leading, and controlling.

Planning is choosing appropriate organizational goals and the correct directions to achieve those goals. Organizing involves determining the tasks and the relationships that allow employees to work together to achieve the planned goals. With leading, managers motivate and coordinate employees to work together to achieve organizational goals. When controlling, managers monitor and measure the degree to which the organization has reached its goals.

The degree to which top, middle, and supervisory managers perform each of these functions is presented in Exhibit 1. Note that top managers do considerably more planning, organizing, and controlling than do managers at any other level. However, they do much less leading. Most of the leading is done by first-line managers. The amount of planning, organizing, and controlling decreases down the hierarchy of management; leading increases as you move down the hierarchy of management.

MANAGEMENT ROLES

In addition to the broad categories of management functions, managers in different levels of the hierarchy fill different managerial roles. These roles were categorized by researcher Henry Mintzberg, and they can be grouped into three major types: decisional, interpersonal, and informational.

Decisional Roles

Decisional roles require managers to plan strategy and utilize resources. There are four specific roles that are decisional. The *entrepreneur* role requires the manager to assign resources to develop innovative goods and services, or to expand a business. Most of these roles will be held by top-level managers, although middle managers may be given some ability to make such decisions. The *disturbance handler* corrects unanticipated problems facing the organization from the internal or external environment. Managers at all levels may take this role. For example, first-line managers may correct a problem halting the assembly line or a middle level manager may attempt to address the aftermath of a store robbery. Top managers are more likely to deal with major crises, such as requiring a recall of defective products. The third decisional role, that of *resource allocator,* involves determining which work units will get which resources. Top managers are likely to make large, overall budget decisions, while middle mangers may make more specific allocations. In some organizations, supervisory managers are responsible for determine allocation of salary raises to employees. Finally, the *negotiator* works with others, such as suppliers, distributors, or labor unions, to reach agreements regarding products and services. First-level managers may negotiate with employees on issues of salary increases or overtime hours, or they may work with other supervisory managers when needed resources must be shared. Middle managers also negotiate with other managers and are likely to work to secure preferred prices from suppliers and distributors. Top managers negotiate on larger issues, such as labor contracts, or even on mergers and acquisitions of other companies.

Interpersonal Roles

Interpersonal roles require managers to direct and supervise employees and the organization. The *figurehead* is typically a top of middle manager. This manager may communicate future organizational goals or ethical guidelines to employees at company meetings. A *leader* acts as an example for other employees to follow, gives commands and directions to subordinates, makes decisions, and mobilizes employee support. Managers must be leaders at all levels of the organization; often lower-level managers look to top management for this leadership example. In the role of *liaison,* a manger must coordinate the work of others in different work units, establish alliances between others, and work to share resources. This role is particularly critical for middle managers, who must often compete with other managers for important resources, yet must maintain successful working relationships with them for long time periods.

Informational Roles

Informational roles are those in which managers obtain and transmit information. These roles have changed dramatically as technology has improved. The *monitor* evaluates the performance of others and takes corrective action to improve that performance. Monitors also watch for changes in the environment and within the company that may affect individual and organizational performance. Monitoring occurs at all levels of management, although managers at higher levels of the organization are more likely to monitor external threats to the environment than are middle or first-line managers. The role of *disseminator* requires that managers inform employees of changes that affect them and the organization. They also communicate the company's vision and purpose.

Managers at each level disseminate information to those below them, and much information of this nature trickles from the top down. Finally, a *spokesperson* communicates with the external environment, from advertising the company's goods and services, to informing the community about the direction of the organization. The spokesperson for major announcements, such as a change in strategic direction, is likely to be a top manager. But, other, more routine information may be provided by a manager at any level of a company. For example, a middle manager may give a press release to a local newspaper, or a supervisor manager may give a presentation at a community meeting.

MANAGEMENT SKILLS

Regardless of organizational level, all managers must have five critical skills: technical skill, interpersonal skill, conceptual skill, diagnostic skill, and political skill.

Technical Skill

Technical skill involves understanding and demonstrating proficiency in a particular workplace activity. Technical skills are things such as using a computer word processing program, creating a budget, operating a piece of machinery, or preparing a presentation. The technical skills used will differ in each level of management. First-level managers may engage in the actual operations of the organization; they need to have an understanding of how production and service occur in the organization in order to direct and evaluate line employees. Additionally, first-line managers need skill in scheduling workers and preparing budgets. Middle managers use more technical skills related to planning and organizing, and top managers need to have skill to understand the complex financial workings of the organization.

Interpersonal Skill

Interpersonal skill involves human relations, or the manager's ability to interact effectively with organizational members. Communication is a critical part of interpersonal skill, and an inability to communicate effectively can prevent career progression for managers. Managers who have excellent technical skill, but poor interpersonal skill are unlikely to succeed in their jobs. This skill is critical at all levels of management.

Conceptual Skill

Conceptual skill is a manager's ability to see the organization as a whole, as a complete entity. It involves understanding how organizational units work together and how the organization fits into its competitive environment. Conceptual skill is crucial for top managers, whose ability to see "the big picture" can have major repercussions on the success of the business. However, conceptual skill is still necessary for middle and supervisory managers, who must use this skill to envision, for example, how work units and teams are best organized.

Diagnostic Skill

Diagnostic skill is used to investigate problems, decide on a remedy, and implement a solution. Diagnostic skill involves other skills—technical, interpersonal, conceptual, and politic. For instance, to determine the root of a problem, a manager may need to speak with many organizational members or understand a variety of informational documents. The difference in the use of diagnostic skill across the three levels of management is primarily due to the types of problems that must be addressed at each level. For example, first-level managers may deal primarily with issues of motivation and discipline, such as determining why a particular employee's performance is flagging and how to improve it. Middle managers are likely to deal with issues related to larger work units, such as a plant or sales office. For instance, a middle-level manager may have to diagnose why sales in a retail location have dipped. Top managers diagnose organization-wide problems, and may address issues such as strategic position, the possibility of outsourcing tasks, or opportunities for overseas expansion of a business.

Political Skill

Political skill involves obtaining power and preventing other employees from taking away one's power. Managers use power to achieve organizational objectives, and this skill can often reach goals with less effort than others who lack political skill. Much like the other skills described, political skill cannot stand alone as a manager's skill; in particular, though, using political skill without appropriate levels of other skills can lead to promoting a manager's own career rather than reaching organizational goals. Managers at all levels require political skill; managers must avoid others taking control that they should have in their work positions. Top managers may find that they need higher levels of political skill in order to successfully operate in their environments. Interacting with competitors, suppliers, customers, shareholders, government, and the public may require political skill.

CHANGES IN MANAGEMENT HIERARCHIES

There are a number of changes to organizational structures that influence how many managers are at each level of the organizational hierarchy, and what tasks they perform each day.

Flatter Organizational Structures

Organizational structures can be described by the number of levels of hierarchy; those with many levels are called "tall" organizations. They have numerous levels of middle management, and each manager supervises a small number of employees or other managers. That is, they have a small span of control. Conversely, "flat" organizations have fewer levels of middle management, and each manager has a much wider span of control. Examples of organization charts that show tall and flat organizational structures are presented in Exhibit 2.

Many organizational structures are now more flat than they were in previous decades. This is due to a number of factors. Many organizations want to be more flexible and increasingly responsive to complex environments. By becoming flatter, many organizations also become less centralized. Centralized organizational structures have most of the decisions and responsibility at the top of the organization, while decentralized organizations allow decision-making and authority at lower levels of the organization. Flat organizations that make use of decentralization are often more able to efficiently respond to customer needs and the changing competitive environment.

As organizations move to flatter structures, the ranks of middle-level managers are diminishing. This means that there a fewer opportunities for promotion for first-level managers, but this also means that employees at all levels are likely to have more autonomy in their jobs, as flatter organizations promote decentralization. When organizations move from taller to flatter hierarchies, this may mean that middle managers lose their jobs, and are either laid off from the organization, or are demoted to lower-level management positions. This creates a surplus of labor of middle level managers, who may find themselves with fewer job opportunities at the same level.

Increased use of Teams

A team is a group of individuals with complementary skills who work together to achieve a common goal. That is, each team member has different capabilities, yet they collaborate to perform tasks. Many organizations are now using teams more frequently to accomplish work because they may be capable of performing at a level higher than that of individual employees. Additionally, teams tend to be more successful when tasks require speed, innovation, integration of functions, and a complex and rapidly changing environment.

Another type of managerial position in an organization that uses teams is the team leader, who is sometimes called a project manager, a program manager, or task force leader. This person manages the team by acting as a facilitator and catalyst. He or she may also engage in work to help accomplish the team's goals. Some teams do not have leaders, but instead are self-managed. Members of self-managed teams hold each other accountable for the team's goals and manage one another without the presence of a specific leader.

Outsourcing

Outsourcing occurs when an organization contracts with another company to perform work that it previously performed itself. Outsourcing is intended to reduce costs and promote efficiency. Costs can be reduced through outsourcing, often because the work can be done in other countries, where labor and resources are less expensive than in the United States. Additionally, by having an out-sourcing company aid in production or service, the contracting company can devote more attention and resources to the company's core competencies. Through outsourcing, many jobs that were previously performed by American workers are now performed overseas. Thus, this has reduced the need for many first-level and middle-level managers, who may not be able to find other similar jobs in another company.

There are three major levels of management: top-level, middle-level, and first-level. Managers at each of these levels have different responsibilities and different functions. Additionally, managers perform different roles within those managerial functions. Finally, many organizational hierarchies are changing, due to changes to organizational structures due to the increasing use of teams, the flattening of organizations, and outsourcing.

NEW PARADIGM IN MANAGEMENT

Driving Forces of Change

Around the 1960s and on to today, the environment of today's organizations has changed a great deal. A variety of driving forces provoke this change. Increasing telecommunications has "shrunk" the world substantially. Increasing diversity of workers has brought in a wide array of differing values, perspectives and expectations among workers. Public consciousness has become much more sensitive and demanding that organizations be more socially responsible. Much of the third-world countries has joined the global marketplace, creating a wider arena for sales and services. Organizations became responsible not only to stockholders (those who owned stock) but to a wider community of "stakeholders."

As a result of the above driving forces, organizations were required to adopt a "new paradigm," or view on the world, to be more sensitive, flexible and adaptable to the demands and expectations of stakeholder demands. Many organizations have abandoned or are abandoning the traditional top-down, rigid and hierarchical structures to more "organic" and fluid forms.

Today's leaders and/or managers must deal with continual, rapid change. Managers faced with a major decision can no longer refer back to an earlier developed plan for direction. Management techniques must continually notice changes in the environment and organization, assess this change and manage change. Managing change does not mean controlling it, rather understanding it, adapting to it where necessary and guiding it when possible.

Managers can't know it all or reference resources for every situation. Managers must count on and listen more to their employees. Consequently, new forms of organizations are becoming more common, *e.g.*, worker-centered teams, self-organizing and self-designing teams, etc.

Traits of the New Paradigm

Marilyn Ferguson, in The New Paradigm: Emerging Strategic for Leadership and Organizational Change (Michael Ray and Alan Rinzler, Eds., 1993, New Consciousness Reader), provides a very concise overview of the differences between the old and new paradigm. (The following is summarized.)

Old Paradigm	New Paradigm
promote consumption at all costs	appropriate consumption
people to fit jobs	jobs to fit people
imposed goals, top-down decision making	autonomy encouraged, worker participation
fragmentation in work and roles	cross-fertilization by specialists seeing wide relevance
identification with job	identity transcends job description
clock model of company	recognition of uncertainty
aggression, competition	cooperation
work and play separate	blurring of work and play
manipulation and dominance	cooperation with nature
struggle for stability	sense of change, of becoming
quantitative	qualitative as well as quantitative
strictly economic motives	spiritual values transcend material gain
polarized	transcends polarities
short-sighted	ecologically sensitive
rational	rational and intuitive
emphasis on short-term solutions	recognition that long-range efficiency must take in to account harmonious work environment
centralized operations	decentralized operations when possible
runaway, unbridled technology	appropriate technology
allopathic treatment of symptoms	attempt to understand the whole, locate deep underlying causes of disharmony

APPENDIX II

BASICS OF INFORMATION

DATA, INFORMATION AND KNOWLEDGE

Data

Raw data are numbers, characters, images or other outputs from devices to convert physical quantities into symbols, in a very broad sense. Such data are typically further processed by a human or input into a computer, stored and processed there, or transmitted (output) to another human or computer. *Raw data* is a relative term; data processing commonly occurs by stages, and the "processed data" from one stage may be considered the "raw data" of the next.

Data is raw. It simply exists and has no significance beyond its existence (in and of itself). It can exist in any form, usable or not. It does not have meaning of itself. In computer parlance, a spreadsheet generally starts out by holding data.

Information

Information is data that has been given meaning by way of relational connection. This "meaning" can be useful, but does not have to be. In computer parlance, a relational database makes information from the data stored within it. When the data is processed, grouped, organized, sequences and presented in an easy to understand manner become information.

Knowledge

Knowledge is the appropriate collection of information, such that it's intent is to be useful. Knowledge is a deterministic process. When someone "memorizes" information (as less-aspiring test-bound students often do), then they have amassed knowledge. This knowledge has useful meaning to them, but it does not provide for, in and of itself, integration such as would infer further knowledge. For example a pre school child can answer only those questions whose answers are written in his/her answer book, like $3 \times 2 = 6$. If we ask a typical question like "3216×23" the child can not answer it correctly, because it is not written in his/her answer book and student could not have knowledge.

Understanding

Understanding is an interpolative and probabilistic process. It is cognitive and analytical. It is the process by which I can take knowledge and synthesize new knowledge from the previously held knowledge. The difference between understanding and knowledge is the difference between "learning" and "memorizing". People who have understanding can undertake useful actions because they can synthesize new knowledge, or in some cases, at least new information, from what is previously known (and understood). That is, understanding can build upon currently held information, knowledge and understanding itself. In computer parlance, AI systems possess understanding in the sense that they are able to synthesize new knowledge from previously stored information and knowledge.

Wisdom

Wisdom is an extrapolative and non-deterministic, non-probabilistic process. It calls upon all the previous levels of consciousness, and specifically upon special types of human programming (moral, ethical codes, etc.). It beckons to give us understanding about which there has previously been no understanding, and in doing so, goes far beyond understanding itself. It is the essence of philosophical probing. Unlike the previous four levels, it asks questions to which there is no (easily-achievable) answer, and in some cases, to which there can be no humanly known answer period. Wisdom is therefore, the process by which we also discern, or judge, between right and wrong, good and bad. I personally believe that computers do not have, and will never have the ability to posses wisdom. Wisdom is a uniquely human state, or as I see it, wisdom requires one to have a soul, for it resides as much in the heart as in the mind. And a soul is something machines will never possess (or perhaps I should reword that to say, a soul is something that, in general, will never possess a machine).

Data Vs Information

Even data is not meaningless but it is not as relevant to a decision maker as information. Data is not easily understood because it is not organized in an intuitive manner, complex and unclear. So we can say data is a row material for information, after passing through in many processes data becomes information.

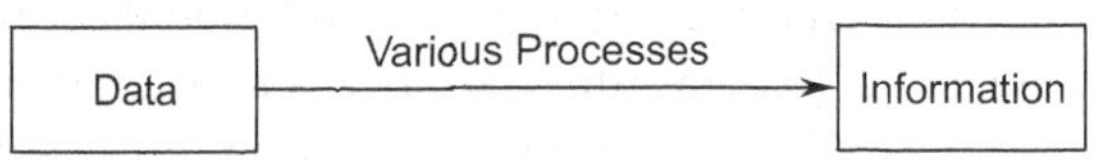

Data

- Facts, statistics used for reference or analysis.
- Numbers, characters, symbols, images etc., which can be processed by a computer.
- Data must be interpreted, by a human or machine, to derive meaning
- "Data is a representation of information"
- Latin 'datum' meaning "that which is given"
- Data plural, datum singular

Information

- Knowledge derived from study, experience (by the senses), or instruction.
- Communication of intelligence.

- "Information is any kind of knowledge that is exchangeable amongst people, about things, facts, concepts, etc., in some context." *
- "Information is interpreted data".

Information Vs Knowledge

Knowledge refers to the practical use of information. While information can be transported, stored or shared without many difficulties the same can not be said about knowledge. Knowledge necessarily involves a personal experience. Referring back to the scientific experiment, a third person reading the results will have information about it, while the person who conducted the experiment personally will have knowledge about it.

INFORMATION: DEFINITION

Initially, while opening our discussions about MIS, we have said that MIS is a System, which provides information to the Management. We have also said that we are living in an information Age. Information is of critical importance for setting up, running, survival and prosperity of a Business Organization. Information is also imperative today as it enables an organization to gain and retain competitive edge and emerge winner.

We will now discuss the concepts of information in more details as MIS is centered around information. But what is Information?

Information is derived from data. Data is nothing but a random, unorganized collection of indications or measurements of certain qualities or attributes relating to an entity, recorded either in alphabetical, numerical, alphanumerical, voice, image, text or any other form.

Data could also be described as unstructured raw facts, observations or unevaluated messages in isolation. Data, per se, does not convey much or is not of much use. It is like a material, which is simply available in an unfinished form. Data are facts and figures, which are not currently being used in a decision process and usually take of office/historical records that are recorded and filed without immediate intent to retrieve for decision-making.

Information, on the other hand, is like a finished product. Information, therefore, is defined as data that is collected, collated, processed, logically organized and analyzed so as to be of use to the decision maker.

Information, according to Davis and Olson, is "data that has been processed into a form that is meaningful to the recipient and is of real or perceived value in current or prospective actions or decisions". Information is, therefore, the difference, which makes the difference.

It will thus, be observed that for data to be converted into information, it has to undergo processing as illustrated hereunder:

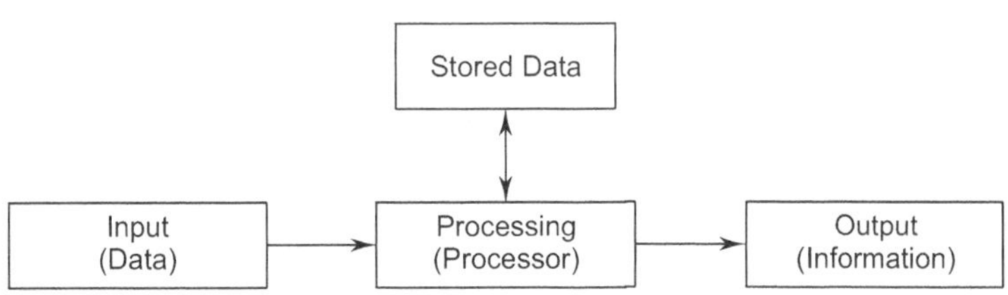

INFORMATION PROCESS

As stated, data has to be processed before information could be available. Hence, various operations have to be carried out in converting data into meaningful information as follows:

• Capturing	Data from an event/transaction has to be recorded
• Verifying	Data has to be checked/validated for correctness
• Classifying	Data has to be placed in specific categories
• Arranging/Sorting	Data has to be placed in a particular Order/Sequence
• Summarizing	Data elements have to be combined/aggregated
• Calculating	Arithmetical/Logical calculations/computations have to be carried out
• Storing	Data has to be placed in some storage media
• Retrieving	Specific data elements have to be searched for and accessed
• Reproducing	Data has to be duplicated from one medium to another
• Dissemination	Data has to be transmitted from one place Communication (device) to another (user).

INFORMATION AND DECISION-MAKER

Information is not only relevant but also critical for the decision maker as the quality of decision-making is dependent on the quality of information. More specifically, information is useful for the decision maker as:

1. Information helps in minimizing, if not eliminating altogether, the elements of risk and uncertainty in decision making.
2. Information minimizes the element of 'surprise' and uncertainty in decision making.
3. Information improves the quality of decision making.
4. Information helps to achieve the most optimum results within given constraints and
5. Information affects the decision making behaviour and makes the difference.

SOURCES OF INFORMATION

Data is the foundation of all information. A few aspects of data, sources of data and methods of collecting the data for the purposes of converting them into information are described in the paragraphs, which follow.

Primary and Secondary Data: Data are the raw materials used for obtaining information. Data is derived from a number of sources, both internal as well as external. If the data is collected for the first time by the researcher, it is classified as *Primary Data.* If, however, the researcher from other sources borrows data, it is referred to as *Secondary Data.*

Primary data could be gathered directly from the respondent. Different techniques like observations, questionnaires, interviews etc. can be used for obtaining primary data, which can then be converted into information.

Secondary sources of data/information include internal records as well as external records. Sources like newspapers, magazines, trade journals, government publications, government policy documents, research reports, web sites etc. are included hereunder.

TYPES OF INFORMATION

Information is to be used for decision-making. The process of decision-making is generally divided into three types:

(*a*) Strategic Level
(*b*) Tactical Level
(*c*) Operational Level

For Strategic decision making, one needs strategic information, which is wholistic, unstructured and draws heavily from the external environment. It would also require more futuristic inputs like the emerging technologies, competition, consumer preferences, social-eco-political changes etc. as these inputs would be used for long-term planning.

Tactical information would be used for medium/short-term planning by the Middle Management, Budgets, forecasts, analysis; cash/funds flow projections are part of the tactical information. Such information is mostly from internal environment and partly from external environment like customer perceptions, competitor's strategy, pricing etc. It has medium term impact.

Operational information is mainly for/from operating people ranging from a 'shift' to a day or a week or a month. It is basically about what is currently happening around within the organization and is mainly drawn from internal sources. It also covers a specific product, specific activity and a smaller group/number of people.

Apart from the three types as stated above, we could also divide information into *Planning Information* and *Control Information.* The planning and control information could be differentiated as explained hereafter.

Planning Information	Control Information
• It covers the whole organization	• It is concerned with small, specific part of organization.
• It has a longer time span	• It has a shorter time span
• It looks for an analyses trends/patterns	• It looks for specific details for functional activity.
• Used for working futuristic trends/forecast.	• Used for assessing actual performance vis-à-vis budgeted.

ATTRIBUTES OF INFORMATION

Information, to be of use for the decision maker, has to possess certain attributes as stated hereunder:

- Timely availability
- Currency
- Periodicity/Frequency
- Pertinent/Relevant
- Completeness
- Consistency
- Accuracy

- Reliability
- Verifiability
- Clarity
- Comprehensibility
- Brevity
- Cost effectiveness

Needless to add, more attributes the 'information' possesses, better the quality it would have, leading to higher value of such information for the organization and decision maker.

HUMAN AS INFORMATION PROCESSORS

A human being can hear, see, touch, feel and smell. These senses are then transmitted to the brain, which analyses them and then comes out with appropriate response. This human behavior could be seen/explained in terms of information processing.

The sensory receptors (ears, eyes, nose, etc) pick up/receive signals which are then transmitted to the brain. The brain then processes the signals and appropriate responses are communicated. Thus, the signals from sensory receptors become inputs. These signals are transmitted through the nervous system, which acts as a channel or medium. These signals are communicated to brain where, while processing the signals, the brain acts as a Central Processing Unit. The processing leads to responses, which can be considered as outputs.

The above-mentioned steps could be referred to as "Model of Human as Information Processor".

The Model of Human as Information Processor can be presented as follows :

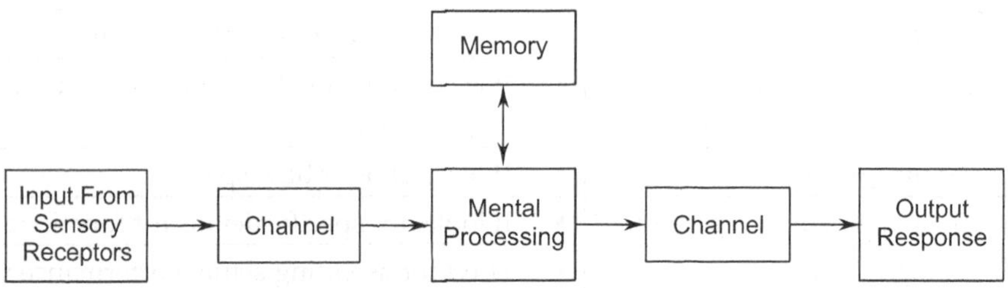

However, human beings cannot go on accepting unlimited inputs and keep coming up with unlimited outputs, as the human capacity to accept inputs and offer outputs is rather limited. If there is too much of input, the human capacity will simply be unable to accept the input and correspondingly, the output will also be reduced/ restricted. This "too much of inputs" affecting the output is considered as " overloading'.

To avoid this eventuality, humans restrict input to a manageable quantity by being selective in accepting some inputs and blocking other inputs. This process leads to creation of filters resulting from:

(*a*) Frame of reference of the person concerned, based on prior knowledge and experience.

(*b*) Normal decision procedure.

(*c*) Decision making under stress.

This process of filtering can be illustrated as follows :

(*a*) **Filtering under normal decision making conditions**

(*b*) **Filtering under decision making stress**

It may be noted that, filtering, apart from blocking unwanted data, may also block data which is not considered to be consistent with the established frame of reference. This, in turn, may result in errors of perception like omission, distortion, inferences etc. These errors of perception may reduce information content.

The typical human information processing mechanism and decision-making process may now be illustrated as follows:

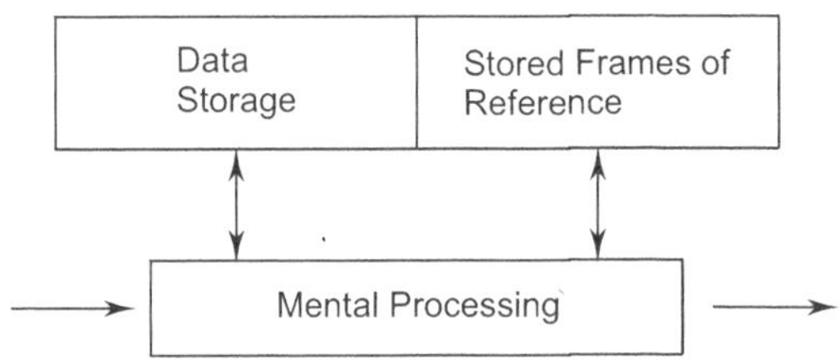

The Newell-Simon Model

Allel Newell and Herbert Simon have proposed a model of human problem solving and human information processing system. According to the model, the human information processing system consists of a processor, sensory inputs, motor output and three different memories- Long Term Memory (LTM), Short Term Memory (STM) and External Memory (EM) as illustrated hereafter:

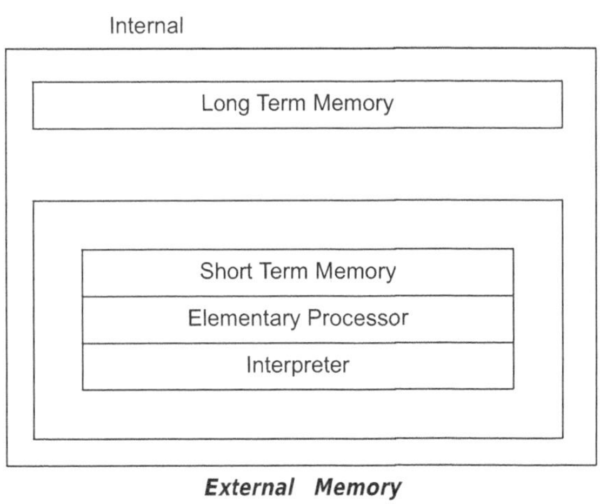

The human memory can perform only one information-processing task at a time (known as Serial Processing).

In view of our earlier discussions, the comparative presentation of Newell-Simon Model and Computer System Model can now be shown as follows:

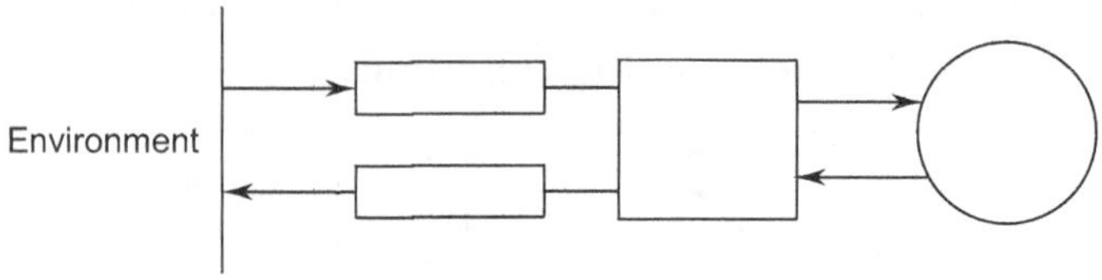

(*a*) Human Information Processing System

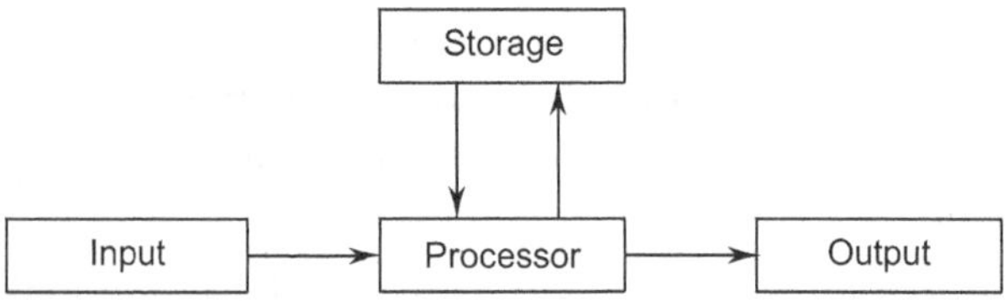

(*b*) Computer Information Processing System.

INFORMATION REQUIREMENT

Introduction

As discussed earlier, information today has become a strategic tool organization. Information is now also considered as a resource, much like capital and labor. As such, it becomes imperative to analyze and assess the information requirement/needs of business organizations activity wise, function wise, level wise as well as for organization as a whole, as the information required at each level is different.

Obviously, then, defining the specific information requirements becomes the most critical and therefore the most difficult-task for the Systems Analyst. This is one area where many large system efforts could go wrong, bringing the edifice of the organizational information system crumbling down as faulty requirements analysis is a leading cause of systems failure and high systems development costs. Analyzing and assessing information requirements/needs, therefore, must be given the attention and importance it deserves.

The Information Requirements within an organization, Hierarchy level wise, activity wise & function wise, could be presented as follows:

There are four reasons, which make it difficult to obtain a correct and complete set of information requirements:

1. The constraints on humans as information processors and problem solvers.
2. The variety and complexity of information requirements.
3. The complex patterns of interaction among users and analyst in defining requirements.
4. Unwillingness of some users to provide requirements.

But, what do we mean by information requirement?

Information requirement is a detailed statement of the information needs that a new system must satisfy. It involves identifying who needs what information, where, when and how.

Information requirement analysis carefully defines the objectives of the new or modified system and develops a detailed description of the functions that the new system is expected to perform. Requirements must consider economic, technical and time constraints as well as the goals, procedures and decision processes of the organization.

Information Requirements: Different Levels

Information requirements need to be established at three levels for the purpose of developing/ implementing organizational information system. The three levels are as follows:

1. Organizational Information Requirements.
2. The requirements for each database defined by data models and other specifications.
3. The detailed information requirements for an application.

Organizational Level Information Requirement

Information requirements are required at the organization-wide level for information system planning, identifying applications and planning information architecture. It is, however, imperative that the organization has a clear understanding of both its long-term and short-term information requirements. The process of organization-level information requirement determination obtains, organizes and documents a complete set of high level, strategic requirements. These requirements are then factored into databases and sub-systems, which can be scheduled for development.

Obtaining organizational information requirements would mainly consist of the following steps:

(*a*) Defining underlying sub-system,

(*b*) Developing manager by sub-system matrix,

(*c*) Defining and evaluating information requirement for organizational sub-system.

(*a*) **Defining underlying sub-system:** Every organization, viewed as a system, would consist of a number of sub-systems. These sub-systems could be obtained by an interactive process of discussing all the organizational functions/activities and arriving at the broad classification of the sub-systems. This activity enables the systems person to subdivide requirements determination by major organizational activity and makes the process more manageable.

(*b*) **Developing manager by sub-system matrix:** After defining the underlying organizational sub-systems, the next step is to relate specific managers to organizational sub-systems using a matrix format. The matrix can be prepared by reviewing the major decision responsibilities of each manager - middle to top - and associating decision making with specific sub-system. Thus, one gets a clear picture of the decision making responsibility, sub-systemwise, which, in turn, helps clarify responsibilities and identify those managers to be interviewed relative to each sub-system. An illustrative manager by sub-system matrix is presented hereafter:

(*c*) **Define and evaluate information requirements for organizational sub-system:** At this stage the information requirements of each sub-system of the organization are obtained by conducting group interviews of those managers having major decision-making responsibility for the sub-systems.

While conducting interviews, three sets of questions are asked to improve the chances of obtaining a complete set of requirements. The three sets of questions are:

1. What problem does the managers have and what information is needed for solving them? What decisions do the managers make and what information do they need for decision-making?

2. What factors are critical to the success of the manager's activity and what information do they need to achieve success in them or monitor progress?
3. What are the outputs (ends) from managerial activities and what do they need to measure effectiveness in achieving the outputs? What resources are used in producing the outputs and what information is needed to measure efficiency in use of the resources?

(These questions are derived from three approaches viz., Business System Planning, Critical Success Factors and Ends - Means Analysis, which are discussed later).

Data Base Requirements

Data base requirements arise both from applications and ad-hoc queries. The overall architecture for the database to meet these requirements is defined as part of the organizational information requirement. Major classes of data are then defined and associated with organization process that require them.

The process of obtaining and organizing more detailed database requirements can be divided into defining datd requirements as perceived by the users[conceptual or logical requirements] and defining requirements for physical design of the database,

Application Level Information Requirements

An application, basically a sub-system of the overall information-system, provides information Processing for a specific organization unit/activity. The process for the determination of information requirement at the application level defines and documents specific information content as also design and implementation requirements.

Application level information requirements are mainly of tow types;

(*a*) Social or Behavioral Requirements and

(*b*) Technical requirements

The social/behavioral requirements, based on job design, specially objectives and assumptions like, for example:

- Individual Role Assumptions.
- Responsibility Assumptions.
- Organizational Design Objectives.
- Organizational Policies.

The technical requirements, based on information needed for performing task/job, specify inputs, outputs, stored data and information processes. The structure and format of data are important in arriving at technical requirement.

The technical requirement also includes interface requirements between the user system and the applications system. The interface requirements include data presentation format, screen design, user language structure, feedback and assistance provisions, and error control and response time.

TECHNIQUES FOR ASSESSING INFORMATION REQUIREMENT

Let us now discuss some of the major ways/tools/methods/techniques for assessing information requirement/needs.

Asking Questions

Asking questions is one of the more frequently used modes of assessing information requirement. Questions are asked to persons associated with use of system/application to obtain their requirements.

Some 'asking' methods are mentioned below with comments on conditions that suggest their use:

Asking Method	Description	Conditions Suggesting Use
Closed Questions	Each question has a defined set of possible answers from which the respondent selects.	When set of factual responses is known or respondent may not be able to recall all possibilities. Analyst must know all possible responses.
Open Questions	No answers provided. Respondent is allowed to formulate responses.	When feelings or opinions are important or when respondent has knowledge and ability to formulate responses.
Brainstorming	Group method for eliciting wide variety of suggestions by open flow of ideas.	Used to extend boundaries of problem spaces of participants and elicit non-conventional solutions.
Guided Brainstorming	Participants are asked to define ideal solutions and then select the best feasible ideal solution.	Used to guide brainstorming to 'ideal' solutions. Useful where participants have system knowledge, but may be locked into anchoring and adjustment behavior.
Group Consensus	The participants are asked for their estimates or expectations regarding significant variables. Delphi Method and Group Norming are examples.	Used to arrive at 'best' judgmental estimate of variables that are difficult or impossible to estimate quantitatively.

One or more asking methods can be used either alone or in conjunction with other tools, to assess information requirement.

Deriving From an Existing Information System

Information systems, currently in operation or having operational history, can be used to arrive at information requirement for a proposed information system. The type of existing information systems which could be useful in this regards are motioned below;

(*a*) Existing system to be replaced by new system.

(*b*) Existing system in another, similar organization

(*c*) Information available from Handbooks, Industry, Specific Studies or subject Text Books.

Ends-Means Analysis

The ends-means analysis is a technique used for determining information requirements of the organization at the department and / or individual manager's level.

The technique separates the definition of ends [or outputs] generated by an organization process, from the means [inputs] used to accomplished them.As the end/output from one process is the input for next/some other process, the ends-means analysis brings out information requirement effectively.

The ends-means analysis is based on the systems Theory. A model of the ends-means analysis is provided hereunder:

APPENDIX III

BASICS OF SYSTEM

INTRODUCTION

The concept of systems is of pivotal importance in the MIS. The system concept is basically a way of thinking about managing optimally, in a wholistic perspective. It could also be consider as a framework for visualizing and analyzing both internal and external environments and the factors affecting these environments in an integrated manner.

When we refer to system, it generally indicates an arrangement, a way of organizing things in an orderly manner. A method or even a well thought-out plan. System also means a regularly interacting interdependent group of items forming a united whole.

A system can also mean an assemblage or combination of things or parts forming a complex or unitary whole.

For MIS purposes, let us put it in this way a system consists of a set of elements, which can be identified as belonging together because of common purpose, goal or objective.

The elements work/function in an integrated, coordinated and interdependent manner to achieve objective as well as synergy.

Alternatively, we may look at system as any group of componet_functions,people, activities etc. Which complement and interface with one another to achieve one or more predetermined goals.

As can we see from above the term wholistic, integrated, interdependent are used frequently. The idea is to emphasise the need for synergy. When the numerical total of individual elements leads to much higher output effectiveness. E.g. 1 + 2 + 3 + 4 + 5 = 15 which is the sum-total of individual elements. However, if these elements become part of the whole are integrated, then the result become 1 * 2 * 3 * 4 * 5 = 120 which is eight times better/higher than earlier.

The systems concept is therefore, important wire developing MIS. As it allows us to view individual elements. Sub-systems in the larger perspective of the whole system leading to optimal solutions and synergy.

A schematic representation of a closed system and its boundary **System** (from Latin *systēma*, in turn from Greek σ′υστημα systēma) is a set of interacting or interdependent entities, real or abstract, forming an integrated whole.

The concept of an "integrated whole" can also be stated in terms of a system embodying a set of relationships which are differentiated from relationships of the set to other elements, and from relationships between an element of the set and elements not a part of the relational regime.

The scientific research field which is engaged in the study of the general properties of systems include systems theory, systems science and systemics. They investigate the abstract properties of the matter and organization, searching concepts and principles which are independent of the specific domain, substance, type, or temporal scales of existence.Most systems share the same common characteristics. **These common characteristics include the following**

- Systems are abstractions of reality.
- Systems have structure which is defined by its parts and their composition.
- Systems have behavior, which involves inputs, processing and outputs of material, information or energy.
- The various parts of a system have functional as well as structural relationships between each other.

The term *system* may also refer to a set of rules that governs behavior or structure.

System Details

A system consists of elements, component and sub-systems. Indeed, a system itself can also be a part of a super system, as shown below:

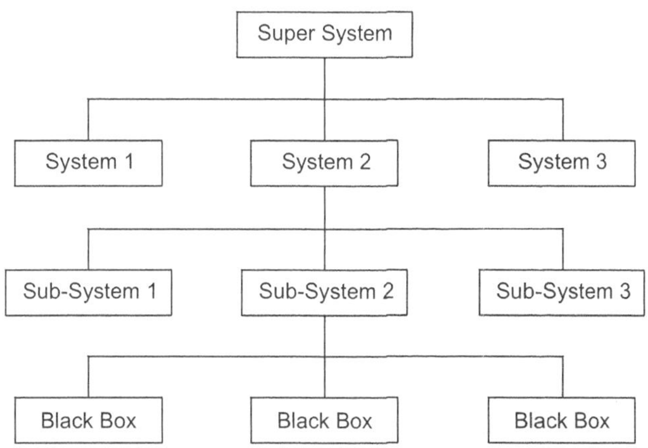

Fig. 1 *System Details*

HISTORY

The term *System* has a long history which can be traced back to the Greek language.

In the 19th century the first to develop the concept of a "system" in the natural sciences was the French physicist Nicolas Léonard Sadi Carnot who studied thermodynamics. In 1824 he studied what he called the *working substance* (system), *i.e.* typically a body of water vapor, in steam engines, in regards to the system's ability to do work when heat is applied to it. The working substance could be put in contact with either a boiler, a cold reservoir (a stream of cold water), or a piston (to which the working body could do work by pushing on it). In 1850, the German physicist Rudolf

Clausius generalized this picture to include the concept of the surroundings and began to use the term "working body" when referring to the system.

One of the pioneers of the general systems theory was the biologist Ludwig von Bertalanffy. In 1945 he introduced *models, principles, and laws that apply to generalized systems or their subclasses, irrespective of their particular kind, the nature of their component elements, and the relation or 'forces' between them,*

Significant development to the concept of a *system* was done by Norbert Wiener and Ross Ashby who pioneered the use of mathematics to study systems .

In the 1980s the term complex adaptive system was coined at the interdisciplinary Santa Fe Institute by John H. Holland, Murray Gell-Mann and others.

SYSTEM CONCEPTS

Environment and Boundaries

Systems theory views the world as a complex system of interconnected parts. We scope a system by defining its *boundary*; this means choosing which entities are inside the system and which are outside - part of the *environment*. We then make simplified representations (models) of the system in order to understand it and to predict or impact its future behavior. These models may define the structure and/or the behaviour of the system.

Natural and Man-Made Systems

There are natural and man-made (designed) systems. Natural systems may not have an apparent objective but their outputs can be interpreted as purposes. Man-made systems are made with purposes that are achieved by the delivery of outputs. Their parts must be related; they must be "designed to work as a coherent entity" - else they would be two or more distinct systems.

Open System

An open system usually interacts with some entities in their environment. A closed system is isolated from its environment.

Process and Transformation Process

A system can also be viewed as a bounded transformation process, that is, a process or collection of processes that transforms inputs into outputs. Inputs are consumed; outputs are produced. The concept of input and output here is very broad. E.g., an output of a passenger ship is the movement of people from departure to destination.

Subsystem

A *subsystem* is a set of elements, which is a system itself, and a part of a larger system.

TYPES OF SYSTEMS

Conceptual and Empirical Systems: Philosophy, Theology are classic examples of Conceptual Systems. Some systems are theoretical, explanatory and provide clarification.

Conceptual Systems provide a theoretical framework for which there may or may not be any real life counterpart *e.g.*, conceptual theory may refer to "Moksha", "Nirvana" which cannot really be experienced here and now.

The Empirical Systems, on the other hand, are practical, specific and operational. They may be based upon conceptual system, but differ from them in as much as one can see/experience the empirical system in operation. Production system, examination system, surgery can be referred to be as examples of the empirical systems.

Natural and Artificial Systems: Natural systems exist and abound in nature and are not the result of human endeavours. Rivers, mountains, minerals are illustrations of natural systems.

Artificial systems, on the other hand, are manufactured and hence man-made. Thus, while river or oceans are natural system, dams, canals, roads, machine and factories are artificial system.

Open and Close Systems: Open system is that system which is always interacting with the environment and exchanges information, material or energy with the environment. Open system is also open, self-organising and adoptive/adaptive to the changing environment as it flexible.

Close system, of course, is one, which shuns any kind of exchange with environment. It is rigid and is not amenable to change. It is self-contained and relatively isolated as it has a well defined boundary. It is also not adoptive.

Thus, while democracy is considered to be open system; communism or Nazism was considered as closed system. While USSR was having iron curtain and China Bamboo curtain, there was no such hindrance as regards USA or INDIA.

Probabilistic and Deterministic Systems: This type of systems will be based upon the predictability of behaviour or outcome.

In a deterministic system, the interaction of elements is known and hence the outcome predictable. In such a system, the behaviour of elements is predetermined and hence the reaction can be worked out-well in advance.

Mathematical formulae, chemical formulae are examples of deterministic system *i.e.*, there is a specific relationship between the inputs and the output. This, however, is not applicable to probabilistic system as in case of, say, human behaviour. In fact, the same person may react in different manner in the same situation on different occasions, or to illustrate further, schedule of examination can be deterministic, but the percentage of the result is probabilistic.

Apart from these systems, there are other types of system like:

- Social and Machine Systems
- Physical and Abstract Systems
- Permanent and Temporary Systems

APPLICATION OF THE SYSTEM CONCEPT

Systems modeling is generally a basic principle in engineering and in social sciences. The system is the representation of the entities under concern. Hence inclusion to or exclusion from system context is dependent of the intention of the modeler.

No model of a system will include all features of the real system of concern, and no model of a system must include all entities belonging to a real system of concern.

Systems in Information and Computer Science

In computer science and information science, system could also be a method or an algorithm. Again, an example will illustrate: There are systems of counting, as with Roman numerals, and various systems for filing papers, or catalogues, and various library systems, of which the Dewey Decimal System is an example. This still fits with the definition of components which are connected together (in this case in order to facilitate the flow of information).

System can also be used referring to a framework, be it software or hardware, designed to allow software programs to run.

Systems in Engineering

In engineering, the concept of a system is usually well defined. It is used in numerous different concrete contexts, and it is the subject of the basic engineering activities, such as: planning, design, implementation, building, and maintaining. Systems engineering is also a generalized theoretical branch of the different engineering approaches and paradigms.

Systems in Social and Cognitive Sciences and Management Research

Social and cognitive sciences recognize systems in human person models and in human societies. They include human brain functions and human mental processes as well as normative ethics systems and social/cultural behavioral patterns.

In management science, operations research and organizational development (OD), human organizations are viewed as systems (conceptual systems) of interacting components such as subsystems or system aggregates, which are carriers of numerous complex processes and organizational structures. Organizational development theorist Peter Senge developed the notion of organizations as systems in his book the Fifth Discipline.

Systems thinking is a style of thinking/reasoning and problem solving. It starts from the recognition of system properties in a given problem. It can be a leadership competency. Some people can think globally while acting locally. Such people consider the potential consequences of their decisions on other parts of larger systems. This is also a basis of systemic coaching in psychology.

Organizational theorists such as Margaret Wheatley have also described the workings of organizational systems in new metaphoric contexts, such as quantum physics, chaos theory, and the self-organization of systems.

SYSTEM FACILIATING ACTIVITIES

Factoring: A system is organized in a particular manner. The various elements or components have a distinctive role to play, which is assigned to them. A system for the sake of operational efficiency is divided into sub-systems. Each sub-system can then be further divided into lower level of sub-systems until we get a unit which is considered easy to manage. This process is known as Factoring.

Boundary: A system is divided into sub-systems. Each sub-system is delineated by its boundaries. The environment remains outside the Boundary.

Inter-Connections: The inter-connection and interaction between the sub-systems are called interfaces. Interfaces occur at the boundary and take the form of input and output (Which could be information, energy or material.)

Why Systems?

Systems are put together, directly or indirectly, for the purpose of ensuring control and feedback. Hence, control and feedback are considered the key system concepts as they 'pervade and permeate the whole idea of systems'.

What is Control?

Control is one of the most important concept, element and process in management. However, in the olden days, control was considered necessary if something went wrong. Control was, then, also confused with lack of freedom and *"puppet-on-string"* syndrome. Today, it has been realized that control and freedom are fully consistent and interdependent. It has also been realised that the total absence of control is not freedom but invitation for chaos or anarchy.

Today, control is seen as a pro-active response to ensure that things move the way they are expected to. In fact, controlling is one of the four major functions of management along with planning, organising, directing and leading. According to Koontz and O'Donnell, *"Control implies measurement of accomplishment against the standard and correction of deviation to assure attainment of objectives according to plans"*.

Anthony has defined control as *"process by which manager assures that resources are obtained and used effectively and efficiently in the accomplishment of an organisation's objectives"*.

Controlling, therefore, can be defined as the process of determining what is to be accomplished, that is, the standard, what is being accomplished that is, the performance, evaluating the performance and, if necessary, applying corrective measures so that performance takes place according to plans that is, in conformity with the standard.

Control, hence, means brining/maintaining:

- Performance of group/individual etc.
- Characteristics of group/individual etc.
- Characteristics or value of a variable within prescribed limit.
- Controlling can, therefore, be viewed as
- Setting standards of performance.
- Measuring performance against standards.
- Taking corrective action to reduce deviation from standards.

Control Process

The control process consists of:

- Determining what should be done or expected.
- Finding out what is being done.
- Comparing results with expectations.
- Approving/disapproving results.
- Applying necessary corrective actions.

CONTROL ELEMENTS AND ANALYSIS OF CONTROL

While authority, knowledge, guidance, direction, constraint and restraints are the six elements of control, the real nature of the controlling can be expressed as follows:

(*a*) Planning is the basis of control.
(*b*) Action is the essence of control.
(*c*) Delegation is the key to control.
(*d*) Information is the guide of control.

Control Cycle

The control process, popularly referred to as *'Control Cycle'*, has be represented hereafter.

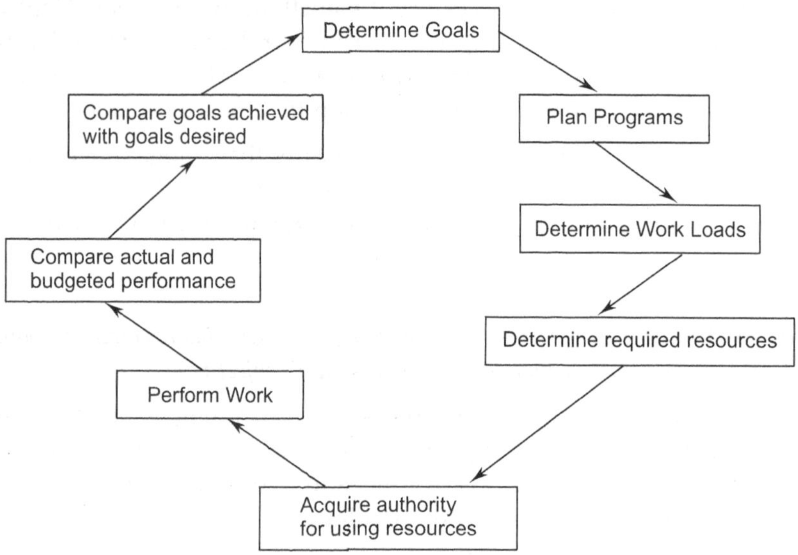

Fig. 2 *Control Process Cycle*

Requirements of Good Control System:

1. **Objective:** The control system should be definite and determinable.
2. **Suitable:** The control system should be conformity with the nature and need of the activity sought to be controlled and the culture/structure of organization.
3. **Intelligible:** The control system should be easily understandable by all concerned.
4. **Flexible:** The system should be able to work even when the plans change or fail.
5. **Prompt reporting:** The system must be able to report deviation from the plain/goals without loss of valuable time.
6. **Forward looking:** The system should enable the manager to plan for the future.
7. **Economical:** It should be cost-effective and economical.
8. **Suggestions of remedial action:** The control system should not only indicate/disclose the performance, but also show where failures are occurring, who is responsible for them and what should be done about them.
9. **Focus on strategic points:** The system should view the performance in strategic perspective and disclose the strategic implication.

10. **Principle of critical point control:** The system should follow the principle, which states "effective control requires attention to those factors critical to evaluating against plans".

FEEDBACK

Feedback is the system that provides information on the deviation between output and control standard and delivers this information as input into process from which the output is desired. This facilitates corrective action and hence, feedback is an integral part of the system Theory as could be evident from the following:

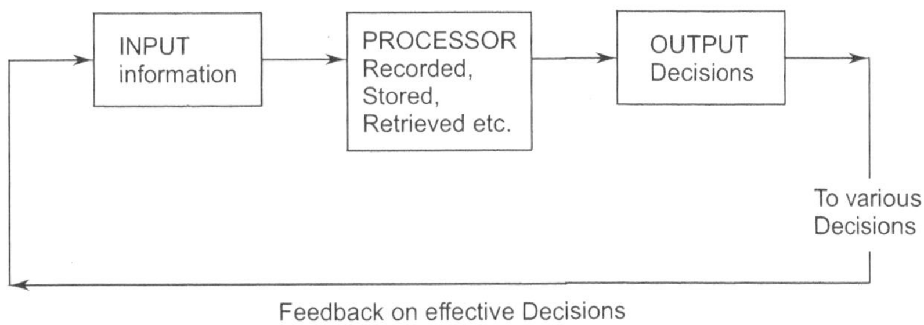

Fig. 3 *Feedback as Integral Part of a System*

The feedback may be positive or negative. Feedback is useful for exercising control in an organization by the management as illustrated below:

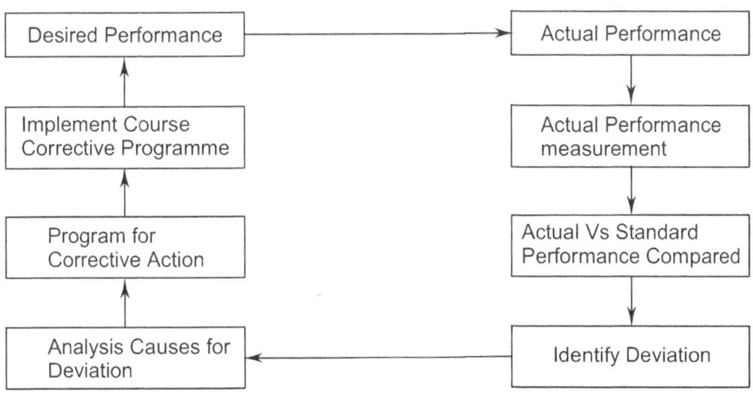

Fig. 4 *Usefulness of Feedback*

CONTROL SYSTEMS

The control system based on Feedback could be categorized into 3 types as follows:

(*a*) ***Closed Loop System:*** Under this system, feedback is based on output measurement. Appropriate feedback is passed on to the input so that suitable corrections could be made at the input stage itself. Control is internalised. Inventory control, cost control, quality control, inspection can be said to be examples of closed loop system.

(*b*) ***Open Loop system:*** Under this system, control is not internalised. Instead, it is extended to the system and there is no feedback or feedback loop. Action to initiate control is also not taken automatically.

(*c*) ***Cybernetic System:*** The science of communication and control is known as cybernetics. These systems, however, refer to systems which are very complex, probabilistic, yet self-regulating.

LAW OF REQUISITE VARITY

As we have studied earlier, control is one of the integral functions of the System Theory. *Law of Requisite Variety deals with the control mechanism of System Theory.*

But before we elaborate the Law of requisite variety, let us remember Murphy's Law which states that *"if a thing can go wrong, it will go wrong and it will go wrong at atime you least expect it to go wrong".*

In the context of systems theory and law of requisite variety, what it means is that the elements constituting a system may malfunction and there has to be appropriate mechanism to ensure that their malfunctioning is detected and also corrected.

The Law of Requisite variety implies to control each possible state of the system elements; there must be a corresponding control state. To put it another way, there must be at least as many variation of control to be supplied as there ways for the system to get out of control. The law of requisite variety also means that for a system to be controlled, each controller-human and machine-must be provided with:

(*a*) Enough control responses (What to do in each case) to cover all possible conditions the system may face.

(*b*) Decision Rules for generating all possible control responses.

(*c*) The authority to become a self-organizing system in order to generate control responses.

These various methods for providing system control responses are presented hereafter:

State of Variable Element	Control Response
S1	C1
S2	C2
S3	C3
⋮	⋮
Sn	Cn
(A) Enough Control Responses	

S1 S2 S3 … Sn → Decision Rules → C1 C2 C3 … Cn
(B) Decision Rules for Control Responses

S1 S2 S3 … Sn → Decision Rules + Judgment → C1 C2 C3 … Cn
(C) Self-organising Control Response

Fig. 5 *LRV Control Responses*

APPENDIX IV

COMPUTERS AND IT RELATED TECHNIQUES

INTRODUCTION

Let us begin with the word 'compute'. It means 'to calculate'. We all are familiar with calculations in our day-to-day life. We apply mathematical operations like addition, subtraction, multiplication, etc. and many other formulae for calculations. Simpler calculations take less time. But complex calculations take much longer time. Another factor is accuracy in calculations. So man explored with the idea to develop a machine, which can perform this type of arithmetic calculation faster, and with full accuracy. This gave birth to a device or machine called '**computer**'.

The computer we see today is quite different from the one made in the beginning. The number of applications of a computer has increased, the speed and accuracy of calculation has increased. You must appreciate the impact of computers in our day to day life. Reservation of tickets in Air Lines and Railways, payment of telephone and electricity bills, deposits and withdrawals of money from banks, business data processing, medical diagnosis, weather forecasting, etc. are some of the areas where computer has become extremely useful.

However, there is one limitation of the computer. Human beings do calculations on their own. But computer is a dumb machine and it has to be given proper instructions to carry out its calculation. This is why we should know how a computer works.

HISTORY OF COMPUTER

History of computer could be traced back to the effort of man to count large numbers. This process of counting of large numbers generated various systems of numeration like Babylonian system of numeration, Greek system of numeration, Roman system of numeration and Indian system of numeration. Out of these the Indian system of numeration has been accepted universally. It is the basis of modern decimal system of numeration (0, 1, 2, 3, 4, 5, 6, 7, 8, 9). Later you will know how the computer solves all calculations based on decimal system. But you will be surprised to know that the computer does not understand the decimal system and uses binary system of numeration for processing.

We will briefly discuss some of the path-breaking inventions in the field of computing devices.

Calculating Machines

It took over generations for early man to build mechanical devices for counting large numbers. The first calculating device called ABACUS was developed by the Egyptian and Chinese people.

The word ABACUS means calculating board. It consisted of sticks in horizontal positions on which were inserted sets of pebbles. A modern form of ABACUS is given in Fig. 1. It has a number of horizontal bars each having ten beads. Horizontal bars represent units, tens, hundreds, etc.

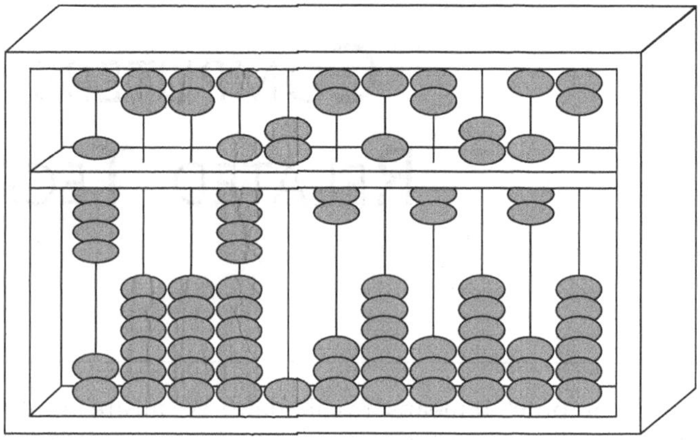

Fig. 1 *Abacus Computer*

Napier's Bones

English mathematician John Napier built a mechanical device for the purpose of multiplication in 1617 A D. The device was known as Napier's bones.

Slide Rule

English mathematician Edmund Gunter developed the slide rule. This machine could perform operations like addition, subtraction, multiplication, and division. It was widely used in Europe in 16th century.

Pascal's Adding and Subtractory Machine

You might have heard the name of Blaise Pascal. He developed a machine at the age of 19 that could add and subtract. The machine consisted of wheels, gears and cylinders.

Leibniz's Multiplication and Dividing Machine

The German philosopher and mathematician Gottfried Leibniz built around 1673 a mechanical device that could both multiply and divide.

Babbage's Analytical Engine

It was in the year 1823 that a famous English man Charles Babbage built a mechanical machine to do complex mathematical calculations. It was called *difference engine*. Later he developed a general-purpose calculating machine called *analytical engine*. You should know that Charles Babbage is called the *father of computer*.

Mechanical and Electrical Calculator

In the beginning of 19th century the mechanical calculator was developed to perform all sorts of mathematical calculations. Up to the 1960s it was widely used. Later the rotating part of mechanical calculator was replaced by electric motor. So it was called the electrical calculator.

Modern Electronic Calculator

The electronic calculator used in 1960 s was run with electron tubes, which was quite bulky. Later it was replaced with *transistors* and as a result the size of calculators became too small.

The modern electronic calculator can compute all kinds of mathematical computations and mathematical functions. It can also be used to store some data permanently. Some calculators have in-built programs to perform some complicated calculations.

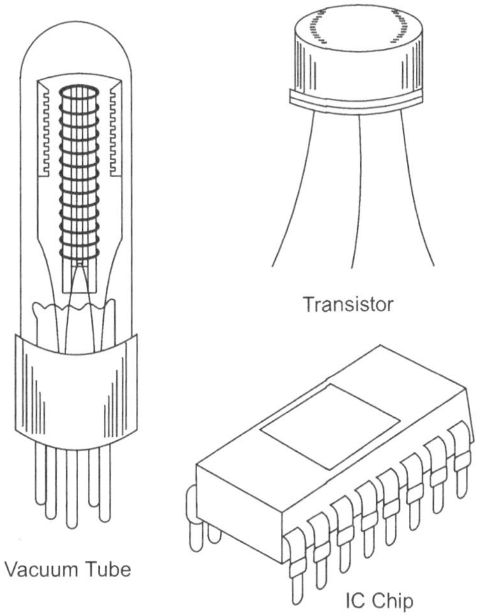

Fig. 2 *Vacuum Tube, Transistor, IC*

COMPUTER GENERATIONS

You know that the evolution of computer started from 16th century and resulted in the form that we see today. The present day computer, however, has also undergone rapid change during the last fifty years. This period, during which the evolution of computer took place, can be divided into five distinct phases known as *Generations of Computers*. Each phase is distinguished from others on the basis of the type of *switching circuits* used.

First Generation Computers

First generation computers used *Thermion valves*. These computers were large in size and writing programs on them was difficult. Some of the computers of this generation were:

ENIAC: It was the first electronic computer built in 1946 at University of Pennsylvania, USA by John Eckert and John Mauchy. It was named Electronic Numerical Integrator and Calculator

(ENIAC). The ENIAC was 30? 50 feet long, weighed 30 tons, contained 18,000 vacuum tubes, 70,000 registers, 10,000 capacitors and required 150,000 watts of electricity. Today your favorite computer is many times as powerful as ENIAC, still size is very small.

EDVAC: It stands for Electronic Discrete Variable Automatic Computer and was developed in 1950. The concept of storing data and instructions inside the computer was introduced here. This allowed much faster operation since the computer had rapid access to both data and instructions. The other advantages of storing instruction was that computer could do logical decision internally.

Other Important Computers of First Generation

EDSAC: It stands for Electronic Delay Storage Automatic Computer and was developed by M.V. Wilkes at Cambridge University in 1949.

UNIVAC-1: Ecker and Mauchly produced it in 1951 by Universal Accounting Computer setup.

Limitations of First Generation Computer

Followings are the major drawbacks of First generation computers.

1. The operating speed was quite slow.
2. Power consumption was very high.
3. It required large space for installation.
4. The programming capability was quite low.

Second Generation Computers

Around 1955 a device called *Transistor* replaced the bulky electric tubes in the first generation computer. Transistors are smaller than electric tubes and have higher operating speed. They have no filament and require no heating. Manufacturing cost was also very low. Thus the size of the computer got reduced considerably.

It is in the second generation that the concept of Central Processing Unit (CPU), memory, programming language and input and output units were developed. The programming languages such as COBOL, FORTRAN were developed during this period. Some of the computers of the Second Generation were

1. IBM 1620: Its size was smaller as compared to First Generation computers and mostly used for scientific purpose.
2. IBM 1401: Its size was small to medium and used for business applications.
3. CDC 3600: Its size was large and is used for scientific purposes.

Third Generation Computers

The third generation computers were introduced in 1964. They used *Integrated Circuits* (ICs). These ICs are popularly known as *Chips*. A single IC has many transistors, registers and capacitors built on a single thin slice of silicon. So it is quite obvious that the size of the computer got further reduced. Some of the computers developed during this period were IBM-360, ICL-1900, IBM-370, and VAX-750. Higher level language such as BASIC (Beginners All purpose Symbolic Instruction Code) was developed during this period.

Computers of this generations were small in size, low cost, large memory and processing speed is very high.

Fourth Generation Computers

The present day computers that you see today are the fourth generation computers that started around 1975. It uses *large scale Integrated Circuits* (LSIC) built on a single silicon chip called microprocessors. Due to the development of microprocessor it is possible to place computer's *central processing unit* (CPU) on single chip. These computers are called microcomputers. Later *very large scale Integrated Circuits* (VLSIC) replaced LSICs.

Thus the computer which was occupying a very large room in earlier days can now be placed on a table. The personal computer (PC) that you see in your school is a Fourth Generation Computer.

Fifth Generation Computer

The computers of 1990s are said to be Fifth Generation computers. The speed is extremely high in fifth generation computer. Apart from this it can perform *parallel processing*. The concept of *Artificial intelligence* has been introduced to allow the computer to take its own decision. It is still in a developmental stage.

WHAT IS A COMPUTER?

Computer is an electronic device. As mentioned in the introduction it can do arithmetic calculations faster. But as you will see later it does much more than that. It can be compared to a magic box, which serves different purpose to different people. For a common man computer is simply a calculator, which works automatic and quite fast. For a person who knows much about it, computer is a machine capable of solving problems and manipulating data. It accepts data, processes the data by doing some mathematical and logical operations and gives us the desired output.

Therefore, we may define *computer as a device that transforms data*. Data can be anything like marks obtained by you in various subjects. It can also be name, age, sex, weight, height, etc. of all the students in your class or income, savings, investments, etc., of a country. Computer can be defined in terms of its functions. It can i) accept data ii) store data, iii) process data as desired, and iv) retrieve the stored data as and when required and v) print the result in desired format. You will know more about these functions as you go through the later lessons.

Fig. 3 below depicts a personal computer.

Fig. 3 *Personal Computer*

General Definition of Computer

A computer is an electronic machine that

1. takes in data and instructions (input)
2. works with the data (processing)
3. puts out information (output)

World famous software company **Microsoft** Inc. has defined computer as:

Any device capable of processing information to produce a desired result. No matter how large or small they are, computers typically perform their work in three well-defined steps: (1) accepting input, (2) processing the input according to predefined rules (programs), and (3) producing output.

CHARACTERISTICS OF COMPUTER

Let us identify the major characteristics of computer. These can be discussed under the headings of speed, accuracy, diligence, versatility and memory.

Speed

As we know computer can work very fast. It takes only few seconds for calculations that we take hours to complete. Suppose you are asked to calculate the average monthly income of one thousand persons in your neighborhood. For this you have to add income from all sources for all persons on a day to day basis and find out the average for each one of them. How long will it take for you to do this? One day, two days or one week? Do you know your small computer can finish this work in few seconds? The weather forecasting that you see every day on TV is the results of compilation and analysis of huge amount of data on temperature, humidity, pressure, etc. of various places on computers. It takes few minutes for the computer to process this huge amount of data and give the result.You will be surprised to know that computer can perform millions (1,000,000) of instructions and even more per second. Therefore, we determine the speed of computer in terms of microsecond (10^{-6} part of a second) or nano-second (10^{-9} part of a second). From this you can imagine how fast your computer performs work.

Accuracy

Suppose some one calculates faster but commits a lot of errors in computing. Such result is useless. There is another aspect. Suppose you want to divide 15 by 7. You may work out up to 2 decimal places and say the dividend is 2.14. I may calculate up to 4 decimal places and say that the result is 2.1428. Some one else may go up to 9 decimal places and say the result is 2.142857143. Hence, in addition to speed, the computer should have accuracy or correctness in computing.

The degree of accuracy of computer is very high and every calculation is performed with the same accuracy. The accuracy level is determined on the basis of design of computer. The errors in computer are due to human and inaccurate data.

Diligence

A computer is free from tiredness, lack of concentration, fatigue, etc. It can work for hours without creating any error. If millions of calculations are to be performed, a computer will perform every calculation with the same accuracy. Due to this capability it overpowers human being in routine type of work.

Versatility

It means the capacity to perform completely different type of work. You may use your computer to prepare payroll slips. Next moment you may use it for inventory management or to prepare electric bills.

Power of Remembering

Computer has the power of storing any amount of information or data. Any information can be stored and recalled as long as you require it, for any numbers of years. It depends entirely upon you how much data you want to store in a computer and when to lose or retrieve these data.

No IQ

Computer is a dumb machine and it cannot do any work without instruction from the user. It performs the instructions at tremendous speed and with accuracy. It is you to decide what you want to do and in what sequence. So a computer cannot take its own decision as you can.

No Feeling

It does not have feelings or emotion, taste, knowledge and experience. Thus it does not get tired even after long hours of work. It does not distinguish between users.

Storage

The Computer has an in-built memory where it can store a large amount of data. You can also store data in secondary storage devices such as floppies, which can be kept outside your computer and can be carried to other computers.

Word Length

A digital computer operates on binary digits — 0 and 1. It can understand information only in binary form *i.e.,* 0 and 4. A binary digit is called bit. The numbers of bits that a computer can process at a time in parallel is called its word length. Word length is the measure of the computing power of a computer. Examples of word lengths are 8, 16, 24, 64, 128 & 256.

TYPES OF COMPUTERS

Personal or Micro Computer

Computers for personal use come in all shapes and sizes, from tiny PDAs (personal digital assistant) to hefty PC (personal computer) towers. More specialized models are announced each week - trip planners, expense account pads, language translators.

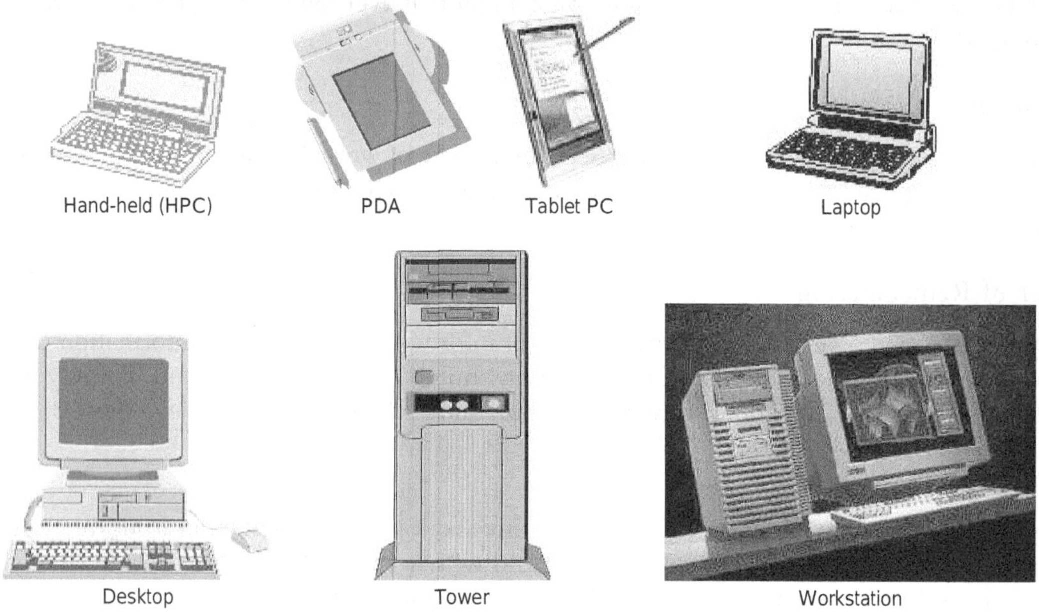

Fig. 4

When talking about PC computers, most people probably think of the **desktop** type, which are designed to sit on your desk. (Bet you figured that one out!) The **tower** and the smaller mini-tower style cases have become popular as people started needing more room for extra drives inside. Repairmen certainly appreciate the roominess inside for all the cables and circuit boards ... and their knuckles.

Workstation

A **workstation** is part of a computer network and generally would be expected to have more than a regular desktop PC of most everything, like memory, storage space, and speed.

The market for the smallest PCs is expanding rapidly. Software is becoming available for the small types of PC like the **palmtop** (**PPC**) and **handheld** (**HPC**). This new software is based on new operating systems like Windows CE (for Consumer Electronics). You may find simplified versions of the major applications you use. One big advantage for the newer programs is the ability to link the small computers to your home or work computer and coordinate the data. So you can carry a tiny computer like a PalmPilot around to enter new phone numbers and appointments and those great ideas you just had. Then later you can move this information to your main computer.

With a Tablet PC you use an electronic stylus to write on the screen, just like with a pen and paper, only your words are in digital ink. The Tablet PC saves your work just like your wrote it (as a picture), or you can let the Hand Recognition (HR) software turn your chicken-scratches into regular text.

Mainframe Computer

1. The mainframe computer is the workhorse of the business world. A mainframe computer is the heart of a network of computers or terminals, which allows hundreds of people to work at the same time on the same data. It requires a special environment cold and

dry. Mainframe computers are big in size, capable of handling all kinds of tasks and require more space. Mainframe computers can support more than 1000 terminals and are capable of accepting all high-level languages. They can transfer data at very high rate. Example of mainframes are DEC, ICL and IBM 3000 series.

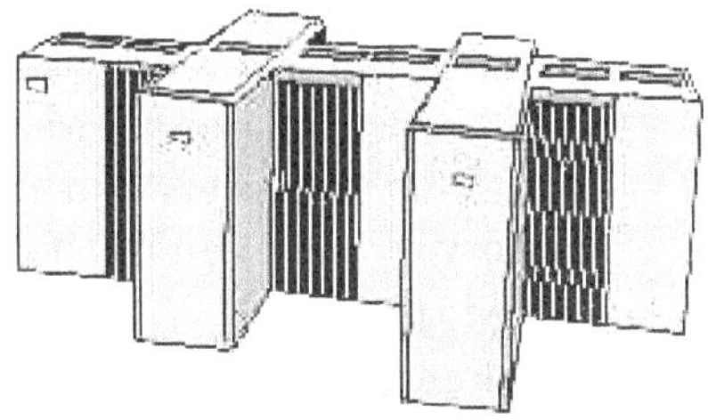

Fig. 5

Supercomputers

2. Super computers are capable of using several processors simultaneously. They process at a rapid speed and the main memory ranges 8 to 64 megabytes. The supercomputer is the top of the heap in power and expense. The capacity, function, speed, accuracy, etc. are very high. These are used for jobs that take massive amounts of calculating, like weather forecasting, engineering design and testing, serious decryption, economic forecasting, etc. Examples of supercomputers are CRAY YMP, CRAY2, NEC SX-3, CRAY XMP and PARAM from India.

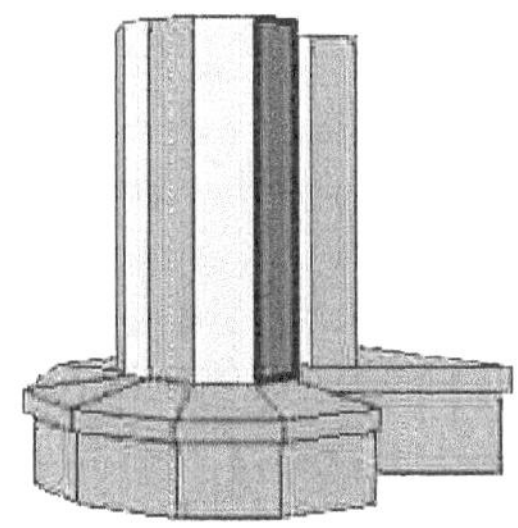

Fig. 6

Minicomputer

The **minicomputer** has become less important since the PC has gotten so powerful on its own. In fact, the ordinary new PC is much more powerful than minicomputers used to be. Originally this size was developed to handle specific tasks, like engineering and CAD calculations, that tended to tie up the main frame.

COMPONENTS OF A COMPUTER

Components of a computer include hardware components and software components.

- **Hardware** is the electric, electronic, and mechanical equipment that makes up a computer.
- **Software** is the series of instructions that tells the hardware how to perform tasks

Computer Hardware

Computer hardware components include input devices, output devices, a system unit, storage devices, and communications devices.

- An **input device** is any hardware component that allows a user to enter data and instructions into a computer. Six commonly used input devices are the keyboard, mouse, microphone, scanner, digital camera, and PC camera.
  - **Keyboard** - This is where the user enters text commands into the computer.
  - **Mouse** - A point and click interface for entering commands, which works well in graphical environments.
- An **output device** is any hardware component that can convey information to a user. Three commonly used output devices are a printer, a monitor, and speakers.
  - **Monitor** - This device which operates like a TV set lets the user see how the computer is responding to their commands.
  - **Printer**
  - **Speaker**

- The **system unit** is a box-like case made from metal or plastic that protects the internal electronic components of the computer from damage. The system unit contains the central processing unit and memory. The **central processing unit** (**CPU**) is the electronic device that interprets and carries out the basic instructions that operate the computer. **Memory** is a temporary holding place for data and instructions.
    - **Motherboard** — This is where the core components of your computer reside which are listed below. Also the support cards for video, sound, networking and more are mounted into this board.
        1. **Microprocessor** — This is the brain of your computer. It performs commands and instructions and controls the operation of the computer.
        2. **Memory** — The RAM in your system is mounted on the motherboard. This is memory that must be powered on to retain its contents.
        3. **Drive controllers** — The drive controllers control the interface of your system to your hard drives. The controllers let your hard drives work by controlling their operation. On most systems, they are included on the motherboard, however you may add additional controllers for faster or other types of drives.
- A **storage device** records and retrieves data to and from a storage medium. Six common storage devices are a floppy disk drive, a Zip® drive, a hard disk drive, a CD-ROM drive, a CD-RW drive, a DVD-ROM drive, and a DVD+RW drive.
    - **Hard disk drive(s)** — This is where your files are permanently stored on your computer. Also, normally, your operating system is installed here.
    - **CD-ROM drive(s)** — This is normally a read only drive where files are permanently stored. There are now read/write CD-ROM drives that use special software to allow users to read from and write to these drives.
    - **Floppy drive(s)** — A floppy is a small disk storage device that today typically has about 1.4 Megabytes of memory capacity.
    - Other possible file storage devices include DVD devices, Tape backup devices, and some others.
- **Power Supply** — The power supply comes with the case, but this component is mentioned separately since there are various types of power supplies. The one you should get depends on the requirements of your system.
- A **communications device** enables computer users to communicate and exchange items such as data, instructions, and information with another computer. A **modem** is a communications device that enables computers to communicate usually via telephone lines or cable.

Computer Software(s)

There are two categories of computer software: system software and application software.

System software consists of the programs that control the operations of a computer and its devices. Two types of system software are the operating system and utility programs.

- An **operating system** (**OS**) coordinates all activities among hardware devices and contains instructions that allow you to run application software.
- A **utility program** performs specific tasks, usually related to managing a computer, its devices, or its programs. You interact with software through its user interface.

Application software consists of programs that perform specific tasks for users. Popular application software includes word processing software, spreadsheet software, database software, and presentation graphics software. Application software can be

- **packaged software** (copyrighted software that meets the needs of a variety of users),
- **custom software** (tailor-made software developed at a user's request),
- **freeware** (copyrighted software provided at no cost),
- **public-domain software** (software donated for public use with no copyright restrictions), or
- **shareware** (copyrighted software distributed free for a trial period).

BASIC COMPUTER OPERATIONS

A computer as shown in Fig. 7 performs basically five major operations or functions irrespective of their size and make. These are 1) it accepts data or instructions by way of input, 2) it stores data, 3) it can process data as required by the user, 4) it gives results in the form of output, and 5) it controls all operations inside a computer. We discuss below each of these operations.

1. **Input:** This is the process of entering data and programs in to the computer system. You should know that computer is an electronic machine like any other machine which takes as inputs raw data and performs some processing giving out processed data. Therefore, the input unit takes data from us to the computer in an organized manner for processing.

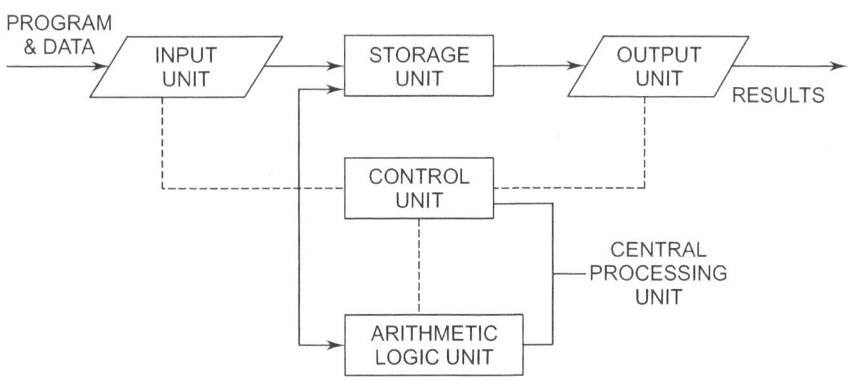

Fig. 7 *Basic Computer Operations*

2. **Storage:** The process of saving data and instructions permanently is known as storage. Data has to be fed into the system before the actual processing starts. It is because the processing speed of Central Processing Unit (CPU) is so fast that the data has to be provided to CPU with the same speed. Therefore the data is first stored in the storage unit for faster access and processing. This storage unit or the primary storage of the computer system is designed to do the above functionality. It provides space for storing data and instructions.

   The storage unit performs the following major functions:

   - All data and instructions are stored here before and after processing.
   - Intermediate results of processing are also stored here.

3. **Processing:** The task of performing operations like arithmetic and logical operations is called processing. The Central Processing Unit (CPU) takes data and instructions from

the storage unit and makes all sorts of calculations based on the instructions given and the type of data provided. It is then sent back to the storage unit.

4. **Output:** This is the process of producing results from the data for getting useful information. Similarly the output produced by the computer after processing must also be kept somewhere inside the computer before being given to you in human readable form. Again the output is also stored inside the computer for further processing.
5. **Control:** The manner how instructions are executed and the above operations are performed. Controlling of all operations like input, processing and output are performed by control unit. It takes care of step-by-step processing of all operations in side the computer.

DATA COMMUNICATION

Today computer is available in many offices and homes and therefore there is a need to share data and programs among various computers with the advancement of data communication facilities. The communication between computers has increased and it thus it has extended the power of computer beyond the computer room. Now a user sitting at one place can communicate computers of any remote sites through communication channel. The aim of this chapter is to introduce you the various aspects of computer network.

We all are acquainted with some sorts of communication in our day to day life. For communication of information and messages we use telephone and postal communication systems. Similarly data and information from one computer system can be transmitted to other systems across geographical areas. Thus data transmission is the movement of information using some standard methods. These methods include electrical signals carried along a conductor, optical signals along an optical fibers and electromagnetic areas.

Suppose a manager has to write several letters to various clients. First he has to use his PC and Word Processing package to prepare his letter. If the PC is connected to all the client's PCs through networking, he can send the letters to all the clients within minutes. Thus irrespective of geographical areas, if PCs are connected through communication channel, the data and information, computer files and any other program can be transmitted to other computer systems within seconds. The modern form of communication like *e-mail* and *Internet* is possible only because of computer networking.

Basic Elements of a Communication System

The following are the basic requirements for working of a communication system.

1. A *sender* (source) which creates the message to be transmitted.
2. A *medium* that carries the message.
3. A *receiver* (sink) which receives the message.

In data communication four basic terms are frequently used. They are

- **Data:** A collection of facts in raw forms that become information after processing.
- **Signals:** Electric or electromagnetic encoding of data.
- **Signaling:** Propagation of signals across a communication medium.
- **Transmission:** Communication of data achieved by the processing of signals.

Communication Protocols

You may be wondering how do the computers send and receive data across communication links. The answer is *data communication software*. It is this software that enables us to communicate with other systems. The data communication software instructs computer systems and devices as to how exactly data is to be transferred from one place to another. The procedure of data transformation in the form of software is commonly called *protocol*.

The data transmission software or protocols perform the following functions for the efficient and error free transmission of data.

1. **Data sequencing:** A long message to be transmitted is broken into smaller packets of fixed size for error free data transmission.
2. **Data Routing:** It is the process of finding the most efficient route between source and destination before sending the data.
3. **Flow control:** All machines are not equally efficient in terms of speed. Hence the flow control regulates the process of sending data between fast sender and slow receiver.
4. **Error Control:** Error detecting and recovering is the one of the main function of communication software. It ensures that data are transmitted without any error.

Data Transmission Modes

There are three ways for transmitting data from one point to another

1. **Simplex:** In simplex mode the communication can take place in one direction. The *receiver* receives the signal from the transmitting device. In this mode the flow of information is Uni.-directional. Hence it is rarely used for data communication.
2. **Half-duplex:** In half-duplex mode the communication channel is used in both directions, but only in one direction at a time. Thus a half-duplex line can alternately send and receive data.
3. **Full-duplex:** In full duplex the communication channel is used in both directions at the same time. Use of full-duplex line improves the efficiency as the line turn-around time required in half-duplex arrangement is eliminated. Example of this mode of transmission is the telephone line.

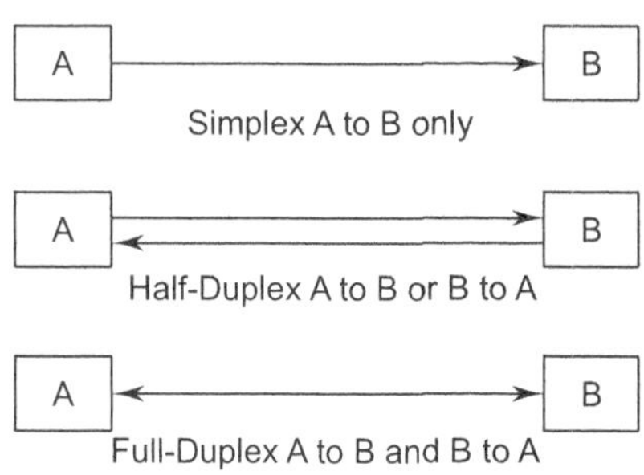

Fig. 8

Digital and Analog Transmission

Data is transmitted from one point to another point by means of electrical signals that may be in digital and analog form. So one should know the fundamental difference between analog and digital signals. In analog signal the transmission power varies over a continuous range with respect to sound, light and radio waves. On the other hand a digital signal may assume only discrete set of values within a given range. Examples are computer and computer related equipment.

Analog signal is measured in *Volts* and its frequency in *Hertz* (Hz). A digital signal is a sequence of voltage represented in *binary form*. When digital data are to be sent over an analog form the digital signal must be converted to analog form. So the technique by which a digital signal is converted to analog form is known as *modulation*. And the reverse process, that is the conversion of analog signal to its digital form, is known as demodulation. The device, which converts digital signal into analog, and the reverse, is known as *modem*.

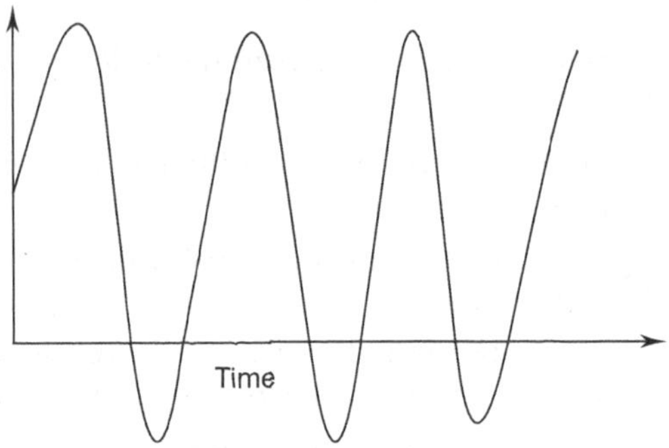

Fig. 9 *Analog Signal*

Asynchronous and Synchronous Transmission

Data transmission through a medium can be either asynchronous or synchronous. In asynchronous transmission data is transmitted character by character as you go on typing on a keyboard. Hence there is irregular gaps between characters. However, it is cheaper to implement, as you do not have to save the data before sending. On the other hand, in the synchronous mode, the saved data is transmitted block by block. Each block can contain many characters. Synchronous transmission is well suited for remote communication between a computer and related devices like card reader and printers.

Following are the major communication devices used to day.

1. **Wire Pairs:** Wire pairs are commonly used in local telephone communication and for short distance digital data communication. They are usually made up of copper and the pair of wires is twisted together. Data transmission speed is normally 9600 bits per second in a distance of 100 meter.
2. **Coaxial Cables:** Coaxial cable is groups of specially wrapped and insulted wires that are able to transfer data at higher rate. They consist of a central copper wire surrounded by an insulation over which copper mesh is placed. They are used for long distance telephone lines and local area network for their noise immunity and faster data transfer.
3. **Microwave:** Microwave system uses very high frequency radio signals to transmit data through space. The transmitter and receiver of a microwave system should be in line-of-sight because the radio signal cannot bend. With microwave very long distance transmission is not possible. In order to overcome the problem of line of sight and power amplification of weak signal, repeaters are used at intervals of 25 to 30 kilometers between the transmitting and receiving end.
4. **Communication Satellite:** The problem of line-sight and repeaters are overcome by using satellites which are the most widely used data transmission media in modern days. A communication satellite is a microwave relay station placed in outer space. INSAT-1B is such a satellite that can be accessible from anywhere in India. In satellite communication,

microwave signal is transmitted from a transmitter on earth to the satellite at space. The satellite amplifies the weak signal and transmits it back to the receiver. The main advantage of satellite communication is that it is a single microwave relay station visible from any point of a very large area. In microwave the data transmission rate is 16 giga bits per second. They are mostly used to link big metropolitan cities.

COMPUTER NETWORK

A computer network is an interconnection of various computer systems located at different places. In computer network two or more computers are linked together with a medium and data communication devices for the purpose of communicating data and sharing resources. The computer that provides resources to other computers on a network is known as *server*. In the network the individual computers, which access shared network resources, are known as *workstations* or *nodes*.

Computer Networks may be classified on the basis of geographical area in two broad categories.

1. Local Area Network (LAN)
2. Wide Area Network (WAN).

Local Area Network

Networks used to interconnect computers in a single room, rooms within a building or buildings on one site are called Local Area Network (LAN). LAN transmits data with a speed of several megabits per second (10^6 bits per second). The transmission medium is normally *coaxial cables*.

LAN links computers, *i.e.*, software and hardware, in the same area for the purpose of sharing information. Usually LAN links computers within a limited geographical area because they must be connected by a cable, which is quite expensive. People working in LAN get more capabilities in data processing, work processing and other information exchange compared to *stand-alone computers*. Because of this information exchange most of the business and government organisations are using LAN.

Major Characteristics of LAN

- Every computer has the potential to communicate with any other computers of the network
- High degree of interconnection between computers
- Easy physical connection of computers in a network
- Inexpensive medium of data transmission
- High data transmission rate.

Advantages

- The reliability of network is high because the failure of one computer in the network does not effect the functioning for other computers.
- Addition of new computer to network is easy.
- High rate of data transmission is possible.
- Peripheral devices like magnetic disk and printer can be shared by other computers.

Disadvantages

If the communication line fails, the entire network system breaks down.

Use of LAN

Followings are the major areas where LAN is normally used

- File transfers and Access
- Word and text processing
- Electronic message handling
- Remote database access
- Personal computing
- Digital voice transmission and storage.

Wide Area Network

The term Wide Area Network (WAN) is used to describe a computer network spanning a regional, national or global area. For example, for a large company the head quarters might be at Delhi and regional branches at Bombay, Madras, Bangalore and Calcutta. Here regional centers are connected to head quarters through WAN. The distance between computers connected to WAN is larger. Therefore the transmission medium used are normally telephone lines, microwaves and satellite links.

Characteristics of WAN

Followings are the major characteristics of WAN.

1. **Communication Facility:** For a big company spanning over different parts of the country the employees can save long distance phone calls and it overcomes the time lag in overseas communications. Computer conferencing is another use of WAN where users communicate with each other through their computer system.
2. **Remote Data Entry:** Remote data entry is possible in WAN. It means sitting at any location you can enter data, update data and query other information of any computer attached to the WAN but located in other cities. For example, suppose you are sitting at Madras and want to see some data of a computer located at Delhi, you can do it through WAN.
3. **Centralised Information:** In modern computerised environment you will find that big organisations go for centralised data storage. This means if the organisation is spread over many cities, they keep their important business data in a single place. As the data are generated at different sites, WAN permits collection of this data from different sites and save at a single site.

Examples of WAN

1. **Ethernet:** Ethernet developed by Xerox Corporation is a famous example of WAN. This network uses coaxial cables for data transmission. Special integrated circuit chips called *controllers* are used to connect equipment to the cable.
2. **Arpanet:** The Arpanet is another example of WAN. It was developed at Advanced Research Projects Agency of U. S. Department. This Network connects more than 40 universities and institutions throughout USA and Europe.

Difference between LAN and WAN

- LAN is restricted to limited geographical area of few kilometers. But WAN covers great distance and operate nationwide or even worldwide.

- In LAN, the computer terminals and peripheral devices are connected with wires and coaxial cables. In WAN there is no physical connection. Communication is done through telephone lines and satellite links.
- Cost of data transmission in LAN is less because the transmission medium is owned by a single organisation. In case of WAN the cost of data transmission is very high because the transmission medium used are hired, either telephone lines or satellite links.
- The speed of data transmission is much higher in LAN than in WAN. The transmission speed in LAN varies from 0.1 to 100 megabits per second. In case of WAN the speed ranges from 1800 to 9600 bits per second (bps).
- Few data transmission errors occur in LAN compared to WAN. It is because in LAN the distance covered is negligible.

NETWORK TOPOLOGY

The term topology in the context of communication network refers to the way the computers or workstations in the network are linked together. According to the physical arrangements of workstations and nature of work, there are three major types of network topology. They are star topology, bus topology and ring topology.

Star Topology

In star topology a number of workstations (or nodes) are directly linked to a central node (see, Fig. 10). Any communication between stations on a star LAN must pass through the central node. There is *bi-directional* communication between various nodes. The central node controls all the activities of the nodes. The advantages of the star topology are:

- It offers flexibility of adding or deleting of workstations from the network.
- Breakdown of one station does not affect any other device on the network.

The major disadvantage of star topology is that failure of the central node disables communication throughout the whole network.

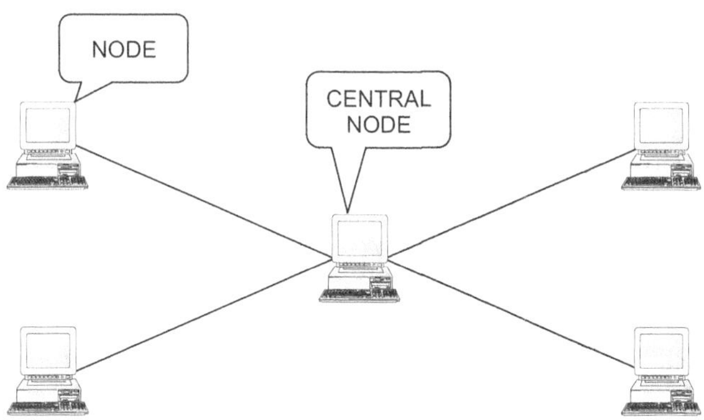

Fig. 10 *Star Topology*

Bus Topology

In bus topology all workstations are connected to a single communication line called *bus*. In this type of network topology there is no central node as in star topology. Transmission from any station travels the length of the bus in both directions and can be received by all workstations. The advantage of the bus topology is that

- It is quite easy to set up.
- If one station of the topology fails it does not affect the entire system.

The disadvantage of bus topology is that any break in the bus is difficult to identify.

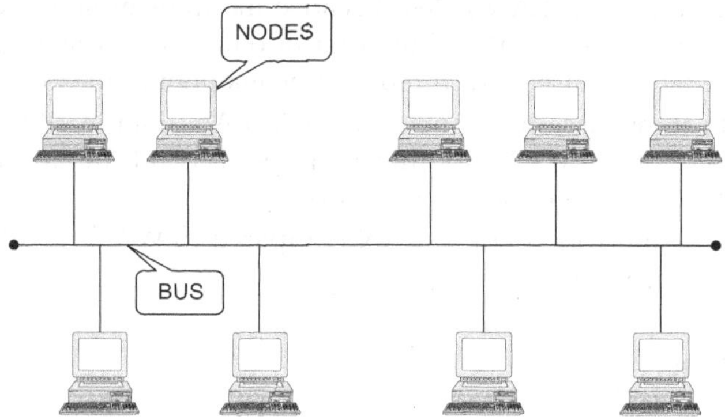

Fig. 11 *Bus Topology*

Ring Topology

In ring topology each station is attached nearby stations on a point to point basis so that the entire system is in the form of a ring. In this topology data is transmitted in one direction only. Thus the data packets circulate along the ring in either clockwise or anticlockwise direction. The advantage of this topology is that any signal transmitted on the network passes through all the LAN stations. The disadvantage of ring network is that the breakdown of any one station on the ring can disable the entire system.

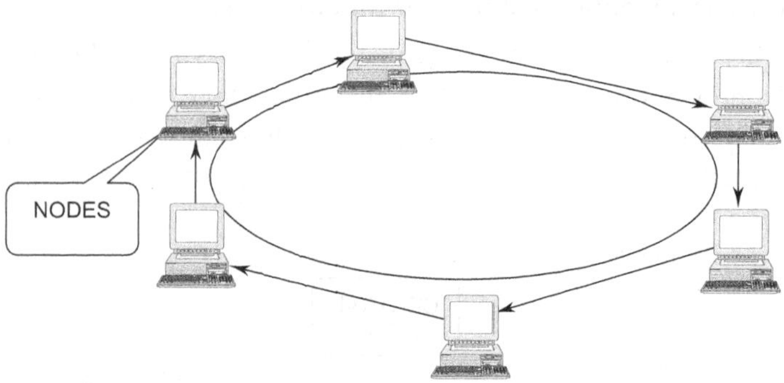

Fig. 12 *Ring Topology*

Hierarchical Topology

The hierarchical topology (also called vertical or tree structure) is one of the most common networks. The hierarchical topology is attractive for several reasons. The software to control the network is simple and the topology provides a concentration point for control and error resolution. However, it also presents potential bottleneck and reliability problems. It is possible that network capabilities may be completely lost in the event of a failure at a higher level.

Mesh Topology

The mesh topology provides a very reliable, though complex, network. Its structure makes it relatively immune to bottlenecks and other failures. The multiplicity of paths makes it relatively easy to route traffic around failed components or busy nodes.

OSI REFERENCE MODEL VIA TCP/IP REFERENCE MODEL

OSI (Open System Interconnection) Reference Model

The OSI model is shown is figure below:

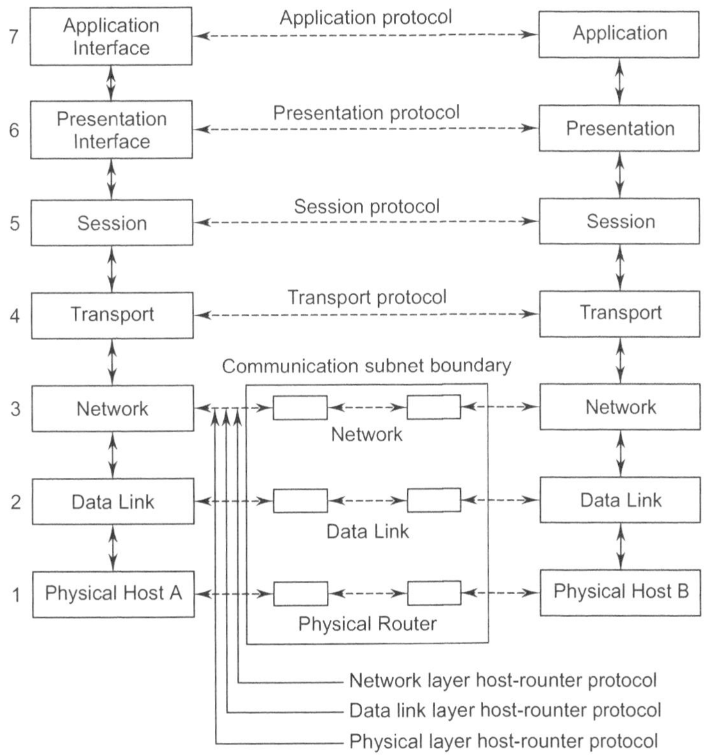

Fig. 13

This model deals with connecting open systems — that is, systems that are open for communication with other systems. Note that the OSI model itself is not a network architecture because it does not specify the exact services and protocols to be used in each layer. However, common standards were produced by ISO (International Standards Organization) for each layer:

Physical Layer

The **physical** layer is concerned with transmitting raw bits over communication channel under assumption, that it is 100% reliable.

Data Link Layer

The **data link** layer takes a raw transmission facility and transforms it into a line that appears free of undetected transmission errors to the network layer. This task is accomplished by using data and acknowledgment frames and error detection algorithms (like code Humming).

Network Layer

The **network** layer is concerned with controlling the operation of the subnet. That is routing the packets from the source to destination. Routes can be based on static or dynamic routing tables as will be reviewed later. *(This layer is the one that we are actually interested in)*.

Transport Layer

The **transport** layer basic function is to accept data from the session layer derive it into packet (if necessary), pass these to the network layer and restore the data on the other end.

The **session, presentation and application** layers are less interesting for us, however you can find their reviews in "Computer Network" of Andrew Tanenbaum (3-*d* edition).

TCP/IP Reference Model

This model was developed on the base of first computer networks (like ARPANET) and has only 4 layers:

Internet Layer

The **internet** layer is the linchpin that holds the whole architecture together. It allows hosts to inject their packets into any network and have them travel independently to their destination. This layer defines official protocol called **IP**.

Transport Layer

The **transport** layer lies above the internet layer and it's functionality is much alike to the same layer in **OSI** model — it allows peer entities on the source and destination hosts to carry on a conversation (2 end-to-end protocols were defined here: TCP and UDP).

There are tow more layers **application and host-to-network** that less interest us (the host-to-network layer plays minor part in TCP/IP protocol, steel being significant enough by itself) , you can find further information at the same reference as before.

OSI Via TCP/IP

Our major interest is in deference's at the network layer, them we will focus on:

~ The OSI model supports both connectionless and connection-oriented communication in the network layer, but only connection-oriented communication in the transport layer.

~ The TCP\IP model has only one mode in the network layer — connectionless, but supports both modes in transport layer, giving the user a choice. This choice is especially important for simple request-response protocols.

Generally the OSI model has proven to be exceptionally useful for discussing computer networks, but OSI protocols did not become popular .The reverse is true of TCP/IP: the model is practically nonexistent, but the protocols are widely used.

INTERNET

The Internet is a network of networks. Millions of computers all over the world are connected through the Internet. Computer users on the Internet can contact one another anywhere in the world. If your computer is connected to the Internet, you can connect to millions of computers. You can gather information and distribute your data. It is very much similar to the telephone connection where you can talk with any person anywhere in the world.

In Internet a huge resource of information is accessible to people across the world. Information in every field starting from education, science, health, medicine, history and geography to business, news, etc. can be retrieved through Internet. You can also download programs and software packages from anywhere in the world. Due to the tremendous information resources the Internet can provide, it is now indispensable to every organization.

Origin of Internet

In 1969 Department of Defence (DOD) of USA started a network called ARPANET (Advanced Research Projects Administration Network) with one computer at California and three at Utah. Later on other universities and R & D institutions were allowed to connect to the Network. APARNET quickly grew to encompass the entire American continent and became a huge success. Every university in the country wanted to become a part of ARPANET. So the network was broken into two smaller parts MILNET for managing military sites and ARPANET (smaller) for managing non-military sites. Around 1980, NSFNET (National Science Foundation Network) was created. With the advancement of modern communication facilities, other computers were also allowed to be linked up with any computer of NSFNET. By 1990 many computers were looking up to NSFNET giving birth to Internet.

How Internet Functions

Internet is not a governmental organization. The ultimate authority of the Internet is the Internet Society. This is a voluntary membership organization whose purpose is to promote global information exchange. Internet has more than one million computers attached to it.

E-mail

E-mail stands for *electronic mail*. This is one of the most widely used features of Internet. Mails are regularly used today where with the help of postage stamp we can transfer mails anywhere in the world. With electronic mail the service is similar. But here data are transmitted through Internet and therefore within minutes the message reaches the destination may it be anywhere in the world. Therefore the mailing system is excessively fast and is being used widely for mail transfer.

EXERCISE

Short Answer Questions

1. What is data communication?
2. Discuss basic elements of a communication system.
3. What do you mean by communication protocols?
4. Differentiate LAN vs. WAN.
5. What is email?
6. How Internet functions?
7. Discuss history of Internet in brief.
8. What is Internet?

Long Answer Questions

1. Discuss various data transmission models.
2. Discuss asynchronous and synchronous transmission.
3. Describe various network topologies.
4. Discuss ISO - OSI Model.

APPENDIX V

GLOSSARY ON MANAGEMENT INFORMATION SYSTEM

Ad-Hoc Query — Any spontaneous or unplanned question or query. It is a query that consists of dynamically constructed SQL, which is usually constructed by desktop-resident query tools.

Ad-Hoc Query Tool — An end-user tool that accepts an English-like or point-and-click request for data and constructs an ad-hoc query to retrieve the desired data from a database.

Agents — Self contained processes that run in the background on a client or server and that perform useful functions for a specific user/owner. Agents may monitor exceptions based on criteria or execute automated tasks. For example once an event occurs a daemon performs a pre-defined action and then it returns to a monitoring state. See daemon.

Aggregate or Aggregated Data — Data that is results from applying a process to combine data elements. Data that is summarized.

Alerts — A notification from an event that a trigger has exceeded a pre-defined threshold. See agents.

Analytical Hierarchy Process — An approach to decision making that involves structuring multiple choice criteria into a hierarchy, assessing the relative importance of these criteria, comparing alternatives for each criterion, and determining an overall ranking of the alternatives.

Business Data — Data about people, places, things, business rules, and events used to operate a business. It is not metadata.

Business Intelligence — BI is a popularized, umbrella term introduced by Howard Dresner of the Gartner Group in 1989 to describe a set of concepts and methods to improve business decision making by using fact-based support systems. The term is sometimes used interchangeably with briefing books and executive information systems. A Business Intelligence System is a DSS.

Business Model — In a data warehouse it is the designer's view of how the business functions. The view can be from a process, data, event or resource perspective, and can be the past, present or future state of the business.

Business Transaction — According to Microstrategy, it is a unit of work acted upon by a data capture system to create, modify, or delete business data. Each transaction represents a single valued fact describing a single business event.

Client/server architecture — A network architecture in which computers on a network act as a server managing files and network services OR as a client where users run applications and access servers. Clients rely on servers for resources like web pages, data, files, printing and OLAP.

Cognitive Overload — A psychological phenomenon characterized by an overload of information for a decision maker. The amount of information exceeds the person's cognitive capacity. DSS can reduce or increase cognitive overload.

Communications-Driven DSS — A Decision Support Systems that uses network and communications technologies to facilitate collaboration and communication. The communications technologies is central to supporting decision-making. Technologies include: LANs, WANs, Internet, ISDN, Virtual Private Networks. Tools used include groupware, Videoconferencing, Bulletin Boards.

Computer-mediated Communication — The use of computers to create, store, deliver, and process communications.

Computer Supported Cooperative Work — The use of computers to support cooperative work among multiple participants (e.g., collaborative authoring), as distinct from work that may not be cooperative.

Conferencing, Videoconferencing or Teleconferencing — Real-time, two-way communications. Audio-video telecommunication support of simultaneous interactions among participants (e.g., involving conference calls or videoconferencing).

Controllable Variables — Decision variables that can be changed and manipulated by a decision maker, such as quantity to produce, amount of resources to allocate, etc. .

Corporate Planning System — A decision support system that holds and derives knowledge relevant to planning decisions that cut across organizational units and involve all of an organization's functions (*i.e.*, its operations, finance, marketing, personnel, etc.).

Critical Success Factors key areas of business activity in which favorable results are necessary for a company to reach its goals.

Data — Binary (digital) representations of atomic facts, text, graphics, bit-mapped images, sound, analog or digital live-video segments. Data is the raw material of a system supplied by data producers and is used by information consumers to create information.

Data Conferencing — This term refers to a communication session in which two or more participants are sharing computer-based data in real-time. Any participants' keyboard/mouse can control screens of other participants. Voice communication can be out-of-band using a totally separate voice connection or in-band using a simultaneous voice and data technology.

Data Dictionary — A database about data and database structures. A catalog of all data elements, containing their names, structures, and information about their usage. A central location for metadata. Normally, data dictionaries are designed to store a limited set of available metadata, concentrating on the information relating to the data elements, databases, files and programs of implemented systems.

Data-Driven DSS — This type of DSS emphasizes access to and manipulation of a time-series of internal company data and sometimes external data. Simple file systems accessed by query and retrieval tools provide the most elementary level of functionality. Data warehouse systems that allow the manipulation of data by computerized tools tailored to a specific task and setting or by more general tools and operators provide additional functionality. Data-Driven DSS with On-line Analytical Processing (OLAP) or data mining tools provide the highest level of functionality and decision support that is linked to analysis of large collections of historical data. Early, very limited versions of data-driven DSS were called Retrieval-Only DSS by Bonczek, Holsapple and Whinston (1981).

Data Element — The most elementary unit of data that can be identified and described in a dictionary or repository which cannot be subdivided.

Data Mining — A class of analytical applications that search for patterns in a data base. Data mining is the process of sifting through large amounts of data to produce data content relationships. Data mining tools use a variety of techniques including case-based reasoning, data visualization, fuzzy query and analysis, and neural networks. Case-based reasoning tools provide a means to find records similar to a specified record or records. These tools let the user specify the "similarity" of retrieved records. Data visualization tools let the user easily and quickly view graphical displays of information from different perspectives.

Data Quality — High quality data is accurate, timely, meaningful, and complete. DSS must have high quality data; low quality data can result in bad decisions. Assessing or measuring data quality is a preliminary task associated with evaluating the feasibility of a data-driven DSS project.

Data Warehouse — A database designed to support decision making in organizations. It is batch updated and structured for rapid online queries and managerial summaries. Data warehouses contain large amounts of data. A data warehouse is a subject-oriented, integrated, time-variant, nonvolatile collection of data in support of management's decision making process. According to Ralph Kimball "A data warehouse is a copy of transaction data specifically structured for query and analysis"

Data Visualization — This term refers to presenting data and summary information using graphics, animation, 3-D displays, and other multimedia DSS tools.

Decision — The choice of one from among a number of alternatives; a statement indicating a commitment to a specific course of action.

Decision Analysis Tools — DA tools help decision makers decompose and structure problems. The aim of these tools is to help a user apply models like decision trees, multi-attribute utility models, bayesian models, Analytical Hierarchy Process (AHP), etc. Examples of DA software packages include AliahThink, BestChoice3, Criterium Decision Plus, DecideRight, DecisionMaker, Demos, DPL, Expert Choice, Strad, Supertree, and Which and Why.

Decision Room — A physical arrangement for a group DSS in which workstations are available to participants. The objective for using a Decision Roomis to enhance and improve the group's decision-making process.

Decision Systems are computer based programs and technologies intended to make routine decisions, monitor and control processes, and aid or assist decision makers in semi-structured and/or non-routine decision situations.

Decision Support Systems (DSS) are interactive computer-based systems intended to help decision makers utilize data and models to identify and solve problems and make decisions. The "system must aid a decision maker in solving unprogrammed, unstructured (or "semistructured") problems...the system must possess an interactive query facility, with a query language that ...is ...easy to learn and use (Bonczek, Holsapple & Whinston, 1981; p. 19)". DSS help managers/decision makers use and manipulate data; apply checklists and heuristics; and build and use mathematical models. According to Turban (1990), a DSS has four major characteristics: DSS incorporate both data and models; they are designed to assist managers in their decision processes in semistructured (or unstructured) tasks; they support, rather than replace, managerial judgment; and their objective is to improve the effectiveness of the decisions, not the efficiency with which decisions are being made (cf., p. 9).

Decision Variables — In a model-driven DSS a decision variable is a changing factor in the model that is determined by a decision maker. They are sometimes called independent variables and the range of values for the decision variables constrain the choices of the decision maker.

Demon or Daemon — A computer program or procedure that is automatically activated when it recognizes a specific, predefined state or condition.

Descriptive Model — Physical, conceptual or mathematical models that describe situations as they are or as they actually appear.

Deterministic Model — Mathematical models that are constructed for a condition of assumed certainty. The models assume there is only one possible result (which is known) for each alternative course or action.

Development Environment — The DE is used by a designer/builder. A development environment typically includes software for creating and maintaining a knowledge base and software for the inference engine.

Dialog Generation and Management System (DGMS) — A software management package in a DSS whose functions in the dialog subsystem is similar to that of a DBMS in a database.

Dialog System — The hardware and software that create and implement a user interface for a DSS. A DSS dialog system creates the human-computer interface.

Document-Driven DSS — It integrates a variety of storage and processing technologies to provide complete document retrieval and analysis. The Web provides access to large document databases including databases of hypertext documents, images, sounds and video. Examples of documents that would be accessed by a Document-Based DSS are policies and procedures, product specifications, catalogs, and corporate historical documents, including minutes of meetings, corporate records, and important correspondence. A search engine is a powerful decision-aiding tool associated with a Document-Driven DSS.

Domain Expert — A person who has expertise in the domain in which a specific expert system is being developed. A domain expert works closely with a developer (known as a knowledge engineer) to capture the expert's knowledge (especially rule and relationship information) in a computer readable representation often called a knowledge base.

Drill Down/Up — An analytical technique that lets a DSS user navigate among levels of data ranging from the most summarized (up) to the most detailed (down).

DSS Generator — Computer software package that provides tools and capabilities that help a developer quickly and easily build a specific Decision Support System (cf., Sprague and Carlson, 1982, p. 11). Excel is an example of a DSS Generator. Many companies market tools for building DSS and EIS, see

DSS Development Tools — Software components (such as editors, code libraries, specific objects, visual interfaces) that facilitate the development of a specific DSS.

e-Meetings — A term for a meeting supported by full-motion video, audio, and Web meeting tools. One or more participants in the meeting is participating remotely in the meeting. It is possible that all participants are in different physical locations.

Enterprise-wide DSS — A DSS that supports a large group of managers in a networked client-server environment with a specialized data warehouse as part of the DSS architecture.

Evolutionary (Iterative) Design Process — A systematic process for system development that is recommended for use in creating DSS. A portion of the DSS system is quickly constructed, then tested, improved, and enlarged in systematic steps.

Exception Reporting — A reporting philosophy and approach that supports Management by Exception. Reports should be designed to display significant exceptions in results and data. The idea is to "flag" important information and bring it quickly to the attention of managerial users of the report. Exception reporting can be implemented in any type of DSS, but it is particularly useful in data-driven DSS and EIS.

Executive Information Systems (EIS) — A computerized system intended to provide current and appropriate information to support executive decision making for managers using a networked workstation. The emphasis is on graphical displays and an easy to use interface that present information from the corporate database. They are tools to provide canned reports or briefing books to top-level executives. They offer strong reporting and drill-down capabilities.

Executive Support Systems (ESS) — An executive information system (EIS) that includes specific decision aiding and/or analysis capabilities.

Expert Systems are man-machine systems with specialized problem-solving expertise. The "expertise" consists of knowledge about a particular domain, understanding of problems within that domain, and "skill" at solving some of these problems.

Facilitator — A person(s) who manages the use of a group decision support system from initial planning through actual operation.

Feasibility Study — A study of the technical and economic prospects for developing a system prior to actually committing resources to actually developing it.

Functional DSS — A decision support system that holds and derives knowledge relevant for decisions about some function an organization performs (e.g., a marketing function, a production function).

Generators — Software packages that are designed to expedite programming efforts that are required to build information systems, especially expert and decision support systems.

Goal-seeking — The capability of asking the computer software what values certain variables must have in order to attain desired goals. It is a tool that uses iterative calculations to find the value required in one cell (variable) in order to achieve a desired value in another cell. A common use of the goal-seeking feature in a spreadsheet is calculating a break-even quantity.

Geographic Information Systems (GIS) — A support system that represents data using maps. It helps people access, display and analyze data that have geographic content and meaning. Check U.S.Examples of software packages include ArcView, Map/IDIS, Proximity, and TargetView.

Graphical User Interface (GUI) — A program interface that uses a computer's graphics capabilities to make the program easier to use. Graphical interfaces use a pointing device to select objects, including icons, menus, text boxes, etc. A GUI includes standard formats for representing text and graphics.

Group Decision Support Systems (GDSS) — An interactive, computer-based system that facilitates solution of unstructured problems by a set of decision-makers working together as a group. It aids groups, especially groups of managers, in analyzing problem situations and in performing group decision-making tasks.

Groupware — Is software designed to support more than one person working on a shared task. Groupware is an evolving concept that is more than multiuser software which allows access to the same data. Groupware provides a mechanism that helps users coordinate and keep track of on-going projects. It allows people to work together through computer-supported communication, collaboration, and coordination. Lotus Notes, Microsoft Exchange, Communicator, Novell GroupWise, Netscape SuiteSpot, Eclipse, Team Talk, and Internet Explorer/NetMeeting are examples of groupware products.

Heuristics — The informal, judgmental knowledge of an application area that constitutes the "rules of good judgment" in the field. Heuristics also encompass the knowledge of how to solve problems efficiently and effectively, how to plan steps in solving a complex problem, how to improve performance, and so forth. From the Greek— Heuriskein to discover.

Hypermedia — Combination of several types of media such as text, graphics, audio, and video.

Hypertext — An approach for handling text and other information by allowing the users to jump from a given topic, whenever he or she wishes, to related topics. A knowledge management technique in which knowledge is represented in linked documents and processed in a way that allows a user to select a highlighted marker on the currently viewed page to access a linked page about a topic indicated by the marker.

Icon — A visual, graphic representation of an object, word, or concept.

Independent Variables — Variables in a model that are controlled by the environment and that influence the results of a decision (also called Input Variables, parameters, givens).

Inference — The process of drawing a conclusion from given evidence. To reach a decision by reasoning.

Inference Engine — That part of an expert system that actually performs the reasoning function.

Information — Data that has been processed to add or create meaning and hopefully knowledge for the person who receives it. Information is the output of information systems.

Information Economics — This term refers to an approach to evaluating DSS/IS projects using a scoring approach to cost/benefit analysis that assesses technical and company tangible and intangible benefits and costs (see Parker, Trainor and Benson, Information Strategy and Economics, 1989.

Information Systems Architecture — A formal definition of the business processes and rules, systems structure, technical framework, and product technologies for business information systems. An information systems architecture consists of four layers: business process architecture, systems architecture, technical architecture, and product delivery architecture.

Interdependent Decisions — A series of decisions that are interrelated. A sequential set of decisions are usually interdependent.

Internet — The Internet (capitalized) refers specifically to the DARPA Internet and the TCP/IP protocols it uses. The Internet is a collection of packet-switching networks and routers that uses the TCP/IP protocol suit and functions as a single, cooperative virtual network. A global web connecting more than one million computers.

Intranet — An internal organizational network using TCP/IP with at least one web server that is only accessible by an organization's members or others who have specific authorization. A firewall and password protection limit access to the network. The intranet is used to share corporate information, including DSS capabilities.

Knowledge — Knowledge refers to what one knows and understands. Knowledge is sometimes categorized as either unstructured, structured, explicit or tacit. What we know we know is explicit knowledge. Knowledge that is unstructured and understood, but not clearly expressed is implicit knowledge. If the knowledge is organized and easy to share then it is called structured knowledge. To convert implicit knowledge into explicit knowledge, it must be extracted and formatted.

Knowledge Acquisition — The extraction and formulation of knowledge derived from various sources, especially from experts.

Knowledge Base — A collection of facts, rules, and procedures organized into schemas. The assembly of all the information and knowledge of a specific field of interest.

Knowledge-Driven DSS — Knowledge-Driven DSS can suggest or recommend actions to managers. These DSS are person-computer systems with specialized problem-solving expertise. The "expertise" consists of knowledge about a particular domain, understanding of problems within that domain, and "skill" at solving some of these problems. A related concept is Data Mining. It refers to a class of analytical applications that search for hidden patterns in a database. Data mining is the process of sifting through large amounts of data to produce data content relationships. Tools used for building Knowledge-Driven DSS are sometimes called Intelligent Decision Support methods (cf., Dhar and Stein, 1997). Data Mining tools can be used to create hybrid DSS that have major data and knowledge components.

Knowledge Engineer — An AI specialist responsible for the technical side of developing an expert system. The knowledge engineer works closely with the domain expert to capture the expert's knowledge in a knowledge base.

Knowledge Engineering (KE) — The engineering discipline that involves integrating knowledge into computer systems in order to solve complex problems normally requiring a high level of human expertise.

Knowledge Management (KM) — KM is the distribution, access and retrieval of unstructured information about "human experiences" between interdependent individuals or among members of a workgroup. Knowledge management involves identifying a group of people who have a need to share knowledge, developing technological support that enables knowledge sharing, and creating a process for transferring and disseminating knowledge.

Knowledge Management Software (KMS) — Software that can store and manage unstructured information in a variety of electronic formats. The software may assist in knowledge capture, categorization, deployment, inquiry, discovery, or communication. Products include electronic document management systems (EDMS).

Linear Programming — A mathematical model for optimal solution of resource allocation problems.

Metadata or Meta Data — Data about the data in a data warehouse. Metadata provides a a directory to help the DSS locate the contents of the data warehouse; it is a guide to mapping data as it is transformed from the operational environment to the data warehouse environment; and it serves as a guide to the algorithms used for summarization of current detailed data. Metadata is semantic information associated with a given variable. Metadata must include business definitions of the data and clear, accurate descriptions of data types, potential values, original source system, data formats, and other characteristics. Metadata defines and describes business data. Examples of metadata include data element descriptions, data type descriptions, attribute/property descriptions, range/domain descriptions, and process/method descriptions. The repository environment encompasses all corporate metadata resources: database catalogs, data dictionaries, and navigation services. Metadata includes things like the name, length, valid values, and description of a data element. Metadata is stored in a data dictionary and repository. It insulates the data warehouse from changes in the schema of operational systems.

Methodology — A system of principles, practices, and procedures applied to a specific branch of knowledge.

Middleware — A communications layer that allows applications to interact across hardware and network environments.

Model Base — A collection of preprogrammed quantitative models (e.g., statistical, financial, optimization) organized as a single unit.

Model-Driven DSS or Model-oriented DSS — This type of DSS emphasizes access to and manipulation of a model, e.g., statistical, financial, optimization and/or simulation. Simple statistical and analytical tools provide the most elementary level of functionality. Some OLAP systems that allow complex analysis of data may be classified as hybrid DSS systems providing both modeling and data retrieval and data summarization functionality. Data mining is also a hybrid approach to DSS. In general, model-driven DSS use complex financial, simulation, optimization and/or rule (expert) models to provide decision support. Model-driven DSS use data and parameters provided by decision makers to aid decision makers in analyzing a situation, but they are not usually data intensive, that is very large data bases are usually not need for model-driven DSS. Early versions of model-driven DSS were called Computationally Oriented DSS by Bonczek, Holsapple and Whinston (1981).

Modeling Tools — Software programs that help developers/users build mathematical models quickly. Spreadsheets and planning languages like IFPS are modeling tools.

Multi-dimensional Database (MDBS and MDBMS) — A database that lets users analyze large amounts of data. An MDBS captures and presents data as arrays that can be arranged in multiple dimensions. Variables are the objects that hold data in a multidimensional database. These are simply arrays of values (usually numeric) that are "dimensioned" by the dimensions in a database. For example, a UNITS variable may be dimensioned by MONTH, PRODUCT, and REGION. This three-dimensional variable or array is often visualized as a cube of data. Multi-dimensional databases can have multiple variables, with common or a unique set of dimensions. This multi-dimensional view of data is especially powerful for OLAP applications.

Multiparticipant DSS — A decision support system that supports multiple participants engaged in a decision-making task (or functions as one of the participants). See group DSS.

Multipoint Conference — An audio, data and/or video conference among more than tworemote participants.

Multipoint Control Unit (MCU) — A device used to link remote sites into a single conference call or a device to manage several simultaneous, independent conferences.

Normalization — The process of reducing a complex data structure into its simplest, most stable structure. In general, the process entails the removal of redundant attributes, keys, and relationships from a conceptual data model.

Object — A person, place, thing, or concept that has characteristics of interest to an environment. In terms of an object-oriented system, an object is an entity that combines descriptions of data and behavior.

On-line Analytical Processing (OLAP) — Software for manipulating multidimensional data from a variety of sources that has been stored in a data warehouse. The software can create various views and representations of the data. OLAP software provides fast, consistent, interactive access to shared, multidimensional data.

Operational or Transaction Database — The database-of-record for a transaction-update system. The operational database is the source of data for the data warehouse. It contains detailed data used to run the day-to-day operations of the business. The data continually changes as updates are made, and reflect the current value of the last transaction.

Optimize — The decision strategy of choosing the alternative that gives the best or optimal overall value.

Organizational DSS — A multiparticipant DSS designed to support a decision maker in a setting that has a more elaborate infrastructure than a group (*i.e.*, involving specialized roles, restricted communication patterns, differing authority levels). See enterprise-wide DSS.

Pivot — Changing the dimensional orientation of a display or report.

Planning — A managerial function concerned with making forecasts, formulating outlines of things to do, and identifying methods to accomplish them.

Prototyping — A strategy in system development in which a scaled down system or portion of a system is constructed in a short time, tested, and improved in several iterations. A prototype is an initial version of a system that is quickly developed to test the effectiveness of the overall design being used to solve a particular problem. Prototyping is similar to the Evolutionary (Iterative) Design Process. It is sometimes termed rapid prototyping and is similar to rapid application development (RAD).

Query — Generically query means question. Usually it refers to a complex SQL SELECT statement for decision support. See Ad-Hoc Query or Ad-Hoc Query Software.

Rapid Application Development (RAD) — Part of a methodology that specifies incremental development with constant feedback from the customers. The point is to keep projects focused on delivering value and to keep clear and open lines of communication. Oral and written communication is not completely adequate for specification of computer systems. RAD overcomes the limitations of language by minimizing the time between concept and implementation.

Rational Decision Behavior — Behavior that is goal-oriented in reaching a decision. Behavior is guided by the consequences likely to result from the selection of a given alternative. A decision maker believes based upon analysis that a chosen alternative will result in achieving one or more desired objectives. Rational decision behavior should be supported by DSS.

Record — A group of data values consisting of one value for each of a prescribed set of relational fields; an occurrence of a record type.

Report and Query Tools — These tools produce a of tabular list of information from data stored in a relational database. Examples include Microsoft Access and Brio Query.

Representation — The formulation or view of a problem. Developed so the problem will be easier to solve.

Result Variables — In a model-driven DSS a result variable shows the consequences of changing decision variables. Result variable are also referred to as dependent variables.

ROMC (Representation, Operations, Memory Aids, Mechanism Control) Design Approach — A Systematic approach for developing large-scale DSS, especially user interfaces. It is user-oriented approach for stating system performance requirements (cf., Sprague and Carlson, 1982).

Rule — A formal way of specifying a recommendation, directive, or strategy, expressed as IF premise THEN conclusion.

Scalability — The ability to scale hardware and software to support larger or smaller volumes of data and more or less users. The ability to increase or decrease size or capability in cost-effective increments with minimal impact on the unit cost of business and the procurement of additional services.

Semistructured Decisions — Decisions in which some aspect of the problem are structured and others are unstructured.

Sensitivity Analysis — Running a decision model several times with different inputs so a modeler can analyze the alternative results.

Shell — An expert system development tool consisting of two stand-alone pieces of software: a rule set manager and an inference engine capable of reasoning with rules set built with the rule set manager. A shell is a complete expert system stripped of its specific knowledge.

Simulation — A technique for conducting one or more experiments that test various outcomes resulting from a quantitative model of a system.

Specific DSS — A computer-based system that actually helps a person accomplish a specific task. "Specific DSS are the hardware/software that allow a specific decision maker or group of them to deal with specific sets of related problems."

Spreadsheet — In the accounting world a spreadsheet was and is a large sheet of paper that lays everything out for a businessperson. It spreads or shows all of the costs, income, taxes, etc. on a single sheet of paper for a manager to look at when making a decision. An electronic spreadsheet organizes information into columns and rows. The data can then be "added up" by a formula to give a total or sum. The spreadsheet summarizes information from many sources in one place and presents the information in a format to help a decision maker see the financial "big picture" for the company. A program that has a collection of cells whose values can be displayed on a computer screen. By changing cell definitions and having all cell values reevaluated, a user can readily observe the effects of those changes. Decision support systems built using spreadsheet software are sometimes called Spreadsheet DSS.

Star Schema — A relational database schema organized around a central table (fact table) joined to a few smaller tables (dimension tables) using foreign key references. The fact table contains raw numeric items that represent relevant business facts (price, discount values, number of units sold, dollar value, etc.) The facts are typically additive and are accessed via dimensions. Since the fact tables are presummarized and aggregated along business dimensions, these tables tend to be very large. The basic premise of star schemas is that information can be classified into two groups: facts and dimensions. Facts are the core data element being analyzed. For example, units of individual items sold are facts, while dimensions are attributes about the facts. Dimensions are the product types purchased and the date of purchase. The star schema has also been called a star-join schema, data cube, data list, grid file, and multidimensional schema. The name star schema comes from the pattern formed by the entities and relationships when they are represented as an entity-relationship diagram (ERD). The results of a business activity are at the center of the star surrounded by the people, places, and things that come together to perform this activity. These dimensions are the points of the star.

Strategic Planning — A decision-making process in which decisions are made about establishing organizational purposes/mission, determining objectives, selecting strategies and setting policies.

Structured Decisions — Standard or repetitive decisions situations for which solution techniques are already available (also sometimed called routine or programmed decisions). The structural elements in the situation, *e.g.*, alternatives, criteria, environmental conditions, are known, defined and understood.

Symbolic Processing — Use of symbols, rather than numbers, combined with rules-of-thumb (or heuristics), in order to process information and solve problems.

Systems Development Life Cycle (SDLC) — A process by which systems analysts, software engineers, programmers, and end-users build systems. It is a project management tool, used to plan, execute,, and control systems develpment projects. The steps in the cycle include: 1) Determine user requirements; 2) Systems analysis; 3) Overall system design; 4) Detailed system design; 5) Programming; 6) Testing; and 7) Implementation. Each step is concluded by developing a written document that must be reviewed and approved before the next step begins.

Ticker — A small Java Applet that displays a specific set of headlines, information, etc. Every web page that wants to display a Ticker must add some special HTML code into the page. This code ensures that the JAVA Applet is loaded from a server. Some parameters control the visible output like coloring and of course they control which news are loaded.

Unstructured Decisions — This type of decision situation is complex and no standard solutions exist for resolving the situation. Some or all of the structural elements of the decision situation are undefined, ill-defined or unknown. For example, goals may be poorly defined, alternatives may be incomplete or non-comparable, choice criteria may be hard to measure or difficult to link to goals.

User-Friendly — An evaluative term for a Decision Support System's user interface. The phrase indicates that users judge the user interface as to easy to learn, understand, and use.

User Interface (or "Human-Computer Interface") — The component of a computerized support system that allows bidirectional communication between the system and its user. This is also called the dialogue component of a DSS. An interface is a set of commands or menus through which a user communicates with a program.

Web-based DSS – A computerized system that delivers decision support information or decision support tools to a manager or business analyst using a "thin-client" Web browser like Netscape Navigator or Internet Explorer. The computer server that is hosting the DSS application is linked to the user's computer by a network with the TCP/IP protocol. In many companies, a Web-based DSS is synonymous with an enterprise-wide DSS that is supporting large groups of managers in a networked client-server environment with a specialized data warehouse as part of the DSS architecture.

"What If" Analysis – The capability of "asking" the software package what the effect will be of changing some of the input data or independent variables.

INDEX

A

Access Controls 207
Adam Smith 105
Agile Competitor 140, 144
Agility 140
APO 181
Artificial Intelligence 117
ASPs 190
Atomicity 9
Attractive Web Sites 128
Automated processes 191

B

B2G 128, 131
Baan 150
Batch 14
Batch processing 9
BB 113
Bill Gates 197
Biometric controls 207
BPR 107
Breaking Business Barriers 144
Breaking Structural Barriers 139
Business Drivers 196
business enterprise 5
business environment 5
Business ethics 215, 222
Business Information system 5
Business Plan 90
Business Processes 151
business processes 132

C

CEO 114, 199
Channel Management 131
chief information officer 3
CIO 199
Cognitive psychology 117
Cohen and Lee 180
Common sense 116
Community Collaboration 93
Competitive Forces 145
Competitive Strategies 145
computer based information processing 2
Consistency 9
Constituency 92
Consumer Protection 241
Continuous 14
Contract Law 240
control data resources 5
Controlled processing 9
COQUAMO 228
corporate database 5
Corporate ethics policies 220
Credit Card 128
CRM 88, 161
CRM technology 170
Cyber crimes 235
Cyber law 238
Cyber Laws 236
Cyber Societies 236
Cyber Space 238

D

data driven 28
data placement 10
Data security 208
data warehouse 11
Databases and files 10
DBA 5
DBMS 4
decentralization 3
decision-making procedures 3
Deliver 177
Dell 201
Discrete 14

Distribution 176
Distribution Management 131
DSS 18
Durability 10

E

E-Procurement 192
Economies of Information 139
ECRM 165
ECS 15
EDI 127
EIS 18
Electronic Catalogues 129
Electronic Cheques 128
Electronic Data Processing 2
Electronic Marketing 128
Electronic Payments 128, 240
ERP 148
ERP Software 151
ERP System 151
ERP Users 151
Ethics 213
Ethics of human resource management 217
Ethics of production 217
Ethics of sales and marketing 217
Ethics officers 221
EUC 85
EUC Ranges 86
Experimental Psychology 117
expert system 21
Extranets 133

F

Facial themography 208
federal 4
Financial management 131
Financial Resources 92
Fingerprints 208
Firewall 209
Fuzzy logic 39
fuzzy logic 22

G

GB 113
Global Decisions 176
Global Marketing 129
goal driven 25
Governance 93

H

Hand geometry 207
hardware, software 2
Hierarchical structure 10
High normalisation 11
Historical data 11
HRMS, EHRMS 19
HTTP 190
Human Resource Management 98
human resources 5
Hyper text 129

I

IBM 201
Inbound Logistics 98
Inflexibility 9
Information strategy 84
Information Technology 205
Infrastructure Managed Services 203
initial concept 1
Integration 106
Intellectual Property Rights 241
Intelligence 116
Intentional Threats 206
International business ethics 218
International Private Law 241
Intranet 134
intranet 133
Inventory management 130
ISO 108
Isolation 10
ISP 190
IT infrastructure 5
ITEC 174

K

Keystroke dynamics 208
KMS 142

L

Liability 240
Logistics 176

M

Make 177
manual information system 1
Manufacturing 176
Marketing and Sales 98
Master file 11
MBB 112
MBO 16
Micro Payments 129
MRP 148
MRP-II 149

N

Navigation 129
Network interface 202
Network Services 203
Network structure 10
networked collaboration 161
Neural networks 29
New Technology Products 129

O

Operating managers 4
Operations 98
Optimizer 181
Oracle 150
Organization Control 94
Organizational Plan 90
organizational structure 3
OSS 8
Outbound Logistics 98

P

Payment Management 131
PeopleSoft 150
Personal finance management 131
Personalization 129
Physical Resources 93
Physical security 207
Plan 177
Plan Evaluation 90
PLANETS 180
PO 112
Price attractiveness 128
Primary Activities 97
Privacy Issues 241
Process control 13
Procurement 98, 176
procurement 192
Procurement Management 191
Program file 11
Program/Services 92
Purchasing products and information 131

Q

QL/QM 112

R

rapid development 234
Rapid response 9
Raw data 6
Real-time backup 10
Real-time processing 9
Relational structure 10
Reliability 9
Report file 11
Resource 205
Return 177
RFID 185
ROI 193
Rough Cut Methods 181
RTSC 189

S

Sales and Marketing 194
Sales force management 131
SAP 150, 181
SCM 148, 177, 182, 188
Service Oriented Architecture 185
Set Goals 89

Set Tasks 89
SFA 163
Short transactions 10
SIS 21
Six sigma 111
Smart Card 128
SMB 170
SOA 186
Social interaction 131
Socialising 129
Software Quality Assurance 224
Source 177
SPC 14
Storing and retrieving 10
strategic decisions 178
Strategic Plan 90
strategic planning 4
Strategic Roles 136
strategic tool 2
Supplier management 130
Supply chain management 174
Supply Management 175
system approach 105
System Vulnerability 205

T

Taxation Law 240
Technology Development 98
TPS 9
TQM 108
Transaction file 11

U

Unintentional threats 206

V

Value Chain Analysis 97
virtual company 122, 141
virtual organization 197

W

W3C 239
Wal-Mart store 183
Web based CRM 165
widening customer relationships 163
Wintel 198
Wisdom 7
Work file 11
Workforce 92
www 127